Taste *of* Home

MEAL PLANNING

THE 500+ RECIPES, SECRETS & TIPS THAT BUSY MEAL PLANNERS RELY ON MOST

T0355856

TASTE OF HOME BOOKS • RDA ENTHUSIAST BRANDS, LLC • MILWAUKEE, WI

Taste of Home

Visit us at **tasteofhome.com** for other
Taste of Home books and products.

International Standard Book Number:
978-1-61765-930-0

Library of Congress Control Number:
2019954152

Executive Editor: Mark Hagen
Senior Art Director: Raeann Thompson
Art Director: Maggie Conners
Designer: Arielle Jardine
Copy Editor: Ann Walter

Cover:
Photographer: Mark Derse
Set Stylist: Stacey Genaw
Food Stylist: Diane Armstrong

Pictured on front cover:
On-the-Go Breakfast Muffins, p. 22; Chopped
Greek Salad in a Jar, p. 147; Turkey Ranch
Wraps, p. 175; Make-Ahead Lasagna, p. 188;
Honey-Lime Roasted Chicken, p. 42; Antipasto
Skewers, p. 93

Pictured on back cover:
Spinach & Cheese Lasagna Rolls, p. 42; Fluffy
Banana Pancakes, p. 237; Bacon Swiss Quiche,
p. 217

Printed in China
3 5 7 9 10 8 6 4 2

CONTENTS

MEAL PLANNING YOUR WAY
LET'S GET STARTED!

MEALS ON THE GO
NOT YOUR MAMMA'S BROWN-BAG STAPLES

PREP NOW, EAT LATER
LIVEN UP MEAL PLANS WITH MAKE-AHEAD GREATS

FREEZER MEAL PREPS
SIMPLIFY YOUR LIFE WITH FREEZER-TO-TABLE BITES

PLANNED OVERS
COOK ONCE, EAT ALL WEEK WITH DISHES THAT USE UP LEFTOVERS

EXTRAS
QUICK MENU ADD-ONS THAT SAVE TIME AND MONEY

P. 257

GET SOCIAL WITH US

TO FIND A RECIPE: tasteofhome.com
TO SUBMIT A RECIPE: tasteofhome.com/submit
TO FIND OUT ABOUT OTHER *TASTE OF HOME* PRODUCTS: shoptasteofhome.com

MEAL PLANNING YOUR WAY

Beat the clock, crush grocery bills, eat heathier—it's a snap with *Taste of Home Meal Planning!* Inside you'll find all of the recipes, tips and tools you need to succeed when it comes to preparing pre-planned entrees, on-the-go breakfasts, make-ahead lunches and more.

Meal planning can mean many different things to today's home cooks. To some, it means creating detailed monthly calendars spotlighting foods for every meal of the day. For others, it's all about scheduling which dinners hit the table over the course of a week.

Some plan to stock their freezers with handy entrees, and others refrigerate several grab-and-go breakfasts or lunches for busy weekdays.

Many family cooks spend Saturdays or Sundays preparing recipes in bulk. Then they use those foods to pack individual meals, streamline weeknight kitchen prep or simply plan all sorts of delicious ideas for leftovers.

No matter what meal planning means to you, this book has you covered. Take a look inside, and you'll find:

- 475 recipes for meal-planning success
- A 30-day dinner planner
- 140+ freezer-friendly dishes with reheating directions
- Snacks, breakfasts and other bites to eat on the run
- 10 plans to cook once and eat all week

Take the stress out of meal planning and beat the "what's for dinner" blues when you dig in to comforting goodness all day long. It's easy when you start taking control of your kitchen today! With *Taste of Home Meal Planning,* success is just around the corner.

AT-A-GLANCE ICONS HELP YOU PLAN

Freezer-Friendly
These recipes freeze well. Stock up today!

Slow Cooker
Let your slow cooker do the work for you.

Eat Smart
Plan to stay healthy when you cut down on calories, fat, carbs and/or sodium.

5 Ingredients
These dishes call for 5 items or fewer, not including water, salt, pepper, oils or optional items such as garnishes.

P. 338

P. 384

MEAL PLANNING 101

THESE BITES OF KITCHEN WISDOM MAKE YOUR PLANNING A SNAP.

Before You Begin...

Start Slowly. If you're new to menu planning, don't overdo it. Start out by planning a week's worth of dinners or lunches. As you feel more comfortable, add days and meals to your plan.

Try Crowdsourcing. Ask your family what they might like to see on the meal plan. Kids (and some adults) are more likely to get excited about meals when they feel they have a say in the plan.

Think Seasonally. Plan around using fresh produce, as in-season foods are often cheaper. Don't forget to hit farmers markets before making your meal plan so you can best take advantage of those delicious finds.

Do a Double Take. Simplify things by using one ingredient a few times. See the Planned Overs chapter on page 334, where you'll learn how to cook up a batch of taco meat, for example, that can be used in numerous dishes later in your meal plan.

Focus on Favorites. Why reinvent the wheel? Repeat hit dinners a few times monthly to make planning quicker with well-received results.

Keep It Simple. Try to pair entrees with no-fuss sides such as frozen veggies, green salads, seasoned rice or beans. Check out the Meal Planning Extras chapter on page 376 for easy ideas to round out menus.

Shopping & Storage Made Simple

Now that you've planned, you're ready to shop! Check which ingredients you have on hand before creating your shopping list, and remember to take your meal plan to the grocery store with you for reference. Try not to shop on Sunday afternoons, as that's traditionally the busiest time for grocery stores. (Save Sundays for planning meals or cooking in bulk instead.) Off-hours at supermarkets are typically early morning and late evening on weekdays.

When you arrive home, unpack dry goods, such as pasta and rice, and immediately store them in clear, airtight canisters. This way, you'll easily see when it's time to restock them.

When putting groceries into your pantry or cabinets, create zones. Store baking items together, stack canned goods in one area, and line up oils and cooking sprays in a particular spot.

INGREDIENTS
TO KEEP
ON HAND

Keep the following staples handy. You'll use them in recipes throughout this book—a few of which are listed below to get you started.

Canned Diced Tomatoes
- Lone Star Chicken Enchiladas (p. 247)
- Italian Pot Roast (p. 337)

Canned/Jarred Mushrooms
- Two-for-One Chicken Tetrazzini (p. 246)
- Italian Pork Chops (p. 275)

Chicken Broth
- Rustic Italian Tortellini Soup (p. 56)
- Slow-Cooker Sweet-and-Sour Pork (p. 304)

Salsa
- Sassy Salsa Meat Loaves (p. 265)
- Spicy Egg Bake (p. 351)

Rice
- California Roll in a Jar (p. 154)
- Pork Spanish Rice (p. 347)

Potatoes
- Favorite Chicken Potpie (p. 273)
- Meat-and-Potato Quiche (p. 350)

Cornbread/Muffin Mix
- Beans & Franks Bake (p. 241)
- Cheddar Corn Dog Muffins (p. 315)

Frozen Meatballs
- Mama Mia Meatball Taquitos (p. 85)
- Meatball Flatbread (p. 366)

Pasta/Spaghetti Sauce
- Best Italian Sausage Sandwiches (p. 52)
- Cheesy Veggie Lasagna (p. 243)

Canned Beans
- Gnocchi with White Beans (p. 60)
- Zesty Sausage & Beans (p. 280)

Spaghetti/Linguine
- Vegetarian Linguine (p. 40)
- Quick Gingered Spaghetti (p. 158)

Frozen Corn
- Lime Chicken Tacos (p. 59)
- Corn Pasta Salad (p. 155)

Cream of Chicken Soup
- Chicken Cordon Bleu Bake (p. 261)
- Chicken Crescent Wreath (p. 66)

Canned/Pouched Tuna
- Crunchy Tuna Salad with Tomatoes (p. 157)
- Comforting Tuna Patties (p. 261)

FREEZER KNOW-HOW

LEARNING THE RIGHT WAY TO KEEP FOODS COLD CAN MAKE PLANNING EASIER AND PREVENT FOOD WASTE.

FREEZE FOODS IN:

- Freezer bags
- Rigid plastic or glass freezer containers
- Plastic wrap
- Vacuum-sealed packages
- Heavy-duty foil
- Freezer paper
- Wide-mouth freezer or canning jars (leave room at the top for foods to expand)

AVOID FREEZING FOODS IN:

- Glass jars from food products (no pickle or pasta-sauce jars)
- Margarine or cottage cheese tubs
- Milk cartons
- Food storage bags

Want to save your casserole dish from spending months in the freezer? Before you place the casserole ingredients in the dish, line it with heavy-duty foil. Once the food is cooked and cooled, use the foil to help remove it from the dish. Wrap securely and freeze. To defrost, be sure to replace it in the same casserole dish.

EASY FREEZING

Your freezer is a great tool when planning ahead. Use these kitchen hacks today for fast freezer success.

- Start with fresh, high-quality food. Any food past its prime will not improve upon freezing.

- Always chill freshly made food in the fridge to at least room temperature before moving it to the freezer. If you want to cool something quickly, place it in an ice bath while it's still in its container.

- Remove as much air as possible before sealing freezer bags, and lay them flat when freezing. That way, you can stack several bags and packages after they're solidly frozen, saving space.

- Freezer burn is not a food-safety issue, but it is a food-quality issue. You may cut off the burnt areas before or after cooking. Discard produce that is icy, blackened and/or shriveled.

- Leave some space around packages so air can circulate.

- Always label and date freezer packages.

30-Day Dinner Plan Solves Your 'What's for Dinner?' Dilemmas

DAY 1
Rosemary
Turkey Breast, p. 353

MENU ADD-ON
• Simple Lemon Parsley
Potatoes, p. 388

DAY 2
Pizza Pasta
Casserole, p. 239

MENU ADD-ON
• Great Garlic Bread, p. 401

DAY 3
Turkey Lattice Pie, p. 353

MENU ADD-ON
• Cheesecake Berry
Parfaits, 420

DAY 4
Double-Duty Chicken with
Olives & Artichokes, p. 374

MENU ADD-ON
• Quick Mango Sorbet,
p. 418

DAY 5
Meatball Flatbread,
p. 366

MENU ADD-ON
• Caesar Salad

DAY 11
Slow-Cooked Ham, p. 359

MENU ADD-ON
• Cheddar Mashed
Cauliflower, p. 383

DAY 12
Two-For-One Chicken
Tetrazzini, p. 246

MENU ADD-ON
• Mini Italian Biscuits,
p. 381

DAY 13
Cheddar Ham Soup,
p. 360

MENU ADD-ON
• Turkey Ranch Wraps,
p. 175

DAY 14
Grilled Buttermilk Chicken,
p. 341

MENU ADD-ON
• Roasted Asparagus

DAY 15
Pork Burritos, p. 75

MENU ADD-ON
• Festive Corn & Broccoli,
p. 384

DAY 21
Double-Duty Hearty Chili
Without Beans, p. 373

MENU ADD-ON
• Buffalo Chicken Biscuits,
p. 71

DAY 22
Garlic-Apple Pork Roast,
p. 345

MENU ADD-ON
• Honey Garlic
Green Beans, p. 382

DAY 23
Double-Duty Layered
Enchilada Casserole,
p. 373

MENU ADD-ON
• Confetti Corn, p. 394

DAY 24
Feta Chicken Burgers,
p. 64

MENU ADD-ON
• Orange Fluff, p. 170

DAY 25
Pork Spanish Rice, p. 347

MENU ADD-ON
• Cornbread

Whether you're new to meal planning or a longtime pro, consider this handy guide that relies on recipes from this book with simple add-ons to round out meals. Be on the lookout for leftovers. For instance, extras from Rosemary Turkey Breast from Day 1 are used to quickly prepare Turkey Lattice Pie on Day 3.

Similarly, watch for dishes stored in the freezer. Southwestern Casserole makes two entrees, for example. Serve one on Day 7 and freeze the other. Then, enjoy that savory dinner when you reheat the frozen dish on Day 20.

DAY 6
Double-Duty Chicken &
Feta Spinach Salad, p. 374

MENU ADD-ON
• Colorful Quinoa Salad,
p. 171

DAY 7
Southwestern Casserole,
p. 267

MENU ADD-ON
• Tortilla Chips

DAY 8
Italian Pot Roast, p. 337

MENU ADD-ON
• Lemon Rice Pilaf, p. 387

DAY 9
Pan-Roasted Chicken &
Vegetables, p. 55

MENU ADD-ON
• Monkey Bread Biscuits,
p. 384

DAY 10
Asparagus Cashew Stir-Fry,
p. 338

MENU ADD-ON
• Fortune Cookies

DAY 16
Creamy Chicken Soup,
p. 341

MENU ADD-ON
• Whole Wheat Bread

DAY 17
Sausage Bread Sandwiches,
p. 262

MENU ADD-ON
• Summer Salad, p. 391

DAY 18
Reheat frozen Pizza Pasta
Casserole, p. 239

MENU ADD-ON
• Gorgonzola-Pear Mesclun
Salad, p. 380

DAY 19
Flaky Chicken Wellington,
p. 343

MENU ADD-ON
• Steamed Carrots

DAY 20
Reheat frozen
Southwestern Casserole,
p. 267
MENU ADD-ON
• Spinach & Turkey
Pinwheels, p. 71

DAY 26
Pizza Roll-Ups, p. 76

MENU ADD-ON
• Green Salad

DAY 27
Reheat frozen Two-For-One
Chicken Tetrazzini,
p. 246
MENU ADD-ON
• Nectarine & Beet Salad,
p. 387

DAY 28
Slow-Cooked Turkey Sloppy
Joes, p. 49

MENU ADD-ON
• Frozen French Fries

DAY 29
Reheat frozen Sausage
Bread Sandwiches, p. 262

MENU ADD-ON
• Thymed Zucchini Saute,
p. 393

DAY 30
Tangy Sweet & Sour
Meatballs, p. 363

MENU ADD-ON
• Creamy Pineapple Pie,
p. 411

MEALS ON THE GO

PUT A TASTY TWIST ON YOUR MAMMA'S BROWN BAG STAPLES.

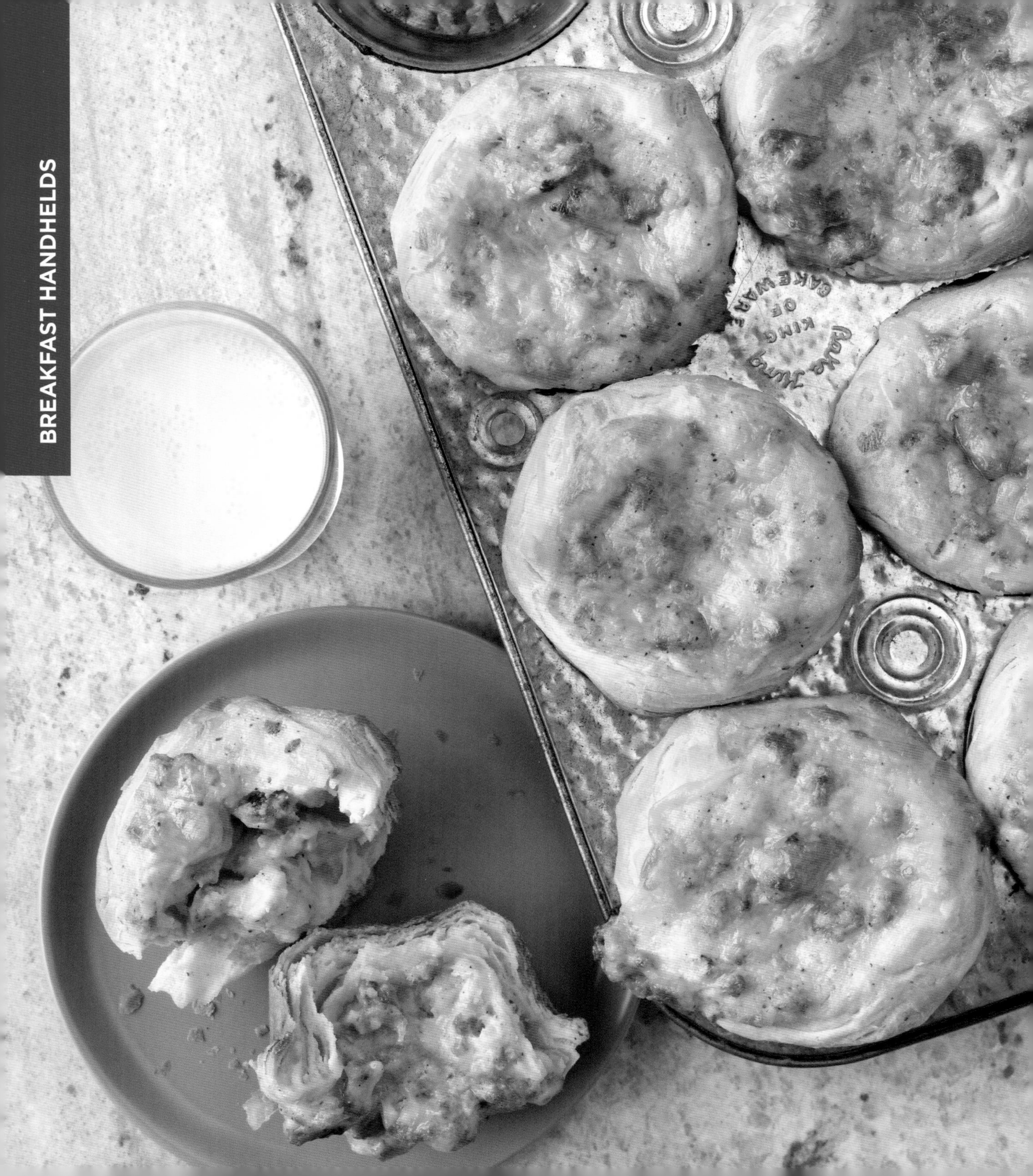

❄ BREAKFAST BISCUIT CUPS

The first time I made these cups, my husband and his friend came into the kitchen as I pulled the pan from the oven. They devoured the biscuits!
—*Debra Carlson, Columbus Junction, IA*

Prep: 30 min. • **Bake:** 20 min.
Makes: 8 servings

- ⅓ lb. bulk pork sausage
- 1 Tbsp. all-purpose flour
- ⅛ tsp. salt
- ½ tsp. pepper, divided
- ¾ cup plus 1 Tbsp. 2% milk, divided
- ½ cup frozen cubed hash brown potatoes, thawed
- 1 Tbsp. butter
- 2 large eggs
- ⅛ tsp. garlic salt
- 1 can (16.3 oz.) large refrigerated flaky biscuits
- ½ cup shredded Colby-Monterey Jack cheese

1. In a large skillet, cook sausage over medium heat until no longer pink; drain. Stir in flour, salt and ¼ tsp. pepper until blended; gradually add ¾ cup milk. Bring to a boil; cook and stir for 2 minutes or until thickened. Remove from the heat and set aside.
2. In another large skillet over medium heat, cook potatoes in butter until tender. Whisk the eggs, garlic salt and remaining milk and pepper; add to skillet. Cook and stir until almost set.
3. Press each biscuit onto the bottom and up the sides of 8 ungreased muffin cups. Spoon the egg mixture, half the cheese, and sausage into cups; sprinkle with remaining cheese.

4. Bake at 375° for 18-22 minutes or until golden brown. Cool 5 minutes before removing from pan.
Freeze option: Freeze cooled biscuit cups in a freezer container, separating layers with waxed paper. To use, microwave 1 frozen biscuit cup on high for 50-60 seconds or until heated through.
1 biscuit cup: 303 cal., 18g fat (6g sat. fat), 72mg chol., 774mg sod., 26g carb. (7g sugars, 1g fiber), 9g pro.

TEST KITCHEN TIP
A touch of maple syrup added to the sausage (or poured over the top) makes for an addictive sweet and savory treat.

5i CRANBERRY-BANANA SMOOTHIES

During the holidays, I enjoy smoothies made with leftover cranberry sauce. Don't have a frozen banana? Use a regular banana and add more ice.
—*Gina Fensler, Cincinnati, OH*

Takes: 5 min. • **Makes:** 2 servings

- 1 large banana, peeled, quartered and frozen
- ⅔ cup whole-berry cranberry sauce
- ½ cup fat-free vanilla yogurt
- ½ cup ice cubes

Place all ingredients in a blender; cover and process until smooth. Serve immediately.
1 cup: 230 cal., 0 fat (0 sat. fat), 2mg chol., 21mg sod., 56g carb. (35g sugars, 3g fiber), 3g pro.

GLAZED LEMON BLUEBERRY MUFFINS

Bursting with berries and drizzled with a light lemony glaze, these muffins are moist, tender and truly something special. This is one recipe you simply must introduce to family and friends.
—*Kathy Harding, Richmond, MO*

Prep: 30 min. • **Bake:** 25 min.
Makes: 11 muffins

- ½ cup butter, softened
- 1 cup sugar
- 2 large eggs, room temperature
- ½ cup 2% milk
- 2 Tbsp. lemon juice
- 2 tsp. grated lemon zest
- 2 cups all-purpose flour
- 2 tsp. baking powder
  Dash salt
- 2 cups fresh or frozen blueberries

GLAZE
- 1½ cups confectioners' sugar
- 2 Tbsp. lemon juice
- 1 tsp. butter, melted
- ¼ tsp. vanilla extract

1. Preheat oven to 400°. In a large bowl, cream butter and sugar until light and fluffy. Add eggs, 1 at a time, beating well after each addition. Beat in milk, lemon juice and zest. Combine flour, baking powder and salt; add to the creamed mixture just until moistened. Fold in blueberries.

2. Fill paper-lined regular-size muffin cups three-fourths full. Bake 25-30 minutes or until a toothpick inserted in muffin comes out clean. Cool 5 minutes before removing from pan to a wire rack.

3. In a small bowl, combine confectioners' sugar, lemon juice, butter and vanilla; drizzle over warm muffins.

Freeze option: Freeze cooled muffins in freezer container. To use, thaw muffins at room temperature or, if desired, microwave each muffin on high for 20-30 seconds or until heated through.

Note: If using frozen blueberries to prepare the muffins, use without thawing to avoid discoloring the batter.

1 muffin: 327 cal., 10g fat (6g sat. fat), 62mg chol., 166mg sod., 56g carb. (37g sugars, 1g fiber), 4g pro.

CINNAMON-RAISIN GRANOLA BARS

I make these chewy bars with cinnamon, raisin and maple for quick breakfasts and road trips. You can use chocolate chips instead of raisins.
—*Kristina Miedema, Houghton, NY*

Prep: 15 min. • **Bake:** 25 min. + cooling
Makes: 2 dozen

2   cups old-fashioned oats
1   cup all-purpose flour
1   cup golden raisins
¾   cup packed brown sugar
½   cup toasted wheat germ
¾   tsp. ground cinnamon
¾   tsp. salt
1   large egg, room temperature
½   cup canola oil
½   cup maple syrup
2   tsp. vanilla extract

1. Preheat oven to 350°. Line a 13x9-in. baking pan with foil, letting ends extend up sides; grease foil. In a large bowl, combine the first 7 ingredients. In a small bowl, combine egg, oil, maple syrup and vanilla; pour over oat mixture and mix well. (Batter will be sticky.)
2. Press batter into prepared pan. Bake 25-30 minutes or until set and edges are lightly browned. Cool in the pan on a wire rack. Lifting with foil, remove from pan; cut into 24 bars.
1 bar: 160 cal., 6g fat (1g sat. fat), 8mg chol., 80mg sod., 26g carb. (15g sugars, 1g fiber), 3g pro.

5i 🍎

FRUITY FRAPPE

Making a taste-alike of a restaurant drink is fun, but better yet, I know exactly what's in this one. My frappe gets its sweetness from berries, juice and honey.
—*Patty Crouse, Warren, PA*

Takes: 10 min. • **Makes:** 4 servings

1 cup water
1 cup fat-free milk
⅔ cup thawed orange
   juice concentrate
3 Tbsp. honey
½ tsp. vanilla extract
1 cup ice cubes
1 cup frozen unsweetened
   mixed berries

Place all ingredients in a blender; cover and process until blended. Serve immediately.
1¼ cups: 166 cal., 0 fat (0 sat. fat), 1mg chol., 28mg sod., 39g carb. (37g sugars, 1g fiber), 3g pro.

❄ HAM & CHEESE BREAKFAST STRUDELS

These get the morning off to a great start! Sometimes I assemble the strudels ahead and freeze them individually before baking.
—*Jo Groth, Plainfield, IA*

- -

Prep: 25 min. • **Bake:** 10 min.
Makes: 6 servings

3	Tbsp. butter, divided
2	Tbsp. all-purpose flour
1	cup whole milk
⅓	cup shredded Swiss cheese
2	Tbsp. grated Parmesan cheese
¼	tsp. salt
5	large eggs, lightly beaten
¼	lb. ground fully cooked ham (about ¾ cup)
6	sheets phyllo dough (14x9-in. size)
½	cup butter, melted
¼	cup dry bread crumbs

TOPPING
2	Tbsp. grated Parmesan cheese
2	Tbsp. minced fresh parsley

1. In a small saucepan, melt 2 Tbsp. butter. Stir in flour until smooth; gradually add milk. Bring to a boil; cook and stir 2 minutes or until thickened. Stir in cheeses and salt.
2. In a large nonstick skillet, melt remaining butter over medium heat. Add eggs to pan; cook and stir until almost set. Stir in ham and cheese sauce; heat through. Remove from heat.
3. Preheat oven to 375°. Place 1 sheet of phyllo dough on a work surface. (Keep the remaining phyllo covered with a damp towel to prevent it from drying out.) Brush with melted butter. Sprinkle with 2 tsp. bread crumbs. Fold in half lengthwise; brush again with butter. Spoon ½ cup filling onto phyllo about 2 in. from a short side. Fold side and edges over filling and roll up. Brush with butter. Repeat with the remaining phyllo, butter, bread crumbs and filling.
4. Place on a greased baking sheet; sprinkle each with 1 tsp. cheese and 1 tsp. parsley. Bake 10-15 minutes or until golden brown. Serve immediately.

Freeze option: After topping strudels with cheese and parsley, freeze unbaked on a waxed paper-lined baking sheet until firm. Transfer to a freezer container; return to freezer. To use, bake strudels as directed, increasing time to 30-35 minutes or until heated through and golden brown.

1 strudel: 439 cal., 33g fat (18g sat. fat), 255mg chol., 754mg sod., 20g carb. (4g sugars, 1g fiber), 16g pro.

CHUNKY BREAKFAST COOKIES

Who says cookies aren't for breakfast? We devour these hearty oatmeal cookies, especially on the run. Add any dried fruits or nuts you might have on hand.
—Lea Langhoff, Round Lake, IL

Prep: 20 min. • **Bake:** 15 min./batch
Makes: 16 cookies

- ⅔ cup butter, softened
- ⅔ cup packed brown sugar
- 1 large egg, room temperature
- 1 large egg yolk, room temperature
- 1½ cups old-fashioned oats
- ¾ cup all-purpose flour
- ¾ cup whole wheat flour
- 1 tsp. baking soda
- ½ tsp. salt
- 1 cup semisweet chocolate chunks
- 1 cup chopped dates
- ½ cup sweetened shredded coconut

1. Preheat oven to 350°. In a large bowl, cream butter and brown sugar until light and fluffy. Beat in egg and egg yolk. In another bowl, mix oats, flours, baking soda and salt; gradually beat into creamed mixture. Stir in remaining ingredients.
2. Shape ¼ cupfuls of dough into balls; flatten to ¾-in. thickness. Place 2 in. apart on ungreased baking sheets.
3. Bake for 13-15 minutes or until golden brown. Cool on pans 2 minutes. Remove to wire racks to cool. Serve warm or at room temperature. To reheat, microwave each cookie on high for 15-20 seconds or just until warmed.
Freeze option: Freeze unbaked cookies in a freezer container, separating layers with waxed paper. To use, place dough portions 2 in. apart on ungreased baking sheets; let stand at room temperature 30 minutes before baking. Bake as directed, increasing time by 1-2 minutes.
1 cookie: 291 cal., 15g fat (9g sat. fat), 44mg chol., 239mg sod., 40g carb. (24g sugars, 3g fiber), 4g pro.

MICROWAVE EGG SANDWICH

If you are looking for a great grab-and-go breakfast for busy mornings, this sandwich is it. High in protein and low in calories and fat, it keeps me full all morning.
—Brenda Otto, Reedsburg, WI

Takes: 15 min. • **Makes:** 1 serving

- 1 piece Canadian bacon
- ¼ cup egg substitute
- 1 Tbsp. salsa
- 1 Tbsp. shredded reduced-fat cheddar cheese
- 1 whole wheat English muffin, split, toasted
- 3 spinach leaves

1. Place Canadian bacon on bottom of a 6-oz. ramekin or custard cup coated with cooking spray. Pour the egg substitute over the top. Microwave, uncovered, on high for 30 seconds; stir. Microwave 15-30 seconds or until egg is almost set. Top with salsa; sprinkle with cheese. Microwave just until cheese is melted, about 10 seconds.
2. Line bottom of English muffin with spinach. Place egg and Canadian bacon over spinach; replace English muffin top.
1 sandwich: 218 cal., 4g fat (2g sat. fat), 12mg chol., 751mg sod., 30g carb. (7g sugars, 5g fiber), 17g pro. **Diabetic exchanges:** 2 starch, 2 lean meat.

CREAMY BERRY SMOOTHIES

No one can tell there's tofu in these silky smoothies. For me, the blend of berries and pomegranate juice is a welcome delight.
—*Sonya Labbe, West Hollywood, CA*

Takes: 10 min. • **Makes:** 2 servings

- ½ cup pomegranate juice
- 1 Tbsp. agave syrup or honey
- 3 oz. silken firm tofu (about ½ cup)
- 1 cup frozen unsweetened mixed berries
- 1 cup frozen unsweetened strawberries

Place all ingredients in a blender; cover and process until blended. Serve immediately.

1 cup: 157 cal., 1g fat (0 sat. fat), 0 chol., 24mg sod., 35g carb. (29g sugars, 3g fiber), 4g pro.

BACON QUICHE TARTS

Here's a fun way to make single-serving quiche that people of all ages are sure to enjoy. Flavored with bacon, cheese and veggies, these little bites are just the thing for your next brunch spread.
—*Kendra Schertz, Nappanee, IN*

- -

Prep: 15 min. • **Bake:** 20 min.
Makes: 8 servings

6	oz. cream cheese, softened
5	tsp. 2% milk
2	large eggs
½	cup shredded Colby cheese
2	Tbsp. chopped green pepper
1	Tbsp. finely chopped onion
1	tube (8 oz.) refrigerated crescent rolls
5	bacon strips, cooked and crumbled Thinly sliced green onions, optional

1. In a small bowl, beat cream cheese and milk until smooth. Add the eggs, cheese, green pepper and onion.

2. Separate crescent dough into 8 triangles; press onto the bottom and up the sides of greased muffin cups. Sprinkle half of the bacon into cups. Pour egg mixture over bacon; top with remaining bacon.

3. Bake, uncovered, at 375° until a knife inserted in the center comes out clean, 18-22 minutes. Serve warm. If desired, top with chopped green onion.

Freeze option: Freeze cooled baked tarts in a freezer container. To use, reheat tarts on a baking sheet in a preheated 375° oven until heated through.

1 tart: 258 cal., 19g fat (9g sat. fat), 87mg chol., 409mg sod., 12g carb. (3g sugars, 0 fiber), 8g pro.

ON-THE-GO BREAKFAST MUFFINS

I usually prepare these on Sunday night, so when we're running late on weekday mornings, the kids can grab these to eat on the bus. They all request that I make these muffins regularly, and I'm happy to oblige.
—*Irene Wayman, Grantsville, UT*

- -

Prep: 30 min. • **Bake:** 15 min.
Makes: 1½ dozen

- 1 lb. bulk Italian sausage
- 7 large eggs, divided use
- 2 cups all-purpose flour
- ⅓ cup sugar
- 3 tsp. baking powder
- ½ tsp. salt
- ½ cup 2% milk
- ½ cup canola oil
- 1 cup shredded cheddar cheese, divided

1. Preheat oven to 400°. In a large nonstick skillet, cook sausage over medium heat until no longer pink, 6-8 minutes, breaking into crumbles. Remove with a slotted spoon; drain on paper towels. Wipe skillet clean.
2. In a small bowl, whisk 5 eggs. Pour into same skillet; cook and stir over medium heat until thickened and no liquid egg remains. Remove from heat.
3. In a large bowl, whisk flour, sugar, baking powder and salt. In another bowl, whisk remaining eggs, milk and oil until blended. Add to the flour mixture; stir just until moistened. Fold in ⅔ cup cheese, sausage and scrambled eggs.
4. Fill greased or paper-lined muffin cups three-fourths full. Sprinkle the tops with remaining cheese. Bake 12-15 minutes or until a toothpick inserted in center comes out clean. Cool 5 minutes before removing from pans to wire racks. Serve warm.
Freeze option: Freeze cooled muffins in an airtight container. To use, microwave each muffin on high for 45-60 seconds or until heated through.
1 muffin: 238 cal., 16g fat (4g sat. fat), 93mg chol., 357mg sod., 15g carb. (4g sugars, 0 fiber), 8g pro.

CHOCOLATE-PEANUT GRANOLA BARS

Nutella and peanut butter meet to make some amazing granola bars. Everyone always thinks they're eating something naughty but the morning bites are full of oats and healthy fats.

—*Brenda Caughell, Durham, NC*

Takes: 30 min. • **Makes:** 2 dozen

2½ cups old-fashioned oats
¾ cup lightly salted dry roasted peanuts, coarsely chopped
¾ cup wheat germ
¾ cup sunflower kernels
½ cup honey
¼ cup packed brown sugar
3 Tbsp. butter
⅓ cup creamy peanut butter
⅓ cup Nutella

1. Preheat oven to 400°. In an ungreased 15x10x1-in. baking pan, combine the oats, peanuts, wheat germ and sunflower kernels. Bake, stirring occasionally, until toasted, 8-12 minutes. Cool in pan on a wire rack.
2. In a small saucepan, combine honey, brown sugar and butter. Cook and stir over medium heat until mixture comes to a boil; cook 2 minutes longer. Remove from heat; stir in the creamy peanut butter and Nutella until blended.
3. Transfer oat mixture to a large bowl; add honey mixture and toss to coat. Press into a greased 13x9-in. pan. Cool. Cut into bars.
1 bar: 178 cal., 10g fat (2g sat. fat), 4mg chol., 75mg sod., 20g carb. (11g sugars, 2g fiber), 5g pro.

🍎 ❄️ EGG BURRITOS

Quickly zap one of these frozen burritos in the microwave and you'll stave off hunger all morning. This recipe is my family's favorite combo, but I sometimes use breakfast sausage instead of bacon.
—Audra Niederman, Aberdeen, SD

Takes: 25 min. • **Makes:** 10 burritos

12 bacon strips, chopped
12 large eggs
½ tsp. salt
¼ tsp. pepper
10 flour tortillas (8 in.), warmed
1½ cups shredded cheddar cheese
4 green onions, thinly sliced

1. In a large cast-iron or other heavy skillet, cook the bacon until crisp; drain on paper towels. Remove all but 1-2 Tbsp. drippings from pan.
2. Whisk together eggs, salt and pepper. Heat skillet over medium heat; pour in egg mixture. Cook and stir until the eggs are thickened and no liquid egg remains; remove from heat.
3. Spoon about ¼ cup egg mixture onto center of each tortilla; sprinkle with cheese, bacon and green onions. Roll into burritos.
Freeze option: Cool eggs before making burritos. Individually wrap burritos in paper towels and foil; freeze in an airtight container. To use, remove foil; place paper towel-wrapped burrito on a microwave-safe plate. Microwave on high until heated through, turning once. Let stand 15 seconds.
1 burrito: 376 cal., 20g fat (8g sat. fat), 251mg chol., 726mg sod., 29g carb. (0 sugars, 2g fiber), 19g pro.

BANANA OAT BREAKFAST COOKIES

I used to buy name-brand breakfast cookies from the supermarket, but since I found this recipe I've enjoyed making my cookies more than buying them.
—Linda Burciaga, tasteofhome.com

Prep: 20 min. • **Bake:** 15 min./batch
Makes: 1 dozen

1 cup mashed ripe bananas (about 2 medium)
½ cup chunky peanut butter
½ cup honey
1 tsp. vanilla extract
1 cup old-fashioned oats
½ cup whole wheat flour
¼ cup nonfat dry milk powder
2 tsp. ground cinnamon
½ tsp. salt
¼ tsp. baking soda
1 cup dried cranberries or raisins

1. Preheat oven to 350°. Beat the bananas, peanut butter, honey and vanilla until blended. In another bowl, combine next 6 ingredients; gradually beat into the wet mixture. Stir in dried cranberries.
2. Drop cookie dough by ¼ cupfuls 3 in. apart onto greased baking sheets; flatten to ½-in. thickness.
3. Bake until golden brown, 14-16 minutes. Cool on pans 5 minutes. Remove to wire racks. Serve warm or at room temperature. To reheat, microwave each cookie on high just until warmed, 15-20 seconds.
1 cookie: 212 cal., 6g fat (1g sat. fat), 0 chol., 186mg sod., 38g carb. (25g sugars, 4g fiber), 5g pro.

✳ MORNING MAPLE MUFFINS

Maple combines with a subtle touch of cinnamon and nuts to give these muffins the flavor of a hearty pancake breakfast. But you don't have to sit down to enjoy them. Our 2-year-old comes back for seconds, and even my husband—who doesn't normally like muffins—likes these.
—*Elizabeth Talbot, Lexington, KY*

- -

Takes: 30 min. • **Makes:** 16 muffins

2	cups all-purpose flour
½	cup packed brown sugar
2	tsp. baking powder
½	tsp. salt
¾	cup 2% milk
½	cup butter, melted
½	cup maple syrup
¼	cup sour cream
1	large egg, room temperature
½	tsp. vanilla extract

TOPPING

3	Tbsp. all-purpose flour
3	Tbsp. sugar
2	Tbsp. chopped nuts
½	tsp. ground cinnamon
2	Tbsp. cold butter

1. Preheat oven to 400°. In a large bowl, combine flour, brown sugar, baking powder and salt. In another bowl, combine milk, butter, syrup, sour cream, egg and vanilla. Stir into dry ingredients just until moistened.

2. Fill greased or paper-lined muffin cups two-thirds full. For topping, combine flour, sugar, nuts and cinnamon; cut in butter until crumbly. Sprinkle over batter.

3. Bake 16-20 minutes or until a toothpick inserted in center comes out clean. Cool 5 minutes before removing from pans to wire racks. Serve warm.

Freeze option: Freeze cooled muffins in freezer containers. To use, thaw at room temperature or, if desired, microwave each muffin on high for 20-30 seconds or until heated through.

1 muffin: 212 cal., 9g fat (5g sat. fat), 36mg chol., 211mg sod., 30g carb. (16g sugars, 1g fiber), 3g pro.

Bacon Maple Muffins: Omit vanilla and topping. Cook 10 bacon strips until crisp; remove to paper towels to drain. Cool and crumble bacon. Fold into batter.

Hazelnut Maple Muffins: Omit topping. Fold in ¾ cup chopped hazelnuts.

5j

HARD-BOILED EGGS

Here's a foolproof technique for making hard-cooked egg. Prepare them on the weekend for fast bites on busy mornings.
—Taste of Home *Test Kitchen*

- -

Prep: 20 min. + cooling • **Makes:** 12 servings

12 large eggs
    Cold water

1. Place the eggs in a single layer in a large saucepan; add enough cold water to cover by 1 in. Cover and quickly bring to a boil. Remove from the heat. Let stand for 15 minutes for large eggs (18 minutes for extra-large eggs, and 12 minutes for medium eggs).
2. Rinse eggs in cold water and place in ice water until completely cooled. Drain and refrigerate.
1 egg: 75 cal., 5g fat (2g sat. fat), 213mg chol., 63mg sod., 1g carb. (1g sugars, 0 fiber), 6g pro.

⑤i

APPLE YOGURT PARFAITS

Get the morning started right with this super-simple four-ingredient parfait. Try chunky or flavored applesauce or swap the nutmeg with cinnamon for quick and easy variations.
—*Rebekah Radewahn, Wauwatosa, WI*

Takes: 10 min. • **Makes:** 4 servings

 1 **cup sweetened applesauce**
   Dash ground nutmeg
 ½ **cup granola with raisins**
 1⅓ **cups vanilla yogurt**

In a small bowl, combine applesauce and nutmeg. Spoon 1 Tbsp. granola into each of 4 parfait glasses. Layer each with ⅓ cup yogurt and ¼ cup applesauce; sprinkle with remaining granola. Serve immediately.

1 parfait: 158 cal., 2g fat (1g sat. fat), 4mg chol., 70mg sod., 30g carb. (24g sugars, 1g fiber), 5g pro.

WALNUT ZUCCHINI MUFFINS

Shredded zucchini adds moisture to these tender muffins dotted with raisins and chopped walnuts. If you have a surplus of zucchini in summer as many of us do, this is a good way to use some of it.
—*Harriet Stichter, Milford, IN*

Prep: 20 min. • **Bake:** 20 min.
Makes: 1 dozen

1	cup all-purpose flour
¾	cup whole wheat flour
⅔	cup packed brown sugar
2	tsp. baking powder
¾	tsp. ground cinnamon
½	tsp. salt
2	large eggs, room temperature
¾	cup 2% milk
½	cup butter, melted
1	cup shredded zucchini
1	cup chopped walnuts
½	cup raisins

1. Preheat oven to 375°. In a large bowl, whisk the first 6 ingredients. In another bowl, whisk eggs, milk and melted butter until blended. Add to flour mixture; stir just until moistened. Fold in zucchini, walnuts and raisins.

2. Fill 12 greased muffin cups three-fourths full. Bake 18-20 minutes or until a toothpick inserted in center comes out clean. Cool 5 minutes before removing from pan to a wire rack. Serve warm.

Freeze option: Freeze cooled muffins in freezer containers. To use, thaw at room temperature or, if desired, microwave each muffin on high until heated through, roughly 20-30 seconds.

1 muffin: 281 cal., 15g fat (6g sat. fat), 53mg chol., 250mg sod., 33g carb. (17g sugars, 2g fiber), 6g pro.

BREAKFAST WRAPS

We like quick and simple morning meals during the week, and these wraps can be prepped ahead of time. With just a minute in the microwave, breakfast is ready to go.
—*Betty Kleberger, Florissant, MO*

Takes: 15 min. • **Makes:** 4 servings

- 6 **large eggs**
- 2 **Tbsp. milk**
- ¼ **tsp. pepper**
- 1 **Tbsp. canola oil**
- 1 **cup shredded cheddar cheese**
- ¾ **cup diced fully cooked ham**
- 4 **flour tortillas (8 in.), warmed**

1. In a small bowl, whisk the eggs, milk and pepper. In a large skillet, heat oil. Add egg mixture; cook and stir over medium heat until eggs are completely set. Stir in cheese and ham.
2. Spoon egg mixture down the center of each tortilla; roll up.
Freeze option: Wrap cooled egg wrap in foil and freeze in a freezer container. To use, thaw in refrigerator overnight. Remove foil; wrap the tortilla in a moist paper towel. Microwave on high for 30-60 seconds or until heated through. Serve immediately.
1 serving: 436 cal., 24g fat (10g sat. fat), 364mg chol., 853mg sod., 28g carb. (1g sugars, 0 fiber), 25g pro.
Pizza Breakfast Wraps: Prepare recipe as directed, replacing cheddar cheese and ham with mozzarella cheese and cooked sausage. Serve with warm marinara sauce on the side.
Pulled Pork Breakfast Wraps: Prepare recipe as directed, replacing cheddar cheese and ham with smoked Gouda cheese and precooked pulled pork. Serve with warm barbecue sauce on the side.

RICHARD'S BREAKFAST BARS

These are so addictive! For clean slices, use a pizza cutter coated with cooking spray.
—*Richard Cole, Richmond, TX*

Prep: 10 min. • **Bake:** 25 min. + cooling
Makes: 2 dozen

- 1 **can (14 oz.) sweetened condensed milk**
- 2 **large eggs, beaten**
- 2 **cups Fiber One bran cereal**
- 2 **cups quick-cooking oats**
- 1½ **cups chopped pecans**
- 1 **cup miniature semisweet chocolate chips**
- 1 **cup golden raisins**
- 1 **cup sweetened shredded coconut**
- 1 **can (8 oz.) unsweetened crushed pineapple, undrained**

1. Preheat oven to 350°. Whisk together condensed milk and eggs; mix in remaining ingredients. Firmly press mixture evenly into a greased 13x9-in. baking dish.
2. Bake, uncovered, until edges are golden brown, 25-30 minutes. Cool completely in dish on wire rack. Chill 1 hour; cut into bars. Store refrigerated in an airtight container.
1 bar: 219 cal., 11g fat (4g sat. fat), 21mg chol., 57mg sod., 31g carb. (20g sugars, 5g fiber), 4g pro.

GRANOLA BLUEBERRY MUFFINS

I wanted to put a new spin on muffins, so I mixed in some granola. I brought a batch to work the next morning—success. The granola I used contained lots of nuts, pumpkin seeds and shredded coconut.
—*Megan Weiss, Menomonie, WI*

- -

Prep: 20 min. • **Bake:** 15 min.
Makes: 1 dozen

1½ cups whole wheat flour
½ cup all-purpose flour
¼ cup packed brown sugar
2 tsp. baking powder
½ tsp. salt
½ tsp. baking soda
1 cup granola without raisins, divided
1 large egg, room temperature
1 cup buttermilk
¼ cup canola oil
2 Tbsp. orange juice
1 Tbsp. lemon juice
1 cup fresh or frozen unsweetened blueberries

1. Preheat oven to 400°. In a small bowl, whisk flours, brown sugar, baking powder, salt and baking soda. Stir in ½ cup granola. In another bowl, whisk egg, buttermilk, oil and juices until blended. Add to the flour mixture; stir just until moistened. Fold in the blueberries.

2. Fill 12 greased muffin cups three-fourths full; sprinkle remaining granola over batter. Bake for 12-15 minutes or until a toothpick inserted in center comes out clean. Cool 5 minutes before removing from pan to a wire rack.

Freeze option: Freeze cooled muffins in freezer containers. To use, thaw at room temperature or, if desired, microwave each muffin on high for 20-30 seconds or until heated through.

Note: If using frozen berries, use without thawing to avoid discoloring the batter.

1 muffin: 188 cal., 7g fat (1g sat. fat), 18mg chol., 251mg sod., 28g carb. (8g sugars, 4g fiber), 6g pro. **Diabetic exchanges:** 2 starch, 1 fat.

HAM CHEDDAR BISCUITS

My husband often skipped breakfast until I created these savory biscuits that have become his favorite. I keep a batch in the freezer, and he reheats a few in the microwave before he heads out the door.
—*Sarah Marshall, Broken Arrow, OK*

- -

Takes: 20 min. • **Makes:** 20 biscuits

2¼ **cups biscuit/baking mix**
¾ **cup 2% milk**
¾ **cup shredded cheddar cheese**
½ **cup chopped fully cooked ham**

1. In a bowl, combine the biscuit mix and milk just until moistened. Stir in the cheese and ham. Drop by rounded tablespoonfuls onto greased baking sheets.
2. Bake at 450° for 8-10 minutes or until golden brown. Serve warm.
1 serving: 81 cal., 4g fat (2g sat. fat), 8mg chol., 245mg sod., 9g carb. (1g sugars, 0 fiber), 3g pro.

CHEWY HONEY GRANOLA BARS

There's sweetness from honey, chewiness from raisins, a lovely hint of chocolate and cinnamon, and bit of crunch in these rustic bars. Wrap individual bars and place in a resealable freezer container. When you want a nibble on a hectic morning, just grab one and let it thaw for a few minutes.
—*Tasha Lehman, Williston, VT*

- -

Prep: 10 min. • **Bake:** 15 min. + cooling
Makes: 20 servings

3	cups old-fashioned oats
2	cups unsweetened puffed wheat cereal
1	cup all-purpose flour
⅓	cup chopped walnuts
⅓	cup raisins
⅓	cup miniature semisweet chocolate chips
1	tsp. baking soda
1	tsp. ground cinnamon
1	cup honey
¼	cup butter, melted
1	tsp. vanilla extract

1. Preheat oven to 350°. In a large bowl, combine the first 8 ingredients. In a small bowl, combine honey, butter and vanilla; pour over oat mixture and mix well. (Mixture will be sticky.)
2. Press into a 13x9-in. baking pan coated with cooking spray. Bake 14-18 minutes or until set and edges are lightly browned. Cool on a wire rack. Cut into bars.

1 bar: 178 cal., 5g fat (2g sat. fat), 6mg chol., 81mg sod., 32g carb. (17g sugars, 2g fiber), 3g pro. **Diabetic exchanges:** 2 starch, ½ fat.

❄ MAKE-AHEAD BREAKFAST BURRITOS

Burritos for breakfast? Why not! These zesty little handfuls will wake up your taste buds and start your day with a smile. And you can make and freeze them ahead, then just pop them into the microwave for a quick meal.
—*Linda Wells, St. Mary's, GA*

- -

Takes: 30 min. • **Makes:** 12 burritos

     1   lb. bulk pork sausage
   1½   cups frozen cubed hash
           brown potatoes
     ¼   cup diced onion
     ¼   cup diced green or red pepper
     4   large eggs, lightly beaten
   12   flour tortillas (8 in.), warmed
     ½   cup shredded cheddar cheese
           Optional: Picante sauce and sour
           cream

1. In a large skillet, cook pork sausage over medium heat until no longer pink; drain. Add the potatoes, onion and pepper; cook and stir for 6-8 minutes or until tender. Add eggs; cook and stir until set.

2. Spoon filling off center on each tortilla. Sprinkle with cheese. Fold sides and ends over filling and roll up. Serve with picante sauce and sour cream if desired.

Freeze option: Wrap each burrito in waxed paper and foil. Freeze burritos for up to 1 month. To use, remove foil and waxed paper. Place 1 burrito on a microwave-safe plate. Microwave on high for 2-2¼ minutes or until a thermometer reads 165°, turning burrito over once. Let stand for 20 seconds.

1 burrito: 303 cal., 15g fat (5g sat. fat), 87mg chol., 521mg sod., 30g carb. (0 sugars, 2g fiber), 12g pro.

MINI CHEESEBURGERS

Burger toppings are cooked right into the meat in these hearty sliders. Preparation is quick and easy, so make a bunch for future meals and snacks.
—Taste of Home *Test Kitchen*

Takes: 30 min. • **Makes:** 5 servings

1 large egg, lightly beaten
¼ cup quick-cooking oats
2 Tbsp. dill pickle relish
2 Tbsp. ketchup
2 tsp. prepared mustard
2 tsp. Worcestershire sauce
¼ tsp. pepper
⅛ tsp. garlic powder
1 lb. ground beef
3 to 4 slices American cheese
10 dinner rolls, split

1. Preheat broiler. In a large bowl, combine the first 8 ingredients. Add the beef; mix lightly but thoroughly. Shape into 10 patties. Transfer to a 15x10x1-in. baking pan. Broil 3-4 in. from heat 4-6 minutes on each side or until a thermometer reads 160°.
2. Meanwhile, cut cheese slices into thirds. Immediately place on burgers; serve on dinner rolls.
Freeze option: Place patties on a waxed paper-lined baking sheet; wrap and freeze until firm. Remove from pan and transfer to a large freezer container; return to freezer. To use, broil the frozen patties as directed, increasing time as necessary.
1 mini cheeseburger: 217 cal., 8 g fat (3 g sat. fat), 65 mg chol., 387 mg sod., 21 g carb., 2 g fiber, 13 g pro.

GROUND BEEF NOODLE SOUP

My heartwarming specialty combines ground beef with onions, celery and carrots. Whip it up on Saturday or Sunday for savory, satisfying lunches during the busy work week.
—*Judy Brander, Two Harbors, MN*

Prep: 15 min. • **Cook:** 20 min.
Makes: 8 servings (2 qt.)

1½ lbs. lean ground beef (90% lean)
½ cup each chopped onion, celery and carrot
7 cups water
1 envelope au jus mix
2 Tbsp. beef bouillon granules
2 bay leaves
⅛ tsp. pepper
1½ cups uncooked egg noodles

1. In a large saucepan, cook the beef, onion, celery and carrot over medium heat until meat is no longer pink; drain.
2. Add the water, au jus mix, bouillon, bay leaves and pepper; bring to a boil. Stir in the noodles. Return to a boil. Cook, uncovered, for 15 minutes or until noodles are tender, stirring occasionally. Discard bay leaves.
1 cup: 203 cal., 9g fat (3g sat. fat), 32mg chol., 471mg sod., 10g carb. (0 sugars, 1g fiber), 20g pro. **Diabetic exchanges:** 2 lean meat, 1 starch.

❄ PEPPERONI PIZZA LOAF

Because this hearty stromboli relies on frozen bread dough, it comes together in no time. The golden loaf is stuffed with cheese, pepperoni, mushrooms, peppers and olives. I often add a few thin slices of ham, too. It's tasty served with warm pizza sauce for dipping.
—*Jenny Brown, West Lafayette, IN*

- -

Prep: 20 min. • **Bake:** 35 min.
Makes: 12 slices

1	loaf (1 lb.) frozen bread dough, thawed
2	large eggs, separated
1	Tbsp. grated Parmesan cheese
1	Tbsp. olive oil
1	tsp. minced fresh parsley
1	tsp. dried oregano
½	tsp. garlic powder
¼	tsp. pepper
8	oz. sliced pepperoni
2	cups shredded part-skim mozzarella cheese
1	can (4 oz.) mushroom stems and pieces, drained
¼	to ½ cup pickled pepper rings
1	medium green pepper, diced
1	can (2¼ oz.) sliced ripe olives
1	can (15 oz.) pizza sauce

1. Preheat oven to 350°. On a greased baking sheet, roll out dough into a 15x10-in. rectangle. In a small bowl, combine the egg yolks, Parmesan cheese, oil, parsley, oregano, garlic powder and pepper. Brush over the dough.

2. Sprinkle with the pepperoni, mozzarella cheese, mushrooms, pepper rings, green pepper and olives. Roll up, jelly-roll style, starting with a long side; pinch seam to seal and tuck ends under.

3. Position loaf with seam side down; brush with egg whites. Do not let rise. Bake until golden brown and the dough is cooked through, 35-40 minutes. Warm the pizza sauce; serve with sliced loaf.

Freeze option: Freeze cooled unsliced pizza loaf in heavy-duty foil. To use, remove from freezer 30 minutes before reheating. Remove from foil and reheat loaf on a greased baking sheet in a preheated 325° oven until heated through. Serve as directed.

1 slice: 296 cal., 17g fat (6g sat. fat), 66mg chol., 827mg sod., 24g carb. (4g sugars, 2g fiber), 13g pro.

ITALIAN PULLED PORK SANDWICHES

Savor the flavors of Italian sausage sandwiches made with a healthier alternative—pulled pork! Let your slow cooker do the work, and you'll have meat to use in these sandwiches or other dishes.
—*Mike Dellario, Middleport, NY*

- -

Prep: 20 min. • **Cook:** 8 hours
Makes: 12 servings

- 1   **Tbsp. fennel seed, crushed**
- 1   **Tbsp. steak seasoning**
- 1   **tsp. cayenne pepper, optional**
- 1   **boneless pork shoulder butt roast (3 lbs.)**
- 1   **Tbsp. olive oil**
- 2   **medium green or sweet red peppers, thinly sliced**
- 2   **medium onions, thinly sliced**
- 1   **can (14½ oz.) diced tomatoes, undrained**
- 12 **whole wheat hamburger buns, split**

1. In a small bowl, combine the fennel seed, steak seasoning and cayenne if desired. Cut roast in half. Rub the seasoning mixture over pork. In a large skillet, brown roast in oil on all sides. Place in a 4- or 5-qt. slow cooker. Add the peppers, onions and tomatoes; cover and cook on low for 7-9 hours or until meat is tender.
2. Remove roast; cool slightly. Skim fat from cooking juices. Shred pork with 2 forks and return to slow cooker; heat through. Using a slotted spoon, place ½ cup meat mixture on each bun.
1 sandwich: 288 cal., 8g fat (2g sat. fat), 56mg chol., 454mg sod., 27g carb. (7g sugars, 5g fiber), 26g pro. **Diabetic exchanges:** 3 lean meat, 2 starch.

VEGETARIAN LINGUINE

This colorful pasta lunch, which is the brainchild of my oldest son, is truly a stick-to-the-ribs meal that includes fresh mushrooms, zucchini and other vegetables as well as basil and provolone cheese. Divide the dish into several containers for fast lunches.

—*Jane Bone, Cape Coral, FL*

Takes: 30 min. • **Makes:** 6 servings

6	oz. uncooked linguine
2	Tbsp. butter
1	Tbsp. olive oil
2	medium zucchini, thinly sliced
½	lb. fresh mushrooms, sliced
1	large tomato, chopped
2	green onions, chopped
1	garlic clove, minced
½	tsp. salt
¼	tsp. pepper
1	cup shredded provolone cheese
3	Tbsp. shredded Parmesan cheese
2	tsp. minced fresh basil

1. Cook linguine according to package directions. Meanwhile, in a large skillet, heat butter and oil over medium heat. Add zucchini and mushrooms; saute for 3-5 minutes. Add tomato, onions, garlic and seasonings. Reduce heat; simmer, covered, about 3 minutes.

2. Drain the linguine; add to vegetable mixture. Sprinkle with cheeses and basil. Toss to coat.

1½ cups: 260 cal., 13g fat (7g sat. fat), 25mg chol., 444mg sod., 26g carb. (3g sugars, 2g fiber), 12g pro. **Diabetic exchanges:** 1½ starch, 1½ fat, 1 medium-fat meat, 1 vegetable.

QUINOA TURKEY CHILI

This heart-healthy chili is not only tasty, it's a vitamin and protein powerhouse! Quinoa and beans are a nutritious way to stretch a half-pound of turkey for fast, easy and cost-efficient meal planning.
—*Sharon Giljum, Arlington, VA*

- -

Prep: 40 min. • **Cook:** 35 min.
Makes: 9 servings (2¼ qt.)

  1   **cup quinoa, rinsed**
  3½ **cups water, divided**
  ½   **lb. lean ground turkey**
  1   **large sweet onion, chopped**
  1   **medium sweet red pepper, chopped**
  4   **garlic cloves, minced**
  1   **Tbsp. chili powder**
  1   **Tbsp. ground cumin**
  ½   **tsp. ground cinnamon**
  2   **cans (15 oz. each) black beans, rinsed and drained**
  1   **can (28 oz.) crushed tomatoes**
  1   **medium zucchini, chopped**
  1   **chipotle pepper in adobo sauce, chopped**
  1   **Tbsp. adobo sauce**
  1   **bay leaf**
  1   **tsp. dried oregano**
  ½   **tsp. salt**
  ¼   **tsp. pepper**
  1   **cup frozen corn, thawed**
  ¼   **cup minced fresh cilantro**
      Optional toppings: Cubed avocado, shredded Monterey Jack cheese

1. In a large saucepan, bring quinoa and 2 cups water to a boil. Reduce heat; cover and simmer for 12-15 minutes or until water is absorbed. Remove from the heat; fluff with a fork and set aside.

2. Meanwhile, in a large saucepan coated with cooking spray, cook turkey, onion, red pepper and garlic over medium heat until meat is no longer pink and vegetables are tender; drain. Stir in the chili powder, cumin and cinnamon; cook 2 minutes longer.

3. Add the black beans, tomatoes, zucchini, chipotle pepper, adobo sauce, bay leaf, oregano, salt, pepper and remaining water. Bring to a boil. Reduce heat; cover and simmer for 30 minutes. Stir in the corn and quinoa; heat through. Discard the bay leaf; stir in cilantro. Serve with optional toppings as desired.

Freeze option: Freeze cooled chili in freezer containers. To use, partially thaw chili in the refrigerator overnight. Heat through in a saucepan, stirring occasionally; add broth or water if necessary.

Note: Look for quinoa in the cereal, rice or organic food aisle.

1 cup: 264 cal., 5g fat (1g sat. fat), 20mg chol., 514mg sod., 43g carb. (4g sugars, 9g fiber), 15g pro. **Diabetic exchanges:** 2 starch, 2 lean meat, 2 vegetable.

SPINACH & CHEESE LASAGNA ROLLS

These Italian-inspired roll-ups are fast to make. Toss one in a microwave-safe container for a quick, tasty lunch that reheats easily. Yum!
—*Cindy Romberg, Mississauga, ON*

- -

Prep: 25 min. + chilling • **Bake:** 35 min.
Makes: 6 servings

- 1 pkg. (10 oz.) frozen chopped spinach, thawed and squeezed dry
- 1 cup shredded part-skim mozzarella cheese
- 1 cup 2% cottage cheese
- ¾ cup grated Parmesan cheese, divided
- 1 large egg, lightly beaten
- 6 lasagna noodles, cooked and drained
- 1 jar (24 oz.) marinara sauce

1. In a small bowl, combine the chopped spinach, mozzarella, cottage cheese, ½ cup Parmesan cheese and egg. Spread a heaping ⅓ cupful over each noodle. Roll up; place seam side down in a 9-in. square baking dish coated with cooking spray. Cover and refrigerate overnight.
2. Remove from the refrigerator 30 minutes before baking. Pour marinara sauce over the roll-ups.
3. Cover and bake at 350° until bubbly, 33-38 minutes. Sprinkle with the remaining Parmesan cheese.
Note: This recipe was tested with Hunt's seasoned tomato sauce for lasagna.
1 lasagna roll: 301 cal., 11g fat (5g sat. fat), 56mg chol., 963mg sod., 33g carb. (9g sugars, 4g fiber), 18g pro.

🔵5i

HONEY-LIME ROASTED CHICKEN

This chicken dish starts with only a few ingredients. It's simple, light and so good. Prepare the whole chicken, and then cut it up for lunches during the week.
—*Lori Carbonell, Springfield, VT*

- -

Prep: 10 min. • **Bake:** 2½ hours + standing
Makes: 10 servings

- 1 whole roasting chicken (5 to 6 lbs.)
- ½ cup lime juice
- ¼ cup honey
- 1 Tbsp. stone-ground mustard or spicy brown mustard
- 1 tsp. salt
- 1 tsp. ground cumin

1. Carefully loosen the skin from the entire chicken. Place breast side up on a rack in a roasting pan. In a small bowl, whisk the lime juice, honey, mustard, salt and cumin.
2. Using a turkey baster, baste under the chicken skin with ⅓ cup lime juice mixture. Tie drumsticks together. Pour remaining lime juice mixture over chicken.
3. Roast until a thermometer inserted in the thickest part of thigh reads 170°-175°, 2-2½ hours. (Cover loosely with foil if the chicken browns too quickly.) Let stand for 10 minutes before carving. If desired, remove and discard skin before serving.
4 oz. cooked chicken: 294 cal., 16g fat (4g sat. fat), 90mg chol., 354mg sod., 8g carb. (7g sugars, 0 fiber), 28g pro.

MOM'S SWEDISH MEATBALLS

Enjoy this dish for dinner one night and for a hearty lunch the following day. Mom fixed these meatballs for all sorts of family meals, potluck suppers and PTA meetings. After smelling the aromas of browning meat and caramelized onions, we'd all be ready to eat!
—*Marybeth Mank, Mesquite, TX*

- -

Prep: 30 min. • **Cook:** 40 min.
Makes: 6 servings

- ¾ cup seasoned bread crumbs
- 1 medium onion, chopped
- 2 large eggs, lightly beaten
- ⅓ cup minced fresh parsley
- 1 tsp. coarsely ground pepper
- ¾ tsp. salt
- 2 lbs. ground beef

GRAVY
- ½ cup all-purpose flour
- 2¾ cups 2% milk
- 2 cans (10½ oz. each) condensed beef consomme, undiluted
- 1 Tbsp. Worcestershire sauce
- 1 tsp. coarsely ground pepper
- ¾ tsp. salt

NOODLES
- 1 pkg. (16 oz.) egg noodles
- ¼ cup butter, cubed
- ¼ cup minced fresh parsley

1. In a large bowl, combine the first 6 ingredients. Add beef; mix lightly but thoroughly. Shape into 1½-in. meatballs (about 36). In a large skillet over medium heat, brown meatballs in batches. Using a slotted spoon, remove to paper towels to drain, reserving drippings in pan.
2. For gravy, stir flour into drippings; cook over medium-high heat until light brown (do not burn). Gradually whisk in the milk until smooth. Stir in the consomme, Worcestershire sauce, pepper and salt. Bring to a boil over medium-high heat; cook and stir for 2 minutes or until thickened.
3. Reduce heat to medium-low; return meatballs to pan. Cook, uncovered, until meatballs are cooked through, stirring occasionally, 15-20 minutes longer.
4. Meanwhile, cook the noodles according to package directions. Drain; toss with butter. Serve with meatball mixture; sprinkle with parsley.
6 meatballs with 1¾ cups noodles and about ⅓ cup gravy: 837 cal., 33g fat (14g sat. fat), 256mg chol., 1744mg sod., 82g carb. (10g sugars, 4g fiber), 50g pro.

TEST KITCHEN TIP
Feel free to omit the salt in the gravy if you're watching the sodium levels in family dishes. Instead, add a dash of nutmeg or even allspice for a little extra boost of flavor.

ITALIAN SUB SANDWICHES

Add these to your meal plan for hearty change-of-pace lunches and casual dinners.
—*Judy Long, Effingham, IL*

- -

Prep: 15 min. • **Cook:** 40 min.
Makes: 8 servings

1½	lbs. Italian sausage links, cut into ½-in. pieces
2	medium red onions, thinly sliced
2	medium sweet red peppers, thinly sliced
2	medium green peppers, thinly sliced
1	garlic clove, minced
3	medium tomatoes, chopped
1	tsp. dried oregano
	Salt and pepper to taste
8	submarine sandwich buns (about 10 in.), split

1. In a large cast-iron or other heavy skillet, cook sausage over medium heat just until no longer pink; drain. Add onions, peppers and garlic. Cover and cook 25 minutes or until vegetables are tender, stirring occasionally. Add tomatoes and oregano. Cover and simmer 5-6 minutes or until tomatoes are cooked. Season with salt and pepper.

2. Meanwhile, hollow out bottom of each roll, leaving a ½-in. shell. (Discard removed bread or save for another use.) Toast rolls. Fill with sausage mixture.

Freeze option: Freeze cooled meat mixture in freezer containers. To use, partially thaw in refrigerator overnight. Heat through in a saucepan, stirring occasionally; add water if necessary.

1 sandwich: 442 cal., 24g fat (7g sat. fat), 46mg chol., 843mg sod., 42g carb. (7g sugars, 4g fiber), 17g pro.

DIY RAMEN SOUP

This jarred version of ramen soup is a healthier alternative to most commercial varieties. You can customize the veggies to your taste. The jars are ideal for grab-and-go lunches.
—*Michelle Clair, Seattle, WA*

- -

Takes: 25 min. • **Makes:** 2 servings

1	pkg. (3 oz.) ramen noodles
1	Tbsp. reduced-sodium chicken base
1	to 2 tsp. Sriracha chili sauce
1	tsp. minced fresh gingerroot
½	cup shredded carrots
½	cup shredded cabbage
2	radishes, halved and sliced
½	cup sliced fresh shiitake mushrooms
1	cup shredded cooked chicken breast
¼	cup fresh cilantro leaves
1	large hard-boiled egg, halved
2	lime wedges
4	cups boiling water

1. Cook ramen according to package directions; cool. In each of two 1-qt. wide-mouth canning jars, divide and layer ingredients in the following order: ramen noodles, chicken base, chili sauce, ginger, carrots, cabbage, radishes, mushrooms, chicken and cilantro. Place egg and lime wedge in 4-oz. glass jars or other airtight containers. Cover all 4 containers and refrigerate until serving.

2. To serve, pour 2 cups boiling water into each 1-qt. glass jar; let stand until warmed through or until chicken base has dissolved. Stir to combine seasonings. Squeeze lime juice over soup and place egg on top.

1 serving: 401 cal., 14g fat (6g sat. fat), 153mg chol., 1092mg sod., 35g carb. (4g sugars, 2g fiber), 31g pro.

HEARTY PAELLA

You can divide this dish into containers for great lunches that travel well and reheat quickly. I first had paella in Spain, and I instantly set on a quest to re-create the rich flavors of that dish. We love the shrimp, chicken, veggies and olives in this easy make-at-home version.
—*Elizabeth Godecke, Chicago, IL*

- -

Prep: 25 min. • **Cook:** 30 min.
Makes: 6 servings

1¼	lbs. boneless skinless chicken breasts, cut into 1-in. cubes
1	Tbsp. olive oil
1	cup uncooked long grain rice
1	medium onion, chopped
2	garlic cloves, minced
2¼	cups reduced-sodium chicken broth
1	can (14½ oz.) diced tomatoes, undrained
1	tsp. dried oregano
½	tsp. paprika
¼	tsp. salt
¼	tsp. pepper
⅛	tsp. saffron threads
⅛	tsp. ground turmeric
1	lb. uncooked medium shrimp, peeled and deveined
¾	cup frozen peas
12	pimiento-stuffed olives
1	medium lemon, cut into 6 wedges

1. In a large skillet over medium heat, cook chicken in oil until no longer pink. Remove and keep warm. Add rice and onion to the pan; cook until rice is lightly browned and onion is tender, stirring frequently. Add the garlic; cook 1 minute longer.

2. Stir in the broth, tomatoes, oregano, paprika, salt, pepper, saffron and turmeric. Bring to a boil. Reduce heat to low; cover and cook for 10 minutes.

3. Add the shrimp, peas and olives. Cover and cook 10 minutes longer or until rice is tender, shrimp turn pink and liquid is absorbed. Add chicken; heat through. Serve with lemon wedges.

1⅓ cups: 367 cal., 8g fat (1g sat. fat), 144mg chol., 778mg sod., 36g carb. (5g sugars, 3g fiber), 37g pro. **Diabetic exchanges:** 5 lean meat, 2 starch, 1 vegetable, 1 fat.

PRESSURE-COOKER CHAR SIU PORK

Save time when you let your Instant Pot® do the work to create this juicy pork. Plan on serving it with veggies and rice for easy meal planning. Or, enjoy it on buns for lip-smacking sandwiches.
—*Karen Naihe, Kamuela, HI*

- -

Prep: 25 min. + marinating
Cook: 1¼ hours + releasing
Makes: 8 servings

- ½ cup honey
- ½ cup hoisin sauce
- ¼ cup soy sauce
- ¼ cup ketchup
- 4 garlic cloves, minced
- 4 tsp. minced fresh gingerroot
- 1 tsp. Chinese five-spice powder
- 1 boneless pork shoulder
   butt roast (3 to 4 lbs.)
- ½ cup chicken broth
   Fresh cilantro leaves

1. Combine the first 7 ingredients; pour into a large shallow dish. Cut roast in half; add to dish and turn to coat. Cover and refrigerate overnight.
2. Transfer pork and marinade to a 6-qt. electric pressure cooker. Add chicken broth. Lock lid; close pressure-release valve. Adjust to pressure-cook on high for 75 minutes. Allow pressure to naturally release for 10 minutes, then quick-release any remaining pressure.
3. Remove pork; when cool enough to handle, shred meat using 2 forks. Skim fat from cooking juices. Return pork to pressure cooker. Select saute setting and adjust for low heat; heat through. Press cancel. Top pork with fresh cilantro.
1 serving: 392 cal., 18g fat (6g sat. fat), 102mg chol., 981mg sod., 27g carb. (24g sugars, 1g fiber), 31g pro.

SLOW-COOKED TURKEY SLOPPY JOES

This tangy sandwich filling is so easy to prepare in the slow cooker. I frequently take it to potlucks, and I'm always asked for my secret ingredient.
—*Marylou LaRue, Freeland, MI*

- -

Prep: 15 min. • **Cook:** 4 hours
Makes: 8 servings

- 1 lb. lean ground turkey
- 1 small onion, chopped
- ½ cup chopped celery
- ¼ cup chopped green pepper
- 1 can (10¾ oz.) reduced-sodium
   condensed tomato soup, undiluted
- ½ cup ketchup
- 2 Tbsp. prepared mustard
- 1 Tbsp. brown sugar
- ¼ tsp. pepper
- 8 hamburger buns, split

1. In a large skillet coated with cooking spray, cook the turkey, onion, celery and green pepper over medium heat until meat is no longer pink; drain. Stir in the soup, ketchup, mustard, brown sugar and pepper.
2. Transfer to a 3-qt. slow cooker. Cover and cook on low for 4 hours. Serve on buns.
1 sandwich: 264 cal., 7g fat (2g sat. fat), 39mg chol., 614mg sod., 34g carb. (13g sugars, 2g fiber), 16g pro. **Diabetic exchanges:** 2 starch, 1½ lean meat.

GARLICKY CHICKEN PIZZA

I cook extra chicken during the week to include on this white pizza. Make sure the tomatoes are well drained to keep the crust nice and crispy. Then, you can wrap up individual slices to toss in your lunch.
—*Teri Otte, Cannon Falls, MN*

Takes: 25 min. • **Makes:** 6 servings

- 1 tube (13.8 oz.) refrigerated pizza crust
- 2 Tbsp. olive oil
- 2 garlic cloves, minced
- 1 can (14½ oz.) diced tomatoes, well drained
- 1 large onion, thinly sliced (about 1 cup)
- ⅓ cup pitted kalamata olives, halved
- 2 cups cubed or shredded cooked chicken
- 1⅓ cups crumbled goat cheese
- 1 tsp. minced fresh rosemary or ¼ tsp. dried rosemary, crushed
- ½ tsp. garlic salt
- ½ tsp. pepper

1. Preheat oven to 400°. Unroll and press dough onto bottom and ½ in. up sides of a greased 15x10x1-in. baking pan. Bake until edges are lightly browned, 8-10 minutes.
2. Mix oil and garlic; brush over crust. Top with tomatoes, onion, olives, chicken and goat cheese. Sprinkle with rosemary, garlic salt and pepper. Bake 10-12 minutes or until crust is golden.

1 piece: 418 cal., 19g fat (6g sat. fat), 73mg chol., 957mg sod., 39g carb. (7g sugars, 3g fiber), 25g pro.

GRILLED STEAK FAJITAS

Marinating this meat overnight makes it very tender and perfect to use in lunches during the week. I usually plan on using the flavorful steak slices for fajita dinners with Spanish rice and refried beans.
—*Pamela Pogue, Quitman, TX*

- -

Prep: 10 min. + marinating • **Grill:** 20 min.
Makes: 6 servings

  1   beef flank steak (1½ lbs.)
  1   large onion, cut into wedges
  1   medium green pepper, julienned
  1   can (4 oz.) chopped green chiles
  ½   cup lemon juice
  ½   cup cider vinegar
  ½   cup vegetable oil
  4   garlic cloves, minced
  1   Tbsp. Worcestershire sauce
  1   tsp. dried oregano
  ½   tsp. salt
  ½   tsp. pepper
 12   flour tortillas (6 in.), warmed
  1   medium avocado, peeled
       and sliced, optional
       Sour cream, optional

1. In a shallow dish, add beef. In another shallow dish, add onion and green pepper.

2. In a large bowl, combine the green chiles, lemon juice, vinegar, oil, minced garlic, Worcestershire sauce, oregano, salt and pepper. Pour 1½ cups over meat. Pour the remaining marinade over vegetables. Cover and refrigerate overnight.

3. Drain the meat and vegetables, discarding marinade. Grill the steak, covered, over medium-hot heat for 10 minutes on each side or until the meat reaches desired doneness (for medium-rare, a thermometer should read 135°; medium, 140°; medium-well, 145°).

4. Meanwhile, cut 2 pieces of heavy-duty foil into 18x12-in. rectangles. Wrap tortillas in 1 piece and vegetables in the other; seal foil tightly. Grill, covered, over indirect heat for 5-7 minutes, turning occasionally.

5. Cut steak into ⅛-in. slices across the grain; place on tortillas. Top with vegetables and roll up. Serve with avocado and sour cream if desired.

2 fajitas: 466 cal., 22g fat (7g sat. fat), 54mg chol., 703mg sod., 38g carb. (3g sugars, 4g fiber), 27g pro.

- 4 bacon strips, finely chopped
- 1½ lbs. turkey breast tenderloins, cut into 1-in. pieces
- 4 medium carrots, sliced
- 2 small onions, quartered
- 2 celery ribs, sliced
- 1 bay leaf
- ¼ tsp. dried rosemary, crushed
- 2 cups water, divided
- 1 can (14½ oz.) reduced-sodium chicken broth
- 3 Tbsp. all-purpose flour
- ½ tsp. salt
- ⅛ to ¼ tsp. pepper
- 1 cup reduced-fat biscuit/baking mix
- ⅓ cup plus 1 Tbsp. fat-free milk
  Optional: Coarsely ground pepper and chopped fresh parsley

BEST ITALIAN SAUSAGE SANDWICHES

This rich tomato sauce simmers on its own in the slow cooker, ready to top freshly grilled Italian sausages. It's a great flavor combo with meal-planning appeal.
—Taste of Home *Test Kitchen*

- -

Prep: 10 min. • **Cook:** 4 hours
Makes: 10 servings

- 2 jars (24 oz. each) pasta sauce
- 2 medium green peppers, cut into strips
- 2 medium onions, thinly sliced
- ½ tsp. garlic powder
- ½ tsp. fennel seed, crushed
- 2 pkg. (20 oz. each) Italian turkey sausage links
- 10 hoagie buns, split

1. In a 3-qt. slow cooker, combine the first 5 ingredients. Cook, covered, on low until vegetables are tender, about 4 hours.

2. Grill sausages according to package directions. Serve on buns with sauce.
Freeze option: Freeze cooled sauce in freezer containers. To use, partially thaw in refrigerator overnight. Heat through in a saucepan, stirring occasionally; add water if necessary. Continue grilling sausages and assembling the sandwiches as directed.
1 sandwich: 454 cal., 15g fat (3g sat. fat), 68mg chol., 1716mg sod., 52g carb. (17g sugars, 4g fiber), 29g pro.

TURKEY DUMPLING STEW

My mom made this stew when I was young, and it was always a hit. Since it's not too time-consuming, I often make it on weekends for fast and easy meals during the week. My children simply love the tender dumplings.
—*Becky Mohr, Appleton, WI*

- -

Prep: 20 min. • **Cook:** 50 min.
Makes: 6 servings

1. In a Dutch oven, cook bacon over medium heat until crisp, stirring occasionally. Remove with a slotted spoon; drain on paper towels. Reserve 2 tsp. drippings.
2. In drippings, saute turkey over medium-high heat until lightly browned. Add the vegetables, herbs, 1¾ cups water and broth; bring to a boil. Reduce heat; simmer, covered, for 30 minutes.
3. Mix the flour and remaining water until smooth; stir into turkey mixture. Bring to a boil; cook and stir until thickened, about 2 minutes. Discard bay leaf. Stir in the salt, pepper and bacon.
4. In a small bowl, mix biscuit mix and milk to form a soft dough; drop in 6 mounds on top of simmering stew. Cover; simmer for 15 minutes or until a toothpick inserted in dumplings comes out clean. If desired, sprinkle with pepper and chopped parsley before serving.
1 serving: 284 cal., 6g fat (1g sat. fat), 52mg chol., 822mg sod., 24g carb. (6g sugars, 2g fiber), 34g pro. **Diabetic exchanges:** 4 lean meat, 1 starch, 1 vegetable, ½ fat.

PORK NOODLE SOUP

Add this to your meal plan when you're making a pork roast. My daughter created the quick recipe that uses up leftover pork deliciously. Try it with mushroom-flavored ramen noodles, too.
—*Eleanor Niska, Twin Falls, ID*

- -

Takes: 30 min. • **Makes:** 10 servings (2½ qt.)

- ½ cup chopped celery
- ½ cup chopped onion
- 1 Tbsp. olive oil
- ½ tsp. minced garlic
- 7 cups water
- 1½ cups cut fresh asparagus (1-in. pieces)
- ½ cup chopped cabbage
- 1½ tsp. minced fresh parsley
- ¾ tsp. dried tarragon
   Dash cayenne pepper, optional
- 2 pkg. (3 oz. each) pork ramen noodles
- 2 cups cubed cooked pork

1. In a Dutch oven, saute celery and onion in oil until tender. Add garlic; cook 1 minute longer. Stir in the water, asparagus, cabbage, parsley, tarragon and cayenne if desired. Bring to a boil.

2. Coarsely crush ramen noodles. Add the noodles with the contents of the seasoning packets to the pan. Bring to a boil. Reduce heat; simmer, uncovered, for 3-5 minutes or until the noodles and vegetables are tender. Add pork; heat through.

1 cup: 116 cal., 5g fat (2g sat. fat), 25mg chol., 205mg sod., 8g carb. (2g sugars, 1g fiber), 9g pro.

Chicken Ramen Soup: Substitute chicken ramen noodles for the pork ramen noodles and cubed cooked chicken for the pork.

PAN-ROASTED CHICKEN & VEGETABLES

This one-dish meal tastes as if it took hours of hands-on time, but the ingredients can be prepped in minutes. The rosemary gives it a rich flavor, and the meat juices cook the veggies to perfection. Prepare the recipe as instructed, then divide the chicken and veggies into containers for complete grab-and-go lunches.
—*Sherri Melotik, Oak Creek, WI*

- -

Prep: 15 min. • **Bake:** 45 min.
Makes: 6 servings

2 lbs. red potatoes (about 6 medium), cut into ¾-in. pieces
1 large onion, coarsely chopped
2 Tbsp. olive oil
3 garlic cloves, minced
1¼ tsp. salt, divided
1 tsp. dried rosemary, crushed, divided
¾ tsp. pepper, divided
½ tsp. paprika
6 bone-in chicken thighs (about 2¼ lbs.), skin removed
6 cups fresh baby spinach (about 6 oz.)

1. Preheat oven to 425°. In a large bowl, combine potatoes, onion, oil, garlic, ¾ tsp. salt, ½ tsp. rosemary and ½ tsp. pepper; toss to coat. Transfer to a 15x10x1-in. baking pan coated with cooking spray.
2. In a small bowl, mix paprika and the remaining salt, rosemary and pepper. Sprinkle chicken with paprika mixture; arrange over vegetables. Roast until a thermometer inserted in chicken reads 170°-175° and vegetables are just tender, 35-40 minutes.
3. Remove chicken to a serving platter; keep warm. Top vegetables with spinach. Roast until vegetables are tender and spinach is wilted, 8-10 minutes longer. Stir vegetables to combine; serve with chicken.

1 chicken thigh with 1 cup vegetables:
357 cal., 14g fat (3g sat. fat), 87mg chol., 597mg sod., 28g carb. (3g sugars, 4g fiber), 28g pro. **Diabetic exchanges:** 4 lean meat, 1½ starch, 1 vegetable, 1 fat.

TEST KITCHEN TIPS

Prepare your sheet pan the night before your day of cooking and just pop it in the preheated oven to bake it off. This actually helps to flavor the chicken, a win-win. If you want a richer dish, you can use skin-on chicken, and if you want a lighter dish, use bone-in chicken breasts. Be sure to cook bone-in breasts just to 165-170 degrees, since leaner meat can become dry at higher temperatures.

RUSTIC ITALIAN TORTELLINI SOUP

This is my favorite soup recipe. It's quick to fix and full of healthy, tasty ingredients. It originally called for spicy sausage links, but I've found that ground turkey or turkey sausage is just as good, and I usually have those on hand.

—*Tracy Fasnacht, Irwin, PA*

Prep: 20 min. • **Cook:** 20 min.
Makes: 6 servings (2 qt.)

- ¾ lb. Italian turkey sausage links, casings removed
- 1 medium onion, chopped
- 6 garlic cloves, minced
- 2 cans (14½ oz. each) reduced-sodium chicken broth
- 1¾ cups water
- 1 can (14½ oz.) diced tomatoes, undrained
- 1 pkg. (9 oz.) refrigerated cheese tortellini
- 1 pkg. (6 oz.) fresh baby spinach, coarsely chopped
- 2¼ tsp. minced fresh basil or ¾ tsp. dried basil
- ¼ tsp. pepper
  Dash crushed red pepper flakes
  Shredded Parmesan cheese, optional

1. Crumble sausage into a Dutch oven; add onion. Cook and stir over medium heat until meat is no longer pink. Add garlic; cook for 1 minute longer. Stir in the broth, water and tomatoes. Bring to a boil.

2. Add tortellini; return to a boil. Cook for 5-8 minutes or until almost tender, stirring occasionally. Reduce heat; add the spinach, basil, pepper and pepper flakes. Cook for 2-3 minutes longer or until spinach is wilted and tortellini are tender. Serve with cheese if desired.

Freeze option: Place individual portions of cooled soup in freezer containers and freeze. To use, partially thaw in the refrigerator overnight. Heat through in a saucepan, stirring occasionally; add broth if necessary.

1⅓ cups: 203 cal., 8g fat (2g sat. fat), 40mg chol., 878mg sod., 18g carb. (5g sugars, 3g fiber), 16g pro.

Rustic Italian Ravioli Soup: Substitute ravioli for the tortellini.

ROASTED KIELBASA & VEGETABLES

I really like this dish featuring kielbasa and veggies for two reasons. First, it's so hearty. Second, it's a one-pan meal. That makes this a win-win recipe for family cooks who plan out the week's meals.
—*Marietta Slater, Justin, TX*

- -

Prep: 20 min. • **Bake:** 40 min.
Makes: 6 servings

  3 **medium sweet potatoes, peeled and cut into 1-in. pieces**
  1 **large sweet onion, cut into 1-in. pieces**
  4 **medium carrots, cut into 1-in. pieces**
  2 **Tbsp. olive oil**
  1 **lb. smoked kielbasa or Polish sausage, halved and cut into 1-in. pieces**
  1 **medium yellow summer squash, cut into 1-in. pieces**
  1 **medium zucchini, cut into 1-in. pieces**
  ¼ **tsp. salt**
  ¼ **tsp. pepper**
    Dijon mustard, optional

1. Preheat oven to 400°. Divide sweet potatoes, onion and carrots between 2 greased 15x10x1-in. baking pans. Drizzle with oil; toss to coat. Roast 25 minutes, stirring occasionally.
2. Add kielbasa, squash and zucchini to pans; sprinkle with salt and pepper. Roast until vegetables are tender, 15-20 minutes longer. Transfer to a serving bowl; toss to combine. If desired, serve with mustard.

1⅔ cups: 378 cal., 25g fat (8g sat. fat), 51mg chol., 954mg sod., 26g carb. (12g sugars, 4g fiber), 13g pro.

LIME CHICKEN TACOS

This simple recipe is perfect for tacos, but set some of the meat aside to toss into zesty garden-fresh salads during the busy work week.
—*Tracy Gunter, Boise, ID*

Prep: 10 min. • **Cook:** 5½ hours
Makes: 6 servings

- 1½ lbs. boneless skinless chicken breast halves
- 3 Tbsp. lime juice
- 1 Tbsp. chili powder
- 1 cup frozen corn, thawed
- 1 cup chunky salsa
- 12 fat-free flour tortillas (6 in.), warmed
  Optional: Sour cream, pickled onions, shredded lettuce and shredded cheddar or Cotija cheese

1. Place the chicken in a 3-qt. slow cooker. Combine lime juice and chili powder; pour over chicken. Cook, covered, on low until chicken is tender, 5-6 hours.
2. Remove the chicken. When cool enough to handle, shred meat with 2 forks; return to slow cooker. Stir in corn and salsa. Cook, covered, on low until heated through, about 30 minutes. Place the filling on tortillas; if desired, serve with sour cream, pickled onions, lettuce and cheese.
2 tacos: 291 cal., 3g fat (1g sat. fat), 63mg chol., 674mg sod., 37g carb. (2g sugars, 2g fiber), 28g pro. **Diabetic exchanges:** 3 lean meat, 2½ starch.

BACON ALFREDO PASTA IN A JAR

I captured my favorite summery pasta in a jar. So delicious. So simple. Assemble these jars and store them in the fridge. For lunch just tip one into a bowl and enjoy!
—*Keri Whitney, Castro Valley, CA*

Takes: 20 min. • **Makes:** 4 servings

- 6 cups cooked penne pasta
- 1 cup refrigerated Alfredo sauce
- 1 jar (8 oz.) roasted sweet red peppers, drained and coarsely chopped
- ¾ cup frozen peas
- 6 ready-to-serve fully cooked bacon strips, chopped
- ¼ cup fresh basil leaves, coarsely chopped
- ¼ cup grated Parmesan cheese

In each of four 1-pint wide-mouth canning jars, divide and layer ingredients in the following order: pasta, Alfredo sauce, red pepper, peas, bacon, basil and Parmesan cheese. Cover and refrigerate until serving. Transfer into microwave-safe bowls; toss to combine. Microwave until heated through.
1 serving: 488 cal., 18g fat (9g sat. fat), 34mg chol., 787mg sod., 60g carb. (6g sugars, 4g fiber), 19g pro.

GNOCCHI WITH WHITE BEANS

Here's one of those no-fuss recipes you can toss together and cook in one skillet. Ideal for busy days, it's also good with crumbled Italian chicken sausage if you need to please meat lovers.
—Juli Meyers, Hinesville, GA

- -

Takes: 30 min. • **Makes:** 6 servings

1	**Tbsp. olive oil**
1	**medium onion, chopped**
2	**garlic cloves, minced**
1	**pkg. (16 oz.) potato gnocchi**
1	**can (15 oz.) cannellini beans, rinsed and drained**
1	**can (14½ oz.) Italian diced tomatoes, undrained**
1	**pkg. (6 oz.) fresh baby spinach**
¼	**tsp. pepper**
½	**cup shredded part-skim mozzarella cheese**
3	**Tbsp. grated Parmesan cheese**

1. In a large skillet, heat oil over medium-high heat. Add onion; cook and stir until tender. Add garlic; cook 1 minute longer. Add gnocchi; cook and stir 5-6 minutes or until golden brown. Stir in beans, tomatoes, spinach and pepper; heat through.

2. Sprinkle with cheeses; cover and remove from heat. Let stand 3-4 minutes or until cheese is melted.

Note: Look for potato gnocchi in the pasta or frozen foods section.

1 cup: 307 cal., 6g fat (2g sat. fat), 13mg chol., 789mg sod., 50g carb. (10g sugars, 6g fiber), 13g pro.

SIRLOIN STIR-FRY WITH RAMEN NOODLES

I created this recipe when craving Chinese food. The leftovers taste just as yummy when reheated the next day for lunch.
—*Annette Hemsath, Sutherlin, OR*

- -

Takes: 30 min. • **Makes:** 4 servings

- 2 **pkg. (3 oz. each) beef ramen noodles**
- 2 **Tbsp. cornstarch**
- 2 **cups beef broth, divided**
- 1 **lb. beef top sirloin steak, cut into thin strips**
- 2 **Tbsp. canola oil**
- 2 **Tbsp. reduced-sodium soy sauce**
- 2 **cans (14 oz. each) whole baby corn, rinsed and drained**
- 2 **cups fresh broccoli florets**
- 1 **cup diced sweet red pepper**
- 1 **cup shredded carrots**
- 4 **green onions, cut into 1-in. pieces**
- ½ **cup unsalted peanuts**

1. Set aside seasoning packets from noodles. Cook noodles according to package directions.

2. Meanwhile, in a small bowl, combine cornstarch and ¼ cup broth until smooth; set aside. In a large skillet or wok, stir-fry beef in oil until no longer pink. Add soy sauce; cook until liquid has evaporated, 3-4 minutes. Remove beef and keep warm.

3. Add the corn, broccoli, red pepper, carrots, onions and remaining broth to the pan. Sprinkle with contents of seasoning packets. Stir-fry until vegetables are crisp-tender, 5-7 minutes.

4. Stir the cornstarch mixture and add to skillet. Bring to a boil; cook and stir until thickened, about 2 minutes. Drain noodles. Add beef and noodles to pan; heat through. Garnish with peanuts.

1½ cups: 593 cal., 28g fat (8g sat. fat), 46mg chol., 2022mg sod., 49g carb. (8g sugars, 8g fiber), 38g pro.

STROMBOLI SANDWICH

This is a big sandwich, so it's perfect for parties as well as busy moms who love to plan out lunches and casual dinners. Feel free to add ingredients and spices to suit your taste. The recipe is so good I just had to share it!

—Leigh Lauer, Hummelstown, PA

Prep: 20 min. + rising • **Bake:** 30 min.
Makes: 10 servings

2	loaves (1 lb. each) frozen bread dough, thawed
¼	lb. sliced ham
¼	lb. sliced pepperoni
¼	cup chopped onion
¼	cup chopped green pepper
1	jar (14 oz.) pizza sauce, divided
¼	lb. sliced mozzarella cheese
¼	lb. sliced bologna
¼	lb. sliced hard salami
¼	lb. slice Swiss cheese
1	tsp. dried basil
1	tsp. dried oregano
¼	tsp. garlic powder
¼	tsp. pepper
2	Tbsp. butter, melted

1. Let the dough rise in a warm place until doubled. Punch down. Roll loaves together into one 15x12-in. rectangle.

2. Layer ham and pepperoni on half of the dough (lengthwise). Sprinkle with onion and green pepper. Top with ¼ cup of pizza sauce. Layer mozzarella, bologna, salami and Swiss cheese over sauce. Sprinkle with basil, oregano, garlic powder and pepper. Spread another ¼ cup of pizza sauce on top. Fold plain half of dough over filling and seal edges well.

3. Place on a greased 15x10x1-in. baking pan. Bake at 375° 30-35 minutes or until golden brown. Brush with melted butter. Heat the remaining pizza sauce and serve with sliced stromboli.

1 piece: 388 cal., 23g fat (10g sat. fat), 60mg chol., 1175mg sod., 28g carb. (5g sugars, 2g fiber), 19g pro.

SOUTHWESTERN GOULASH

I had some extra cilantro in the fridge and didn't want to throw it away. That inspired this fast and filling family recipe—sure to please cilantro fans. It also travels well and reheats in a pinch for lunches at work.
—*Vikki Rebholz, West Chester, OH*

Takes: 25 min. • **Makes:** 6 servings

1 cup uncooked elbow macaroni
1 lb. lean ground beef (90% lean)
1 medium onion, chopped
1 can (28 oz.) diced
   tomatoes, undrained
1 can (8 oz.) tomato sauce
⅔ cup frozen corn
1 can (4 oz.) chopped green chiles
½ tsp. ground cumin
½ tsp. pepper
¼ tsp. salt
¼ cup minced fresh cilantro

1. Cook macaroni according to package directions; drain. Meanwhile, in a 6-qt. stockpot, cook and crumble beef with onion over medium heat until meat is no longer pink, 6-8 minutes; drain.
2. Stir in tomatoes, tomato sauce, corn, chiles and dry seasonings; bring to a boil. Reduce heat; simmer, uncovered, until flavors are blended, about 5 minutes. Stir in macaroni and cilantro.
1⅓ cups: 224 cal., 6g fat (2g sat. fat), 37mg chol., 567mg sod., 24g carb. (7g sugars, 4g fiber), 19g pro. **Diabetic exchanges:** 2 lean meat, 2 vegetable, 1 starch.

SHREDDED CHICKEN GYROS

Our family always has a great time at the annual Salt Lake City Greek Festival. One of my favorite parts is the awesome food. These gyros are a great way to use the slow cooker while mixing up your menu plan.
—Camille Beckstrand, Layton, UT

- -

Prep: 20 min. • **Cook:** 3 hours
Makes: 8 servings

- 2   medium onions, chopped
- 6   garlic cloves, minced
- 1   tsp. lemon-pepper seasoning
- 1   tsp. dried oregano
- ½   tsp. ground allspice
- ½   cup water
- ½   cup lemon juice
- ¼   cup red wine vinegar
- 2   Tbsp. olive oil
- 2   lbs. boneless skinless chicken breasts
- 8   whole pita breads
     Optional toppings: Tzatziki sauce, torn romaine and sliced tomato, cucumber and onion

1. In a 3-qt. slow cooker, combine the first 9 ingredients; add chicken. Cook, covered, on low 3-4 hours or until chicken is tender (a thermometer should read at least 165°).
2. Remove chicken from slow cooker. Shred with 2 forks; return to slow cooker. Using tongs, place chicken mixture on pita breads. Serve with toppings.
1 gyro: 337 cal., 7g fat (1g sat. fat), 63mg chol., 418mg sod., 38g carb. (2g sugars, 2g fiber), 29g pro. **Diabetic exchanges:** 3 lean meat, 2½ starch, ½ fat.

FETA CHICKEN BURGERS

Make these chicken patties ahead of time and stash them in the freezer for quick lunches. I sometimes add olives, but I always enjoy them with the mayo topping.
—Angela Robinson, Findlay, OH

- -

Takes: 30 min. • **Makes:** 6 servings

- ¼   cup finely chopped cucumber
- ¼   cup reduced-fat mayonnaise
BURGERS
- ½   cup chopped roasted sweet red pepper
- 1   tsp. garlic powder
- ½   tsp. Greek seasoning
- ¼   tsp. pepper
- 1½ lbs. lean ground chicken
- 1   cup crumbled feta cheese
- 6   whole wheat hamburger buns, split and toasted
     Optional: Lettuce leaves and tomato slices

1. Preheat broiler. Mix the cucumber and mayonnaise. For burgers, mix red pepper and seasonings. Add chicken and cheese; mix lightly but thoroughly (mixture will be sticky). Shape into six ½-in.-thick patties.
2. Broil burgers 4 in. from heat until a thermometer reads 165°, 3-4 minutes per side. Serve in buns with cucumber sauce. If desired, top with lettuce and tomato.
Freeze option: Place uncooked patties on a waxed paper-lined baking sheet; wrap and freeze until firm. Remove from the pan and transfer to an airtight freezer container; return to freezer. To use, broil frozen patties as directed, increasing time as necessary.
1 burger with 1 Tbsp. sauce: 356 cal., 14g fat (5g sat. fat), 95mg chol., 703mg sod., 25g carb. (5g sugars, 4g fiber), 31g pro. **Diabetic exchanges:** 5 lean meat, 2 starch, ½ fat.

CHICKEN CRESCENT WREATH

Here's an impressive-looking dish that's a snap to prepare. Even when my cooking time is limited, I can still serve this delicious crescent wreath. Bake it and freeze it ahead of time when hosting a luncheon. What could be easier?

—Marlene Denissen, St. Croix Falls, WI

- -

Prep: 15 min. • **Bake:** 20 min.
Makes: 16 servings

- 2 tubes (8 oz. each) refrigerated crescent rolls
- 1 cup shredded Colby-Monterey Jack cheese
- ⅔ cup condensed cream of chicken soup, undiluted
- ½ cup chopped fresh broccoli
- ½ cup chopped sweet red pepper
- ¼ cup chopped water chestnuts
- 1 can (5 oz.) white chicken, drained or ¾ cup cubed cooked chicken
- 2 Tbsp. chopped onion

1. Arrange the crescent rolls on a 12-in. pizza pan, forming a ring with the pointed ends facing the outer edge of pan and wide ends overlapping.

2. In a large bowl, combine the remaining ingredients; spoon over wide ends of rolls. Fold points over filling and tuck under wide ends (filling will be visible).

3. Bake at 375° for 20-25 minutes or until golden brown.

Freeze option: Securely wrap the cooled wreath in plastic and foil before freezing. To use, remove from freezer 30 minutes before reheating. Remove the wreath from foil and plastic; reheat on a greased baking sheet in a preheated 325° oven until heated through.

1 piece: 151 cal., 8g fat (2g sat. fat), 11mg chol., 357mg sod., 14g carb. (3g sugars, 0 fiber), 6g pro.

ASIAN TURKEY SLIDERS

We make weeknights fun with easy grilled sliders. I like to serve them with tangy slaw on the side. Double the recipe and freeze for quick meals.
—*Trinity Saffer, Golden, CO*

- -

Takes: 25 min. • **Makes:** 4 servings

- 1 **large egg, lightly beaten**
- ⅓ **cup panko bread crumbs**
- ¼ **cup teriyaki sauce**
- 2 **garlic cloves, minced**
- 2 **tsp. minced fresh gingerroot**
- 1 **tsp. sesame oil**
- ½ **tsp. onion powder**
- ⅛ **tsp. white pepper**
- 1 **lb. lean ground turkey**
- 8 **Hawaiian sweet rolls,**
  split and warmed
  Optional toppings: Sliced
  cucumber, shredded carrot
  and fresh cilantro leaves

1. Combine first 8 ingredients. Add turkey; mix lightly but thoroughly. Shape into eight ½-in.-thick patties.
2. Place the sliders on an oiled grill rack over medium heat; grill, covered, until a thermometer reads 165°, 3-4 minutes per side. Serve in rolls with toppings as desired.
Freeze option: Cover and freeze patties on a waxed paper-lined baking sheet until firm. Transfer to a large freezer container; return to freezer. To use, grill the frozen patties as directed, increasing time as necessary for a thermometer to read 165°.
2 sliders: 433 cal., 16g fat (6g sat. fat), 155mg chol., 868mg sod., 38g carb. (14g sugars, 2g fiber), 34g pro.

SANTA FE CHILI

This has been my husband's favorite chili for years. It makes a lot, so it's perfect for those who like to prepare meals for an entire week. We like the combination of black beans, pinto beans and heirloom shoepeg corn in this meaty specialty.
—*Laura Manning, Lilburn, GA*

- -

Prep: 20 min. • **Cook:** 4 hours
Makes: 16 servings (4 qt.)

2   lbs. ground beef
1   medium onion, chopped
2   cans (16 oz. each) kidney
    beans, rinsed and drained
2   cans (15 oz. each) black
    beans, rinsed and drained
2   cans (15 oz. each) pinto
    beans, rinsed and drained
3   cans (7 oz. each) white or
    shoepeg corn, drained
1   can (14½ oz.) diced
    tomatoes, undrained
1   can (10 oz.) diced tomatoes
    and green chiles
1   can (11½ oz.) V8 juice
2   envelopes ranch salad dressing mix
2   envelopes taco seasoning
    Optional: Sour cream, shredded
    cheddar cheese and corn chips

1. In a large skillet, cook beef and onion over medium heat until meat is no longer pink; drain. Transfer to a 5- or 6-qt. slow cooker. Stir in the beans, corn, tomatoes, juice, salad dressing mix and taco seasoning.
2. Cover and cook on high for 4-6 hours or until heated through. Serve with sour cream, cheese and corn chips if desired.
1 cup: 224 cal., 5g fat (2g sat. fat), 28mg chol., 1513mg sod., 28g carb. (4g sugars, 4g fiber), 15g pro.

MOM'S CHICKEN NOODLE SOUP

Thirty minutes are all you need to prep this heartwarming soup. It's a recipe my mother created, and I always think of her when I taste the divine noodles and flavorful both.
—*Marlene Doolittle, Story City, IA*

- -

Prep: 30 min. • **Cook:** 55 min.
Makes: 6 servings

- 1 broiler/fryer chicken (3 to 4 lbs.), cut up
- 2 qt. water
- 1 medium onion, chopped
- 2 tsp. chicken bouillon granules
- 2 celery ribs, diced
- 2 medium carrots, diced
- 2 medium potatoes, peeled and cubed
- 1½ cups fresh or frozen cut green beans
- 1 tsp. salt
- ¼ tsp. pepper

NOODLES
- 1 cup all-purpose flour
- 1 large egg, lightly beaten
- ½ tsp. salt
- 1 tsp. butter, softened
- ¼ tsp. baking powder
- 2 to 3 Tbsp. milk

1. In a Dutch oven, cook chicken in water; cool slightly. Remove chicken from bones; discard bones. Skim fat from broth. Cut chicken into bite-sized pieces; add to broth with remaining ingredients except noodles. Bring to a boil. Reduce heat and simmer, uncovered, for 50-60 minutes or until vegetables are tender.

2. Meanwhile, for noodles, place flour in a small bowl and make a well in the center. Stir together remaining ingredients; pour into well. Working the mixture with your hands, form a dough ball. Knead the dough for 5-6 minutes.

3. Cover and let rest for 10 minutes. On a floured surface, roll dough out to a square, $\frac{1}{16}$ to $\frac{1}{8}$ in. thick, and cut into ¼-in.-wide strips. Cook noodles in boiling salted water for 2-3 minutes or until done. Drain and add to soup just before serving.

Freeze option: Freeze uncooked noodles on waxed paper-lined baking sheets until firm. Transfer to freezer containers; return to freezer. Prepare soup as directed, reserving potatoes for later. Freeze the cooled soup in freezer containers. To use, partially thaw in refrigerator overnight. Place potatoes in a small saucepan; add water to cover. Simmer 10-15 minutes or until tender. Drain. Meanwhile, cook noodles as directed; drain. Transfer the soup and potatoes to a Dutch oven. Heat through. Just before serving, add the noodles.

1 cup: 429 cal., 16g fat (5g sat. fat), 125mg chol., 1012mg sod., 36g carb. (5g sugars, 4g fiber), 34g pro.

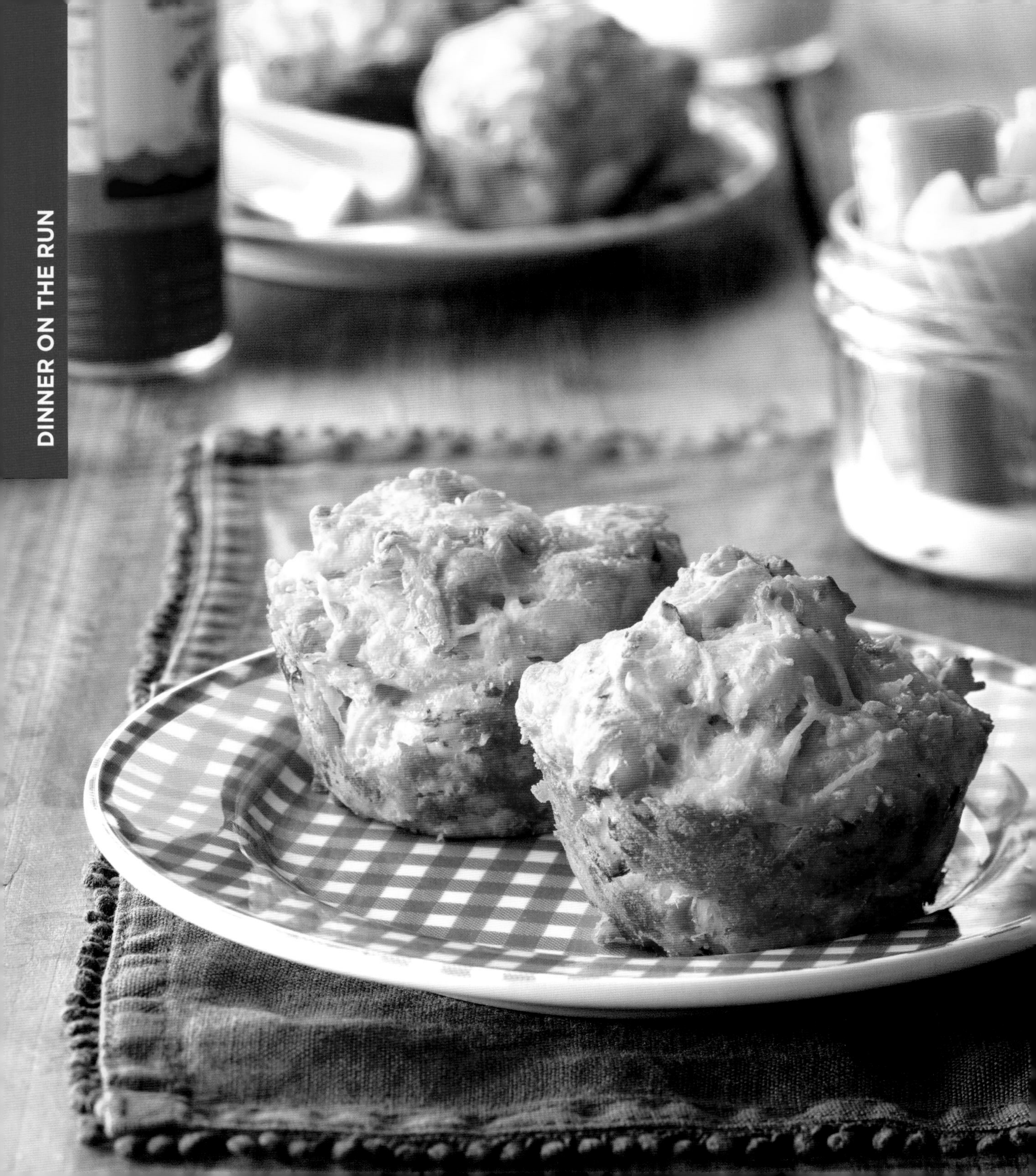

BUFFALO CHICKEN BISCUITS

Bake up these spicy, savory muffins on the weekend, and you'll be set with grab-and-go dinners during the work week. Replace the rotisserie chicken with any cooked chicken you might have worked into your meal planning.
—*Jasmin Baron, Livonia, NY*

Prep: 20 min. • **Bake:** 25 min.
Makes: 1 dozen

- 3 cups chopped rotisserie chicken
- ¼ cup Louisiana-style hot sauce
- 2 cups biscuit/baking mix
- ¼ tsp. celery seed
- ⅛ tsp. pepper
- 1 large egg, room temperature
- ½ cup 2% milk
- ¼ cup ranch salad dressing
- 1½ cups shredded Colby-Monterey Jack cheese, divided
- 2 green onions, thinly sliced
  Optional: Additional ranch dressing and hot sauce

1. Preheat oven to 400°. Toss chicken with hot sauce. In large bowl, whisk together the baking mix, celery seed and pepper. In another bowl, whisk together egg, milk and dressing; add to dry ingredients, stirring just until moistened. Fold in 1 cup cheese, green onions and chicken mixture.
2. Spoon into 12 greased muffin cups. Sprinkle with remaining cheese. Bake until a toothpick inserted in center comes out clean, 25-30 minutes.
3. Cool 5 minutes before removing from pan to a wire rack. Serve warm. If desired, serve with additional dressing and hot sauce. Refrigerate leftovers.
2 biscuits: 461 cal., 24g fat (10g sat. fat), 121mg chol., 1180mg sod., 29g carb. (3g sugars, 1g fiber), 31g pro.

SPINACH & TURKEY PINWHEELS

Toss these quick wraps into a container as you and the kids head out the door before soccer practice or band rehearsal so everyone has a full stomach. Go ahead and make them the day before—they don't get soggy! Best of all, teens can make the bites themselves for snacks or quick meals.
—*Amy Van Hemert, Ottumwa, IA*

Takes: 15 min. • **Makes:** 8 servings

- 1 carton (8 oz.) spreadable garden vegetable cream cheese
- 8 flour tortillas (8 in.)
- 4 cups fresh baby spinach
- 1 lb. sliced deli turkey

Spread cream cheese over tortillas. Layer with spinach and turkey. Roll up tightly; if not serving immediately, wrap and refrigerate. To serve, cut rolls crosswise into 1-in. slices.
6 pinwheels: 307 cal., 13g fat (6g sat. fat), 52mg chol., 866mg sod., 31g carb. (1g sugars, 2g fiber), 17g pro.

CREAMY CAULIFLOWER SOUP

Creamy soups can be soul-warming and so very satisfying. I received this recipe from a friend, and over the years I have served it many times and for many occasions. It makes a lot, so you'll have dinners all week. Or you could ladle it into a thermos for on-the-go dinners or lunches.

—*Doris Watt Davis, Hellertown, PA*

- -

Prep: 30 min. • **Cook:** 30 min.
Makes: 11 servings (2¾ qt.)

6	cups chicken broth
2	celery ribs, chopped
1	small onion, chopped
1	medium carrot, chopped
1	large head cauliflower (2 lbs.), broken into florets
½	cup butter
¾	cup all-purpose flour
2	cups whole milk
1	cup half-and-half cream
1	Tbsp. minced fresh parsley
1	tsp. salt
1	tsp. dill weed
¼	tsp. white pepper

1. In a Dutch oven, combine the broth, celery, onion and carrot. Bring to a boil. Reduce the heat; cover and simmer for 5 minutes. Add cauliflower; cover and simmer 15-20 minutes longer or until vegetables are tender. Cool slightly.

2. Meanwhile, in a saucepan, melt butter. Stir in flour until smooth; gradually stir in milk. Bring to a boil; cook and stir until thickened, 1-2 minutes.

3. In a blender or food processor, process vegetable mixture in batches until smooth; return to pan. Stir in the cream, parsley, salt, dill, white pepper and white sauce; heat through.

1 cup: 195 cal., 12g fat (8g sat. fat), 39mg chol., 874mg sod., 16g carb. (6g sugars, 3g fiber), 6g pro.

CURRIED EGG SALAD

A curry kick gives this egg salad big appeal. We love it for no-fuss dinners when the weather turns warm.

—*Joyce McDowell, West Union, OH*

- -

Takes: 15 min. • **Makes:** 6 servings

- ½ cup mayonnaise
- ½ tsp. ground curry
- ½ tsp. honey
   Dash ground ginger
- 6 hard-boiled large eggs, coarsely chopped
- 3 green onions, sliced
- 6 slices whole wheat bread
   Optional: Tomato slices and cracked pepper

Mix the first 4 ingredients; stir in eggs and green onions. Spread on bread. If desired, top with tomato and sprinkle with pepper.
1 open-faced sandwich: 273 cal., 20g fat (4g sat. fat), 188mg chol., 284mg sod., 14g carb. (2g sugars, 2g fiber), 10g pro.

TEST KITCHEN TIP

A switch to low-fat mayonnaise will save roughly 100 calories and more than 10 grams of fat per serving.

HAM & SWISS ENVELOPES

These clever envelopes will make people eager to look inside. The hot pockets shaped with refrigerated dough are stuffed with a delicious ham and cheese filling.
—*Tammy Burgess, Loveland, OH*

Takes: 30 min. • **Makes:** 4 servings

- ¾ **cup diced fully cooked ham**
- 4 **tsp. finely chopped onion**
- 1 **tsp. canola oil**
- ¾ **cup shredded Swiss cheese**
- 3 **oz. cream cheese, cubed**
- 2 **tubes (8 oz. each) refrigerated crescent rolls**

1. In a large skillet, saute ham and onion in oil until onion is tender. Add cheeses; cook 3-4 minutes or until melted. Remove from the heat; set aside.

2. Unroll crescent dough and separate into 4 rectangles; seal the perforations. Place 2 Tbsp. ham mixture in the center of each rectangle. Starting with a short side, fold a third of the dough over filling. On the other short side, bring both corners together in the center to form a point. Fold over to resemble an envelope. Pinch seams to seal.

3. Place on an ungreased baking sheet. Bake at 400° for 10-12 minutes or until dough is golden brown.

1 sandwich: 603 cal., 36g fat (8g sat. fat), 56mg chol., 1272mg sod., 50g carb. (13g sugars, 0 fiber), 21g pro.

PORK BURRITOS

As a working mother, I depend on my slow cooker to help feed my family. We all love the spicy but slightly sweet flavor of these tender burritos—they'd fit into anyone's monthly meal plan.
—*Kelly Gengler, Theresa, WI*

- -

Prep: 25 min. • **Cook:** 8 hours
Makes: 10 burritos

    1 **boneless pork shoulder**
       butt roast (3 to 4 lbs.)
    1 **can (14½ oz.) diced tomatoes with**
       mild green chiles, undrained
    ¼ **cup chili powder**
    3 **Tbsp. minced garlic**
    2 **Tbsp. lime juice**
    2 **Tbsp. honey**
    1 **Tbsp. chopped seeded**
       jalapeno pepper
    1 **tsp. salt**
   10 **flour tortillas (8 in.), warmed**
       Optional: Sliced avocado, sour
       cream and minced fresh cilantro

1. Cut roast in half; place in a 5-qt. slow cooker. In a blender, combine the tomatoes, chili powder, garlic, lime juice, honey, jalapeno and salt; cover and process until smooth. Pour over pork. Cover and cook on low for 8-10 hours or until meat is tender.
2. Remove roast; cool slightly. Shred pork with 2 forks and return to slow cooker. Using a slotted spoon, place about ½ cup pork mixture down the center of each tortilla; if desired, top with avocado, sour cream and cilantro. Fold sides and ends over filling and roll up.

Freeze option: Omit avocado, sour cream and cilantro. Individually wrap cooled burritos in paper towels and foil; freeze in an airtight container. To use, remove the foil; place paper towel-wrapped burrito on a microwave-safe plate. Microwave on high for 3-4 minutes or until heated through, turning once. Let stand 20 seconds. If desired, serve with sliced avocado, sour cream and cilantro.

Note: Wear disposable gloves when cutting hot peppers; the oils can burn skin. Avoid touching your face.

1 burrito: 420 cal., 18g fat (6g sat. fat), 81mg chol., 745mg sod., 36g carb. (5g sugars, 3g fiber), 28g pro.

FARMHOUSE BARBECUE MUFFINS

Tangy barbecue sauce, fluffy biscuits and cheddar cheese combine to turn muffins into hand-held dinners. Try them with ground turkey or other shredded cheeses to vary the flavor.

—*Karen Kenney, Harvard, IL*

- -

Prep: 20 min. • **Bake:** 20 min.
Makes: 10 servings

- 1 tube (12 oz.) refrigerated buttermilk biscuits
- 1 lb. ground beef
- ½ cup ketchup
- 3 Tbsp. brown sugar
- 1 Tbsp. cider vinegar
- ½ tsp. chili powder
- 1 cup shredded cheddar cheese

1. Separate dough into 10 biscuits; flatten into 5-in. circles. Press each onto bottom and up the sides of a greased muffin cup; set aside.
2. In a skillet, cook beef over medium heat until no longer pink; drain. In a small bowl, combine the ketchup, brown sugar, vinegar and chili powder; add to beef and mix well.
3. Divide the meat mixture among the biscuit-lined muffin cups, using about ¼ cup for each. Sprinkle with cheese. Bake at 375° for 18-20 minutes or until golden brown. Cool for 5 minutes before serving.
1 muffin: 226 cal., 9 g fat (5 g sat. fat), 42 mg chol., 477 mg sod., 21 g carb., trace fiber, 14 g pro.

PIZZA ROLL-UPS

These pizza rolls, made with refrigerated crescent rolls, are great for grab-and-go dinners. Kids of all ages love them, and they can be prepared on the weekend for meals on the run.

—*Donna Klettke, Wheatland, MO*

- -

Prep: 20 min. • **Bake:** 15 min.
Makes: 2 dozen

- ½ lb. ground beef
- 1 can (8 oz.) tomato sauce
- ½ cup shredded part-skim mozzarella cheese
- ½ tsp. dried oregano
- 2 tubes (8 oz. each) refrigerated crescent rolls

1. In a large skillet, cook beef over medium heat until no longer pink; drain. Remove from the heat. Add the tomato sauce, mozzarella cheese and oregano.
2. Separate the crescent dough into 8 rectangles, pinching seams together. Place about 3 Tbsp. of the meat mixture along 1 long side of each rectangle. Roll up, jelly-roll style, starting with a long side. Cut each roll into 3 pieces.
3. Place, seam side down, 2 in. apart on greased baking sheets. Bake at 375° for 15 minutes or until golden brown.
1 roll-up: 94 cal., 5g fat (1g sat. fat), 7mg chol., 206mg sod., 9g carb. (2g sugars, 0 fiber), 4g pro.

HEARTY CHICKEN GYROS

I love reinventing classic recipes to fit our taste and healthy lifestyle. This recipe is quick to prepare and can be served with oven fries or on its own. You can add Greek olives, omit the onion, or even use cubed pork tenderloin for a new taste.

—*Kayla Douthitt, Elizabethtown, KY*

Prep: 30 min. + marinating • **Cook:** 5 min.
Makes: 6 servings

- 1½ lbs. boneless skinless chicken breasts, cut into ½-in. cubes
- ½ cup salt-free lemon-pepper marinade
- 3 Tbsp. minced fresh mint

SAUCE
- ½ cup fat-free plain Greek yogurt
- 2 Tbsp. lemon juice
- 1 tsp. dill weed
- ½ tsp. garlic powder

ASSEMBLY
- 1 medium cucumber, seeded and chopped
- 1 medium tomato, chopped
- ¼ cup finely chopped onion
- 6 whole wheat pita pocket halves, warmed
- ⅓ cup crumbled feta cheese

1. Place chicken, marinade and mint in a shallow dish and turn to coat. Cover and refrigerate up to 6 hours.

2. Drain chicken, discarding marinade. Place a large nonstick skillet over medium-high heat. Add chicken; cook and stir until no longer pink, 4-6 minutes.

3. In a small bowl, mix sauce ingredients. In another bowl, combine cucumber, tomato and onion. Serve chicken in pita pockets with sauce, vegetable mixture and cheese.

1 gyro: 248 cal., 4g fat (2g sat. fat), 66mg chol., 251mg sod., 22g carb. (4g sugars, 3g fiber), 30g pro. **Diabetic exchanges:** 3 lean meat, 1½ starch, ½ fat.

ITALIAN JOES ON TEXAS TOAST

This is perfect for weeknights on the go. I like to double the meat mixture and freeze it so I have another dinner on hand for later in the month.

—*Ashley Armstrong, Kingsland, GA*

Takes: 30 min. • **Makes:** 8 servings

- 1   lb. ground beef
- 1   small green pepper, finely chopped
- 1   medium onion, finely chopped
- 3   garlic cloves, minced
- ½   cup dry red wine or beef broth
- 1   can (14½ oz.) diced tomatoes, undrained
- ¼   cup tomato paste
- ¼   tsp. salt
- ⅛   tsp. pepper
- 1   pkg. (11¼ oz.) frozen garlic Texas toast
- 8   slices part-skim mozzarella cheese

1. Preheat oven to 425°. In a large skillet, cook and crumble beef with green pepper, onion and garlic over medium-high heat until meat is no longer pink, 5-7 minutes; drain. Stir in wine. Bring to a boil; cook until wine is reduced by half, about 2 minutes. Stir in tomatoes, tomato paste, salt and pepper; return to a boil. Reduce the heat; simmer, uncovered, until the mixture is thickened, 2-3 minutes, stirring occasionally.

2. Meanwhile, place the Texas toast on a foil-lined 15x10x1-in. pan; bake until lightly browned, 8-10 minutes.

3. Spoon beef mixture onto toast; top with cheese. Bake until cheese is melted, 3-4 minutes. Serve immediately.

1 open-faced sandwich: 353 cal., 19g fat (7g sat. fat), 58mg chol., 626mg sod., 25g carb. (5g sugars, 2g fiber), 22g pro.

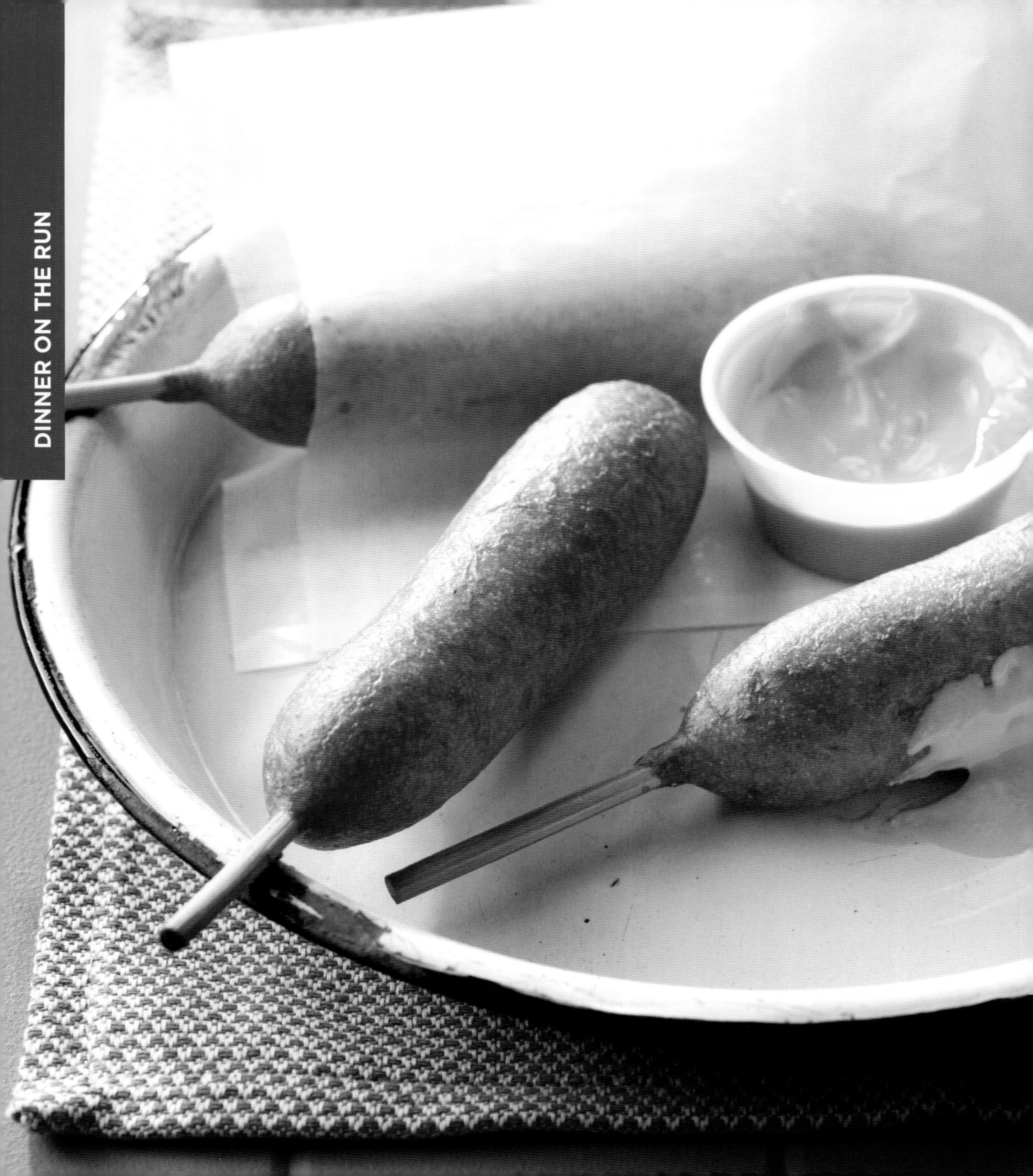

INDIANA-STYLE CORN DOGS

One of the best parts of attending the many fairs and festivals in Indiana is the corn dogs! My family adores corn dogs, so I make them fairly often at home. They're perfect for dinner on the run.
—*Sally Denney, Warsaw, IN*

- -

Prep: 20 min. • **Cook:** 5 min./batch
Makes: 1 dozen

- 1   cup all-purpose flour
- ½   cup yellow cornmeal
- 1   Tbsp. sugar
- 3   tsp. baking powder
- 1   tsp. salt
- ½   tsp. ground mustard
- ¼   tsp. paprika
-     Dash pepper
- 1   large egg, lightly beaten
- 1   cup evaporated milk
-     Oil for deep-fat frying
- 12 wooden skewers
- 12 hot dogs

1. In a bowl, whisk the first 8 ingredients. Whisk in egg and milk just until blended. Transfer batter to a tall drinking glass.
2. In an electric skillet or deep-fat fryer, heat oil to 375°. Insert skewers into hot dogs. Dip hot dogs into batter; allow excess batter to drip off. Fry corn dogs, a few at a time, 2-3 minutes or until golden brown, turning occasionally. Drain on paper towels. Serve immediately.
1 corn dog: 299 cal., 21g fat (7g sat. fat), 47mg chol., 805mg sod., 18g carb. (4g sugars, 1g fiber), 9g pro.

APPLE SQUASH SOUP

I add a ginger and sage to apples and squash to make this creamy soup. Few cream soups freeze as nicely as this one does!
—*Crystal Ralph-Haughn, Bartlesville, OK*

- -

Prep: 10 min. • **Cook:** 35 min.
Makes: 5 servings

- 2   Tbsp. butter
- 1   large onion, chopped
- ½   tsp. rubbed sage
- 1   can (14½ oz.) chicken or vegetable broth
- 2   medium tart apples, peeled and finely chopped
- ¾   cup water
- 1   pkg. (12 oz.) frozen cooked winter squash, thawed
- 1   tsp. ground ginger
- ½   tsp. salt
- ½   cup fat-free milk

1. In a large saucepan, heat butter over medium-high heat. Add onion and sage; cook and stir 2-4 minutes or until tender. Add broth, apples and water; bring to a boil. Reduce heat; simmer, covered, 12 minutes.
2. Add squash, ginger and salt; return to a boil. Reduce heat; simmer, uncovered, for 10 minutes to allow flavors to blend. Remove from heat; cool slightly.
3. Process in batches in a blender until smooth; return to pan. Add milk; heat through, stirring occasionally (do not allow to boil).
Freeze option: Freeze cooled soup in freezer containers. To use, partially thaw in refrigerator overnight. Heat through in a saucepan, stirring occasionally; add broth if necessary.
1 cup: 119 cal., 5g fat (3g sat. fat), 15mg chol., 641mg sod., 18g carb. (8g sugars, 3g fiber), 3g pro. **Diabetic exchanges:** 1 starch, ½ fruit, 1 fat.

5i

SIMPLY ELEGANT TOMATO SOUP

If you've only had tomato soup from a can, you're going to be blown away when you try a bowl of this. It's velvety, creamy and oh, so good!

—*Heidi Blanken, Sedro-Woolley, WA*

Prep: 25 min. • **Cook:** 20 min.
Makes: 4 servings (1 qt.)

- 4   lbs. tomatoes (about 10 medium)
- 1   Tbsp. butter
- 3   Tbsp. minced chives, divided
- 1   tsp. salt
- ½   tsp. pepper
- 2   cups half-and-half cream

1. In a large saucepan, bring 8 cups water to a boil. Using a slotted spoon, place the tomatoes, 1 at a time, in boiling water for 30-60 seconds. Remove each tomato and immediately plunge in ice water. Peel and quarter tomatoes; remove seeds.

2. In another large saucepan, melt butter. Add the tomatoes, 2 Tbsp. chives, salt and pepper. Bring to a boil. Reduce heat; simmer, uncovered, for 6-7 minutes or until tender, stirring occasionally. Remove from the heat. Cool slightly.

3. In a blender, process soup until blended. Return to the pan. Stir in the cream; heat through. Sprinkle each serving with the remaining chives.

1 cup: 268 cal., 16g fat (10g sat. fat), 68mg chol., 693mg sod., 22g carb. (16g sugars, 6g fiber), 8g pro.

LAYERED PICNIC LOAVES

This big sandwich is inspired by one I fell in love with at a New York deli. It's easy to make ahead of time and cart anywhere we might be headed. Kids and adults alike say it's just super.
—*Marion Lowery, Medford, OR*

Prep: 20 min. + chilling
Makes: 2 loaves (12 servings each)

    2   unsliced loaves
        (1 lb. each) Italian bread
    ¼   cup olive oil
    3   garlic cloves, minced
    2   tsp. Italian seasoning, divided
    ½   lb. deli roast beef
   12   slices part-skim mozzarella
        cheese (1 oz. each)
   16   fresh basil leaves
    3   medium tomatoes, thinly sliced
    ¼   lb. thinly sliced salami
    1   jar (6½ oz.) marinated artichoke
        hearts, drained and sliced
    1   pkg. (10 oz.) ready-to-
        serve salad greens
    8   oz. thinly sliced deli chicken
    1   medium onion, thinly sliced
    ¼   tsp. salt
    ⅛   tsp. pepper

1. Cut both loaves in half horizontally; hollow out tops and bottoms, leaving ½-in. shells (discard removed bread or save for another use).

2. Combine oil and garlic; brush inside bread shells. Sprinkle with 1 tsp. Italian seasoning. Layer bottom of each loaf with a fourth of each: roast beef, mozzarella, basil, tomatoes, salami, artichokes, salad greens, chicken and onion. Repeat layers. Season with the salt, pepper and remaining Italian seasoning.

3. Drizzle with remaining oil mixture if desired. Replace bread tops; wrap tightly and refrigerate at least 1 hour before slicing and serving.

1 slice: 341 cal., 18g fat (7g sat. fat), 47mg chol., 991mg sod., 26g carb. (3g sugars, 2g fiber), 19g pro.

CAJUN PORK SANDWICHES

This recipe's simple spice rub gives pork tenderloin an irresistible flavor. You'll watch in delight as these tasty open-faced sandwiches disappear fast.
—*Mae Kruse, Monee, IL*

Prep: 25 min. + chilling
Bake: 25 min. + standing • **Makes:** 3 dozen

- 2 pork tenderloins (1 lb. each), trimmed
- 2 tsp. vegetable oil
- 3 Tbsp. paprika
- 2 tsp. dried oregano
- 2 tsp. dried thyme
- 1½ tsp. garlic powder
- ½ tsp. pepper
- ½ tsp. salt, optional
- ½ tsp. ground cumin
- ¼ tsp. ground nutmeg
- ¼ tsp. cayenne pepper
- 36 French bread slices or mini buns
  Butter or mayonnaise
  Lettuce leaves
  Thin slivers of green and sweet red pepper

1. Place tenderloins in a greased 13x9-in. baking pan. Rub each with 1 tsp. oil.

2. Combine the paprika, oregano, thyme, garlic powder, pepper, salt if desired, cumin, nutmeg and cayenne; pat over tenderloins. Cover and refrigerate overnight.

3. Bake at 425° for 25-30 minutes or until a thermometer reads 160°. Let stand for 10 minutes; thinly slice. Spread bread or buns with butter or mayonnaise; top with lettuce, pork and green and red pepper.

1 sandwich: 112 cal., 3g fat (1g sat. fat), 15mg chol., 127mg sod., 14g carb. (1g sugars, 1g fiber), 8g pro. **Diabetic exchanges:** 1 starch, 1 lean meat.

TEST KITCHEN TIP

Consider adding this pork tenderloin to your meal plan. Use some of the cooked meat for these handy sandwiches, then use the rest of the pork for tacos, wraps and stir fries later in the week.

MAMA MIA MEATBALL TAQUITOS

We love lasagna, but it takes too long on weeknights. My solution? Meatball taquitos! My kids get the flavors they want, I'm out of the kitchen fast and we all enjoy a filling meal as we head out the door.
—*Lauren Wyler, Dripping Springs, TX*

Takes: 30 min. • **Makes:** 1 dozen

12 **frozen fully cooked Italian turkey meatballs, thawed**
2 **cups shredded part-skim mozzarella cheese**
1 **cup whole-milk ricotta cheese**
1 **tsp. Italian seasoning**
12 **flour tortillas (8 in.)**
   Cooking spray
   Warm marinara sauce

1. Preheat oven to 425°. Place meatballs in a food processor; pulse until finely chopped. Transfer to a large bowl; stir in cheeses and Italian seasoning.
2. Spread about ¼ cup meatball mixture down center of each tortilla. Roll up tightly. Place in a greased 15x10x1-in. baking pan, seam side down; spritz with cooking spray.
3. Bake until golden brown, 16-20 minutes. Serve with marinara sauce.
2 taquitos: 617 cal., 28g fat (11g sat. fat), 94mg chol., 1069mg sod., 60g carb. (3g sugars, 3g fiber), 33g pro.

EASY CORNISH PASTIES

These are a bit different from traditional pasties, but the ingredients are probably already in your kitchen. I double the recipe and freeze the extras to have on hand as a quick dinner when we're on the go.
—*Judy Marsden, Ontario, CA*

- -

Prep: 45 min. • **Bake:** 20 min.
Makes: 8 pasties

½ lb. ground beef
2 Tbsp. all-purpose flour
½ to 1 tsp. seasoned salt
1 Tbsp. minced fresh parsley
1 tsp. beef bouillon granules
¼ cup water
1 cup diced peeled potatoes
½ cup diced carrots
2 Tbsp. finely chopped onion
2 pkg. (11 oz. each) pie crust mix
   Water

1. In a skillet, cook beef over medium heat until no longer pink; drain. Add the flour, seasoned salt and parsley; stir until well coated. Dissolve bouillon in water; stir into meat mixture. Add potatoes, carrots and onion. Cover and cook over medium heat until vegetables are crisp-tender. Cool.
2. Meanwhile, prepare pie crusts according to the package directions. On a floured surface, roll each pie crust into a 12-in. square. Cut each square into four 6-in. squares. Place about ⅓ cup meat mixture in center of each square.
3. Moisten edges of pastry with water and fold over meat mixture to form a triangle. Press the edges with a fork to seal. Make a 1-in. slit in the top of each triangle. Place on 2 ungreased baking sheets. Bake at 400° until golden brown, 20-25 minutes.
1 pasty: 289 cal., 18g fat (5g sat. fat), 14mg chol., 521mg sod., 24g carb. (1g sugars, 1g fiber), 8g pro.

CILANTRO-AVOCADO TUNA SALAD SANDWICHES

Lime juice and cilantro in tuna salad — who knew? This recipe came to me as a way to have a protein-packed meal with lots of pizazz . Mix it up early in the week and stash it in the fridge for fast dinners even on your busiest night.
—*Heather Waldorf, Black Mountain, NC*

- -

Takes: 15 min. • **Makes:** 4 servings

2 pouches (5 oz. each) albacore white tuna in water
⅓ cup mayonnaise
3 Tbsp. minced fresh cilantro
2 Tbsp. lime juice
2 garlic cloves, minced
¼ tsp. salt
⅛ tsp. pepper
8 slices whole wheat bread, toasted if desired
4 slices Muenster or provolone cheese
1 medium ripe avocado, peeled and sliced

In a small bowl, mix the first 7 ingredients. Spread tuna mixture over 4 slices of bread; top with cheese, avocado and remaining bread. Serve immediately.
1 sandwich: 506 cal., 30g fat (8g sat. fat), 56mg chol., 908mg sod., 28g carb. (3g sugars, 6g fiber), 30g pro.
Mixed Veggie Tuna Salad Sandwiches: Mix tuna and mayonnaise with ½ cup frozen mixed vegetables, thawed and chopped; 2 Tbsp. chopped onion and 1 Tbsp. ranch salad dressing mix. Serve on buns.

HARVEST SWEET POTATO SOUP

This is truly the easiest soup I've ever made. I always double the recipe when I prepare it, since we love leftovers later in the week. We prefer this thick soup warm, but it can also be served chilled.

—*Gayle Becker, Mount Clemens, MI*

- -

Prep: 30 min. • **Cook:** 25 min.
Makes: 4 servings

1	cup chopped celery
½	cup chopped onion
1	Tbsp. canola oil
3	medium sweet potatoes (about 1 lb.), peeled and cubed
3	cups chicken or vegetable broth
1	bay leaf
½	tsp. dried basil
¼	tsp. salt, optional

1. In a Dutch oven, saute celery and onion in oil until tender. Add remaining ingredients; bring to a boil over medium heat. Reduce heat; simmer for 25-30 minutes or until potatoes are tender.

2. Discard bay leaf. Cool slightly. In a blender, process soup in batches until smooth. Return all to pan and heat through.

1 cup: 133 cal., 5g fat (0 sat. fat), 4mg chol., 116mg sod., 20g carb. (0 sugars, 0 fiber), 4g pro. **Diabetic exchanges:** 1 starch, 1 vegetable, 1 fat.

❄ MUFFIN-CUP CHEDDAR BEEF PIES

My kids love these beef rolls so much that I always make extra and store the savory bites in the freezer, since they heat up so quickly. I give the kids their choice of dipping sauces. Ranch dressing and spaghetti sauce are their top picks.
—*Kimberly Farmer, Wichita, KS*

- -

Prep: 25 min. + standing • **Bake:** 20 min.
Makes: 20 meat pies

2	**loaves (1 lb. each) frozen bread dough**
2	**lbs. ground beef**
1	**can (8 oz.) mushroom stems and pieces, drained**
1¼	**cups shredded cheddar cheese**
1½	**tsp. Italian seasoning**
1	**tsp. garlic powder**
½	**tsp. salt**
¼	**tsp. pepper**
	Spaghetti sauce, warmed

1. Let dough stand at room temperature until softened, about 30 minutes. Preheat oven to 350°. Meanwhile, in a Dutch oven, cook beef over medium heat until no longer pink, breaking into crumbles, 12-15 minutes; drain. Stir in the mushrooms, shredded cheese and seasonings.

2. Divide each loaf into 10 portions; roll each into a 4-in. circle. Top with ¼ cup filling; bring edges of dough up over filling and pinch to seal.

Place meat pies in greased muffin cups, seam side down. Bake until golden brown, 20-25 minutes. Serve with spaghetti sauce.

Freeze option: Freeze cooled beef pies in a freezer container. To use, reheat beef pies on greased baking sheets in a preheated 350° oven until heated through.

2 meat pies: 482 cal., 19g fat (7g sat. fat), 71mg chol., 850mg sod., 45g carb. (4g sugars, 4g fiber), 29g pro.

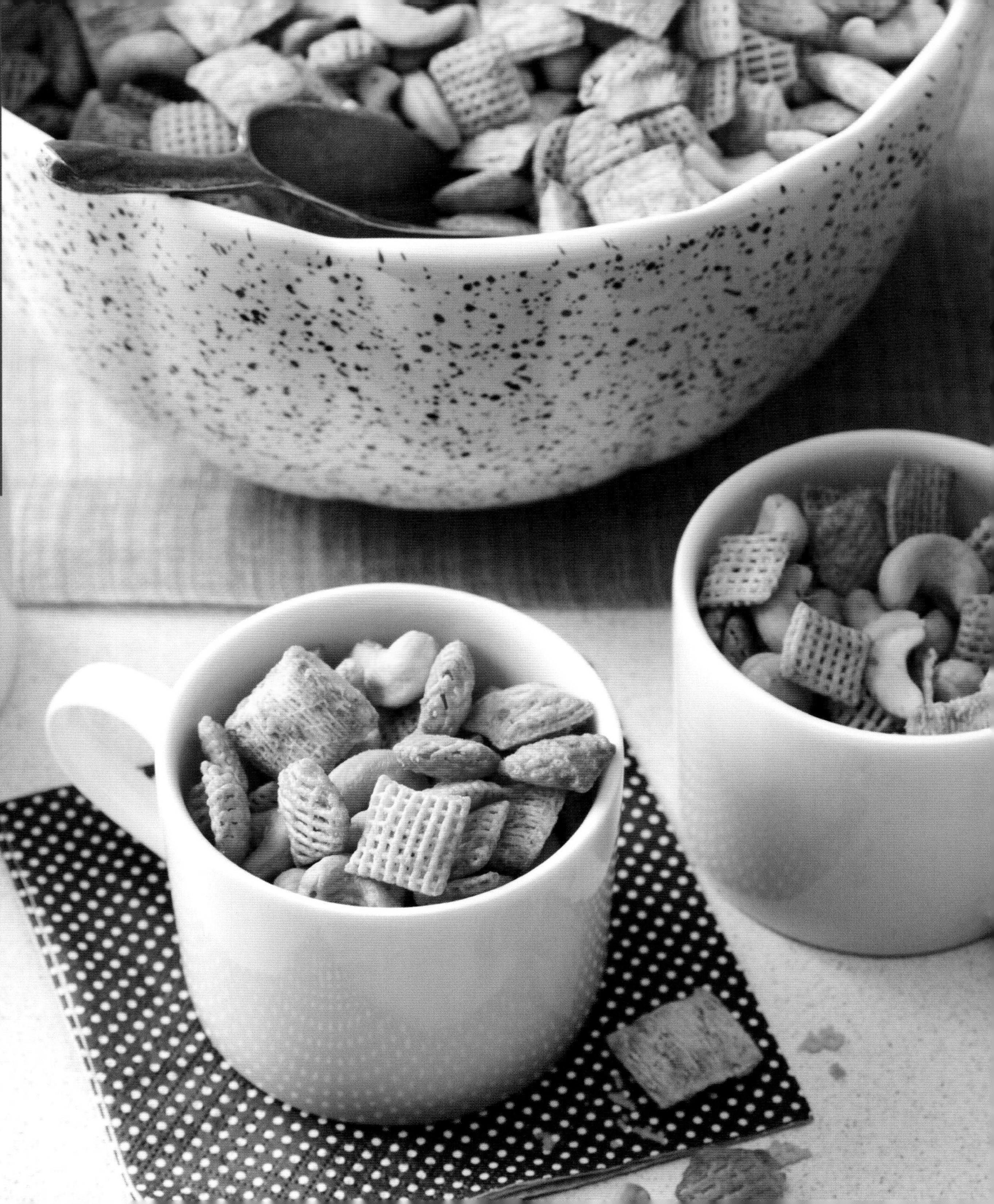

REALLY GOOD SNACK MIX

I got tired of my family picking through a snack mix for their favorite items and leaving the rest. So I experimented using only their favorites and came up with this recipe. Now there's never any left!
—*Lori Genske, Waldo, WI*

- -

Prep: 10 min. • **Bake:** 45 min.
Makes: about 7 cups

- 3 **Tbsp. butter, melted**
- 4 **tsp. Worcestershire sauce**
- 1 **Tbsp. canola oil**
- 1 **tsp. seasoned salt**
- ½ **tsp. garlic powder**
- 2 **cups Corn Chex**
- 2 **cups Crispix**
- 2 **cups bite-sized Shredded Wheat**
- 1½ **cups salted cashews**

1. Preheat the oven to 250°. Mix the first 5 ingredients; toss with cereals and cashews, coating evenly. Spread into a 15x10x1-in. pan coated with cooking spray.

2. Bake 45 minutes, gently stirring every 15 minutes. Cool completely before storing in airtight containers.

½ cup: 180 cal., 11g fat (3g sat. fat), 7mg chol., 269mg sod., 18g carb. (2g sugars, 2g fiber), 4g pro. **Diabetic exchanges:** 1 starch, 2 fat.

TACO PUMPKIN SEEDS

Here's a hot and spicy idea—toast pumpkin seeds in taco seasoning and a bit of garlic salt. The combination packs a tasty punch!
—Taste of Home *Test Kitchen*

- -

Prep: 15 min. • **Bake:** 15 min. + cooling
Makes: 1 cup

- 1 **cup seeds from freshly cut pumpkin, washed and dried**
- 2 **Tbsp. vegetable oil**
- 1 **to 2 Tbsp. taco seasoning**
- ¼ **to ½ tsp. garlic salt**

In a skillet, saute pumpkin seeds in oil for 5 minutes or until lightly browned. Using a slotted spoon, transfer the seeds to an ungreased 15x10x1-in. baking pan. Sprinkle with taco seasoning and garlic salt; stir to coat. Spread into a single layer. Bake at 325° for 15-20 minutes or until crisp. Remove to paper towels to cool completely. Store in an airtight container for up to 3 weeks.

2 Tbsp.: 70 cal., 5g fat (1g sat. fat), 0 chol., 161mg sod., 5g carb. (0 sugars, 0 fiber), 1g pro.

⑤ⱼ SPICY CASHEWS

These seasoned nuts are so good, it's hard to stop eating them. I made them for gift baskets and got many compliments. They are perfect for the holidays but delicious to munch any time of year.
—*Jean Voan, Shepherd, TX*

Takes: 10 min. • **Makes:** 2⅔ cups

- 2   cans (10 oz. each) salted cashews
- 3   Tbsp. butter
- 1   Tbsp. canola oil
- ½   tsp. salt
- ½   tsp. chili powder
- ¼   to ½ tsp. crushed red pepper flakes

In a large skillet, saute cashews in butter and oil for 4-5 minutes or until golden brown. Spread on a paper towel-lined baking sheet; let stand for 2-3 minutes. Transfer to a large bowl. Sprinkle with salt, chili powder and pepper flakes; toss to coat. Store in an airtight container.

⅓ cup: 273 cal., 24g fat (7g sat. fat), 11mg chol., 425mg sod., 9g carb. (2g sugars, 1g fiber), 6g pro.

⑤ⱼ BARBECUED PEANUTS

These zippy peanuts are wonderful for football parties and movie nights, or even as after-school snacks. I like to prepare them ahead of time and stash them away for last-minute snacking.
—*Abbey Boyle, Tampa, FL*

Prep: 10 min. • **Bake:** 20 min. + cooling
Makes: 3 cups

- ⅓   cup barbecue sauce
- 2   Tbsp. butter, melted
- 1   tsp. garlic powder
- ¼   to ½ tsp. cayenne pepper
- 1   jar (16 oz.) dry roasted peanuts

1. In a large bowl, combine the barbecue sauce, butter, garlic powder and cayenne. Add peanuts; stir until evenly coated. Transfer to a greased 13x9-in. baking pan.
2. Bake peanuts, uncovered, at 325° for 20-25 minutes, stirring every 10 minutes. Spread on waxed paper; cool completely. Store in an airtight container.

½ cup: 366 cal., 31g fat (6g sat. fat), 8mg chol., 575mg sod., 14g carb. (4g sugars, 5g fiber), 14g pro.

5i

ANTIPASTO SKEWERS

This elegant-looking appetizer is quick and easy to make. It's perfect for dinner parties, cocktail parties and everything in between!
—*Amanda Pederson, Fargo, ND*

- -

Takes: 15 min. • **Makes:** 1 dozen

 24 grape tomatoes (about 1 pint)
  1 carton (8 oz.) cherry-size
     fresh mozzarella cheese
 12 thin slices hard salami (about ¼ lb.)
 12 pimiento-stuffed Queen olives
     Italian vinaigrette, optional

On 12 wooden 6-in. skewers, alternately thread tomatoes, mozzarella, folded salami slices and olives. Refrigerate until serving. If desired, drizzle skewers with vinaigrette to serve.

1 skewer: 204 cal., 9g fat (4g sat. fat), 24mg chol., 345mg sod., 24g carb. (16g sugars, 7g fiber), 11g pro.

CRISP SUGAR COOKIES

My grandmother always had sugar cookies in her pantry. We grandchildren would empty that big jar fast because those cookies were the absolute best!
—*Evelyn Poteet, Hancock, MD*

- -

Prep: 15 min. + chilling • **Bake:** 10 min./batch
Makes: 8 dozen

- 1 cup butter, softened
- 2 cups sugar
- 2 large eggs, room temperature
- 1 tsp. vanilla extract
- 5 cups all-purpose flour
- 1½ tsp. baking powder
- 1 tsp. baking soda
- ½ tsp. salt
- ¼ cup 2% milk

1. In a large bowl, cream butter and sugar until light and fluffy. Add eggs and vanilla. Combine flour, baking powder, baking soda and salt; add to creamed mixture alternately with milk. Cover and refrigerate until easy to handle, 15-30 minutes.

2. Preheat oven to 350°. On a floured surface, carefully roll out dough to ⅛-in. thickness. Cut into desired shapes using a 2-in. cookie cutter. Place 2 in. apart on greased baking sheets.

3. Bake 10 minutes or until edges are lightly browned. Remove from pans to wire racks to cool completely.

2 cookies: 117 cal., 4g fat (2g sat. fat), 19mg chol., 105mg sod., 18g carb. (8g sugars, 0 fiber), 2g pro.

PEANUT BUTTER POPCORN BALLS

Friends and family are always happy to see these popcorn balls. Make them ahead of time for easy snacking.
—*Betty Claycomb, Alverton, PA*

- -

Prep: 20 min. + standing
Makes: 10 servings

- 5 cups popped popcorn
- 1 cup dry roasted peanuts
- ½ cup sugar
- ½ cup light corn syrup
- ½ cup chunky peanut butter
- ½ tsp. vanilla extract
- 10 lollipop sticks

1. Place popcorn and peanuts in a large bowl; set aside. In a large heavy saucepan over medium heat, bring sugar and corn syrup to a rolling boil, stirring occasionally. Remove from the heat; stir in peanut butter and vanilla. Quickly pour over the popcorn mixture and mix well.

2. When cool enough to handle, quickly shape into ten 2½-in. balls; insert a lollipop stick into each ball. Let stand at room temperature until firm; wrap in plastic.

1 popcorn ball: 281 cal., 16g fat (2g sat. fat), 0 chol., 228mg sod., 32g carb. (25g sugars, 3g fiber), 7g pro.

TEST KITCHEN TIP

To roast your own peanuts, simply preheat the oven to 350° and place shelled peanuts on a baking pan. Put the pan in the oven for about 15 minutes, and you're good to get munching!

CHOCOLATE SNACK MIX

Being gluten-intolerant, I experiment with a lot of recipes. This sweet snack packed with cashews, banana chips and cereal is popular with kids and adults alike.
—*Angela Buchanan, Longmont, CO*

- -

Takes: 25 min. • **Makes:** 3 qt.

5	cups Chocolate Chex
4	cups Cinnamon Chex
1	cup salted cashews
1	cup dried banana chips
6	Tbsp. butter, cubed
1	cup sweetened shredded coconut
¼	cup honey
2	Tbsp. baking cocoa
1	tsp. coconut extract
½	tsp. ground cinnamon

1. In a large microwave-safe bowl, combine the cereals, cashews and banana chips. In a small microwave-safe bowl, melt butter. Add the coconut, honey, cocoa, extract and cinnamon; stir until blended. Pour over the cereal mixture and toss to coat.

2. Microwave, uncovered, on high for 4 minutes, stirring every minute. Spread onto waxed paper to cool. Store in an airtight container.

Note: Read all ingredient labels for possible gluten content prior to use. Ingredient formulas can change, and production facilities vary among brands. If you're concerned that your brand may contain gluten, contact the company.

½ cup: 182 cal., 10g fat (5g sat. fat), 8mg chol., 185mg sod., 23g carb. (11g sugars, 1g fiber), 2g pro.

BLACK FOREST HAM PINWHEELS

I love these treats because I can make them ahead of time. Roll up the tortillas and store in the refrigerator. When you need a quick snack, slice and enjoy. They're perfect for Christmas, but I enjoy them all year.
—*Kate Dampier, Quail Valley, CA*

- -

Prep: 20 min. + chilling
Makes: about 3½ dozen

    1   pkg. (8 oz.) cream cheese, softened
    4   tsp. minced fresh dill
    1   Tbsp. lemon juice
    2   tsp. Dijon mustard
        Dash salt and pepper
    ½   cup dried cherries, chopped
    ¼   cup chopped green onions
    5   flour tortillas (10 in.),
        room temperature
    ½   lb. sliced deli Black Forest ham
    ½   lb. sliced Swiss cheese

1. In a small bowl, beat cream cheese, dill, lemon juice, mustard, salt and pepper until blended. Stir in cherries and onions. Spread over each tortilla; layer with the ham and Swiss cheese.
2. Roll up tightly; wrap securely in waxed paper. Refrigerate at least 2 hours. Cut into ½-in. slices.
1 piece: 78 cal., 4g fat (2g sat. fat), 13mg chol., 151mg sod., 6g carb. (2g sugars, 0 fiber), 4g pro.

Appetizer Pinwheels: Omit dill, lemon juice, mustard, salt, pepper, cherries, onion, ham and cheese. Beat cream cheese with 1 cup sour cream, 1 can (4¼ oz.) drained chopped ripe olives, 1 can (4 oz.) well-drained chopped green chiles, 1 cup shredded cheddar cheese, ½ cup chopped green onions, dash garlic powder and dash salt until blended. Spread over tortillas and proceed as recipe directs.
Reuben Pinwheels: Omit dill, lemon juice, mustard, salt, pepper, cherries, onion, ham and cheese. Beat cream cheese with 3 Tbsp. spicy brown mustard and ¼ tsp. prepared horseradish. Spread 1 heaping Tbsp. of cream cheese mixture over each tortilla; layer each with 8 thin slices deli corned beef, 3 thin slices Swiss cheese and 1 heaping Tbsp. additional cream cheese mixture. Top each with ½ cup well-drained sauerkraut. Proceed as recipe directs.

5i
QUICK & EASY GUMDROPS

These homemade candies are sweet little gummy bites that are softer than the store-bought varieties.
—Leah Rekau, Milwaukee, WI

- -

Prep: 25 min. + chilling
Makes: 64 pieces (1 lb.)

3	envelopes unflavored gelatin
½	cup plus ¾ cup water, divided
1½	cups sugar
¼	to ½ tsp. raspberry extract
	Red food coloring
	Additional sugar

1. In a small bowl, sprinkle gelatin over ½ cup water; let stand 5 minutes. In a small saucepan, bring sugar and remaining water to a boil over medium heat, stirring constantly. Add gelatin; reduce heat. Simmer 5 minutes, stirring frequently. Remove from heat; stir in extract and food coloring as desired.

2. Pour into a greased 8-in. square pan. Refrigerate, covered, 3 hours or until firm.

3. Loosen edges of candy from pan with a knife; turn onto a sugared work surface. Cut into 1-in squares; roll in sugar. Let stand, uncovered, at room temperature until all sides are dry, turning every hour, 3-4 hours. Store between layers of waxed paper in an airtight container in the refrigerator.

Note: For lemon gumdrops, use lemon extract and yellow food coloring. For orange gumdrops, use orange extract, yellow food coloring and a drop of red food coloring.

1 piece: 19 cal., 0 fat (0 sat. fat), 0 chol., 1mg sod., 5g carb. (5g sugars, 0 fiber), 0 pro.

GLUTEN-FREE SNACK MIX

The buttery sweet cinnamon coating in this crunchy mix makes this snack addicting. Because it travels well, it makes an easy on-the-go snack you can make ahead.
—Taste of Home *Test Kitchen*

- -

Prep: 15 min. • **Bake:** 10 min. + cooling
Makes: 10 cups

  8   **cups popped popcorn**
  2   **cups Koala Crisp cereal**
  1   **pkg. (5 oz.) dried cherries**
 ⅓   **cup butter, cubed**
 ⅓   **cup honey**
 ½   **tsp. ground cinnamon**

1. In a large ungreased roasting pan, combine the popcorn, cereal and cherries. In a small saucepan, melt butter. Add honey and cinnamon; cook and stir until heated through. Pour over popcorn mixture and toss to coat.

2. Bake at 325° for 15 minutes, stirring every 5 minutes. Cool completely. Store in airtight containers.

Note: Read all ingredient labels for possible gluten content prior to use. Ingredient formulas can change, and production facilities vary among brands. If you're concerned that your brand may contain gluten, contact the company.

½ cup: 110 cal., 5g fat (2g sat. fat), 8mg chol., 89mg sod., 16g carb. (11g sugars, 1g fiber), 1g pro. **Diabetic exchanges:** 1 starch, 1 fat.

5i SNACKERS

These crispy, chewy treats pack lots of peanut flavor. They're our favorite travel snack. I always make a double batch so we have some left to enjoy when we reach our destination.
—*W.H. Gregory, Roanoke, VA*

- -

Takes: 20 min. • **Makes:** about 1½ dozen

- 3 cups Crispix cereal
- ½ cup salted peanuts
- ⅓ cup packed brown sugar
- ⅓ cup corn syrup
- ¼ cup peanut butter

In a large bowl, combine cereal and peanuts; set aside. In a microwave-safe bowl, combine brown sugar and corn syrup. Microwave on high for 30-60 seconds or until sugar is dissolved, stirring several times. Immediately stir in peanut butter until smooth. Pour over cereal mixture and toss to coat. Drop by rounded tablespoonfuls onto waxed paper. Cool.

2 pieces: 190 cal., 8g fat (1g sat. fat), 0 chol., 156mg sod., 28g carb. (16g sugars, 1g fiber), 5g pro.

5i 🍎 ROSEMARY WALNUTS

My Aunt Mary created this recipe years ago, and each time we visited her she would have a batch ready for us to enjoy. The use of cayenne adds an unexpected spice to the savory combo of rosemary and walnuts. Double the batch for on-hand snacks or when you need a last-minute gift.
—*Renee Ciancio, New Bern, NC*

- -

Takes: 20 min. • **Makes:** 2 cups

- 2 cups walnut halves
  Cooking spray
- 2 tsp. dried rosemary, crushed
- ½ tsp. kosher salt
- ¼ to ½ tsp. cayenne pepper

1. Place walnuts in a small bowl. Spritz with cooking spray. Add seasonings; toss to coat. Place in a single layer on a baking sheet.

2. Bake at 350° for 10 minutes. Serve the walnuts warm, or cool completely and store in an airtight container.

¼ cup: 166 cal., 17g fat (2g sat. fat), 0 chol., 118mg sod., 4g carb. (1g sugars, 2g fiber), 4g pro. **Diabetic exchanges:** 3 fat.

HOMEMADE CRISP CRACKERS

When friends drop by, be ready with cheesy homemade crackers that store easily in an airtight container. Let the snacking begin!
—Taste of Home *Test Kitchen*

- -

Prep: 20 min. + chilling
Bake: 20 min./batch + cooling
Makes: 4 dozen

  1¾ cups all-purpose flour
  ½ cup cornmeal
  ½ tsp. baking soda
  ½ tsp. sugar
  ½ tsp. salt
  ½ tsp. garlic powder
  ¼ tsp. Italian seasoning
  ½ cup cold butter, cubed
  1½ cups shredded Colby-
      Monterey Jack cheese
  ½ cup plus 2 Tbsp. cold water
  2 Tbsp. cider vinegar

1. In a large bowl, combine the first 7 ingredients; cut in butter until crumbly. Stir in cheese. Gradually add water and vinegar, tossing with a fork until dough forms a ball. Wrap securely in waxed paper and refrigerate 1 hour or until firm.
2. Divide into 6 portions. On a lightly floured surface, roll each portion into an 8-in. circle. Cut into 8 wedges and place on greased baking sheets.
3. Bake at 375° for 17-20 minutes or until edges are lightly browned. Cool on wire racks. Store in an airtight container.
2 crackers: 103 cal., 6g fat (4g sat. fat), 16mg chol., 145mg sod., 10g carb. (0 sugars, 0 fiber), 3g pro. **Diabetic exchanges:** 1 fat, ½ starch.

SPICY ALMONDS

We like to venture out into the Selkirk mountain range surrounding our family cabin. These nuts never tasted better than when we enjoyed them together at the peak after an amazing hike. Almonds are extremely nutritious, and, when dressed up with a wonderful blend of spices, they go from ordinary to awesome!
—*Gina Myers, Spokane, WA*

- -

Prep: 10 min. • **Bake:** 30 min. + cooling
Makes: 2½ cups

  1 Tbsp. sugar
  1½ tsp. kosher salt
  1 tsp. paprika
  ½ tsp. ground cinnamon
  ½ tsp. ground cumin
  ½ tsp. ground coriander
  ¼ tsp. cayenne pepper
  1 large egg white, room temperature
  2½ cups unblanched almonds

Preheat oven to 325°. In a small bowl, combine the first 7 ingredients. In another small bowl, whisk egg white until foamy. Add almonds; toss to coat. Sprinkle with spice mixture; toss to coat. Spread in a single layer in a greased 15x10x1-in. baking pan. Bake for 30 minutes, stirring every 10 minutes. Spread on waxed paper to cool completely. Store in an airtight container.
¼ cup: 230 cal., 20g fat (2g sat. fat), 0 chol., 293mg sod., 9g carb. (3g sugars, 4g fiber), 8g pro.

MAPLE SNACK MIX

This savory snack mix offers a sweet hint of maple flavor that folks will love. Keep the buttery, perfectly seasoned and crunchy combination on hand when the munchies come calling.
—Taste of Home *Test Kitchen*

- -

Prep: 10 min. • **Bake:** 1 hour
Makes: 12 servings (about 2¼ qt.)

    2   cups Bugles
    2   cups pretzel sticks
    2   cups cheese-flavored
        snack crackers
    1   cup bite-sized Shredded Wheat
    1   cup Corn Chex
    1   cup pecan halves
    ½   cup butter, cubed
    1   Tbsp. maple syrup
    1½ tsp. Worcestershire sauce
    ¾   tsp. Cajun seasoning
    ¼   tsp. cayenne pepper

1. Preheat the oven to 250°. Place the first 6 ingredients in a large bowl. In a microwave, melt butter; stir in remaining ingredients. Drizzle over snack mixture; toss to combine. Transfer to an ungreased 15x10x1-in. pan.
2. Bake 1 hour, stirring every 15 minutes. Cool completely before storing in an airtight container.
¾ cup: 239 cal., 16g fat (6g sat. fat), 21mg chol., 331mg sod., 22g carb. (2g sugars, 2g fiber), 3g pro.

CINNAMON TOASTED ALMONDS

These crunchy, cinnamon-glazed almonds taste like those sold at carnivals and fairs.
—Janice Thompson, Stacy, MN

- -

Prep: 15 min. • **Bake:** 25 min. + cooling
Makes: about 4 cups

    2   large egg whites
    6   tsp. vanilla extract
    4   cups unblanched almonds
    ⅓   cup sugar
    ⅓   cup packed brown sugar
    1   tsp. salt
    ½   tsp. ground cinnamon

1. In a large bowl, beat the egg whites until frothy; beat in vanilla. Add the almonds; stir gently to coat. Combine the sugars, salt and cinnamon; add to the nut mixture and stir gently to coat.
2. Spread evenly into 2 greased 15x10x1-in. baking pans. Bake at 300° until almonds are crisp, 25-30 minutes, stirring once. Cool. Store in an airtight container.
¼ cup: 250 cal., 18g fat (1g sat. fat), 0 chol., 166mg sod., 16g carb. (10g sugars, 4g fiber), 8g pro.

5i
APRICOT LEATHER

Since it isn't sticky, this tasty, nutritious snack is perfect to take along anywhere. It's also a great addition to lunch boxes, and an easy choice for after-school snacking.
—*Patsy Faye Steenbock, Riverton, WY*

Prep: 50 min. • **Bake:** 2 hours
Makes: 4 dozen pieces

- 8 **oz. dried apricots**
- 2 **Tbsp. sugar**
- 1 **drop almond extract**
  Confectioners' sugar

1. Place apricots in a small saucepan and cover with water by 1 in. Bring to a boil. Reduce heat; simmer, uncovered, until soft, about 30 minutes. Drain and cool slightly.
2. Place apricots in a blender; add sugar. Cover and process until smooth. Add almond extract.
3. Preheat the oven to 175°. Line two 15x10x1-in. baking pans with silicone baking mats. Spoon half of the apricot mixture onto each baking mat, spreading to form a 12x8-in. rectangle; repeat with remaining fruit. Bake 2-2½ hours or until almost dry to the touch. Cool completely on a wire rack.
4. Transfer to a cutting board; dust both sides with confectioners' sugar. Cut into ½x8-in. strips; roll up. Store in an airtight container in a cool, dry place.
Note: If baked fruit sticks to the knife, air-dry for 15-20 minutes, then slice and roll.
1 piece: 16 cal., 0 fat (0 sat. fat), 0 chol., 0 sod., 4g carb. (3g sugars, 0 fiber), 0 pro.

ZUCCHINI-CHOCOLATE CHIP MUFFINS

Whenever I make these muffins, I freeze several. As I'm leaving for work in the morning, I take one out of the freezer to enjoy at the office with a cup of coffee.
—*Janet Pierce DeCori, Rockton, IL*

- -

Prep: 20 min. • **Bake:** 20 min.
Makes: 1 dozen

- 1½ cups all-purpose flour
- ¾ cup sugar
- 1 tsp. baking soda
- 1 tsp. ground cinnamon
- ½ tsp. salt
- 1 large egg, room temperature, lightly beaten
- ½ cup canola oil
- ¼ cup 2% milk
- 1 Tbsp. lemon juice
- 1 tsp. vanilla extract
- 1 cup shredded zucchini
- ¼ cup miniature semisweet chocolate chips
- ¼ cup chopped walnuts

1. In a bowl, combine flour, sugar, baking soda, cinnamon and salt. Beat the egg, oil, milk, lemon juice and vanilla; stir into dry ingredients just until moistened. Fold in zucchini, chocolate chips and walnuts. Fill 12 greased or paper-lined muffin cups two-thirds full.

2. Bake at 350° for 20-25 minutes or until a toothpick comes out clean.

Freeze option: Freeze cooled muffins in an airtight container. To use, thaw at room temperature or, if desired, microwave each muffin on high for 20-30 seconds or until heated through.

1 serving: 234 cal., 13g fat (2g sat. fat), 16mg chol., 213mg sod., 28g carb. (15g sugars, 1g fiber), 3g pro.

WHY YOU'LL LOVE IT:
"I double this recipe since the muffins freeze so well, and then I have them at my beck and call whenever I want."
—GAYLENE2, TASTEOFHOME.COM

EASY DEVILED EGGS

The eggs are delicious, and it's easy to make more for larger gatherings. Best of all, you can customize the bites to the event at which you're serving them.
—*Margaret Sanders, Indianapolis, IN*

- -

Takes: 15 min. • **Makes:** 1 dozen

- 6 **hard-boiled large eggs**
- 2 **Tbsp. mayonnaise**
- 1 **tsp. sugar**
- 1 **tsp. white vinegar**
- 1 **tsp. prepared mustard**
- ½ **tsp. salt**
   Paprika

Slice eggs in half lengthwise; remove yolks and set whites aside. In a small bowl, mash yolks with a fork. Add the mayonnaise, sugar, vinegar, mustard and salt; mix well. Stuff or pipe into egg whites. Sprinkle with paprika. Refrigerate until serving.

2 stuffed egg halves: 114 cal., 9g fat (2g sat. fat), 214mg chol., 293mg sod., 1g carb. (1g sugars, 0 fiber), 6g pro.

Bacon-Cheddar Deviled Eggs: To mashed yolks, add ¼ cup mayonnaise, 2 cooked and crumbled bacon strips. 1 Tbsp. finely shred cheddar cheese, 1½ tsp. honey mustard and ⅛ tsp. pepper. Stuff as directed.

Picnic Stuffed Eggs: To mashed yolks, add ¼ cup mayonnaise, 2 Tbsp. drained sweet pickle relish, 1½ tsp. honey mustard, ½ tsp. garlic salt, ¼ tsp. Worcestershire sauce and ⅛ tsp. pepper. Stuff as directed.

Santa Fe Deviled Eggs: To mashed yolks, add 3 Tbsp. each mayonnaise and canned chopped green chiles, 1½ tsp. chipotle pepper in adobo sauce and ¼ tsp. garlic salt. Stuff as directed. Garnish each with 1 tsp. salsa, and a sliver of ripe olive.

Crab-Stuffed Deviled Eggs: Make 12 hard-cooked eggs. To mashed yolks, add 1 can (6 oz.) crabmeat (drained, flaked and cartilage removed), ⅔ cup mayonnaise, ½ cup finely chopped celery, ½ cup slivered almonds, 2 Tbsp. finely chopped green pepper and ½ tsp. salt. Stuff as directed.

SUNFLOWER POPCORN BARS

Who can resist these grab-and-go bites? They're a smart change from brownie- or cakelike bars, and you can make a batch early in the week for convenient treats. Best of all, they're a no-bake snack the whole family will like.
—*Karen Ann Bland, Gove City, KS*

Takes: 25 min. • **Makes:** 4 dozen

1	cup sugar
½	cup light corn syrup
½	cup honey
½	cup peanut butter
¼	cup butter, softened
1	tsp. vanilla extract
1	cup salted sunflower kernels
4	qt. popped popcorn

1. In a large saucepan over medium heat, bring the sugar, corn syrup and honey to a boil, stirring often. Boil for 2 minutes. Remove from the heat; stir in the peanut butter, butter and vanilla until smooth. Add sunflower kernels.

2. Place popcorn in a large bowl. Add the syrup and stir to coat. Press into 2 greased 13x9-in. pans. Cut into 48 bars. Store in an airtight container.

Note: Reduced-fat peanut butter is not recommended for this recipe.

1 bar: 96 cal., 5g fat (1g sat. fat), 3mg chol., 76mg sod., 13g carb. (9g sugars, 1g fiber), 2g pro.

🖐 PUPPY CHOW

Make this snack mix early in the week so you can enjoy it for late-night treats or midday pick-me-ups. I sometimes take a batch to work, and it's always eaten quickly. It's a slightly different cereal snack because of the chocolate and peanut butter.
—*Mary Obeilin, Selinsgrove, PA*

- -

Takes: 15 min. • **Makes:** about 6 cups

- 1 **cup (6 oz.) semisweet chocolate chips**
- ¼ **cup creamy peanut butter**
- 6 **cups Corn or Rice Chex**
- 1 **cup confectioners' sugar**

1. In a large microwave-safe bowl, melt the chocolate chips on high for 30 seconds. Stir; microwave 30 seconds longer or until the chips are melted. Stir in peanut butter. Gently stir in the cereal until well coated; set aside.

2. Place confectioners' sugar in a 2-gallon plastic storage bag. Add cereal mixture and shake until well coated. Store in an airtight container in the refrigerator.

½ cup: 194 cal., 7g fat (3g sat. fat), 0 chol., 170mg sod., 33g carb. (19g sugars, 1g fiber), 3g pro.

TEST KITCHEN TIP
You can make confectioners' sugar at home my combining 1 cup granulated sugar and 1 tsp. cornstarch.

🖐 PEANUT BUTTER S'MORES SANDWICH

Your favorite s'more flavors come together in this tasty peanut butter sandwich—no campfire required.
—*James Schend, Pleasant Prairie, WI*

- -

Takes: 10 min. • **Makes:** 1 serving

- 1 **Tbsp. creamy peanut butter**
- 1 **slice crusty white bread**
- 1 **Tbsp. milk chocolate chips**
- 2 **Tbsp. miniature marshmallows**

Spread peanut butter over bread. Place on a baking sheet; top with chocolate chips and marshmallows. Broil 4-5 in. from heat until lightly browned, 30-60 seconds.

1 open-faced sandwich: 249 cal., 12g fat (4g sat. fat), 2mg chol., 224mg sod., 29g carb. (12g sugars, 2g fiber), 7g pro.

GARLIC & ONION CASHEWS

You'll be set for either a quick snack or an easy hostess gift with this recipe.
—*Anndrea Bailey, Huntington Beach, CA*

- -

Prep: 15 min. + cooling • **Makes:** 3 cups

4	**tsp. onion salt**
2	**tsp. sugar**
¾	**tsp. garlic powder**
2	**Tbsp. olive oil**
3	**cups salted cashews**
2	**tsp. lemon juice**
4	**tsp. dried parsley flakes**

1. Mix onion salt, sugar and garlic powder. In a large skillet, heat oil over medium heat. Add cashews, seasoning mixture and lemon juice; cook and stir 4-7 minutes or until cashews are toasted.

2. Stir in parsley. Drain on paper towels; cool completely. Store in an airtight container.

¼ cup: 237 cal., 20g fat (4g sat. fat), 0 chol., 754mg sod., 12g carb. (3g sugars, 1g fiber), 5g pro.

5i TURTLE PRETZELS

Who doesn't love the classic combination of chocolate, caramel and pecans? Double the recipe because these sweet and salty treats will be devoured in no time.
—*Barbara Loudenslager, O'Fallon, MO*

Takes: 30 min. • **Makes:** about 2½ dozen

- 1 pkg. (11 oz.) caramels
- 1 Tbsp. water
- 1 pkg. (10 oz.) pretzel rods
- 8 oz. German sweet chocolate or semisweet chocolate, chopped
- 2 tsp. shortening
- 1 cup finely chopped pecans

1. In a double boiler, melt caramels in water. Dip half of each pretzel into the hot caramel. Place on a greased sheet of foil to cool.
2. In a microwave, melt chocolate and shortening; stir until smooth. Dip the caramel-coated end of each pretzel into the chocolate, allowing excess to drip off; sprinkle with nuts. Return to foil to cool.
2 pretzels: 304 cal., 13g fat (5g sat. fat), 2mg chol., 311mg sod., 45g carb. (28g sugars, 2g fiber), 5g pro.

5i GRANOLA TRAIL MIX

My family has always enjoyed this crunchy 4-ingredient snack. When we go camping, each person includes one additional ingredient like mini marshmallows, corn chips or cookie pieces. The taste is never the same, and we're often pleasantly surprised by the combinations.
—*Shelley Riddlespurger, Amarillo, TX*

Takes: 5 min. • **Makes:** 11 cups

- 1 pkg. (16 oz.) banana-nut granola
- 1 pkg. (15 oz.) raisins
- 1 pkg. (12.6 oz.) milk chocolate M&M's
- 1 can (12 oz.) honey-roasted peanuts

Place all ingredients in a large bowl; toss to combine. Store in airtight containers.
½ cup: 331 cal., 15g fat (4g sat. fat), 3mg chol., 73mg sod., 46g carb. (30g sugars, 3g fiber), 7g pro.

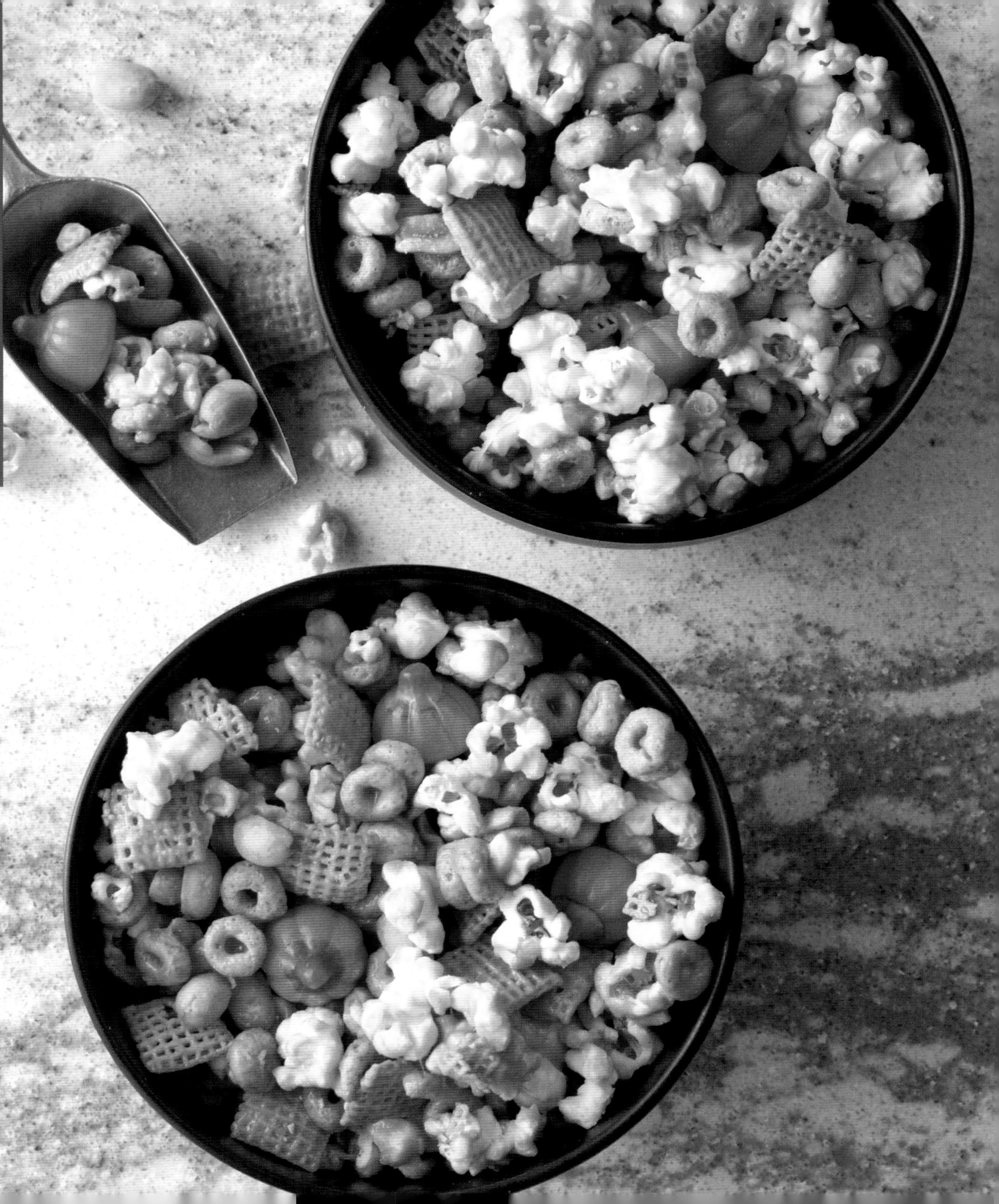

PUMPKIN SNACK MIX

This yummy mix is so munchable, a bowl of it never lasts long. Feel free to use candy corn instead of the candy pumpkins—or a mix of both—if desired.
—*Shirley Engstrom, Genoa, NE*

- -

Prep: 25 min. • **Bake:** 1 hour + cooling
Makes: about 5½ qt.

- 3 qt. popped popcorn
- 4 cups Cheerios
- 4 cups Corn or Rice Chex
- 2 cups salted peanuts
- 1 cup packed brown sugar
- ¾ cup light corn syrup
- ¼ cup butter, cubed
- 2 tsp. vanilla extract
- ½ tsp. baking soda
- 1 pkg. (16 oz.) candy pumpkins

1. In a large greased roasting pan, combine the popcorn, cereal and peanuts. In a large saucepan, combine the brown sugar, corn syrup and butter; bring to a rolling boil. Boil for 6 minutes, stirring occasionally. Remove from the heat; quickly stir in vanilla and baking soda until mixture is light and foamy.
2. Immediately pour over popcorn mixture; toss to coat. Bake, uncovered, at 250° for 1 hour, stirring every 15 minutes. Cool completely. Stir in candy pumpkins.
¾ cup: 216 cal., 8g fat (2g sat. fat), 4mg chol., 223mg sod., 34g carb. (20g sugars, 2g fiber), 4g pro.

OLD BAY® CRISPY KALE CHIPS

These crunchy kale chips are delicious, super healthy and easy to make. The seasoning gives them a nice zing, but if you like things spicy, simply add a dash of cayenne pepper.
—*Luanne Asta, Hampton Bays, NY*

- -

Prep: 10 min. • **Bake:** 30 min.
Makes: 4 servings

- 1 bunch kale, washed
- 2 Tbsp. olive oil
- 1 to 3 tsp. Old Bay Seasoning
  Sea salt, to taste

1. Preheat oven to 300° Remove tough stems from kale and tear leaves into large pieces. Place in a large bowl and toss with olive oil and seasonings. Arrange leaves in a single layer on greased baking sheets.
2. Bake, uncovered, 10 minutes and then rotate pans. Continue baking until crisp and just starting to brown, about 15 minutes. Let stand at least 5 minutes before serving.
1 serving: 101 cal., 7g fat (1g sat. fat), 0 chol., 202mg sod., 8g carb. (0 sugars, 1g fiber), 3g pro. **Diabetic exchanges:** 1 vegetable, 1½ fat.

ROASTED RED PEPPER HUMMUS

My son taught me how to make hummus, which is a tasty and healthy alternative to calorie-filled dips. Fresh roasted red bell peppers make it special.
—Nancy Watson-Pistole, Shawnee, KS

Prep: 30 min. + standing • **Makes:** 3 cups

- 2 large sweet red peppers
- 2 cans (15 oz. each) garbanzo beans or chickpeas, rinsed and drained
- ⅓ cup lemon juice
- 3 Tbsp. tahini
- 1 Tbsp. olive oil
- 2 garlic cloves, peeled
- 1¼ tsp. salt
- 1 tsp. curry powder
- ½ tsp. ground coriander
- ½ tsp. ground cumin
- ½ tsp. pepper
  Optional: Fresh vegetables, pita bread or assorted crackers

1. Broil red peppers 4 in. from the heat until skins blister, about 5 minutes. With tongs, rotate peppers a quarter turn. Broil and rotate until all sides are blistered and blackened. Immediately place peppers in a bowl; cover and let stand for 15-20 minutes.

2. Peel off and discard charred skin. Remove stems and seeds. Place the peppers in a food processor. Add the garbanzo beans, lemon juice, tahini, oil, garlic and seasonings; cover and process until blended.

3. Transfer to a serving bowl. Serve with fresh vegetables, pita bread or assorted crackers as desired.

¼ cup: 113 cal., 5g fat (1g sat. fat), 0 chol., 339mg sod., 14g carb. (3g sugars, 4g fiber), 4g pro. **Diabetic exchanges:** 1 starch, 1 fat.

WHY YOU'LL LOVE IT:
"I've made this recipe a number of times, and it never seems like enough! Great flavor and it's healthy, too. A real winner."
—BECKY66, TASTEOFHOME.COM

5j

BEARY GOOD SNACK MIX

My family loves to hike and be outdoors, and we take this snack mix along for a boost of energy. It makes a lot, and It's cute with all of the fun colors and shapes.
—*Doris Wedige, Elkhorn, WI*

- -

Takes: 10 min. • **Makes:** 10 cups

1   pkg. (10 oz.) honey bear-shaped crackers (about 4 cups)
1   pkg. (7 oz.) dried banana chips (about 2 cups)
2   cups M&M's
1   cup salted peanuts
1   cup dried cranberries

In a large bowl, combine all the ingredients. Store in an airtight container.

¾ cup: 455 cal., 22g fat (11g sat. fat), 4mg chol., 128 sod., 62g carb. (42 sugars, 5g fiber), 7g pro.

PREP NOW, EAT LATER

BUH-BYE BORING, HELLO VARIETY! ADD THESE MAKE-AHEAD DISHES TO YOUR MEAL PLANS TODAY!

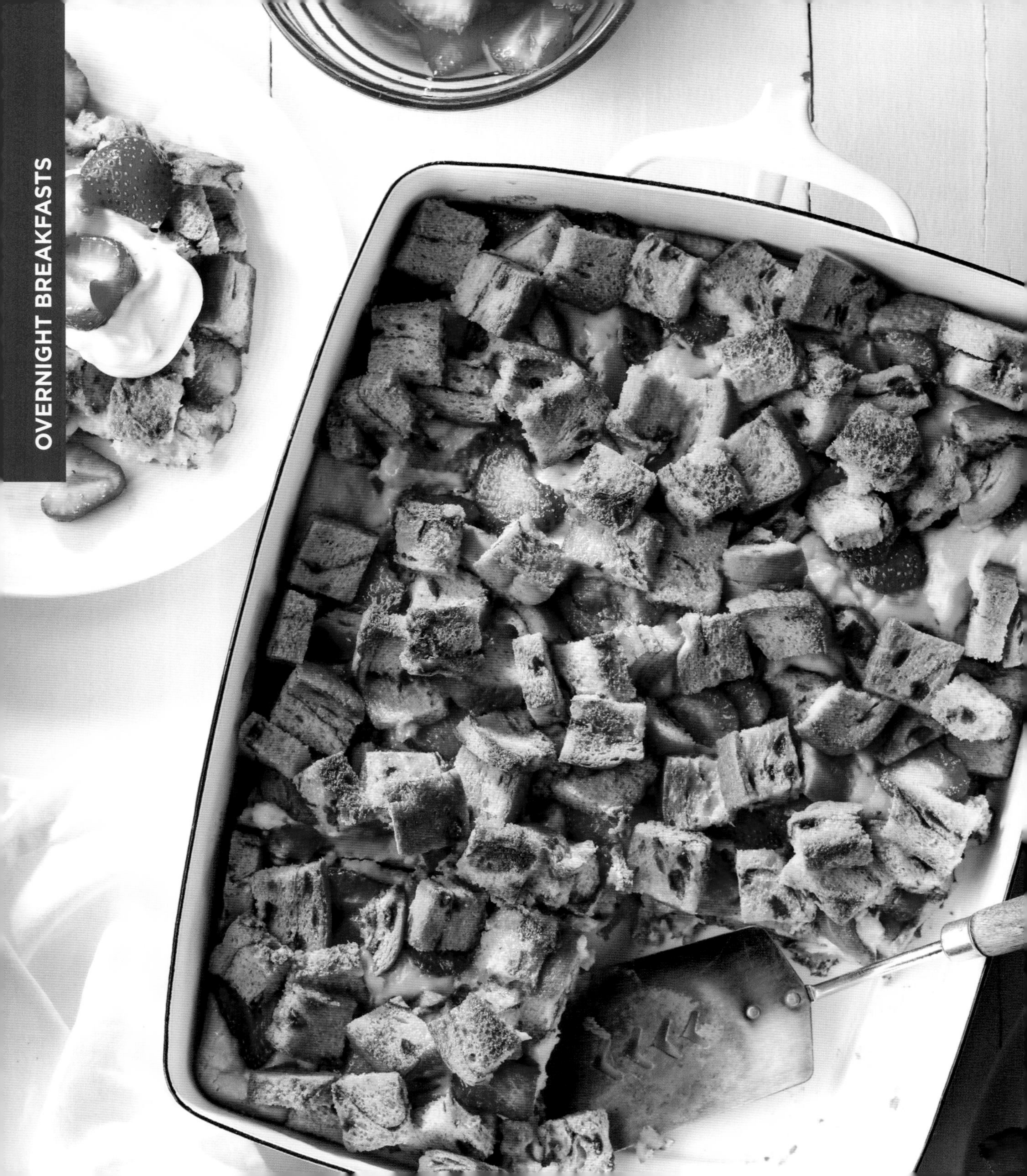

CREAMY STRAWBERRY FRENCH TOAST BAKE

I love this recipe because on Sunday mornings I like to take it easy, but I still want my family to have a nice breakfast. Preparing the dish the night before allows me to sleep in and feel like I'm a great mom at the same time. Win!
—*Alynn Hansen, Mona, UT*

Prep: 30 min. + chilling • **Bake:** 45 min.
Makes: 8 servings

- 3 cups sliced fresh strawberries, divided
- 2 Tbsp. sugar
- 1 pkg. (8 oz.) cream cheese, softened
- ½ cup confectioners' sugar
- 1 Tbsp. grated orange zest
- 1 Tbsp. orange juice
- 1 tsp. vanilla extract
- 1 loaf (1 lb.) cinnamon bread, cut into 1-in. pieces
- 5 large eggs
- 1 cup half-and-half cream
  Sweetened whipped cream

1. Toss 2 cups strawberries with sugar. In another bowl, beat the next 5 ingredients until smooth. Place half the bread in a greased 13x9-in. baking dish. Spoon cream cheese mixture over bread. Layer with strawberry mixture and remaining bread. Whisk eggs and cream until blended; pour over top. Refrigerate, covered, overnight.
2. Preheat oven to 350°. Remove casserole from refrigerator while oven heats. Bake, uncovered, until a knife inserted in the center comes out clean, 40-45 minutes. Let stand 5 minutes before serving. Top with whipped cream and remaining strawberries.
1 piece: 431 cal., 21g fat (10g sat. fat), 160mg chol., 382mg sod., 47g carb. (24g sugars, 5g fiber), 13g pro.

OVERNIGHT VEGETABLE & EGG BREAKFAST

My overnight eggs and veggies make a hearty breakfast for those who have to rush out the door. I set it all the night before so it simmers to perfection while we sleep.
—*Kimberly Clark-Thiry, Anchor Point, AK*

Prep: 15 min. • **Cook:** 7 hours
Makes: 8 servings

- 4 lbs. potatoes, peeled and thinly sliced (about 8 cups)
- 1 medium green pepper, finely chopped
- 1 pkg. (10 oz.) frozen chopped spinach, thawed and squeezed dry
- 1 cup sliced fresh mushrooms
- 1 medium onion, finely chopped
- 8 large eggs
- 1 cup water
- 1 cup 2% milk
- 1¼ tsp. salt
- ¼ tsp. pepper
- 2 cups shredded cheddar cheese

In a greased 6-qt. slow cooker, layer the first 5 ingredients. In a large bowl, whisk the next 5 ingredients; pour over top. Sprinkle with shredded cheese. Cook, covered, on low until potatoes are tender and eggs are set, 7-9 hours.
1½ cups: 354 cal., 15g fat (7g sat. fat), 217mg chol., 668mg sod., 37g carb. (5g sugars, 4g fiber), 19g pro.

CHORIZO EGG CASSEROLE

Growing up on chorizo and egg burritos, I decided it was time for a remake. I prepare the hot bake the night before. The next morning, I simply pop it in the oven and, before I know it, breakfast is ready!
—*Relina Shirley, Reno, NV*

Prep: 30 min. + chilling
Bake: 35 min. + standing • **Makes:** 8 servings

- 1 **lb. fresh chorizo**
- 3 **cups frozen cubed hash brown potatoes**
- 1 **medium onion, diced**
- ¾ **cup chopped sweet red pepper**
- 2 **garlic cloves, minced**
- 5 **large eggs**
- 1½ **cups half-and-half cream**
- 1 **can (4 oz.) chopped green chiles**
- 2 **tsp. chili powder**
- 1 **cup shredded Monterey Jack or pepper jack cheese**
- 1 **cup shredded cheddar cheese**
- 3 **Tbsp. minced fresh cilantro, divided**
  Sour cream
  Hot pepper sauce

1. In a large nonstick skillet, cook and crumble chorizo over medium-high heat until cooked through, 5-7 minutes. Drain on paper towels. In same skillet, cook and stir potatoes, onion and pepper until tender, 5-7 minutes. Add garlic; cook 1 minute longer. Remove from heat; stir in chorizo. Cool 15 minutes.

2. Whisk eggs, cream, green chiles and chili powder. Layer a greased 11x7-in. baking dish with half each of the following: chorizo mixture, cheeses, and egg mixture; sprinkle with 1 Tbsp. cilantro. Top with remaining chorizo and eggs; sprinkle with remaining cheeses and 1 Tbsp. cilantro. Refrigerate, covered, overnight.

3. Preheat oven to 350°. Remove casserole from refrigerator while oven heats. Bake, uncovered, 35-40 minutes or until set and bubbling. Let stand for 10 minutes before serving. Sprinkle with remaining cilantro. Serve with sour cream and pepper sauce.

1 cup: 461 cal., 34g fat (15g sat. fat), 215mg chol., 1017mg sod., 10g carb. (3g sugars, 1g fiber), 25g pro.

PUMPKIN-PECAN BAKED OATMEAL

My husband rarely eats in the morning, but when I make my baked oatmeal, he digs right in. A little planning the night before means we can enjoy this yummy treat without much work.
—*Alex Muehl, Austin, TX*

- -

Prep: 15 min. + chilling • **Bake:** 30 min.
Makes: 6 servings

 2 **large eggs**
 3 **cups quick-cooking oats**
 1 **can (15 oz.) solid-pack pumpkin**
 1 **cup 2% milk**
 ¾ **cup packed brown sugar**
 ½ **cup dried cranberries**
 ⅓ **cup butter, melted**
 1½ **tsp. baking powder**
 1 **tsp. vanilla extract**
 ½ **tsp. ground nutmeg**
 ¼ **tsp. salt**
 ¼ **tsp. ground cloves**
 ¼ **cup chopped pecans**
  Additional 2% milk and brown sugar

1. In a large bowl, combine the first 12 ingredients. Transfer to a greased 11x7-in. baking dish. Refrigerate, covered, 8 hours or overnight.
2. Remove oatmeal from refrigerator 30 minutes before baking. Preheat oven to 350°. Uncover and stir oatmeal; sprinkle with pecans. Bake, uncovered, until a thermometer reads 160°, 30-35 minutes. Serve oatmeal warm with additional milk and brown sugar.
¾ cup: 478 cal., 19g fat (8g sat. fat), 92mg chol., 335mg sod., 71g carb. (39g sugars, 7g fiber), 10g pro.

CROISSANT BREAKFAST CASSEROLE

Turning prepared croissants, orange marmalade and apricot preserves into a classic overnight casserole makes a wonderful treat for family and guests the next morning.
—*Joan Hallford, North Richland Hills, TX*

- -

Prep: 15 min. + chilling • **Bake:** 25 min.
Makes: 12 servings

- 1 jar (18 oz.) orange marmalade
- ½ cup apricot preserves
- ⅓ cup orange juice
- 3 tsp. grated orange zest
- 6 croissants, split
- 5 large eggs
- 1 cup half-and-half cream
- 1 tsp. almond or vanilla extract
  Quartered fresh strawberries

1. In a small bowl, mix the marmalade, preserves, orange juice and zest. Arrange croissant bottoms in a greased 13x9-in. baking dish. Spread with 1½ cups marmalade mixture. Add croissant tops.

2. In another bowl, whisk eggs, cream and extract; pour over croissants. Spoon the remaining marmalade mixture over tops. Refrigerate, covered, overnight.

3. Preheat oven to 350°. Remove casserole from refrigerator while oven heats. Bake, uncovered, 25-30 minutes or until a knife inserted in the center comes out clean. Let stand 5 minutes before serving. Serve with fresh strawberries.

1 serving: 314 cal., 10g fat (5g sat. fat), 117mg chol., 280mg sod., 52g carb. (35g sugars, 1g fiber), 6g pro.

CARAMEL-PECAN MONKEY BREAD

The kids will get a kick out of pulling off gooey pieces of this delectable monkey bread. Everyone loves this—and we love that it can be started the day before.
—Taste of Home *Test Kitchen*

- -

Prep: 20 min. + chilling
Bake: 30 min. + cooling • **Makes:** 20 servings

- 1 pkg. (¼ oz.) active dry yeast
- ¼ cup warm water (110° to 115°)
- 1¼ cups warm 2% milk (110° to 115°)
- 2 large eggs, room temperature
- 5 Tbsp. plus ½ cup melted butter, divided
- 1¼ cups sugar, divided
- 1 tsp. salt
- 5 cups all-purpose flour
- 1 tsp. ground cinnamon

CARAMEL
- ⅔ cup packed brown sugar
- ¼ cup butter, cubed
- ¼ cup heavy whipping cream
- ¾ cup chopped pecans, divided

OPTIONAL GLAZE
- 4 oz. cream cheese, softened
- ¼ cup butter, softened
- 1½ cups confectioners' sugar
- 3 to 5 Tbsp. 2% milk

1. Dissolve yeast in warm water. Add the milk, eggs and 5 Tbsp. melted butter; stir in ¼ cup sugar, salt and 3 cups flour. Beat on medium speed for 3 minutes. Stir in enough remaining flour to form a firm dough.

2. Turn onto a floured surface; knead until smooth and elastic, 6-8 minutes. Place in a greased bowl, turning once to grease the top. Refrigerate, covered, overnight.

3. Punch dough down; shape into 40 balls (about 1¼-in. diameter). Pour remaining melted butter in a shallow bowl. In another shallow bowl, combine cinnamon and remaining sugar. Dip balls in butter, then roll in sugar mixture.

4. For caramel, bring brown sugar, butter and cream to a boil in a small saucepan over medium heat. Cook and stir 3 minutes. Pour half of the caramel into a greased 10-in. fluted tube pan; layer with half the pecans and half the dough balls; repeat. Cover and let rise until doubled, about 45 minutes.

5. Preheat oven to 350°. Bake until golden brown, 30-40 minutes. (Cover loosely with foil for last 10 minutes if top browns too quickly.) Cool 10 minutes before inverting onto a serving plate.

6. For optional glaze, beat cream cheese and butter until blended; gradually beat in confectioners' sugar. Add enough milk to reach desired consistency. Drizzle glaze over warm bread.

2 pieces: 334 cal., 15g fat (8g sat. fat), 52mg chol., 207mg sod., 45g carb. (21g sugars, 1g fiber), 5g pro.

CHICKEN CHILES RELLENOS STRATA

This versatile dish can be made for breakfast or brunch, or as a potluck contribution. It's also one of the easiest meals to assemble on a busy weeknight.
—*Kallee Krong-McCreery, Escondido, CA*

Prep: 20 min. + chilling
Bake: 35 min. + standing
Makes: 10 servings

- 6 cups cubed French bread (about 6 oz.)
- 2 cans (4 oz. each) chopped green chiles
- 2 cups shredded Monterey Jack cheese
- 2 cups shredded cooked chicken
- 12 large eggs
- 1½ cups 2% milk
- 2 tsp. baking powder
- 1 tsp. garlic salt
- 1 cup shredded cheddar cheese
  Salsa

1. In a greased 13x9-in. baking dish, layer half of each of the following: bread cubes, chiles, Monterey Jack cheese and chicken. Repeat layers.
2. In a large bowl, whisk eggs, milk, baking powder and garlic salt until blended. Pour over layers. Sprinkle with cheddar cheese. Refrigerate, covered, overnight.
3. Preheat oven to 350°. Remove strata from refrigerator while oven heats. Bake, uncovered, 35-40 minutes or until puffed and golden at edges. Let stand 10 minutes before serving. Serve with salsa.
1 piece: 338 cal., 20g fat (9g sat. fat), 282mg chol., 820mg sod., 13g carb. (3g sugars, 1g fiber), 27g pro.

WARM & FRUITY BREAKFAST CEREAL

Sleepyheads will love the heartiness of this nutritious cooked cereal with cinnamon. Loaded with chopped fruit and nuts, it simmers on its own overnight.
—*John Vale, Long Beach, WA*

Prep: 10 min. • **Cook:** 6 hours
Makes: 10 servings

- 2 cups seven-grain hot cereal
- 1 medium apple, peeled and chopped
- ¼ cup dried apricots, chopped
- ¼ cup dried cranberries
- ¼ cup chopped dates
- ¼ cup raisins
- 1 tsp. ground cinnamon
- ½ tsp. salt
- 5 cups water
- 1 cup unsweetened apple juice
- ¼ cup maple syrup
  Chopped walnuts, optional

1. Place first 8 ingredients in a 4- or 5-qt. slow cooker coated with cooking spray. Stir in water, juice and syrup.
2. Cook, covered, on low until thickened and cereal is tender, 6-7 hours. If desired, top with walnuts.
Note: This recipe was tested with Bob's Red Mill 7-Grain Hot Cereal.
1 cup: 185 cal., 3g fat (0 sat. fat), 0 chol., 120mg sod., 37g carb. (18g sugars, 5g fiber), 5g pro. **Diabetic exchanges:** 1 starch, 1 fruit, ½ fat.

OVERNIGHT BAKED EGGS BRUSCHETTA

I like to spend as much time as I can with my guests when they stay for the weekend, so I rely on make-ahead recipes to help make that happen. Because most overnight brunch casseroles are similar, I came up with a breakfast bruschetta for a fun change of pace.
—*Judi Berman-Yamada, Portland, OR*

Prep: 45 min. + chilling • **Bake:** 10 min.
Makes: 9 servings

- 1 tube (13.8 oz.) refrigerated pizza crust
- 1 Tbsp. cornmeal
- 3 Tbsp. olive oil, divided
- 1½ cups shredded part-skim mozzarella cheese, divided
- ¾ lb. sliced baby portobello mushrooms
- ¾ tsp. garlic powder
- ¾ tsp. dried rosemary, crushed
- ½ tsp. pepper
- ¼ tsp. salt
- 2 cups pizza sauce
- 1 Tbsp. white vinegar
- 9 large eggs
- 2 oz. fresh goat cheese, crumbled
- ½ cup French-fried onions
  Fresh basil leaves

1. Preheat oven to 400°. Unroll the pizza dough and press onto bottom of a greased 15x10x1-in baking pan that's been sprinkled with cornmeal. Brush dough with 1 Tbsp. oil; sprinkle with ¾ cup mozzarella cheese. Bake 8 minutes.

2. Meanwhile, in a large skillet, heat the remaining oil over medium-high heat. Add mushrooms; cook and stir until tender. Stir in garlic powder, rosemary and seasonings. Stir pizza sauce into mushrooms; spread mushroom mixture over crust.

3. In a large skillet with high sides, bring vinegar and 2-3 in. water to a boil. Reduce heat to maintain a gentle simmer. Break 1 cold egg at a time into a small bowl; holding bowl close to surface of water, gently slip eggs into the water.

4. Cook, uncovered, 3-5 minutes or until whites are completely set and yolks begin to thicken but are not hard. Using a slotted spoon, carefully remove the eggs; place over mushrooms in baking pan. Sprinkle the goat cheese and remaining mozzarella over the eggs and mushrooms. Refrigerate, covered, overnight.

5. Remove pan from the refrigerator 30 minutes before baking. Preheat oven to 400°. Sprinkle onions over top. Bake, uncovered, until golden brown and heated through, 10-15 minutes. Top with basil just before serving.

1 piece: 345 cal., 17g fat (5g sat. fat), 227mg chol., 798mg sod., 29g carb. (6g sugars, 2g fiber), 17g pro.

CHIA ORANGE YOGURT

I love this chia yogurt parfait because it makes me feel as if I'm eating dessert for breakfast. Plus, chia seeds deliver a big dose of omega-3 oils, and they're rich in fiber, calcium, phosphorus, magnesium, manganese, copper, iron and zinc.
—*Marion McNeill, Mayfield Heights, OH*

- -

Prep: 10 min. + chilling • **Makes:** 1 serving

⅓ cup fat-free milk or
   unsweetened almond milk
¼ cup old-fashioned oats
¼ cup reduced-fat plain Greek yogurt
1 Tbsp. orange marmalade
   spreadable fruit
1½ tsp. chia seeds
¼ tsp. vanilla extract
⅓ cup orange segments, chopped

In a jar with a tight-fitting lid, combine the milk, oats, yogurt, marmalade, chia seeds and vanilla. Cover and shake to combine. Stir in orange segments. Cover and refrigerate for 8 hours or overnight.

1 cup: 245 cal., 5g fat (1g sat. fat), 5mg chol., 59mg sod., 39g carb. (20g sugars, 6g fiber), 13g pro. **Diabetic exchanges:** 2½ starch, 1 lean meat.

BUSY MORNING OATMEAL

When I first tried this dish, I was convinced I was eating some yummy apple crisp for breakfast. I even cut down on the butter, but this hearty oatmeal remained moist and scrumptious, and worked great when cooked overnight.

—*Monica Lord, Collegeville, PA*

Prep: 10 min. • **Cook:** 7 hours
Makes: 6 servings

- ⅓ cup packed brown sugar
- 1 tsp. ground cinnamon
- ½ tsp. ground nutmeg
- 2 medium apples, peeled and sliced
- ¾ cup dried cranberries
- 2 Tbsp. butter, cubed
- 2 cups old-fashioned oats
- 2 cups water
- 2 cups cranberry-apple juice
- ½ tsp. salt
- Optional: Chopped pecans, dried cranberries or sliced apples

1. Combine brown sugar, cinnamon and nutmeg. Add apples and cranberries; toss to coat. Transfer to a 3-qt. slow cooker. Dot with butter.

2. In a large bowl, combine oats, water, juice and salt; pour over apple mixture. Cook, covered, on low until liquid is absorbed, 7-8 hours. Serve warm; top as desired.

1 cup: 287 cal., 6g fat (3g sat. fat), 10mg chol., 241mg sod., 58g carb. (35g sugars, 4g fiber), 4g pro.

HAWAIIAN HAM STRATA

I came up with this recipe because I love Hawaiian pizza, and wanted a casserole I could make ahead and pop in the oven at the last minute. This is a perfect main dish to take to a brunch or potluck.

—*Lisa Renshaw, Kansas City, MO*

Prep: 20 min. + chilling
Cook: 35 min. + standing
Makes: 8 servings

- 8 English muffins, cut into eighths and toasted
- 3 cups cubed fully cooked ham
- 1 can (20 oz.) pineapple tidbits, drained
- 4 green onions, chopped
- 1 jar (4 oz.) diced pimientos, drained
- 1½ cups shredded cheddar cheese
- ¼ cup grated Parmesan cheese
- 1 jar (15 oz.) Alfredo sauce
- 1½ cups evaporated milk
- 4 large eggs, lightly beaten
- ½ tsp. salt
- ¼ tsp. cayenne pepper

1. Combine first 5 ingredients. Transfer to a 13x9-in. baking dish; top with cheeses.

2. Whisk together remaining ingredients. Pour sauce over layers, pushing down, if necessary, with the back of a spoon to ensure muffins absorb liquid. Refrigerate, covered, 1 hour or overnight.

3. Preheat oven to 350°. Remove strata from refrigerator while oven heats. Bake, uncovered, until golden brown and bubbly, 30-40 minutes. Let strata stand 10 minutes before serving.

1 piece: 515 cal., 22g fat (12g sat. fat), 177mg chol., 1512mg sod., 48g carb. (16g sugars, 3g fiber), 31g pro.

CARROT CAKE OATMEAL

This warm breakfast cereal made in the slow cooker is a great way to get your veggies in the morning and keep a healthy diet! For extra crunch, I garnish individual servings with ground walnuts or pecans.
—*Debbie Kain, Colorado Springs, CO*

Prep: 10 min. • **Cook:** 6 hours
Makes: 8 servings

- 4½ **cups water**
- 1 **can (20 oz.) crushed pineapple, undrained**
- 2 **cups shredded carrots**
- 1 **cup steel-cut oats**
- 1 **cup raisins**
- 2 **tsp. ground cinnamon**
- 1 **tsp. pumpkin pie spice**
  Brown sugar, optional

In a 4-qt. slow cooker coated with cooking spray, combine the first 7 ingredients. Cover and cook on low for 6-8 hours or until oats are tender and liquid is absorbed. Sprinkle with brown sugar if desired.

1 cup: 197 cal., 2g fat (0 sat. fat), 0 chol., 23mg sod., 46g carb. (26g sugars, 4g fiber), 4g pro.

TEST KITCHEN TIP

For meal-planning ease, simply measure out the oats, cinnamon and pumpkin pie spice into a resealable container. Store in a cool, dry place until ready to make the oatmeal as directed.

ITALIAN APRICOT-PANCETTA STRATA

For me, the combination of sweet and savory along with easy preparation make this Italian-inspired strata a winning dish for home cooks everywhere! It can be served for breakfast, brunch or even as a late afternoon meal.
—*Naylet LaRochelle, Miami, FL*

- -

Prep: 35 min. + chilling • **Bake:** 35 min.
Makes: 12 servings

⅓	lb. pancetta, finely chopped
2	Tbsp. butter, divided
1⅓	cups finely chopped sweet onion
2	cups sliced fresh mushrooms
3	cups fresh baby spinach, coarsely chopped
5	cups cubed multigrain bread
½	cup sliced almonds, optional
6	large eggs
1	cup heavy whipping cream
¼	tsp. salt
¼	tsp. pepper
1	carton (8 oz.) mascarpone cheese
1	cup shredded part-skim mozzarella cheese
½	cup shredded Asiago cheese
1	cup apricot preserves
3	Tbsp. minced fresh basil

1. In large skillet, cook pancetta until crisp, stirring occasionally. Remove with a slotted spoon; drain on paper towels. Discard drippings, reserving 1 Tbsp. in pan.

2. Add 1 Tbsp. butter to drippings; heat over medium-high heat. Add onion; cook and stir for 4-6 minutes or until tender. Transfer onion to a large bowl.

3. Heat remaining butter in pan. Add mushrooms; cook and stir 2-3 minutes or until tender. Stir in spinach; cook until wilted, 30-45 seconds.

4. Add bread cubes, mushroom mixture, pancetta and almonds if desired to onion; toss to combine. Transfer to a greased 13x9-in. baking dish.

5. In a large bowl, beat eggs, cream, salt and pepper until blended. Beat in mascarpone cheese just until blended; pour over bread. Sprinkle with the mozzarella cheese and Asiago cheese; spoon preserves over the top. Refrigerate, covered, several hours or overnight.

6. Preheat oven to 350°. Remove strata from refrigerator while oven heats. Bake, uncovered, 35-45 minutes or until golden brown and a knife inserted in the center comes out clean. Sprinkle with basil. Let stand 5-10 minutes before cutting.

1 piece: 440 cal., 30g fat (15g sat. fat), 165mg chol., 514mg sod., 30g carb. (15g sugars, 3g fiber), 15g pro.

MAPLE-WALNUT STICKY BUNS

Mmm! These ooey-gooey goodies will have everyone licking maple syrup from their fingers—and reaching for seconds. The yeast dough chills beautifully overnight.
—*Nancy Foust, Stoneboro, PA*

- -

Prep: 45 min. + rising • **Bake:** 30 min.
Makes: 2 dozen

- 1 pkg. (¼ oz.) active dry yeast
- 1 cup warm water (110° to 115°)
- ½ cup mashed potatoes (without added milk and butter)
- 1 large egg, room temperature
- 2 Tbsp. shortening
- 2 Tbsp. sugar
- 1 tsp. salt
- 3 to 3½ cups all-purpose flour

TOPPING
- 1 cup maple syrup
- ¾ cup coarsely chopped walnuts

FILLING
- ⅓ cup sugar
- 1½ tsp. ground cinnamon
- 3 Tbsp. butter, softened

1. In a small bowl, dissolve yeast in warm water. In a large bowl, combine potatoes, egg, shortening, sugar, salt, yeast mixture and 1 cup flour; beat on medium speed until smooth. Stir in enough remaining flour to form a soft dough.

2. Turn dough onto a floured surface; knead until smooth and elastic, 6-8 minutes. Place in a greased bowl, turning once to grease the top. Cover and refrigerate overnight.

3. Pour syrup into a greased 13x9-in. baking dish; sprinkle with walnuts. In a small bowl, mix sugar and cinnamon. Punch down the dough; turn onto a lightly floured surface. Roll into a 24x8-in. rectangle. Spread with butter to within ½ in. of edges; sprinkle with cinnamon sugar. Roll up jelly-roll style, starting with a long side; pinch seam to seal. Cut into 24 slices.

4. Place in prepared baking dish, cut side down. Cover with a kitchen towel; let rise in a warm place until doubled, about 30 minutes. Preheat oven to 350°.

5. Bake 30-35 minutes or until golden brown. Cool 5 minutes before inverting buns onto a platter.

1 bun: 159 cal., 5g fat (1g sat. fat), 13mg chol., 114mg sod., 26g carb. (12g sugars, 1g fiber), 3g pro.

HAM & BROCCOLI BAKE

Plan ahead and start this satisfying and comforting casserole the night before you bake it. Best of all, the hearty entree is also an inexpensive dish to add to your family meal plan.

—*Harmony Tardugno, Vernon Center, NY*

- -

Prep: 15 min. + chilling • **Bake:** 35 min.
Makes: 8 servings

1	loaf (8 oz.) day-old French bread, cubed
½	cup butter, melted
2	cups shredded cheddar cheese
2	cups frozen chopped broccoli, thawed
2	cups cubed fully cooked ham
4	large eggs
2	cups 2% milk
¼	tsp. pepper

1. Toss bread cubes with butter. Place half in a greased 13x9-in. baking dish. Layer with half of the cheese and broccoli; sprinkle with ham. Layer with remaining broccoli, cheese and bread cubes.
2. In a large bowl, whisk the eggs, milk and pepper. Pour over casserole. Cover and refrigerate overnight.
3. Remove from the refrigerator 30 minutes before baking. Bake, uncovered, at 350° for 35-40 minutes or until a knife inserted in the center comes out clean. Let stand for 5 minutes before cutting.
1 piece: 422 cal., 27g fat (16g sat. fat), 191mg chol., 951mg sod., 23g carb. (4g sugars, 2g fiber), 22g pro.

MAPLE-BACON FRENCH TOAST

This is my favorite Sunday breakfast. It's easy to put together the night before and pop in the fridge until morning. It gives me more time for enjoying family.
—*Erin Wright, Wallace, KS*

- -

Prep: 20 min. + chilling • **Bake:** 40 min.
Makes: 8 servings

- 6   large eggs
- 1   cup half-and-half cream
- 1   cup 2% milk
- ¼   cup maple syrup
- 2   Tbsp. sugar
- ¼   tsp. ground cinnamon
     Dash salt
- 16 slices French bread (1 in. thick)
- 10 bacon strips, cooked and crumbled
     Additional maple syrup

1. In a shallow bowl, whisk the first 7 ingredients. Dip both sides of bread in egg mixture. Arrange bread slices into 2 overlapping rows in a greased 13x9-in. baking dish. Pour remaining egg mixture over top. Refrigerate, covered, overnight.
2. Preheat oven to 350°. Remove French toast from refrigerator while oven heats. Bake, covered, 30 minutes. Sprinkle with bacon. Bake, uncovered, until lightly browned, 10-15 minutes longer. Serve with additional syrup.
2 slices: 323 cal., 12g fat (5g sat. fat), 167mg chol., 725mg sod., 36g carb. (12g sugars, 1g fiber), 14g pro.

ITALIAN SAUSAGE EGG BAKE

This hearty entree warms up any breakfast or brunch menu with its savory herb-seasoned flavor.
—*Darlene Markham, Rochester, NY*

- -

Prep: 20 min. + chilling • **Bake:** 50 min.
Makes: 12 servings

- 8   slices white bread, cubed
- 1   lb. Italian sausage links, casings removed, sliced
- 2   cups shredded sharp cheddar cheese
- 2   cups shredded part-skim mozzarella cheese
- 9   large eggs, lightly beaten
- 3   cups 2% milk
- 1   tsp. dried basil
- 1   tsp. dried oregano
- 1   tsp. fennel seed, crushed

1. Place bread cubes in a greased 13x9-in. baking dish; set aside. In a large skillet, cook sausage over medium heat until no longer pink; drain. Spoon sausage over bread; sprinkle with cheeses.
2. In a large bowl, whisk the eggs, milk and seasonings; pour over casserole. Cover and refrigerate overnight.
3. Remove from the refrigerator 30 minutes before baking. Bake, uncovered, at 350° for 50-55 minutes or until a knife inserted in the center comes out clean. Let stand for 5 minutes before cutting.
1 piece: 316 cal., 20g fat (10g sat. fat), 214mg chol., 546mg sod., 13g carb. (5g sugars, 1g fiber), 21g pro.

BRUNCH ENCHILADAS

I need just a few ingredients to whip up this make-ahead breakfast. It's a great change-of-pace dish for morning meals, particularly when you have to feed a crowd.
—*Gail Sykora, Menomonee Falls, WI*

Prep: 15 min. + chilling
Bake: 40 min. + standing
Makes: 10 servings

- 2 **cups cubed fully cooked ham**
- ½ **cup chopped green onions**
- 10 **fat-free flour tortillas (8 in.)**
- 2 **cups shredded reduced-fat cheddar cheese**
- 1 **Tbsp. all-purpose flour**
- 2 **cups fat-free milk**
- 1½ **cups egg substitute**

1. Combine ham and onions; place about ⅓ cup down the center of each tortilla. Top with 2 Tbsp. cheese. Roll up and place seam side down in a greased 13x9-in. baking dish.
2. In a large bowl, whisk flour, milk and eggs until smooth. Pour over the tortillas. Cover and refrigerate for 8 hours or overnight.
3. Remove from the refrigerator 30 minutes before baking. Cover and bake at 350° for 25 minutes. Uncover; bake 10 minutes longer. Sprinkle with the remaining cheese; bake 3 minutes or until cheese is melted. Let stand 10 minutes before serving.

1 serving: 258 cal., 7g fat (4g sat. fat), 32mg chol., 838mg sod., 29g carb. (4g sugars, 1g fiber), 19g pro.

CHEESE & CRAB BRUNCH BAKE

Who doesn't love an easy, cheesy seafood casserole that can be pulled together in a matter of minutes, refrigerated overnight and baked up the next morning?
—*Joyce Conway, Westerville, OH*

Prep: 30 min. + chilling • **Bake:** 50 min.
Makes: 12 servings

2	Tbsp. Dijon mustard
6	English muffins, split
8	oz. lump crabmeat, drained
2	Tbsp. lemon juice
2	tsp. grated lemon zest
2	cups shredded white cheddar cheese
12	large eggs
1	cup half-and-half cream
1	cup 2% milk
½	cup mayonnaise
1	tsp. salt
½	tsp. cayenne pepper
½	tsp. pepper
2	cups shredded Swiss cheese
1	cup grated Parmesan cheese
4	green onions, chopped
¼	cup finely chopped sweet red pepper
¼	cup finely chopped sweet yellow pepper

1. Spread mustard over bottom half of muffins. Place in a greased 13x9-in. baking dish. Top with crab, lemon juice and zest. Sprinkle with cheddar cheese. Top with muffin tops; set aside.

2. In a large bowl, whisk eggs, cream, milk, mayonnaise, salt, cayenne and pepper. Pour over muffins; sprinkle with Swiss cheese, Parmesan cheese, onions and peppers. Cover and refrigerate overnight.

3. Remove from refrigerator 30 minutes before baking. Preheat oven to 375°. Cover and bake 30 minutes. Uncover; bake until set, 20-25 minutes longer. Let stand for 5 minutes before serving. If desired, top with additional chopped green onions.

1 serving: 428 cal., 28g fat (13g sat. fat), 286mg chol., 844mg sod., 18g carb. (4g sugars, 1g fiber), 26g pro.

WHY YOU'LL LOVE IT:
"I make this every year on Christmas Eve so I can pop it in on Christmas morning. It's one of my favorite traditions in our house. It's delicious and the flavors work so well together."
—NCMAMA87, TASTEOFHOME.COM

SAVORY ASPARAGUS STRATA

Fresh asparagus and goat cheese combine to make my delectable strata. Assemble it a day ahead and let it chill overnight for an easy morning entree.

—*Lynda Ruce, Minneapolis, MN*

- -

Prep: 30 min. + chilling • **Bake:** 50 min.
Makes: 12 servings

- 2 Tbsp. olive oil
- 1 lb. fresh asparagus, trimmed and cut into 1-in. pieces
- ½ lb. medium fresh mushrooms, quartered
- ½ tsp. garlic salt
- ½ tsp. pepper, divided
- 1 loaf (1 lb.) Italian bread, cut into 1-in. cubes
- 2 pkg. (4 oz. each) herbed fresh goat cheese, cut into ½-in. cubes
- 12 large eggs
- 2 cups 2% milk
- 1½ tsp. dried thyme
- ¼ tsp. salt
- ½ cup grated Parmesan cheese
- 1 envelope hollandaise sauce mix

1. In a large skillet, heat oil over medium-high heat. Add asparagus, mushrooms, garlic salt and ¼ tsp. pepper; cook and stir 3-4 minutes or until the asparagus is crisp-tender.

2. Place half of the bread cubes in a greased 13x9-in. baking dish. Top with asparagus mixture, goat cheese and remaining bread.

3. In a large bowl, whisk eggs, milk, thyme, salt and remaining pepper. Pour over top; sprinkle with Parmesan cheese. Refrigerate, covered, overnight.

4. Preheat oven to 350°. Remove strata from refrigerator while oven heats. Bake, uncovered, 50-60 minutes or until a knife inserted in the center comes out clean. Let stand 5-10 minutes before serving. Meanwhile, prepare sauce mix according to package directions. Serve with strata.

1 piece with a scant 2 Tbsp. sauce: 362 cal., 20g fat (8g sat. fat), 218mg chol., 740mg sod., 26g carb. (5g sugars, 2g fiber), 17g pro.

BANANAS FOSTER BAKED FRENCH TOAST

This yummy baked French toast serves up all the flavor of the spectacular dessert in an eye-opening fashion.
—*Laurence Nasson, Hingham, MA*

Prep: 20 min. + chilling • **Bake:** 35 min.
Makes: 6 servings

- ½ cup butter, cubed
- ⅔ cup packed brown sugar
- ½ cup heavy whipping cream
- ½ tsp. ground cinnamon
- ½ tsp. ground allspice
- ¼ cup chopped pecans, optional
- 3 large bananas, sliced
- 12 slices egg bread or challah (about ¾ lb.)
- 1½ cups 2% milk
- 3 large eggs
- 1 Tbsp. sugar
- 1 tsp. vanilla extract

1. Place butter in a microwave-safe bowl; microwave, covered, 30-45 seconds or until melted. Stir in brown sugar, cream, cinnamon, allspice and, if desired, pecans. Add bananas; toss gently to coat.
2. Transfer to a greased 13x9-in. baking dish. Arrange bread over top, trimming to fit as necessary.
3. Place remaining ingredients in a blender; process just until blended. Pour over bread. Refrigerate, covered, 8 hours or overnight.
4. Preheat oven to 375°. Remove French toast from refrigerator while oven heats. Bake, uncovered, until a knife inserted in the center comes out clean, 35-40 minutes. Let stand 5-10 minutes. Invert to serve.
1 piece: 658 cal., 31g fat (17g sat. fat), 218mg chol., 584mg sod., 84g carb. (39g sugars, 4g fiber), 14g pro.

PUMPKIN-CRANBERRY BREAKFAST BAKE

This bread pudding is a hit with my family for weekend breakfasts.
—*Terri Crandall, Gardnerville, NV*

- -

Prep: 15 min. + chilling • **Bake:** 30 min.
Makes: 12 servings

1	loaf (1 lb.) brioche, cut into 1-in. cubes
½	cup dried cranberries
½	cup chopped walnuts, toasted
2	cups 2% milk
1	cup canned pumpkin
¾	cup packed brown sugar
4	large eggs
½	tsp. grated lemon zest
2	Tbsp. butter, melted
1	tsp. vanilla extract
1	tsp. ground cinnamon
¼	tsp. ground nutmeg
¼	tsp. ground ginger
⅛	tsp. ground cloves
	Maple syrup

1. Place bread cubes in a greased 13x9-in. baking dish; sprinkle with cranberries and walnuts. Whisk together next 11 ingredients until blended; pour over bread. Refrigerate, covered, overnight.

2. Preheat oven to 350°. Remove casserole from refrigerator while oven heats. Bake, uncovered, until puffed, golden and a knife inserted in the center comes out clean, 30-35 minutes. Let stand 5-10 minutes before serving. Serve with syrup.

Note: To toast nuts, bake in a shallow pan in a 350° oven for 5-10 minutes or cook in a skillet over low heat until lightly browned, stirring occasionally.

1 piece: 303 cal., 12g fat (6g sat. fat), 101mg chol., 230mg sod., 43g carb. (26g sugars, 2g fiber), 7g pro.

WESTERN OMELET CASSEROLE

When I'm hosting brunch, I make omelets the easy way—with my slow cooker. My whole family's on board with this dish.
—*Kathleen Murphy, Littleton, CO*

- -

Prep: 15 min. • **Cook:** 6 hours + standing
Makes: 8 servings

1	pkg. (30 oz.) frozen shredded hash brown potatoes, thawed
1	lb. cubed fully cooked ham or 1 lb. bulk pork sausage, cooked and drained
1	medium onion, chopped
1	medium green pepper, chopped
1½	cups shredded cheddar cheese
12	large eggs
1	cup 2% milk
1	tsp. salt
1	tsp. pepper

1. In a greased 5- or 6-qt. slow cooker, layer half of each of the following: potatoes, ham, onion, green pepper and shredded cheese. Repeat layers.

2. Whisk together remaining ingredients; pour over top. Cook, covered, on low until set, 6-7 hours. Turn off the slow cooker. Remove insert; let stand, uncovered, for 15-30 minutes before serving.

1⅓ cups: 363 cal., 17g fat (8g sat. fat), 332mg chol., 1166mg sod., 24g carb. (4g sugars, 2g fiber), 29g pro.

ELEGANT SMOKED SALMON STRATA

This strata is ideal for overnight guests. In the morning, simply let it come to room temperature and whip up sides as it bakes.
—*Lisa Speer, Palm Beach, FL*

Prep: 30 min. + chilling
Bake: 55 min. + standing
Makes: 12 servings

- 4 cups cubed ciabatta bread
- 2 Tbsp. butter, melted
- 2 Tbsp. olive oil
- 2 cups shredded Gruyere or Swiss cheese
- 2 cups shredded white cheddar cheese
- 10 green onions, sliced
- ½ lb. smoked salmon or lox, coarsely chopped
- 8 large eggs
- 4 cups 2% milk
- 4 tsp. Dijon mustard
- ¼ tsp. salt
- ¼ tsp. pepper
  Creme fraiche or sour cream and minced chives

1. In a large bowl, toss bread cubes with butter and oil; transfer to a greased 13x9-in. baking dish. Sprinkle with cheeses, onions and salmon. In another bowl, whisk the eggs, milk, mustard, salt and pepper; pour over top. Cover and refrigerate overnight.

2. Remove from the refrigerator 30 minutes before baking. Preheat oven to 350°. Cover and bake for 30 minutes. Uncover; bake until a knife inserted in the center comes out clean, 25-30 minutes longer. Let stand for 10 minutes before serving. Serve with creme fraiche and chives.

1 piece: 359 cal., 21g fat (11g sat. fat), 194mg chol., 845mg sod., 21g carb. (6g sugars, 1g fiber), 22g pro.

PEACH-STUFFED FRENCH TOAST

With its make-ahead convenience and scrumptious flavor, I think this recipe is ideal for holiday brunches—and for busy hostesses with a hungry crowd to feed.
—*Julie Robinson, Little Chute, WI*

- -

Prep: 25 min. + chilling
Bake: 25 min. • **Makes:** 10 servings

  1   loaf (1 lb.) French bread, cut into 20 slices
  1   can (15 oz.) sliced peaches in juice, drained and chopped
  ¼ cup chopped pecans
  4   large eggs
  4   large egg whites
1½ cups fat-free milk
  3   Tbsp. sugar
1¼ tsp. ground cinnamon, divided
  1   tsp. vanilla extract
  ¼ cup all-purpose flour
  2   Tbsp. brown sugar
  2   Tbsp. cold butter
     Maple syrup, optional

1. Arrange half of the bread in a 13x9-in. baking dish coated with cooking spray. Top with peaches, pecans and remaining bread.
2. In a small bowl, whisk the eggs, egg whites, milk, sugar, 1 tsp. cinnamon and vanilla; pour over bread. Cover and refrigerate for 8 hours or overnight.
3. Remove from the refrigerator 30 minutes before baking. Bake, uncovered, at 400° for 20 minutes.
4. In a small bowl, combine the flour, brown sugar and remaining cinnamon; cut in the butter until crumbly. Sprinkle over French toast. Bake 5-10 minutes longer or until a knife inserted in the center comes out clean. Serve with syrup if desired.

1 piece: 267 cal., 8g fat (3g sat. fat), 92mg chol., 368mg sod., 39g carb. (13g sugars, 2g fiber), 10g pro. **Diabetic exchanges:** 2½ starch, 1½ fat.

SAVORY FRENCH TOAST BAKE

Spend just 15 minutes prepping this casserole the night before, and you'll have extra time to make a fruit salad and pour the coffee as it bakes. It's a keeper!
—*Patricia Nieh, Portola Valley, CA*

- -

Prep: 15 min. + chilling
Bake: 50 min. + standing
Makes: 10 servings

- 1 loaf (8 oz.) day-old French bread, cut into ½-in. slices
- 6 large eggs, beaten
- 2 cups 2% milk
- 4 tsp. Dijon mustard
- ½ tsp. salt
- ½ tsp. pepper
- ½ cup minced chives, divided
- 1½ cups shredded Gruyere or Swiss cheese, divided

1. Arrange half of the bread slices in a greased 13x9-in. baking dish. In a large bowl, combine the eggs, milk, mustard, salt, pepper and ¼ cup chives.
2. Pour half of the egg mixture over bread; sprinkle with 1 cup cheese. Layer with remaining bread and egg mixture. Sprinkle with remaining cheese. Cover and refrigerate overnight.
3. Remove from the refrigerator 30 minutes before baking. Bake, uncovered, at 350° for 50-55 minutes or until a knife inserted in the center comes out clean. Let stand for 10 minutes before cutting. Sprinkle with remaining chives.
1 piece: 241 cal., 13g fat (6g sat. fat), 159mg chol., 466mg sod., 16g carb. (3g sugars, 1g fiber), 16g pro.

FRUITY CROISSANT PUFF

I got this recipe from a good friend. Sweet, tart, tender and light, it tastes like a danish.
—*Myra Almer, Tuttle, ND*

- -

Prep: 10 min. + chilling • **Bake:** 45 min.
Makes: 6 servings

- 4 large croissants, cut into 1-in. cubes (about 6 cups)
- 1½ cups mixed fresh berries
- 1 pkg. (8 oz.) cream cheese, softened
- 1 cup 2% milk
- ½ cup sugar
- 2 large eggs, room temperature
- 1 tsp. vanilla extract
  Maple syrup, optional

1. Place croissants and berries in a greased 8-in. square baking dish. In a medium bowl, beat cream cheese until smooth. Beat in milk, sugar, eggs and vanilla until blended; pour over the croissants. Refrigerate, covered, overnight.
2. Preheat oven to 350°. Remove casserole from refrigerator while oven heats. Bake, covered, 30 minutes. Bake, uncovered, until puffed and golden and a knife inserted in the center comes out clean, 15-20 minutes. Let stand 5-10 minutes before serving. If desired, serve with syrup.
1 piece: 429 cal., 24g fat (14g sat. fat), 132mg chol., 358mg sod., 44g carb. (27g sugars, 2g fiber), 9g pro.

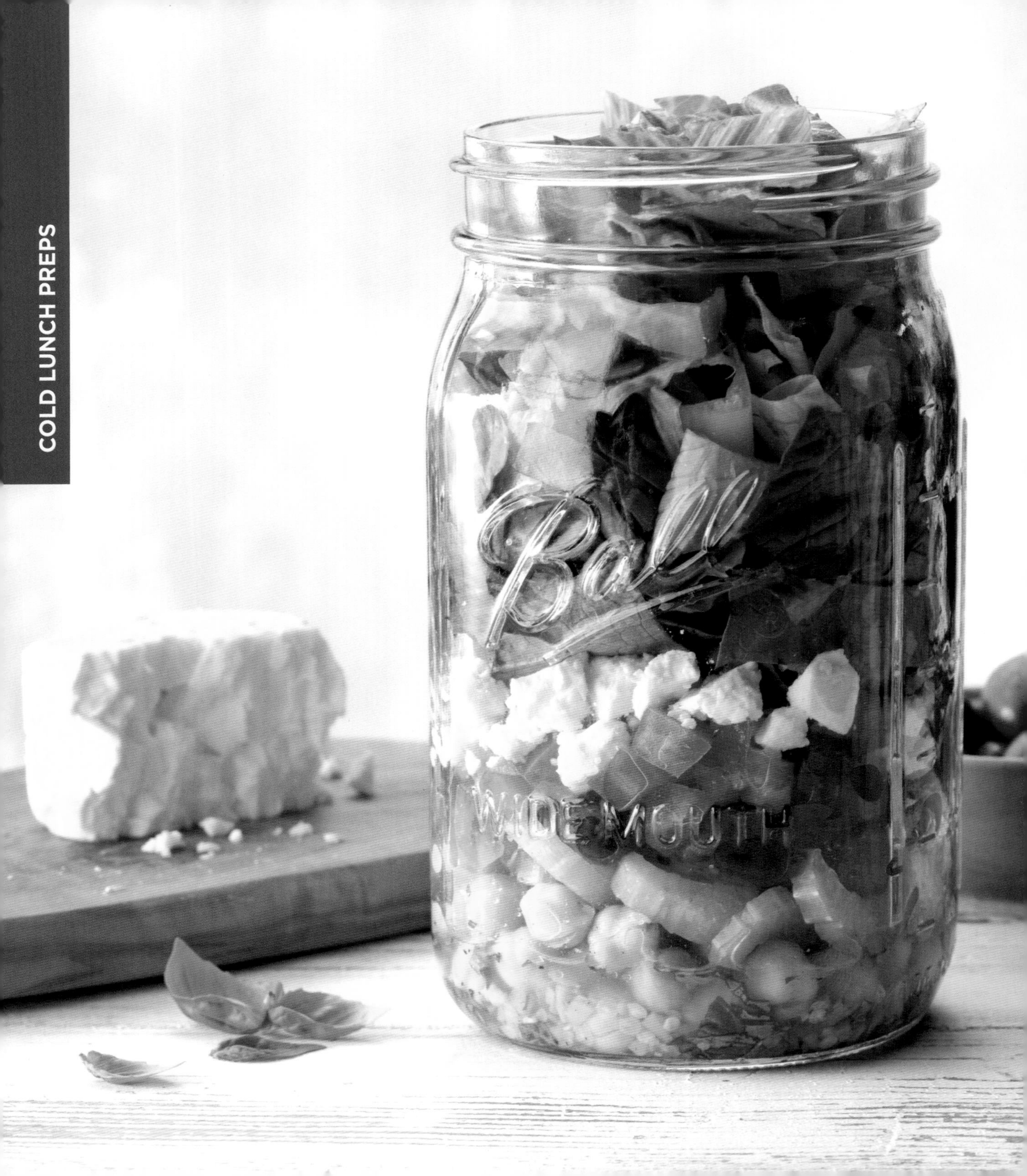
Ball
WIDE MOUTH

CHOPPED GREEK SALAD IN A JAR

Here's a lunchbox-friendly salad with lots of zesty flair. Prepare the jars on Sunday, and you'll have four grab-and-go lunches ready for the workweek.
—Taste of Home *Test Kitchen*

- -

Takes: 20 min. • **Makes:** 4 servings

- ¼ cup pepperoncini juice
- ¼ cup extra virgin olive oil
- ¼ cup minced fresh basil
- 2 Tbsp. lemon juice
- ½ tsp. pepper
- ¼ tsp. salt
- ¼ cup finely chopped pepperoncini
- 1 can (15 oz.) garbanzo beans or chickpeas, rinsed and drained
- 2 celery ribs, sliced
- ½ cup Greek olives
- 1 medium tomato, chopped
- ½ cup crumbled feta cheese
- 8 cups chopped romaine

In a small bowl, whisk the first 6 ingredients. In each of four 1-qt. wide-mouth canning jars, divide and layer the ingredients in the following order: olive oil mixture, pepperoncini, garbanzo beans, celery, Greek olives, tomato, feta and romaine. Cover and refrigerate until serving. Transfer salads into bowls; toss to combine.

1 serving: 332 cal., 23g fat (4g sat. fat), 8mg chol., 795mg sod., 25g carb. (5g sugars, 8g fiber), 9g pro.

TEST KITCHEN TIP
The olives and feta add flavor, but also fat and sodium. Leave them out to save 7 grams of fat and more than 400 milligrams of sodium per serving.

PENNSYLVANIA DUTCH COLESLAW

My mother used to make this salad, which stays crunchy for days and travels well for lunches and potlucks.
—*Deb Darr, Falls City, OR*

- -

Prep: 15 min. + chilling • **Makes:** 16 servings

- 1 medium head green cabbage, shredded (about 8 cups)
- 1 cup shredded red cabbage
- 4 to 5 carrots, shredded
- 1 cup mayonnaise
- 2 Tbsp. cider vinegar
- ½ cup sugar
- 1 tsp. salt
- ¼ tsp. pepper

In a large bowl, combine cabbage and carrots; set aside. In a small bowl, combine all remaining ingredients; pour over cabbage mixture. Toss well and refrigerate overnight.

¾ cup: 146 cal., 11g fat (2g sat. fat), 5mg chol., 239mg sod., 11g carb. (9g sugars, 2g fiber), 1g pro.

DELI-STYLE PASTA SALAD

Pasta provides a base for this tongue-tingling make-ahead salad. It has lots of fresh and satisfying ingredients topped with a flavorful dressing. It makes a lot, so add it to your meal plan for quick lunches or no-fuss side dishes. I like to make it for large backyard barbecues as well as bring-a-dish parties and potlucks.
—*Joyce McLennan, Algonac, MI*

Prep: 20 min. + chilling • **Makes:** 12 servings

7	oz. tricolor spiral pasta
6	oz. thinly sliced hard salami, julienned
6	oz. provolone cheese, cubed
1	can (2¼ oz.) sliced ripe olives, drained
1	small red onion, thinly sliced
1	small zucchini, halved and thinly sliced
½	cup chopped green pepper
½	cup chopped sweet red pepper
¼	cup minced fresh parsley
¼	cup grated Parmesan cheese
½	cup olive oil
¼	cup red wine vinegar
1	garlic clove, minced
1½	tsp. ground mustard
1	tsp. dried basil
1	tsp. dried oregano
¼	tsp. salt
	Dash pepper
2	medium tomatoes, cut into wedges

1. Cook the pasta according to package directions; rinse in cold water and drain. Place pasta in a large bowl; add the next 9 ingredients.

2. In a jar with tight-fitting lid, combine oil, vinegar, garlic, mustard, basil, oregano, salt and pepper; shake well.

3. Pour over salad; toss to coat. Cover and chill for 8 hour or overnight. Toss before serving. Garnish with tomatoes.

1 cup: 273 cal., 18g fat (6g sat. fat), 25mg chol., 536mg sod., 17g carb. (3g sugars, 1g fiber), 11g pro.

5i 🍎

FRESH FRUIT BOWL

The glorious colors used here make this a festive salad. Slightly sweet and chilled, it makes a nice accompaniment to almost any entree or a light snack on its own.
—*Marion Kirst, Troy, MI*

- -

Prep: 15 min. + chilling • **Makes:** 16 servings

8	to 10 cups fresh melon cubes
1	to 2 Tbsp. white corn syrup
1	pint fresh strawberries, halved
2	cups fresh pineapple chunks
2	oranges, sectioned
	Fresh mint leaves, optional

In a large bowl, combine melon cubes and corn syrup. Cover and refrigerate overnight. Just before serving, stir in remaining fruit. Garnish with fresh mint leaves if desired.

¾ cup: 56 cal., 0 fat (0 sat. fat), 0 chol., 14mg sod., 14g carb. (11g sugars, 2g fiber), 1g pro. **Diabetic exchanges:** 1 fruit.

ANN'S SPECIAL TUNA SALAD

This tuna salad features crunchy celery, green onions and pimientos that add a bit of flavor. What a great dish to have in the fridge for fast lunches, quick snacks or even no-fuss side dishes. Trust me, the salad will be gone in no time.

—*Ann Kaiser, Hartland, WI*

- -

Prep: 15 min. + chilling • **Makes:** 6 servings

1   **cup small shell macaroni**
1   **can (14 oz.) tuna,**
     drained and flaked
1   **cup diced celery**
½   **cup chopped green onions with tops**
1   **cup frozen peas, thawed**
1   **jar (2 oz.) diced pimientos,**
     drained, or 1 tomato, seeded
     and diced, or 6 radishes, sliced
1   **cup Miracle Whip**
1   **Tbsp. sweet or dill pickle relish**
1   **Tbsp. ketchup**
1   **tsp. mustard**
¼   **cup half-and-half cream or milk**
     Salt and pepper to taste
     Fresh parsley

Cook macaroni in boiling salted water until tender. Rinse in cold water and drain. Place in a large bowl. Add tuna, celery, onions, peas and pimientos; toss gently to mix. Combine the Miracle Whip, pickle relish, ketchup, mustard and cream; fold into the salad. Add the salt and pepper. Cover and refrigerate for several hours before serving. Garnish with parsley.

1 serving: 434 cal., 31g fat (5g sat. fat), 38mg chol., 536mg sod., 16g carb. (4g sugars, 2g fiber), 21g pro.

SLOW-COOKER FLAN IN A JAR

Spoil yourself with these delightful portable custards! Tuck a jar into your lunchbox for a sweet treat during the day. They're a cute and fun take on the Mexican dessert classic.
—*Megumi Garcia, Milwaukee, WI*

- -

Prep: 25 min. • **Cook:** 2 hours + chilling
Makes: 6 servings

- ½ cup sugar
- 1 Tbsp. plus 3 cups hot water (110°-115°)
- 1 cup coconut or whole milk
- ⅓ cup whole milk
- ⅓ cup sweetened condensed milk
- 2 large eggs plus 1 large egg yolk, room temperature, lightly beaten Pinch salt
- 1 tsp. vanilla extract
- 1 tsp. dark rum, optional

1. In a small heavy saucepan, spread sugar; cook, without stirring, over medium-low heat until it begins to melt. Gently drag the melted sugar to center of pan so sugar melts evenly. Cook, stirring constantly, until the melted sugar turns a deep amber color, about 2 minutes. Immediately remove from heat and carefully stir in 1 Tbsp. hot water. Quickly ladle the hot mixture into 6 hot 4-oz. jars.

2. In a small saucepan, heat coconut milk and whole milk until bubbles form around sides of pan; remove from heat. In a large bowl, whisk condensed milk, eggs, egg yolk and salt until blended but not foamy. Slowly stir in hot milk; stir in vanilla and, if desired, rum. Strain through a fine sieve. Pour egg mixture into prepared jars. Center lids on jars; screw on bands until fingertip tight.

3. Add remaining hot water to a 6-qt. slow cooker; place jars in slow cooker. Cook, covered, on high 2 hours or until centers are set. Cool 10 minutes on a wire rack.

4. Remove jars to a 13x9-in. baking pan filled halfway with ice water; cool for 10 minutes. Refrigerate until cold, about 1 hour. Run a knife around sides of jars; invert flans onto dessert plates.

⅓ cup: 224 cal., 10g fat (8g sat. fat), 100mg chol., 87mg sod., 28g carb. (27g sugars, 0 fiber), 5g pro.

TEST KITCHEN TIP
Not sure rum is a good choice for workplace lunches? You can use rum extract in place of the dark rum.

JUDY'S MACARONI SALAD

After finding this vintage macaroni salad years ago, I tweaked it and bumped up the pickles. Make it on the weekend, then tuck a serving inside your lunch bag.
—*Elizabeth Kirchgatter, Maysville, KY*

- -

Prep: 20 min. + chilling • **Makes:** 12 servings

2½ cups uncooked elbow macaroni
1½ cups mayonnaise
¼ cup sweet pickle juice
½ tsp. salt
¼ tsp. pepper
1 cup shredded cheddar cheese
6 hard-boiled large eggs, chopped
6 sweet pickles, chopped

1. Cook macaroni according to the package directions. Drain macaroni; rinse with cold water and drain well.
2. In a large bowl, combine the mayonnaise, pickle juice, salt and pepper. Stir in cheese, eggs and pickles. Add macaroni; toss gently to coat. Refrigerate, covered, until chilled, at least 2 hours.
¾ cup: 347 cal., 28g fat (6g sat. fat), 113mg chol., 413mg sod., 15g carb. (4g sugars, 1g fiber), 8g pro.

TEST KITCHEN TIP

Pasta salads are a great way to use up extras from your planned meals. Stir in some cooked chicken, add sliced pork from last night's roast or work in a few extra veggies you have sitting in the fridge.

🟢5i SIMPLE CUCUMBERS

This salad can be expanded to make larger quantities to fit whatever type of meal plan you're working on, and it's the perfect way to use up a garden bounty. The cucumbers stay nice and crisp.
—*Betsy Carlson, Rockford, IL*

- -

Prep: 10 min. + chilling • **Makes:** 10 servings

3 medium cucumbers, sliced
1 cup sugar
¾ cup water
½ cup white vinegar
3 Tbsp. minced fresh dill or parsley

Place the cucumbers in a 1½- to 2-qt. glass container. In a jar with a tight-fitting lid, shake remaining ingredients until combined. Pour over cucumbers. Cover and refrigerate overnight. Serve with a slotted spoon.
½ cup: 87 cal., 0 fat (0 sat. fat), 0 chol., 0 sod., 22g carb. (21g sugars, 1g fiber), 1g pro.

CALIFORNIA ROLL IN A JAR

I'm a big sushi fan but don't always have time to make those intricate rolls at home. This jar is layered with my favorite California roll ingredients, for all of the flavor without the fuss. What a treat at lunchtime!
—*James Schend, Pleasant Prairie, WI*

- -

Prep: 20 min. • **Cook:** 15 min. + standing
Makes: 4 servings

- 1 cup uncooked sushi rice
- 1 cup water
- ½ tsp. salt
- 1 Tbsp. rice vinegar
- 1 Tbsp. sugar
- 2 medium ripe avocados, peeled and cubed
- 1 cup lump crabmeat, drained
- 1 cup chopped cucumber
- 2 nori sheets, thinly sliced
   Optional: Pickled ginger slices, soy sauce and toasted sesame seeds

1. Wash rice in a colander until water runs clear. Combine rice, 1 cup water and salt in a large saucepan; bring to a boil. Reduce heat; cover. Simmer until water is absorbed and rice is tender, 15-20 minutes. Remove from heat. Let stand 10 minutes. Combine rice vinegar and sugar, stirring until sugar is dissolved. Stir into rice.

2. Place ⅓ cup rice into each of four 1-pint wide-mouth canning jars; layer with half of the avocados, crabmeat, cucumber and nori. Top with remaining rice and repeat layers. Cover and refrigerate until serving. Transfer into bowls; toss to combine. If desired, serve with optional ingredients.

1 serving: 349 cal., 11g fat (2g sat. fat), 33mg chol., 562mg sod., 52g carb. (6g sugars, 7g fiber), 11g pro.

TEST KITCHEN TIP

Imitation crabmeat is a very acceptable substitution for the more costly lump crabmeat. Tuna fish, smoked salmon or smoked trout are also good replacements for the crab. Have fun and add in some other ingredients, such as matchstick carrots or cubed cream cheese.

CORN PASTA SALAD

After tasting this chilled salad at a family reunion, I immediately asked for the recipe. It has tricolor pasta, crunchy corn, red onion and green pepper to give the zippy dish plenty of color.

—*Bernice Morris, Marshfield, MO*

Prep: 20 min. + chilling • **Makes:** 10 servings

- 2 cups cooked tricolor spiral pasta
- 1 pkg. (16 oz.) frozen corn, thawed
- 1 cup chopped celery
- 1 medium green pepper, chopped
- 1 cup chopped seeded tomatoes
- ½ cup diced pimientos
- ½ cup chopped red onion
- 1 cup picante sauce
- 2 Tbsp. canola oil
- 1 Tbsp. lemon juice
- 1 garlic clove, minced
- 1 Tbsp. sugar
- ½ tsp. salt

1. In a large bowl, combine the first 7 ingredients. In a jar with a tight-fitting lid, combine the picante sauce, oil, lemon juice, garlic, sugar and salt; shake well.
2. Pour over pasta mixture and toss to coat. Cover and refrigerate overnight.

¾ cup: 133 cal., 3g fat (1g sat. fat), 0 chol., 301mg sod., 24g carb. (0 sugars, 3g fiber), 3g pro. **Diabetic exchanges:** 1 starch, 1 vegetable, ½ fat.

SESAME BEEF & ASPARAGUS SALAD

Beat the clock when you plan on using leftover steak in this hearty yet healthy salad. That said, cooking the steak from scratch truly only takes moments. I love this for lunch, particularly in spring when asparagus is at its best.

—*Tamara Steeb, Issaquah, WA*

Takes: 30 min. • **Makes:** 6 servings

- 1 beef top round steak (1 lb.)
- 4 cups cut fresh asparagus (2-in. pieces)
- 3 Tbsp. reduced-sodium soy sauce
- 2 Tbsp. sesame oil
- 1 Tbsp. rice vinegar
- ½ tsp. grated gingerroot
  Sesame seeds
  Optional: Lettuce leaves, julienned carrot and radishes, cilantro leaves and lime wedges

1. Preheat broiler. Place the steak on a broiler pan. Broil 2-3 in. from heat until meat reaches desired doneness (for medium-rare, a thermometer should read 135°), 6-7 minutes per side. Let stand 5 minutes before slicing.

2. In a large saucepan, bring ½ in. water to a boil. Add the asparagus; cook, uncovered, just until crisp-tender, 3-5 minutes. Drain and cool.

3. Mix soy sauce, sesame oil, vinegar and ginger; toss with beef and asparagus. Sprinkle with sesame seeds. If desired, serve over lettuce with carrot, radishes, cilantro and lime wedges.

1 cup: 160 cal., 7g fat (1g sat. fat), 42mg chol., 350mg sod., 5g carb. (2g sugars, 2g fiber), 19g pro. **Diabetic exchanges:** 2 lean meat, 1 vegetable, 1 fat.

CRUNCHY TUNA SALAD WITH TOMATOES

On a hot summer day, there's nothing more refreshing than this salad. I grow a few tomato plants in my garden and the fresh-picked taste makes the dish even more of a treat.

—*Diane Selich, Vassar, MI*

Takes: 20 min. • **Makes:** 4 servings

- ⅔ cup reduced-fat mayonnaise
- ½ cup chopped sweet onion
- 1 celery rib, chopped
- 1 tsp. minced fresh parsley or ¼ tsp. dried parsley flakes
- ¾ tsp. pepper
- 1 can (12 oz.) albacore white tuna in water, drained and flaked
- 4 medium tomatoes, cut into wedges

In a small bowl, combine mayonnaise, onion, celery, parsley and pepper. Stir in the tuna. Serve with tomato wedges.

½ cup tuna salad with 1 tomato: 280 cal., 16g fat (3g sat. fat), 50mg chol., 656mg sod., 12g carb. (7g sugars, 2g fiber), 22g pro. **Diabetic exchanges:** 3 lean meat, 2 fat, 1 vegetable.

ORANGE BUTTERMILK GELATIN SALAD MOLD

Plan on this sweet surprise for a colorful treat at lunch. A friend shared this recipe with me years ago, and now it's one of my favorite dishes. Everyone who tries it asks for the recipe. No one can believe the make-ahead salad comes together with just a handful of ingredients.
—*Juanita Hutto, Mechanicsville, VA*

Prep: 15 min. + chilling • **Makes:** 16 servings

- 1 can (20 oz.) unsweetened crushed pineapple, undrained
- 3 Tbsp. sugar
- 1 pkg. (6 oz.) orange gelatin
- 2 cups buttermilk
- 1 carton (8 oz.) frozen whipped topping, thawed
- 1 cup chopped nuts

In a saucepan, combine pineapple and sugar; bring to a boil, stirring occasionally. When mixture boils, immediately add gelatin and stir until dissolved. Cool slightly. Stir in the buttermilk. Chill until partially set. Fold in whipped topping and nuts. If necessary, chill until mixture mounds slightly. Pour into a lightly oiled 8½-cup mold. Chill overnight.
⅔ cup: 168 cal., 7g fat (3g sat. fat), 1mg chol., 57mg sod., 23g carb. (19g sugars, 1g fiber), 4g pro.

🍎 QUICK GINGERED SPAGHETTI

Here's a unique way to use up any cooked chicken in your meal plan. I sometimes leave the chicken out to make this a meatless dish, and then toss in additional edamame for a midday protein boost.
—*Cindy Heinbaugh, Aurora, CO*

Takes: 30 min. • **Makes:** 8 servings

- 1 pkg. (16 oz.) whole wheat spaghetti
- 1 cup frozen shelled edamame
- 1 tsp. minced fresh gingerroot
- 1 cup reduced-fat sesame ginger salad dressing
- 3 cups cubed cooked chicken breast
- 1 English cucumber, chopped
- 1 medium sweet red pepper, chopped
- 1 small sweet yellow pepper, chopped
- 1 small red onion, finely chopped
- 3 green onions, sliced

1. Cook spaghetti according to the package directions, adding edamame during the last 5 minutes of cooking. Rinse in cold water and drain well. Meanwhile, stir ginger into salad dressing.
2. In a large bowl, combine the spaghetti, chicken, cucumber, peppers and red onion. Add dressing; toss to coat. Sprinkle with green onions.
1¾ cups: 353 cal., 5g fat (1g sat. fat), 40mg chol., 432mg sod., 53g carb. (6g sugars, 8g fiber), 26g pro.

MEDITERRANEAN BULGUR SALAD

It doesn't get any better than this meat-free make-ahead dish. It travels well for lunches, and it is perfect alongside a sandwich or bowl of soup—or enjoy it on its own!
—Taste of Home *Test Kitchen*

- -

Prep: 15 min. • **Cook:** 20 min. + cooling
Makes: 9 servings

- 3 cups vegetable broth
- 1½ cups uncooked bulgur
- 6 Tbsp. olive oil
- 2 Tbsp. lemon juice
- 2 Tbsp. minced fresh parsley
- ½ tsp. salt
- ¼ tsp. pepper
- 1 can (15 oz.) garbanzo beans or chickpeas, rinsed and drained
- 2 cups halved cherry tomatoes
- 1 cup chopped cucumber
- 8 green onions, sliced
- 1 pkg. (4 oz.) crumbled feta cheese
- ½ cup pine nuts, toasted

1. In a large saucepan, bring the broth and bulgur to a boil over high heat. Reduce heat; cover and simmer for 20 minutes or until tender and the broth is almost absorbed. Remove from the heat; let stand at room temperature, uncovered, until the broth is absorbed.

2. In a small bowl, whisk the oil, lemon juice, parsley, salt and pepper.

3. In a large serving bowl, combine the bulgur, beans, tomatoes, cucumber and onions. Drizzle with dressing; toss to coat. Sprinkle with cheese and pine nuts.

1 cup: 298 cal., 17g fat (3g sat. fat), 7mg chol., 657mg sod., 31g carb. (4g sugars, 8g fiber), 10g pro.

SLOW-COOKER CHOCOLATE POTS DE CREME

Lunch on the go just got a lot sweeter. Tuck jars of rich chocolate custard into lunch bags for a midday treat. These desserts in a jar are fun for picnics, too.
—*Nick Iverson, Denver, CO*

- -

Prep: 20 min. • **Cook:** 4 hours + chilling
Makes: 8 servings

  2 cups heavy whipping cream
  8 oz. bittersweet chocolate,
     finely chopped
  1 Tbsp. instant espresso powder
  4 large egg yolks, room temperature
  ¼ cup sugar
  ¼ tsp. salt
  1 Tbsp. vanilla extract
  3 cups hot water
     Optional: Whipped cream, grated
     chocolate and fresh raspberries

1. Place cream, chocolate and espresso in a microwave-safe bowl; microwave on high until chocolate is melted and cream is hot, about 4 minutes. Whisk to combine.
2. In a large bowl, whisk egg yolks, sugar and salt until blended but not foamy. Slowly whisk in cream mixture; stir in extract.
3. Ladle egg mixture into eight 4-oz. jars. Center lids on jars and screw on bands until fingertip tight. Add hot water to a 7-qt. slow cooker; place jars in slow cooker. Cook, covered, on low until set, about 4 hours. Remove jars from slow cooker; cool on the counter for 30 minutes. Refrigerate until cold, about 2 hours.
4. If desired, top with whipped cream, grated chocolate and raspberries.
1 jar: 424 cal., 34g fat (21g sat. fat), 160g chol., 94mg sod., 13g carb. (11g sugars, 1g fiber), 5g pro.

TEST KITCHEN TIP
Store the jars in the refrigerator up to 1 week.

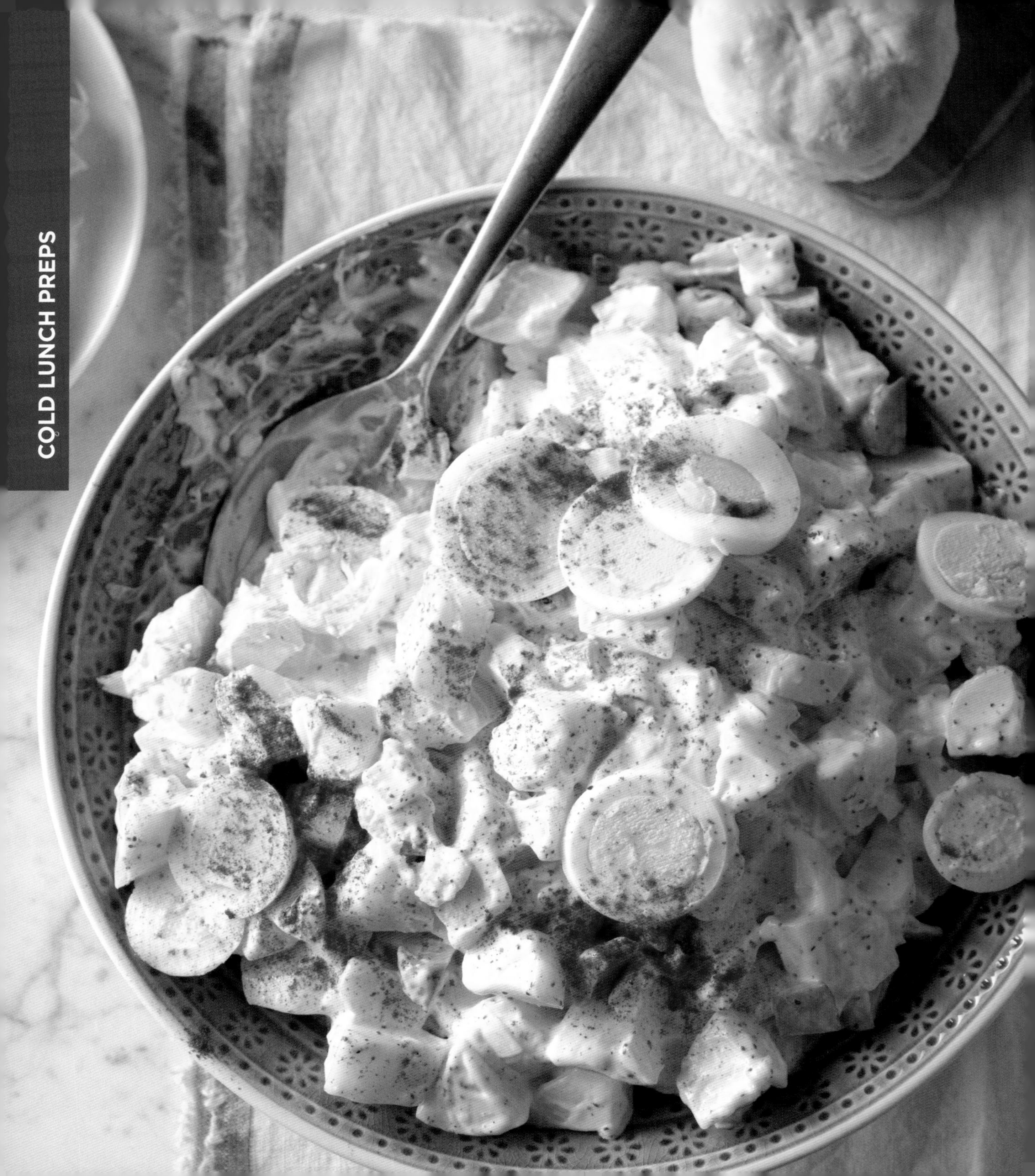

DILLY POTATO & EGG SALAD

Everyone has a favorite potato salad, and this is mine. As a young bride 36 years ago, I was eager to learn how to cook and make things that my husband would love. When I combined my mom's and his mom's recipes, this was the delicious result.

—*Angela Leinenbach, Mechanicsville, VA*

- -

Prep: 20 min. + chilling
Cook: 20 min. + cooling
Makes: 12 servings

- 4 **lbs. medium red potatoes (about 14), peeled and halved**
- 5 **hard-boiled large eggs**
- 1 **cup chopped dill pickles**
- 1 **small onion, chopped**
- 1½ **cups mayonnaise**
- 1 **tsp. celery seed**
- ½ **tsp. salt**
- ¼ **tsp. pepper**
  Paprika

1. Place potatoes in a large saucepan; add water to cover. Bring to a boil. Reduce heat; cook, uncovered, 15-20 minutes or until tender. Drain; cool completely.
2. Cut potatoes into ¾-in. cubes; place in a large bowl. Chop 4 eggs; slice remaining egg. Add chopped eggs, pickles and onion to potatoes. Mix mayonnaise, celery seed, salt and pepper; stir gently into the potato mixture. Top with sliced egg and sprinkle with paprika. Refrigerate, covered, at least 2 hours before serving.
¾ cup: 326 cal., 22g fat (4g sat. fat), 80mg chol., 413mg sod., 25g carb. (2g sugars, 3g fiber), 6g pro.

MEDITERRANEAN SHRIMP SALAD IN A JAR

This Greek salad to go is loaded with so much freshness that it makes any day feel brighter. Just layer it in a jar and pack it up—then serve and enjoy.
—Taste of Home *Test Kitchen*

- -

Prep: 20 min. • **Cook:** 15 min.
Makes: 4 servings

- ¾ **cup uncooked orzo pasta**
- ¾ **cup Greek vinaigrette**
- ½ **cup minced fresh parsley**
- ⅓ **cup chopped fresh dill**
- ¾ **lb. peeled and deveined cooked shrimp (31-40 per lb.)**
- 1 **can (14 oz.) water-packed quartered artichoke hearts, rinsed and drained**
- 1 **medium sweet red pepper, chopped**
- 1 **medium green pepper, chopped**
- 1 **small red onion, thinly sliced**
- ½ **cup pitted Greek olives, sliced**
- ½ **cup crumbled feta cheese**
- 8 **cups fresh arugula**

1. Cook orzo according to the package directions. Drain; rinse with cold water and drain well. Combine orzo with Greek vinaigrette and herbs.
2. In each of four 1-qt. wide-mouth canning jars, divide and layer ingredients in the following order: orzo mixture, shrimp, artichokes, red pepper, green pepper, red onion, Greek olives, feta cheese and arugula. Cover and refrigerate until serving. Transfer salads into bowls; toss to combine.
1 serving: 548 cal., 26g fat (5g sat. fat), 137mg chol., 1287mg sod., 47g carb. (5g sugars, 4g fiber), 29g pro.

NINE-LAYER SALAD

Creamy and crunchy, this delightful dish is loaded with popular salad ingredients such as green pepper, green onions, frozen peas and bacon. It's a colorful accompaniment to just about any lunch staple.
—*Anne Halfhill, Sunbury, OH*

Prep: 30 min. + chilling • **Makes:** 8 servings

- 4 cups torn iceberg lettuce
- 4 cups fresh baby spinach
- 1 cup each chopped green pepper, celery and green onions
- 1 pkg. (10 oz.) frozen peas, thawed and patted dry
- 1½ cups mayonnaise
- ½ cup shredded Parmesan cheese
- ½ cup shredded Romano cheese
- 1 cup crumbled cooked bacon

In a large salad bowl, layer the lettuce, spinach, green pepper, celery, green onions and peas. Spread with the mayonnaise. Combine the cheeses; sprinkle cheeses and bacon over mayonnaise. Cover and refrigerate overnight.
1 cup: 418 cal., 38g fat (7g sat. fat), 31mg chol., 847mg sod., 8g carb. (3g sugars, 3g fiber), 11g pro.

TUNA MACARONI

This jazzed-up tuna recipe came from a nutritionist I worked with. It's so full of protein and flavor that we shared it with many of our patients.
—*Mary Pat Eck, Cincinnati, OH*

Prep: 15 min. + chilling • **Makes:** 2 servings

- ¾ cup cooked small pasta shells
- 1 can (5 oz.) light water-packed tuna, drained and flaked
- 1 hard-boiled large egg, chopped
- ½ cup cubed cheddar cheese
- ¼ cup chopped celery
- 2 Tbsp. pickle relish, drained
- ⅓ cup mayonnaise
- 1½ tsp. Dijon mustard
- ⅛ tsp. salt
  Lettuce leaves

In a small bowl, combine first 6 ingredients. In another bowl, combine the mayonnaise, mustard and salt; stir into tuna mixture. Cover pasta salad and refrigerate for at least 30 minutes. Serve on lettuce-lined plates.
1 cup: 347 cal., 11g fat (5g sat. fat), 156mg chol., 1259mg sod., 25g carb. (9g sugars, 2g fiber), 35g pro.

OVERNIGHT SLAW

I love to make this recipe during the fall and winter months, when salad ingredients are less abundant. I also enjoy the ease of prep when using my food processor.
—*Nancy Brown, Janesville, WI*

Prep: 15 min. + chilling • **Makes:** 8 servings

1	medium head cabbage, shredded
4	mild white onions, thinly sliced
2	large carrots, shredded
½	cup vinegar
½	cup sugar
1	tsp. ground mustard
1	tsp. celery seed
1	tsp. salt
⅛	tsp. pepper
½	cup vegetable oil

In a large bowl, combine the cabbage, onions and carrots; set aside. In a saucepan, combine the vinegar, sugar, mustard, celery seed, salt and pepper; bring to a boil, stirring until sugar is dissolved. Remove from the heat and stir in oil. Pour over the cabbage mixture. Cool to room temperature. Cover and refrigerate overnight; stir several times.
¾ cup: 238 cal., 14g fat (2g sat. fat), 0 chol., 325mg sod., 28g carb. (21g sugars, 5g fiber), 3g pro.

BACON MACARONI PASTA

This pleasing pasta salad is like eating a BLT in a bowl. Chock-full of crispy crumbled bacon, and chopped tomato, celery and green onion, the sensational salad is draped in a tangy mayonnaise and vinegar dressing. It's perfect for lunch, packed with a roll and a piece of fruit.
—*Norene Wright, Manilla, IN*

- -

Prep: 20 min. + chilling • **Makes:** 12 servings

- 2 cups uncooked elbow macaroni
- 1 large tomato, finely chopped
- 2 celery ribs, finely chopped
- 5 green onions, finely chopped
- 1¼ cups mayonnaise
- 5 tsp. white vinegar
- ¼ tsp. salt
- ⅛ to ¼ tsp. pepper
- 1 lb. bacon strips, cooked and crumbled

1. Cook macaroni according to package directions; drain and rinse in cold water. Transfer to a large bowl; stir in tomato, celery and green onions.
2. In a small bowl, whisk the mayonnaise, vinegar, salt and pepper. Pour over the macaroni mixture and toss to coat. Refrigerate, covered, at least 2 hours. Just before serving, stir in bacon.

¾ cup: 290 cal., 25g fat (5g sat. fat), 19mg chol., 387mg sod., 11g carb. (1g sugars, 1g fiber), 6g pro.

CHICKEN SALAD CROISSANTS

This tempting chicken salad gets its special flavor from Swiss cheese and pickle relish. It's my brother's favorite; he insists I make it whenever he visits.
—*Laura Koziarski, Battle Creek, MI*

- -

Takes: 15 min. • **Makes:** 6 servings

- ⅔ cup mayonnaise
- ½ cup dill pickle relish
- 1 Tbsp. minced fresh parsley
- 1 tsp. lemon juice
- ½ tsp. seasoned salt
- ⅛ tsp. pepper
- 2 cups cubed cooked chicken
- 1 cup cubed Swiss cheese
- 6 croissants, split
  Lettuce leaves

Mix first 6 ingredients; stir in chicken and cheese. Serve chicken salad on croissants lined with lettuce.

1 sandwich: 593 cal., 40g fat (14g sat. fat), 102mg chol., 818mg sod., 33g carb. (6g sugars, 2g fiber), 24g pro.

CREAMY EGG SALAD

I love this egg salad's versatility—serve it on a nest of mixed greens, tucked into a sandwich or with your favorite crisp crackers. It's all good!
—*Cynthia Kolberg, Syracuse, IN*

Takes: 10 min. • **Makes:** 3 cups

- 3 oz. cream cheese, softened
- ¼ cup mayonnaise
- ½ tsp. salt
- ⅛ tsp. pepper
- ¼ cup finely chopped green or sweet red pepper
- ¼ cup finely chopped celery
- ¼ cup sweet pickle relish
- 2 Tbsp. minced fresh parsley
- 8 hard-boiled large eggs, chopped

In a bowl, mix cream cheese, mayonnaise, salt and pepper until smooth. Stir in green pepper, celery, relish and parsley. Fold in eggs. Refrigerate, covered, until serving.

½ cup: 228 cal., 19g fat (6g sat. fat), 264mg chol., 456mg sod., 6g carb. (4g sugars, 0 fiber), 9g pro.

TEST KITCHEN TIP
Freshen up this recipe with help from your herb garden. Simply use dill instead of (or in addition to) the parsley. Remember, dill packs quite a punch, so 2 teaspoons instead of 2 tablespoons should do it.

TUNA-CHEESE SPREAD

This thick and creamy spread is perfect in sandwiches and wraps, stuffed into tomatoes or served alongside crackers, carrots or celery sticks. Keep it in the fridge for all to enjoy as they wish.
—*Dorothy Anderson, Ottawa, KS*

Takes: 5 min. • **Makes:** 2 cups (8 servings)

- 1 pkg. (8 oz.) cream cheese, softened
- ½ cup thinly sliced green onions
- ¼ cup mayonnaise
- 1 Tbsp. lemon juice
- ¾ tsp. curry powder
  Dash salt
- 1 can (6 oz.) tuna, drained and flaked
  Bread or crackers

In a bowl, combine the first 6 ingredients. Stir in tuna. Serve with bread or crackers.

¼ cup: 177 cal., 16g fat (7g sat. fat), 40mg chol., 213mg sod., 1g carb. (1g sugars, 0 fiber), 8g pro.

5i

ORANGE FLUFF

My sister gave me this fluffy salad recipe that whips up in a jiffy and keeps well in the fridge. With only a few ingredients, it's a quick and easy addition to your menu plan.
—*Stacey Meyer, Merced, CA*

- -

Takes: 15 min. • **Makes:** 8 servings

- 1 **cup sour cream**
- 1 **pkg. (3 oz.) lemon gelatin**
- 2 **cans (11 oz. each) mandarin oranges, drained**
- 1 **can (21 oz.) pineapple tidbits, drained**
- 1 **carton (8 oz.) frozen whipped topping, thawed Pastel miniature marshmallows, optional**

Place sour cream in a large bowl. Sprinkle with gelatin and stir until blended. Fold in the oranges, pineapple and whipped topping. Sprinkle with marshmallows if desired.

1 cup: 225 cal., 9g fat (8g sat. fat), 19mg chol., 44mg sod., 30g carb. (26g sugars, 1g fiber), 2g pro.

COLORFUL QUINOA SALAD

My youngest daughter recently learned she has to avoid gluten, dairy and eggs, which gave me a new challenge in the kitchen. I put this dish together as a fast lunch or side dish we could all enjoy.
—*Catherine Turnbull, Burlington, ON*

- -

Prep: 30 min. + cooling • **Makes:** 8 servings

2	cups water
1	cup quinoa, rinsed
2	cups fresh baby spinach, thinly sliced
1	cup grape tomatoes, halved
1	medium cucumber, seeded and chopped
1	medium sweet orange pepper, chopped
1	medium sweet yellow pepper, chopped
2	green onions, chopped

DRESSING

3	Tbsp. lime juice
2	Tbsp. olive oil
4	tsp. honey
1	Tbsp. grated lime zest
2	tsp. minced fresh gingerroot
¼	tsp. salt

1. In a large saucepan, bring water to a boil. Add quinoa. Reduce heat; simmer, covered, until the liquid is absorbed, 12-15 minutes. Remove from heat; fluff with a fork. Transfer to a large bowl; cool completely.

2. Stir the spinach, tomatoes, cucumber, peppers and green onions into quinoa. In a small bowl, whisk dressing ingredients until blended. Drizzle over quinoa mixture; toss to coat. Refrigerate until serving.

¾ cup: 143 cal., 5g fat (1g sat. fat), 0 chol., 88mg sod., 23g carb. (6g sugars, 3g fiber), 4g pro. **Diabetic exchanges:** 1 starch, 1 vegetable, 1 fat.

PASTA IN A JAR

If you're planning ahead, this super fast salad is a must. When I pack it for my husband's lunch at work, I sometimes tie a plastic fork onto the jar.
—*Pat Neiheisel, Leetonia, OH*

Takes: 30 min.
Makes: 16 servings

8	oz. each uncooked bow tie pasta, medium pasta shells and wagon wheel pasta
2	cups Greek vinaigrette
3	cups cherry tomatoes, halved
1	medium red onion, finely chopped
1	jar (12 oz.) marinated quartered artichoke hearts, drained and coarsely chopped
1	jar (12 oz.) roasted sweet red peppers, drained and chopped
1	cup chopped fresh basil
1	cup grated Parmesan cheese
1	pkg. (3½ oz.) sliced pepperoni
1	can (2¼ oz.) sliced ripe olives, drained

1. Cook pasta according to the package directions for al dente. Drain pasta; rinse with cold water and drain well. Transfer to a large bowl.

2. Add vinaigrette to pasta; toss to coat. Add vegetables, basil, cheese, pepperoni and olives; toss to combine. If desired, transfer to covered jars. Refrigerate salad until serving.

1 cup: 375 cal., 20g fat (4g sat. fat), 11mg chol., 690mg sod., 37g carb. (5g sugars, 2g fiber), 9g pro.

CHICKEN SALAD

I make this dish ahead so I have it on hand for busy days. I also turn to the recipe when I need to whip something up for family get-togethers.
—*Cathy Rauen, Ridgeway, CO*

Takes: 10 min. • **Makes:** 6 servings

2½	cups diced cooked chicken
4	bacon strips, cooked and crumbled
1	can (8 oz.) sliced water chestnuts, drained
½	cup thinly sliced celery
1	cup halved green grapes
¾	cup Miracle Whip
1	to 2 Tbsp. dried parsley flakes
2	tsp. grated onion
1	tsp. lemon juice
¼	tsp. ground ginger
	Dash Worcestershire sauce
	Salt and pepper to taste

In large bowl, combine the chicken, bacon, water chestnuts, celery and grapes; set aside. In another bowl, whisk together the remaining ingredients; add to salad and toss to coat. Chill until serving.

1 cup: 316 cal., 21g fat (4g sat. fat), 66mg chol., 321mg sod., 14g carb. (8g sugars, 1g fiber), 19g pro.

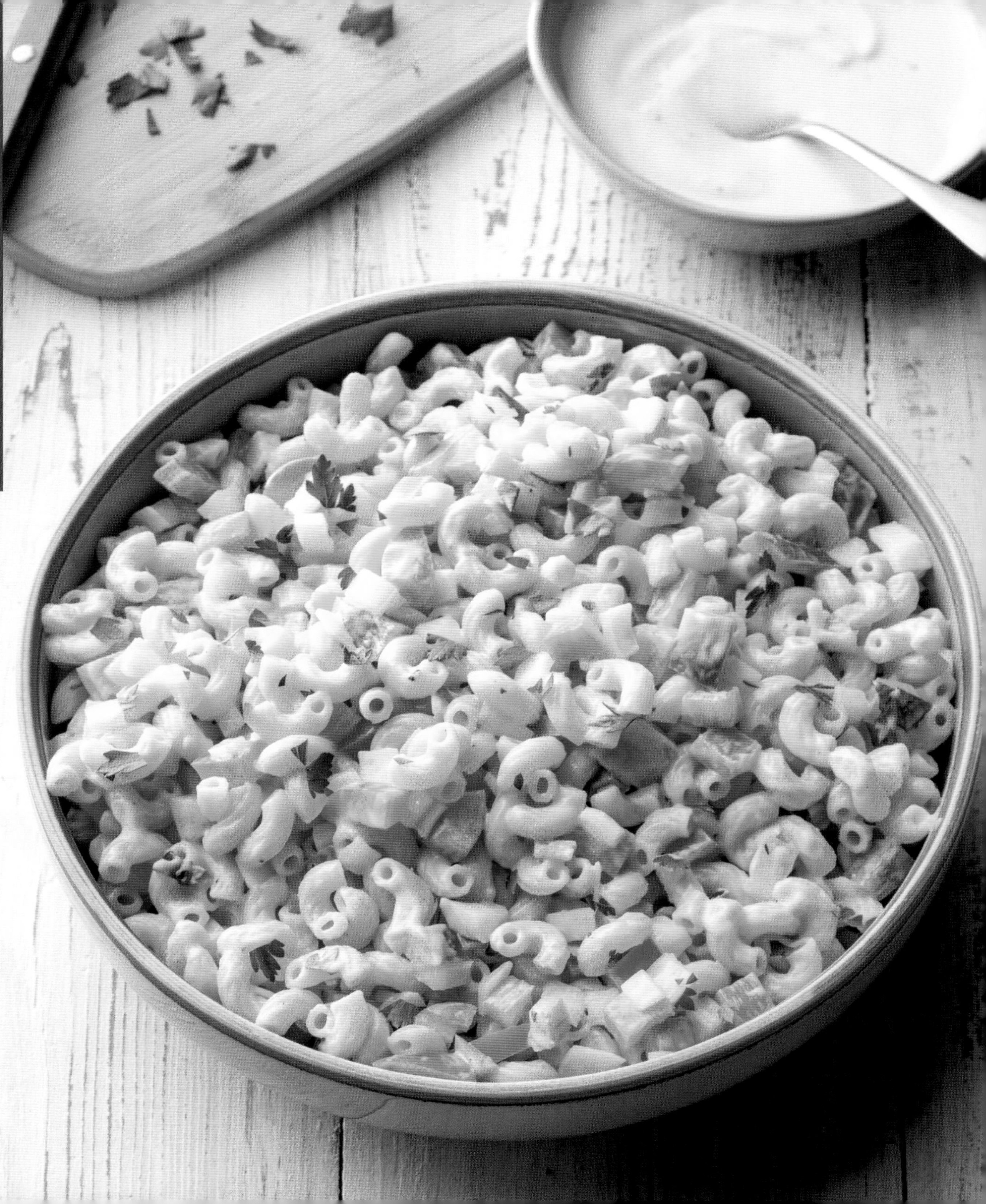

SUMMER MACARONI

If you're making this pasta ahead of time, consider keeping a small amount of the dressing in a separate container and then stirring it in right before lunch.

—*Carly Curtin, Ellicott City, MD*

Prep: 20 min. + chilling • **Cook:** 15 min.
Makes: 16 servings

1	pkg. (16 oz.) elbow macaroni
1	cup reduced-fat mayonnaise
3	to 4 Tbsp. water or 2% milk
2	Tbsp. red wine vinegar
1	Tbsp. sugar
1½	tsp. salt
¼	tsp. garlic powder
¼	tsp. pepper
1	small sweet yellow, orange or red pepper, finely chopped
1	small green pepper, finely chopped
1	small onion, finely chopped
1	celery rib, finely chopped
2	Tbsp. minced fresh parsley

1. Cook macaroni according to package directions. Drain; rinse with cold water and drain again.

2. In a small bowl, mix mayonnaise, water, vinegar, sugar and seasonings until blended. In a large bowl, combine the macaroni, peppers, onion and celery. Add 1 cup dressing; toss gently to coat. Refrigerate, covered, until cold, about 2 hours. Cover and refrigerate remaining dressing to add just before serving.

3. To serve, stir in reserved dressing. Sprinkle with parsley.

¾ cup: 160 cal., 6g fat (1g sat. fat), 5mg chol., 320mg sod., 24g carb. (3g sugars, 1g fiber), 4g pro. **Diabetic exchanges:** 1½ starch, 1 fat.

TURKEY RANCH WRAPS

Here's a cool idea that's ready to gobble up in no time. It's a terrific way to use leftover turkey or simply deli turkey. The wraps are easy to customize, too, for make-ahead lunches for the whole family.

—Taste of Home *Test Kitchen*

Takes: 10 min. • **Makes:** 4 servings

8	thin slices cooked turkey
4	flour tortillas (6 in.), room temperature
1	large tomato, thinly sliced
1	medium green pepper, cut into thin strips
1	cup shredded lettuce
1	cup shredded cheddar cheese
⅓	cup ranch salad dressing

Place 2 slices of turkey on each tortilla. Layer with tomato, green pepper, lettuce and cheese. Drizzle with salad dressing. Roll up tightly.

1 wrap: 403 cal., 25g fat (9g sat. fat), 76mg chol., 601mg sod., 19g carb. (3g sugars, 1g fiber), 26g pro.

CHICKEN PASTA SALAD

For sunny, lazy days, I make a loaded macaroni salad that's like three salads in one. The mix of fresh veggies, sweet peaches and crunchy pistachios is a surprisingly delicious combo.
—*Nancy Heishman, Las Vegas, NV*

- -

Prep: 25 min. + chilling • **Makes:** 16 servings

1½ cups uncooked elbow macaroni
1 rotisserie chicken, skin removed, shredded
¾ cup fresh or frozen peas
5 green onions, finely chopped
2 celery ribs, thinly sliced
⅓ cup loosely packed basil leaves, thinly sliced
¼ cup lemon juice, divided
1 tsp. kosher salt
¾ tsp. coarsely ground pepper
¾ cup plain yogurt
¾ cup reduced-fat mayonnaise
3 medium peaches, peeled and sliced
1 cup sharp cheddar cheese, shredded
½ cup crumbled Gorgonzola cheese
¾ cup pistachios

1. Cook macaroni according to package directions. Meanwhile, mix the chicken, peas, onions, celery, basil, 2 Tbsp. lemon juice, salt and pepper. Drain macaroni; rinse with cold water, then drain again. Add to chicken mixture.

2. Mix yogurt, mayonnaise and remaining lemon juice. Add to the salad and mix well. Add the peaches and cheeses; toss gently. Refrigerate at least 2 hours. Sprinkle with pistachios before serving.

¾ cup: 312 cal., 16g fat (5g sat. fat), 85mg chol., 379mg sod., 13g carb. (5g sugars, 2g fiber), 29g pro.

WHY YOU'LL LOVE IT:
"This salad was very cool and refreshing. It is the perfect summer recipe! I switched the peaches and pistachios with grapes and walnuts."
—RLEWIS7, TASTEOFHOME.COM

SMOKED SALMON CROISSANTS

Smoked salmon and croissants elevate egg salad sandwiches to a delicious, definitely grown-up level. Stash a container in the fridge for quick lunches during the week.
—*Cathy Tang, Redmond, WA*

- -

Takes: 10 min. • **Makes:** 6 servings

- ¾ **cup mayonnaise**
- 1 **tsp. dill weed**
- ½ **tsp. lemon juice**
- ¼ **tsp. salt**
- ⅛ **tsp. pepper**
- 6 **hard-boiled large eggs, chopped**
- 4 **oz. smoked salmon, chopped**
- 6 **croissants, split**
- 1½ **cups fresh baby spinach**

1. In a large bowl, combine the first 5 ingredients. Stir in the eggs and salmon.
2. Place ⅓ cup on the bottom of each croissant; top with spinach leaves and replace croissant tops.
1 sandwich: 533 cal., 40g fat (11g sat. fat), 265mg chol., 889mg sod., 27g carb. (7g sugars, 2g fiber), 15g pro.

CRANBERRY WALDORF GELATIN

We enjoy this easy-to-make salad in the fall when apples are in season. Their crisp freshness adds so much to a favorite dish.
—Debbie Short, Carlisle, IA

Prep: 15 min. + chilling • **Makes:** 12 servings

- 1 envelope unflavored gelatin
- 1 cup cold water, divided
- 1 pkg. (3 oz.) cranberry gelatin
- 2 cups boiling water
- 1 can (14 oz.) whole-berry cranberry sauce
- ½ to 1 tsp. ground cinnamon
- ¼ tsp. ground ginger
- ⅛ to ¼ tsp. salt
- 2 medium tart apples, peeled and diced
- 1 cup chopped walnuts

Sprinkle unflavored gelatin over ¼ cup cold water; let stand for 5 minutes. In a bowl, dissolve softened gelatin and cranberry gelatin in boiling water. Stir in cranberry sauce until blended. Add the cinnamon, ginger, salt and remaining cold water. Cover and refrigerate until almost set. Fold in apples and walnuts. Pour into an ungreased 2½-qt. serving bowl. Refrigerate until firm.
¾ cup: 156 cal., 6g fat (0 sat. fat), 0 chol., 50mg sod., 24g carb. (18g sugars, 1g fiber), 4g pro.

SALAMI & PROVOLONE PASTA SALAD

This pasta salad is the perfect dish when you want something that's fast, light, cool and absolutely delicious.
—Jill Donley, Warsaw, IN

Prep: 25 min. + chilling • **Makes:** 8 servings

- 3 cups uncooked cellentani pasta or elbow macaroni
- 1 medium sweet red pepper, chopped
- 4 oz. provolone cheese, cubed (about 1 cup)
- 4 oz. hard salami, cubed (about 1 cup)
- ⅓ cup prepared Italian salad dressing
  Optional: Additional Italian salad dressing and minced fresh basil

1. Cook pasta according to package directions. Meanwhile, in a large bowl, combine pepper, cheese and salami.
2. Drain the pasta and rinse in cold water. Add to pepper mixture. Drizzle with ⅓ cup dressing and toss to coat. Refrigerate, covered, at least 1 hour. If desired, stir in additional dressing to moisten and sprinkle with basil before serving.
¾ cup: 244 cal., 12g fat (5g sat. fat), 24mg chol., 575mg sod., 23g carb. (2g sugars, 1g fiber), 11g pro.

5i

CURRIED CHICKEN WITH PINEAPPLE & GRAPES

This fun and flavorful beauty turns last night's cooked chicken into a delightful salad that's perfect for lunch.
—*Linda Bevill, Monticello, AR*

Prep: 15 min. + chilling • **Makes:** 6 servings

- 4 cups cubed cooked chicken
- 1 can (20 oz.) pineapple tidbits, drained
- 1 cup halved seedless grapes
- ½ cup mayonnaise
- ½ tsp. curry powder
  Fresh cilantro leaves, optional
  Bibb lettuce leaves, optional

In a large bowl, combine the chicken, pineapple and grapes. In a small bowl, combine mayonnaise and curry; pour over chicken mixture; toss to coat. Cover and refrigerate until serving. If desired, top with cilantro and serve in lettuce leaves.

1 cup: 364 cal., 22g fat (4g sat. fat), 90mg chol., 185mg sod., 14g carb. (13g sugars, 1g fiber), 27g pro.

HAM & SWISS IN A JAR

Here's a fun, creative take on a lunchbox classic. Give it a try when you have leftover ham to use up.
—Taste of Home *Test Kitchen*

- -

Takes: 25 min. • **Makes:** 4 servings

¾	cup mayonnaise
⅓	cup reduced-fat sour cream
2	Tbsp. water
1½	tsp. white wine vinegar
¼	tsp. sugar
⅛	tsp. salt
⅛	tsp. pepper
⅓	lb. cubed fully cooked ham
2	cups frozen peas, thawed
1	small red onion, halved and thinly sliced
6	hard-boiled large eggs, chopped
¼	lb. bacon strips, cooked and crumbled
1	cup shredded Swiss cheese
4	cups torn iceberg lettuce (about ½ head)
6	cups fresh baby spinach

In a small bowl, whisk the first 7 ingredients. In each of four 1-qt. wide-mouth canning jars, divide and layer ingredients in the following order: mayonnaise mixture, ham, peas, onion, eggs, bacon, cheese, lettuce and spinach. Cover and refrigerate until serving. Transfer the salads into bowls; toss to combine.

1 serving: 691 cal., 54g fat (14g sat. fat), 344mg chol., 1110mg sod., 18g carb. (8g sugars, 5g fiber), 36g pro.

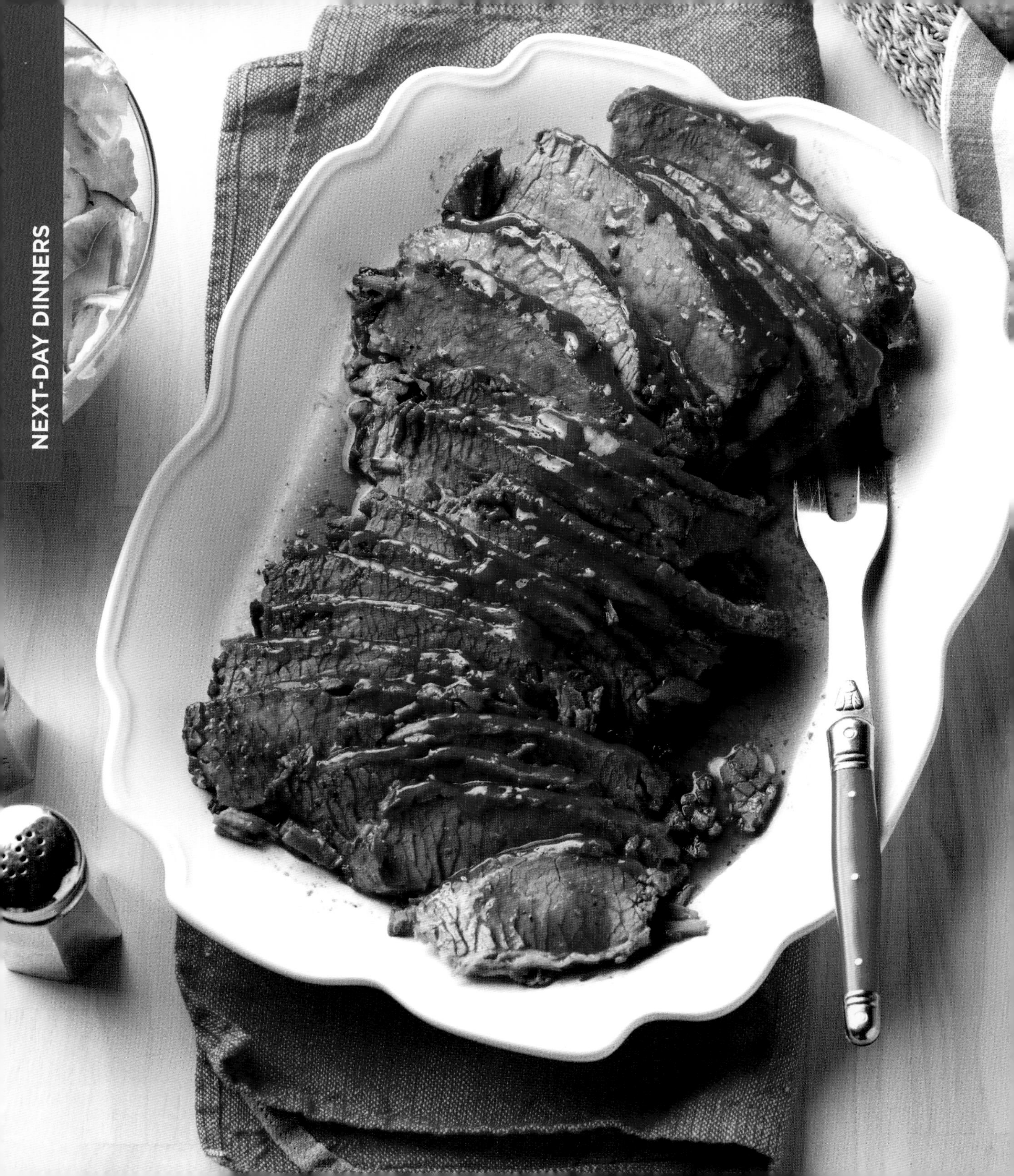

OVEN-BAKED BRISKET

Texans like brisket cooked on the smoker, but this make-ahead recipe offers all the convenience of oven prep.
—*Katie Ferrier, Houston, TX*

- -

Prep: 15 min. + marinating • **Bake:** 4¼ hours
Makes: 8 servings

- 1 fresh beef brisket (4 to 5 lbs.)
- 2 Tbsp. Worcestershire sauce
- 2 Tbsp. soy sauce
- 1 Tbsp. onion salt
- 1 Tbsp. liquid smoke
- 2 tsp. salt
- 2 tsp. pepper
  Dash hot pepper sauce

SAUCE
- ½ cup ketchup
- 3 Tbsp. brown sugar
- 1 Tbsp. lemon juice
- 1 Tbsp. soy sauce
- 1 tsp. ground mustard
- 3 drops hot pepper sauce
  Dash ground nutmeg

1. Place the brisket, fat side down, in a 13x9-in. baking dish. In a small bowl, mix Worcestershire sauce, soy sauce, onion salt, liquid smoke, salt, pepper and pepper sauce; pour over brisket. Turn brisket fat side up; refrigerate, covered, overnight.

2. Remove the brisket from the refrigerator. Preheat oven to 300°. Bake, covered, for 4 hours. In a small bowl, combine the sauce ingredients. Spread over the brisket. Bake, uncovered, 15-30 minutes longer or until tender. Cut diagonally across the grain into thin slices.

Note: This is a fresh beef brisket, not corned beef.

6 oz. cooked beef: 334 cal., 10g fat (4g sat. fat), 97mg chol., 1922mg sod., 11g carb. (10g sugars, 0 fiber), 48g pro.

RANCH-MARINATED CHICKEN BREASTS

The pub-favorite pairing of ranch dressing and chicken comes home to your kitchen. With a little prep time the night before, you can have these savory chicken breasts ready in about half an hour.
—*Barbee Decker, Whispering Pines, NC*

- -

Prep: 10 min. + marinating • **Bake:** 25 min.
Makes: 6 servings

- 2 cups sour cream
- 1 envelope ranch salad dressing mix
- 4 tsp. lemon juice
- 4 tsp. Worcestershire sauce
- 2 tsp. celery salt
- 2 tsp. paprika
- 1 tsp. garlic salt
- 1 tsp. pepper
- 6 boneless skinless chicken breast halves (6 oz. each)
- ¼ cup butter, melted

1. Combine first 8 ingredients in a large shallow dish. Add the chicken; turn to coat. Refrigerate, covered, for 8 hours or overnight.

2. Drain chicken, discarding marinade. Place chicken in a greased 15x10x1-in. baking pan. Drizzle with butter. Bake, uncovered, at 350° for 25-30 minutes or until a thermometer reads 165°.

1 chicken breast half : 421 cal., 28g fat (15g sat. fat), 133mg chol., 733mg sod., 5g carb. (3g sugars, 0 fiber), 37g pro.

SHRIMP & CRAB CASSEROLE

This is a great make-ahead entree. Just assemble, cover and refrigerate, then bake when ready. The melt-in-your-mouth specialty is comforting, easy and elegant.
—*Jan Bartley, Evergreen, NC*

- -

Prep: 25 min. • **Bake:** 40 min.
Makes: 8 servings

- 2 pkg. (8.8 oz. each) ready-to-serve long grain and wild rice
- ¼ cup butter, cubed
- 2 celery ribs, chopped
- 1 medium onion, chopped
- 3 Tbsp. all-purpose flour
- 1½ cups half-and-half cream
- 1 tsp. seafood seasoning
- ¾ tsp. salt
- ½ tsp. hot pepper sauce
- ¼ tsp. pepper
- 1½ lbs. uncooked shrimp (31-40 per lb.), peeled and deveined
- 2 cans (6 oz. each) lump crabmeat, drained
- 1 cup shredded Colby-Monterey Jack cheese

1. Preheat oven to 350°. Spread rice into a greased 13x9-in. baking dish. In a large skillet, heat butter over medium-high heat. Add celery and onion; cook and stir until tender, 6-8 minutes. Stir in the flour until blended; gradually whisk in cream. Bring to a boil, stirring constantly; cook and stir until thickened, 1-2 minutes.

2. Stir in seafood seasoning, salt, pepper sauce and pepper. Fold in shrimp and crab. Spoon over rice. Sprinkle with cheese. Bake, covered, 40-45 minutes or until shrimp turn pink. Let stand 5 minutes.

To Make Ahead: Prepare recipe as directed, cooling sauce slightly before adding shrimp and crab. Cover and refrigerate overnight. Remove from the refrigerator 30 minutes before baking. Bake as directed.

1 serving: 376 cal., 17g fat (10g sat. fat), 195mg chol., 1127mg sod., 24g carb. (3g sugars, 1g fiber), 29g pro.

PERFECT-EVERY-THYME CHICKEN

I prepare this often because I can assemble the marinade one day, and grill it the next. Everyone is pleased with the fantastic flavor. It really is perfect every time!
—*Wayne Snyder, Dalton, GA*

- -

Prep: 5 min. + marinating • **Grill:** 10 min.
Makes: 6 servings

½ cup honey
½ cup olive oil
1 Tbsp. dried thyme
1 tsp. garlic salt
6 boneless skinless chicken breast halves (4 oz. each)

1. In a small saucepan, combine the first 4 ingredients; cook and stir over low heat. Bring to a boil (mixture will foam). Remove from the heat; cool.
2. Pour into a large shallow dish; add chicken and turn to coat. Cover and refrigerate overnight.
3. Drain the chicken, discarding marinade. Grill the chicken, uncovered, over low heat for 5-8 minutes on each side or until a thermometer reads 165°.

1 chicken breast half: 210 cal., 9g fat (2g sat. fat), 63mg chol., 170mg sod., 8g carb. (8g sugars, 0 fiber), 23g pro. **Diabetic exchanges:** 3 lean meat, 1 fat, ½ starch.

NEXT-DAY DINNERS

STEAKS WITH CUCUMBER SAUCE

This recipe combines my family's favorite flavors. Steaks marinated in teriyaki sauce are accompanied by a creamy herbed cucumber sauce.
—*Erika Aylward, Clinton, MI*

Prep: 10 min. + marinating • **Grill:** 10 min.
Makes: 4 servings

- 4 boneless beef New York strip steaks (8 to 10 oz. each)
- ¾ cup teriyaki sauce
- ½ cup chopped seeded peeled cucumber
- ½ cup sour cream
- ½ cup mayonnaise
- 1 Tbsp. minced chives
- ½ to 1 tsp. dill weed
- ¼ tsp. salt

1. Place steaks in a shallow dish; add teriyaki sauce and turn steaks to coat. Cover; refrigerate overnight. In a bowl, combine the cucumber, sour cream, mayonnaise, chives, dill and salt. Cover and refrigerate.
2. Drain steaks, discarding marinade. Grill steaks, covered, over medium-hot heat for 4-5 minutes on each side or until meat reaches desired doneness (for medium-rare, a thermometer should read 135°; medium, 140°; medium-well, 145°). Serve with cucumber sauce.

1 steak with ⅓ cup sauce: 544 calories, 35g fat (10g sat. fat), 101mg chol., 912mg sod., 3g carb. (3g sugars, 0 fiber), 50g pro.

PRESSURE-COOKER BOEUF BOURGUIGNON

I've wanted to make beef Burgundy ever since I got one of Julia Child's cookbooks, but I wanted to find a way to fix it in a pressure cooker. My version of the popular beef stew is still rich, hearty and delicious, but without the need to watch it on the stovetop or in the oven.
—*Crystal Jo Bruns, Iliff, CO*

- -

Prep: 30 min. + marinating
Cook: 35 min. + releasing
Makes: 12 servings

3	lbs. beef stew meat
1¾	cups dry red wine
3	Tbsp. olive oil
3	Tbsp. dried minced onion
2	Tbsp. dried parsley flakes
1	bay leaf
1	tsp. dried thyme
¼	tsp. pepper
8	bacon strips, chopped
1	lb. whole fresh mushrooms, quartered
24	pearl onions, peeled (about 2 cups)
2	garlic cloves, minced
⅓	cup all-purpose flour
1	tsp. salt
	Hot cooked whole wheat egg noodles, optional

1. Place beef in a large shallow dish; add wine, oil and seasonings. Turn beef to coat. Cover and refrigerate overnight.
2. Select saute setting on a 6-qt. electric pressure cooker and adjust for medium heat. Add bacon; cook until crisp, stirring occasionally. Remove with a slotted spoon; drain on paper towels. Discard drippings, reserving 1 Tbsp. in pressure cooker.
3. Add mushrooms and onions to drippings; cook and stir until tender. Add garlic; cook 1 minute longer. Press cancel.
4. Drain beef, reserving marinade. Add beef to the pressure cooker. Sprinkle beef with flour and salt; toss to coat. Top with bacon; add reserved marinade.
5. Lock lid; close pressure-release valve. Adjust to pressure-cook on high for 20 minutes. Let pressure release naturally for 10 minutes, then quick-release any remaining pressure.
6. Select saute setting and adjust for low heat. Simmer, uncovered, until the sauce reaches desired thickness, 15-20 minutes. Remove bay leaf. If desired, serve stew with hot cooked noodles.

⅔ cup beef mixture: 289 cal., 15g fat (5g sat. fat), 77mg chol., 350mg sod., 8g carb. (2g sugars, 1g fiber), 25g pro. **Diabetic exchanges:** 3 lean meat, 1½ fat, 1 vegetable.

MAKE-AHEAD LASAGNA

This is an old standby that's actually a combo of several easy lasagna recipes.
—*Mary Grimm, Williamsburg, IA*

- -

Prep: 35 min. + chilling
Bake: 55 min. + standing
Makes: 12 servings

- 1 lb. ground beef
- 1 lb. bulk hot Italian sausage
- 2 cups marinara sauce
- 1 can (15 oz.) pizza sauce
- 2 large eggs, lightly beaten
- 1 carton (15 oz.) whole-milk ricotta cheese
- ½ cup grated Parmesan cheese
- 1 Tbsp. dried parsley flakes
- ½ tsp. pepper
- 12 no-cook lasagna noodles
- 4 cups shredded part-skim mozzarella cheese

1. In a large skillet, cook and crumble beef and sausage over medium-high heat until no longer pink; drain. Stir in marinara and pizza sauces. In a bowl, mix eggs, ricotta cheese, Parmesan cheese, parsley and pepper.
2. Spread 1 cup meat sauce into a greased 13x9-in. baking dish. Layer with 4 noodles, half of the ricotta cheese mixture, 1 cup meat sauce and 1 cup mozzarella cheese. Repeat the layers. Top with the remaining noodles, meat sauce and mozzarella cheese. Refrigerate, covered, for 8 hours or overnight.
3. Preheat oven to 375°. Remove lasagna from refrigerator while oven heats. Bake, covered, 45 minutes. Bake, uncovered, until cheese is melted, 10-15 minutes. Let stand 10 minutes before cutting.
1 piece: 462 cal., 27g fat (12g sat. fat), 117mg chol., 931mg sod., 26g carb. (7g sugars, 2g fiber), 30g pro.

5i

OVERNIGHT TERIYAKI PORK

I use fresh rosemary and wine to marinate pork chops. It takes time, so plan ahead. The chops are excellent with noodles tossed in parsley.
—*Jane Whittaker, Pensacola, FL*

- -

Prep: 10 min. + marinating • **Bake:** 20 min.
Makes: 4 servings

- 1 cup reduced-sodium teriyaki sauce
- ¾ cup sweet white wine
- ¼ cup packed brown sugar
- 2 Tbsp. minced fresh rosemary or 2 tsp. dried rosemary, crushed
- 4 bone-in pork loin chops (1 in. thick and 10 oz. each)

1. In a 13x9-in. baking dish, mix the teriyaki sauce, wine, brown sugar and rosemary until blended. Add pork; turn to coat. Refrigerate, covered, at least 4 hours.
2. Remove from refrigerator 30 minutes before baking. Preheat oven to 350°.
3. Bake for 20-25 minutes or until a thermometer reads 145°. Let stand 5 minutes before serving.
1 pork chop with ½ cup sauce: 549 cal., 23g fat (9g sat. fat), 139mg chol., 1382mg sod., 27g carb. (26g sugars, 0g fiber), 49g pro.

OVEN-FRIED CHICKEN DRUMSTICKS

This fabulous recipe uses Greek yogurt to create an amazing marinade that makes the chicken incredibly moist. No one will guess the drumsticks are not actually fried. They are a, smart, easy and healthy take on an all-time favorite.

—*Kimberly Wallace, Dennison, OH*

- -

Prep: 20 min. + marinating • **Bake:** 40 min.
Makes: 4 servings

- 1 cup fat-free plain Greek yogurt
- 1 Tbsp. Dijon mustard
- 2 garlic cloves, minced
- 8 chicken drumsticks (4 oz. each), skin removed
- ½ cup whole wheat flour
- 1½ tsp. paprika
- 1 tsp. baking powder
- 1 tsp. salt
- 1 tsp. pepper
  Olive oil-flavored cooking spray

1. In a large bowl, combine yogurt, mustard and garlic. Add chicken and turn to coat. Refrigerate, covered, 8 hours or overnight.

2. Preheat oven to 425°. In another bowl, mix flour, paprika, baking powder, salt and pepper. Remove chicken from marinade and add, 1 piece at a time, to flour mixture; toss to coat. Place on a wire rack over a baking sheet; spritz with cooking spray. Bake 40-45 minutes or until a thermometer reads 170°-175°.

2 chicken drumsticks: 227 cal., 7g fat (1g sat. fat), 81mg chol., 498mg sod., 9g carb. (2g sugars, 1g fiber), 31g pro. **Diabetic exchanges:** 4 lean meat, ½ starch.

TEST KITCHEN TIP

To prepare in air fryer: Preheat air fryer to 375°. Place coated chicken in a single layer in air-fryer basket sprayed with cooking spray. Air-fry until a thermometer reads 170°, about 20 minutes, turning halfway. Repeat with remaining chicken. When the last batch of chicken is cooked, return all chicken to basket and air-fry 2-3 minutes longer to heat through.

BIG DADDY'S BBQ RIBS

There's nothing left on the platter when I make these tender ribs. The spices and brown sugar make an excellent rub.
—*Eric Brzostek, East Islip, NY*

- -

Prep: 30 min. + chilling • **Bake:** 1½ hours
Makes: 8 servings

- ¾ cup packed brown sugar
- 2 Tbsp. mesquite seasoning
- 4½ tsp. garlic powder
- 4½ tsp. paprika
- 1 Tbsp. dried minced onion
- 1 Tbsp. seasoned salt
- 1 Tbsp. ground cinnamon
- 1 Tbsp. ground cumin
- 1 Tbsp. pepper
- 1 tsp. salt
- 8 lbs. pork spareribs, cut into serving size pieces
- 3½ cups barbecue sauce

1. In a small bowl, combine the first 10 ingredients. Rub over ribs; cover and refrigerate overnight.

2. Place ribs bone side down on a rack in a shallow roasting pan. Cover and bake at 350° for 1 hour; drain. Brush some of the barbecue sauce over ribs. Bake, uncovered, for 30-45 minutes or until tender, basting occasionally with barbecue sauce.

1 serving: 1027 cal., 67g fat (24g sat. fat), 255mg chol., 2071mg sod., 40g carb. (35g sugars, 3g fiber), 64g pro.

LISA'S ALL-DAY SUGAR & SALT PORK ROAST

My family loves this tender, juicy roast, so we eat it a lot. The salty crust is so delicious mixed into the pulled pork. Best of all, it cooks to perfection on its own, leaving me plenty of time to do other things.
—*Lisa Allen, Joppa, AL*

Prep: 15 min. + marinating • **Cook:** 6¼ hours
Makes: 12 servings

- 1 cup plus 1 Tbsp. sea salt, divided
- 1 cup sugar
- 1 bone-in pork shoulder butt roast (6 to 8 lbs.)
- ¼ cup barbecue seasoning
- ½ tsp. pepper
- ½ cup packed brown sugar
- 12 hamburger buns or kaiser rolls, split

1. Combine 1 cup sea salt and granulated sugar; rub onto all sides of roast. Place in a shallow dish; refrigerate, covered, overnight.
2. Preheat oven to 300°. Using a kitchen knife, scrape salt and sugar coating from roast; discard any accumulated juices. Transfer pork to a large shallow roasting pan. Rub with barbecue seasoning; sprinkle with pepper. Roast until tender, 6-8 hours.
3. Increase oven temperature to 500°. Combine brown sugar and 1 Tbsp. sea salt; sprinkle over cooked pork. Return pork to oven and roast until a crisp crust forms, 10-15 minutes. Remove; when cool enough to handle, shred meat with 2 forks. Serve warm on fresh buns or rolls.
1 sandwich: 534 cal., 24g fat (9g sat. fat), 135mg chol., 2240mg sod., 33g carb. (14g sugars, 1g fiber), 43g pro.

BEEF SHORT RIBS VINDALOO

My sister shared this dish with me, and I've made a few modifications to fit my tastes. I love the smell of it simmering in the slow cooker all day long.

—*Lorraine Carlstrom, Nelson, BC*

Prep: 30 min. + marinating • **Cook:** 8¼ hours
Makes: 4 servings

- 1 **Tbsp. cumin seeds**
- 2 **tsp. coriander seeds**
- 1 **Tbsp. butter**
- 1 **medium onion, finely chopped**
- 8 **garlic cloves, minced**
- 1 **Tbsp. minced fresh gingerroot**
- 2 **tsp. mustard seed**
- ½ **tsp. ground cloves**
- ¼ **tsp. kosher salt**
- ¼ **tsp. ground cinnamon**
- ¼ **tsp. cayenne pepper**
- ½ **cup red wine vinegar**
- 4 **bay leaves**
- 2 **lbs. bone-in beef short ribs**
- 1 **cup fresh sugar snap peas, halved**
 Hot cooked rice and plain yogurt

1. In a dry small skillet over medium heat, toast cumin and coriander seeds until aromatic, stirring frequently. Cool. Coarsely crush seeds in a spice grinder or with a mortar and pestle.

2. In a large saucepan, heat butter over medium heat. Add the onion, garlic and ginger; cook and stir for 1 minute. Add the mustard seed, cloves, salt, cinnamon, cayenne pepper and crushed seeds; cook and stir 1 minute longer. Cool completely.

3. In a large shallow dish, combine the vinegar, bay leaves and onion mixture. Add the short ribs; turn to coat. Cover and refrigerate overnight.

4. Transfer the rib mixture to a 4-qt. slow cooker. Cover and cook on low until meat is tender, 8-10 hours. Stir in peas; cook until peas are crisp-tender, 8-10 minutes longer. Skim fat; discard bay leaves. Serve rib mixture with rice and yogurt.

1 serving: 266 cal., 15g fat (6g sat. fat), 62mg chol., 180mg sod., 13g carb. (4g sugars, 3g fiber), 21g pro.

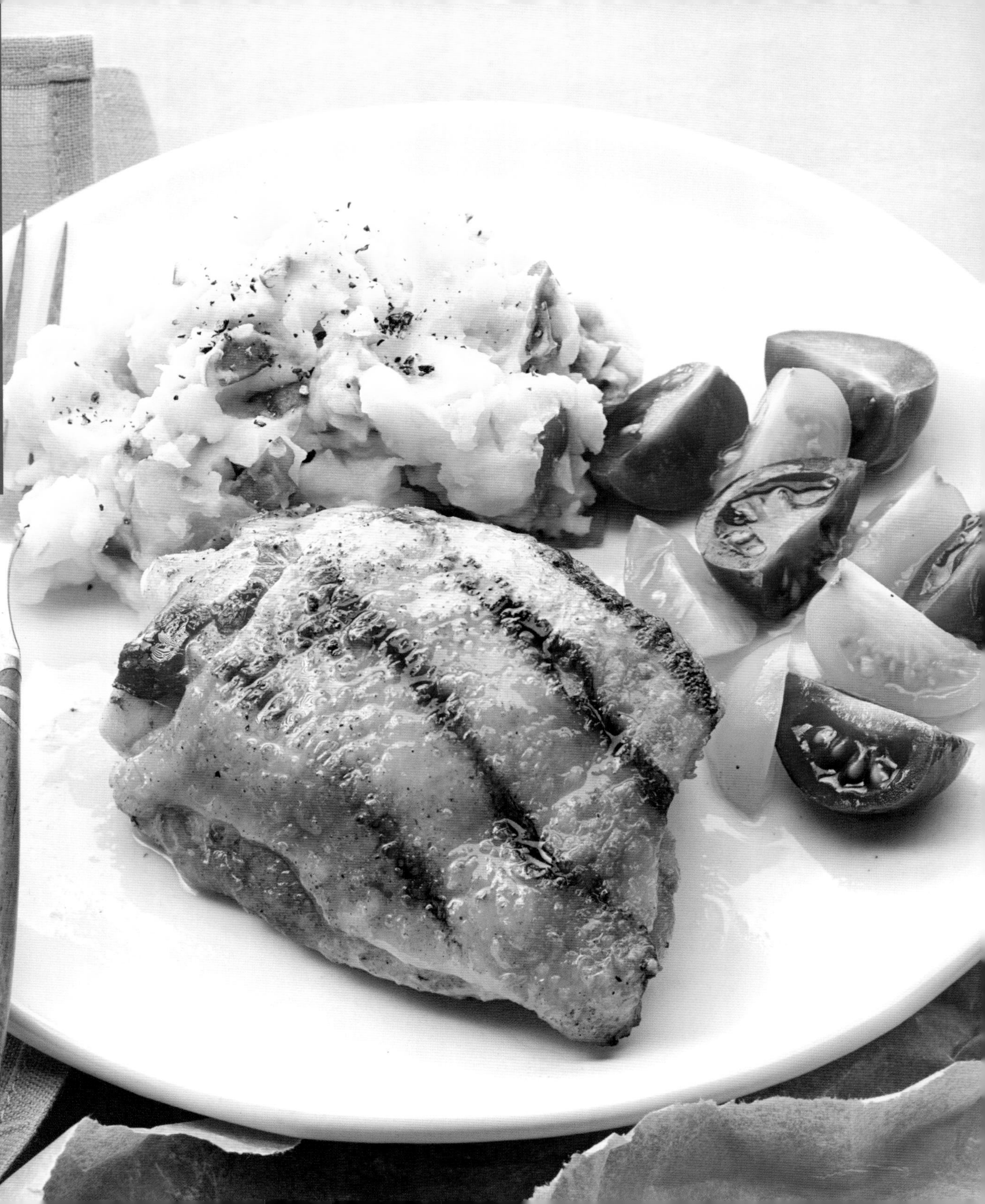

CHIPOTLE-LIME CHICKEN THIGHS

Take meal planning to new heights with this dish. Use the leftover chicken bones to make your own stock and freeze remaining chipotle peppers and sauce for a smoky chili on lazy Sundays.
—Nancy Brown, Dahinda, IL

- -

Prep: 15 min. + chilling • **Grill:** 20 min.
Makes: 4 servings

- 2 garlic cloves, peeled
- ¾ tsp. salt
- 1 Tbsp. lime juice
- 1 Tbsp. minced chipotle pepper in adobo sauce
- 2 tsp. adobo sauce
- 1 tsp. chili powder
- 4 bone-in chicken thighs (about 1½ lbs.)

1. Place garlic on a cutting board; sprinkle with salt. Using the flat side of a knife, mash garlic. Continue to mash until it reaches a paste consistency; transfer to a small bowl.
2. Stir in the lime juice, pepper, adobo sauce and chili powder. Gently loosen skin from chicken thighs; rub garlic mixture under skin. Cover and refrigerate overnight.
3. On a lightly oiled grill rack, grill chicken, covered, over medium-low heat until a thermometer reads 170°-175°, turning once, 20-25 minutes. Remove and discard skin before serving.
1 chicken thigh: 209 cal., 11g fat (3g sat. fat), 87mg chol., 596mg sod., 2g carb. (1g sugars, 0 fiber), 25g pro. **Diabetic exchanges:** 3 lean meat.

SLOW-COOKER CHAR SIU PORK

I based this juicy pork on the influence of Asian flavors here in Hawaii. It's tasty as is, in a bun, over rice, or with fried rice, ramen and salads.
—Karen Naihe, Kamuela, HI

- -

Prep: 25 min. + marinating • **Cook:** 5 hours
Makes: 8 servings

- ½ cup honey
- ½ cup hoisin sauce
- ¼ cup soy sauce
- ¼ cup ketchup
- 4 garlic cloves, minced
- 4 tsp. minced fresh gingerroot
- 1 tsp. Chinese five-spice powder
- 1 boneless pork shoulder butt roast (3 to 4 lbs.)
- ½ cup chicken broth
  Fresh cilantro leaves

1. Combine first 7 ingredients; pour into a large shallow dish. Add pork; turn to coat. Cover and refrigerate overnight.
2. Transfer pork and marinade to a 4-qt. slow cooker. Cook, covered, 5-6 hours on low or until tender. Remove; when cool enough to handle, shred meat using 2 forks. Skim fat from cooking juices; stir in chicken broth. Return pork to slow cooker and heat through. Top with fresh cilantro.
4 oz. cooked pork: 392 cal., 18g fat (6g sat. fat), 102mg chol., 981mg sod., 27g carb. (24g sugars, 1g fiber), 31g pro.

FLANK STEAK SPINACH SALAD

Years ago, a friend gave me the idea for this recipe, and with some tweaking, it's become a favorite of ours

—*Freddie Johnson, San Antonio, TX*

Prep: 15 min. + marinating
Grill: 15 min. + standing
Makes: 16 servings

- 4 **beef flank steaks (about 1 lb. each)**
- 1 **bottle (16 oz.) Italian salad dressing, divided**
- 1¼ **cups uncooked wild rice**
- 2 **pkg. (6 oz. each) fresh baby spinach**
- ½ **lb. fresh mushrooms, sliced**
- 1 **large red onion, thinly sliced**
- 1 **pint grape tomatoes, halved**
- 1 **pkg. (2½ oz.) slivered almonds, toasted**

1. Place steaks in a shallow dish; add ¾ cup salad dressing and turn to coat. Cover and refrigerate overnight. Prepare the rice according to package directions. In a bowl, combine rice with ½ cup salad dressing. Cover and refrigerate overnight.

2. Drain steaks, discarding marinade. Grill steaks, uncovered, over medium heat for 6-8 minutes on each side or until meat reaches desired doneness (for medium-rare, a thermometer should read 135°; medium, 140°; medium-well, 145°). Let stand for 10 minutes. Thinly slice against the grain; cool to room temperature.

3. To serve, arrange spinach on a platter. Top with the rice, mushrooms, onion, tomatoes and steak. Sprinkle with almonds; drizzle with remaining salad dressing.

1 serving: 305 cal., 15g fat (4g sat. fat), 54mg chol., 348mg sod., 15g carb. (3g sugars, 2g fiber), 26g pro.

CRANBERRY CHIPOTLE CHICKEN ENCHILADAS

A little bit sweet, a little bit smoky, these enchiladas are a delightful way to use up leftover chicken or turkey.
—*Julie Peterson, Crofton, MD*

- -

Prep: 30 min. • **Bake:** 30 min.
Makes: 8 servings

2½ cups shredded cooked
    chicken or turkey
1 can (15 oz.) black beans,
    rinsed and drained
1 cup (4 oz.) shredded
    reduced-fat Colby-Monterey
    Jack cheese, divided
1 can (14 oz.) whole-berry
    cranberry sauce, divided
½ cup reduced-fat sour cream
1½ cups salsa, divided
4 green onions, sliced
¼ cup minced fresh cilantro
1 to 2 Tbsp. finely chopped chipotle
    peppers in adobo sauce
1 tsp. ground cumin
1 tsp. chili powder
½ tsp. pepper
8 whole wheat tortilla or flour
    tortillas (8 in.), warmed

1. Preheat oven to 350°. Combine chicken, beans, ¾ cup shredded cheese, ⅔ cup cranberry sauce, sour cream, ½ cup salsa, green onions, cilantro, chipotle peppers, cumin, chili powder and pepper. Place ¾ cup turkey mixture off center on each tortilla. Roll up and place in a greased 13x9-in. baking dish, seam side down.

2. Combine the remaining salsa and cranberry sauce; pour over enchiladas. Cover and bake 25 minutes. Uncover and sprinkle with remaining cheese. Bake until cheese is melted, 5-10 minutes longer.

To Make Ahead: Cover and refrigerate unbaked enchiladas overnight. Remove from refrigerator 30 minutes before baking. Preheat oven to 350°. Cover dish with foil; bake as directed, increasing covered time to 35-40 minutes or until heated through and a thermometer inserted in center reads 165°. Uncover; sprinkle with remaining cheese. Bake until the cheese is melted, 5-10 minutes longer.

1 enchilada: 368 cal., 6g fat (3g sat. fat), 53mg chol., 623mg sod., 54g carb. (15g sugars, 6g fiber), 24g pro.

TEST KITCHEN TIP
Warming the tortillas before filling helps to make them more pliable. If your tortillas are already soft, there's no need to heat them up.

GRILLED PORK NOODLE SALAD

The only complex thing about this entree is the flavor! With smoky barbecued pork and a variety of herbs and vegetables, this is a comforting and tasty home-cooked meal.
—*Rosalyn Nguyen, Astoria, NY*

Prep: 40 min. + marinating • **Grill:** 5 min.
Makes: 6 servings

- 1   jalapeno pepper, seeded and minced
- 3   Tbsp. lime juice
- 2   Tbsp. fish sauce or soy sauce
- 2   tsp. brown sugar
- 2   pork tenderloins (¾ lb. each), cut into ½-in. slices
- 1   pkg. (8.8 oz.) vermicelli-style thin rice noodles

DRESSING
- ¼   cup water
- 2   Tbsp. lime juice
- 1   Tbsp. fish sauce or soy sauce
- ½   tsp. brown sugar

SALAD
- 2   cups shredded lettuce
- 2   plum tomatoes, sliced
- 1   medium cucumber, julienned
- 2   medium carrots, julienned
- ½   cup coarsely chopped fresh cilantro
- ¼   cup loosely packed fresh mint leaves

1. In a large shallow dish, combine jalapeno, lime juice, fish sauce and brown sugar. Add pork; turn to coat. Cover and refrigerate 3 hours or overnight.

2. Drain pork, discarding marinade. On a lightly oiled grill rack, grill pork, covered, over medium heat 1-2 minutes on each side or until a thermometer reads 145°.

3. Cook rice noodles according to package directions. Drain and rinse in cold water; drain well. In a small bowl, whisk dressing ingredients. Divide rice noodles among 6 serving bowls. Arrange vegetables, pork and herbs over noodles; drizzle with dressing and toss to combine.

Note: Wear disposable gloves when cutting hot peppers; the oils can burn skin. Avoid touching your face.

1 serving: 315 cal., 4g fat (1g sat. fat), 64mg chol., 708mg sod., 40g carb. (3g sugars, 3g fiber), 27g pro. **Diabetic exchanges:** 3 lean meat, 2 starch, 1 vegetable.

HAM & PINEAPPLE KABOBS

These tangy kabobs cook in the oven for a tasty change-of-pace main course. The marinade gets its unique zip from hoisin, teriyaki and soy sauces.
—*Chandra Lane Sirois, Kansas City, MO*

- -

Prep: 30 min. + marinating • **Bake:** 15 min.
Makes: 12 servings

- ¼ cup hoisin sauce
- ¼ cup unsweetened pineapple juice
- ¼ cup teriyaki sauce
- 1 Tbsp. honey
- 1½ tsp. rice vinegar
- 1½ tsp. reduced-sodium soy sauce

KABOBS
- 2 lbs. fully cooked boneless ham, cut into 1-in. pieces
- 1 large fresh pineapple, peeled, cored and cut into 1-in. cubes (about 4 cups)

1. In a large shallow dish, combine the first 6 ingredients. Add ham; turn to coat. Cover and refrigerate overnight.
2. Preheat oven to 350°. Drain the ham, reserving marinade. For the glaze, pour marinade into a small saucepan; bring to a boil. Reduce heat; simmer, uncovered, 5-7 minutes or until slightly thickened, stirring occasionally. Remove from heat.
3. On 12 metal or soaked wooden skewers, alternately thread ham and pineapple; place in a foil-lined 15x10x1-in. baking pan. Brush with glaze. Bake, uncovered, 15-20 minutes or until lightly browned.

1 kabob: 144 cal., 3g fat (1g sat. fat), 39mg chol., 1109mg sod., 15g carb. (12g sugars, 1g fiber), 15g pro.

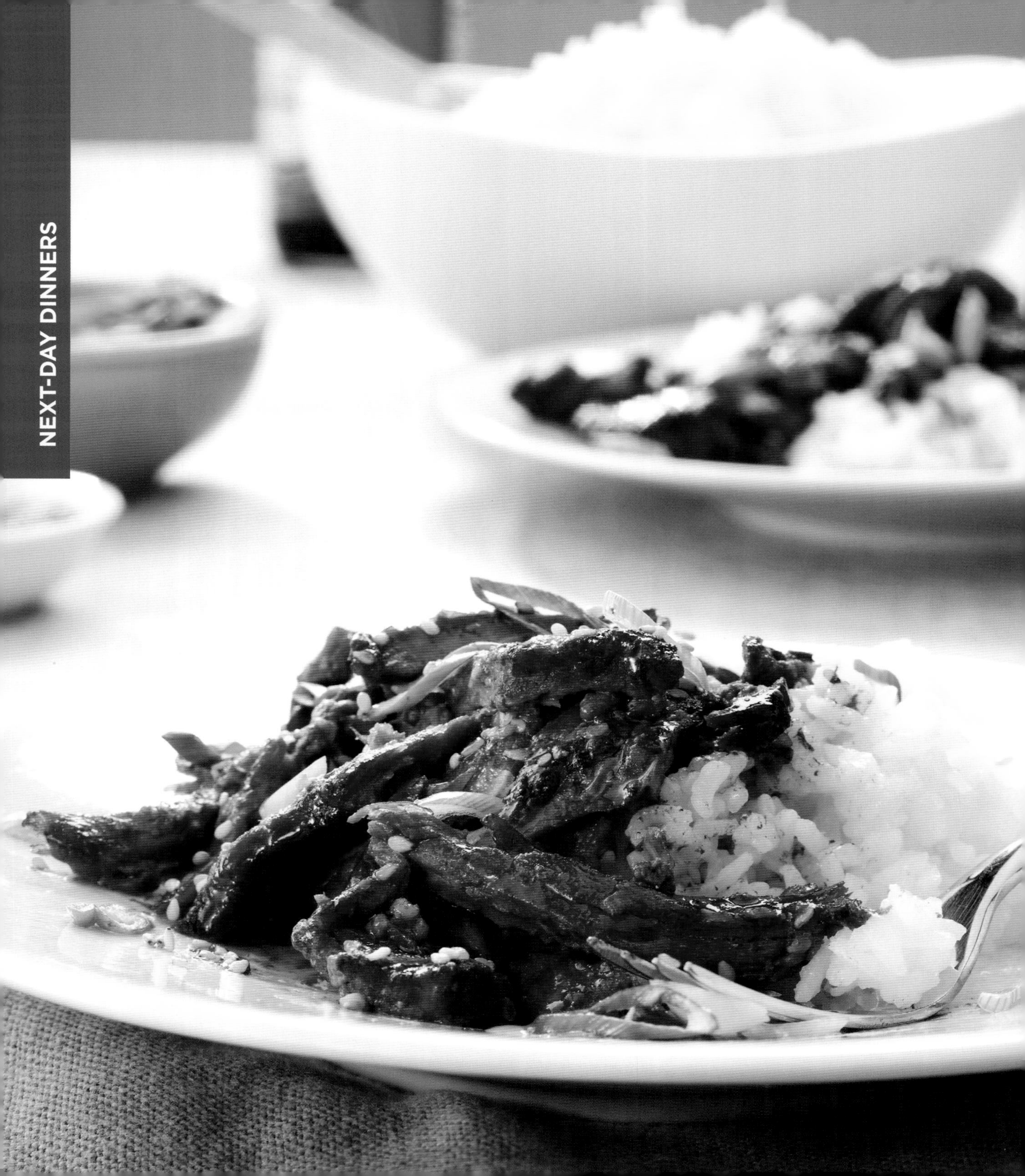

SLOW-COOKER GARLIC-SESAME BEEF

My mom received this marinade recipe from a neighbor while she lived in Seoul, South Korea, which is where I was adopted from. Mom created heritage night for my brother and me, and she served Korean bulgogi with sticky rice, kimchi and chopsticks. As a busy mom of four, I keep her tradition alive but let the slow cooker do the work!
—*Jackie Brown, Fairview, NC*

Prep: 15 min. + marinating • **Cook:** 5 hours
Makes: 6 servings

- 6 green onions, sliced
- ½ cup sugar
- ½ cup water
- ½ cup reduced-sodium soy sauce
- ¼ cup sesame oil
- 3 Tbsp. sesame seeds, toasted
- 2 Tbsp. all-purpose flour
- 4 garlic cloves, minced
- 1 beef sirloin tip roast (3 lbs.), thinly sliced
  Additional sliced green onions and toasted sesame seeds
  Hot cooked rice

1. In a large shallow dish, mix the first 8 ingredients. Add the beef; turn to coat. Cover and refrigerate 8 hours or overnight.
2. Pour beef and marinade into a 3-qt. slow cooker. Cook, covered, on low 5-7 hours or until meat is tender.
3. Using a slotted spoon, remove beef to a serving platter; sprinkle with additional green onions and sesame seeds. Serve with hot cooked rice.
⅔ cup: 384 cal., 16g fat (4g sat. fat), 145mg chol., 471mg sod., 11g carb. (9g sugars, 0 fiber), 47g pro.

GRILLED HULI HULI CHICKEN

I got this grilled chicken recipe from a friend while living in Hawaii. It sizzles with the flavors of brown sugar, ginger and soy sauce. The sweet and savory glaze is fantastic on pork chops, too.
—*Sharon Boling, San Diego, CA*

Prep: 15 min. + marinating • **Grill:** 15 min.
Makes: 12 servings

- 1 cup packed brown sugar
- ¾ cup ketchup
- ¾ cup reduced-sodium soy sauce
- ⅓ cup sherry or chicken broth
- 2½ tsp. minced fresh gingerroot
- 1½ tsp. minced garlic
- 24 boneless skinless chicken thighs (about 5 lbs.)

1. In a small bowl, mix the first 6 ingredients. Reserve 1⅓ cups for basting; cover and refrigerate. Divide remaining marinade between 2 large shallow dishes. Add 12 chicken thighs to each; turn to coat. Cover dishes and refrigerate for 8 hours or overnight.
2. Drain the chicken, discarding marinade.
3. Grill the chicken, covered, on an oiled rack over medium heat for 6-8 minutes on each side or until a thermometer reads 170°; baste occasionally with reserved marinade during the last 5 minutes.
2 chicken thighs: 391 cal., 16g fat (5g sat. fat), 151mg chol., 651mg sod., 15g carb. (14g sugars, 0 fiber), 43g pro.

TEST KITCHEN TIP
This sweet and savory glaze is also fantastic on pork chops.

CRAB-SALAD JUMBO SHELLS

Here's a fun and flavorful way to enjoy chilled crab salad. Serve it over lettuce for a refreshing yet easy meal.
—*Jo Anne Anderson, Knoxville, IA*

- -

Prep: 35 min. + chilling
Makes: 30 stuffed shells

30 uncooked jumbo pasta shells
1 cup finely chopped fresh broccoli florets
1 garlic clove, minced
2 pkg. (8 oz. each) imitation crabmeat, chopped
1 cup sour cream
½ cup mayonnaise
¼ cup finely shredded carrot
¼ cup diced seeded peeled cucumber
1 Tbsp. chopped green onion
1 tsp. dill weed

1. Cook pasta according to the package directions; rinse in cold water and drain well.
2. Meanwhile, in a small microwave-safe bowl, combine the broccoli and garlic. Cover and microwave on high for 1 minute or until crisp-tender.
3. Transfer to a large bowl; stir in the remaining ingredients. Stuff into pasta shells. Cover and refrigerate overnight.
1 stuffed shell: 85 cal., 4g fat (1g sat. fat), 8mg chol., 67mg sod., 9g carb. (1g sugars, 0 fiber), 2g pro.

SLOW-COOKED HERBED TURKEY

I prepare this when herbs are plentiful in my garden. The turkey stays moist in the slow cooker and bursts with herb flavors. It cooks on its own and makes a lot, so you can freeze the extras or use up the cooked poultry in meals later in the week.
—*Sue Jurack, Mequon, WI*

- -

Prep: 15 min. + marinating
Cook: 4 hours + standing
Makes: 16 servings

- 2 cans (14½ oz. each) chicken broth
- 1 cup lemon juice
- ½ cup packed brown sugar
- ½ cup minced fresh sage
- ½ cup minced fresh thyme
- ½ cup lime juice
- ½ cup cider vinegar
- ½ cup olive oil
- 2 envelopes onion soup mix
- ¼ cup Dijon mustard
- 2 Tbsp. minced fresh marjoram
- 3 tsp. paprika
- 2 tsp. garlic powder
- 2 tsp. pepper
- 1 tsp. salt
- 2 boneless skinless turkey breast halves (3 lbs. each)

1. In a blender, combine the first 15 ingredients; cover and process until blended. Pour half the marinade into a bowl; cover and refrigerate. Place turkey breasts in a large, shallow bowl; add the remaining marinade. Turn turkey to coat. Cover and refrigerate overnight, turning occasionally.
2. Drain turkey, discarding marinade. Transfer turkey breasts to a 5-qt. slow cooker. Add reserved marinade; cover and cook on high until a thermometer reads 165°, 4-5 hours. Let stand for 10 minutes before slicing.

5 oz. cooked turkey: 232 cal., 5g fat (1g sat. fat), 97mg chol., 369mg sod., 4g carb. (3g sugars, 0 fiber), 40g pro. **Diabetic exchanges:** 5 lean meat, ½ fat.

WHY YOU'LL LOVE IT:
"This marinade was simple to assemble, and being able to throw the turkey in the slow cooker left me with time to prepare the other dishes."
—LESLIE6479, TASTEOFHOME.COM

SMOKY BRAISED CHUCK ROAST

After tiring of the same sauces, I began experimenting with spices and herbs, coming up with this make-ahead flavor booster. It's excellent with steak, London broil or a roast.

—Karen Brown, Tunkhannock, PA

Prep: 15 min. + marinating • **Bake:** 2½ hours
Makes: 8 servings

    4   tsp. beef bouillon granules
    ¼   cup hot water
    1¾ cups water
    2   Tbsp. brown sugar
    1   tsp. dried rosemary, crushed
    1   tsp. dried basil
    ¾   tsp. dried tarragon
    ½   tsp. garlic powder
    ¼   tsp. dried oregano
        Dash pepper
    ½   tsp. liquid smoke, optional
    1   beef chuck roast (3 to 4 lbs.)

1. In a 13x9-in. baking dish, dissolve the bouillon in hot water. Stir in water, brown sugar, seasonings and, if desired, liquid smoke. Add the beef; turn to coat. Cover and refrigerate overnight.
2. Preheat oven to 325°. Transfer roast to a Dutch oven; pour remaining marinade over top. Bake the roast, covered, 2½-3 hours or until tender.

Freeze option: Place sliced chuck roast in freezer containers; top with cooking juices. Cool and freeze. To use, partially thaw in refrigerator overnight. Microwave, covered, on high, stirring gently and adding broth if necessary, until heated through.

4 oz. cooked beef: 305 cal., 16g fat (6g sat. fat), 111mg chol., 465mg sod., 4g carb. (4g sugars, 0 fiber), 34g pro.

PORK WITH PEACH PICANTE SAUCE

When fresh peaches are in season, I cook these pork ribs for family and friends. I love the recipe because I only need a few ingredients. The slow cooker does most of the work for me and the ribs turn out tender and tasty.

—Connie Jenista, Valrico, FL

Prep: 20 min. + chilling • **Cook:** 5½ hours
Makes: 4 servings

    2   lbs. boneless country-
        style pork ribs
    2   Tbsp. taco seasoning
    ½   cup mild salsa
    ¼   cup peach preserves
    ¼   cup barbecue sauce
    2   cups chopped fresh peeled peaches
        or frozen unsweetened sliced
        peaches, thawed and chopped

1. In a large bowl, toss pork ribs with taco seasoning. Cover and refrigerate overnight.
2. Place pork in a 3-qt. slow cooker. In a small bowl, combine the salsa, preserves and barbecue sauce. Pour over ribs. Cover and cook on low for 5-6 hours or until the meat is tender.
3. Add peaches; cover and cook 30 minutes longer or until peaches are tender.
1 serving: 315 cal., 14g fat (5g sat. fat), 87mg chol., 514mg sod., 18g carb. (13g sugars, 1g fiber), 27g pro.

SPICY AIR-FRYER CHICKEN BREASTS

My family adores this chicken recipe. The coating keeps the chicken nice and moist, and the air fryer makes it oh, so easy.
—*Stephanie Otten, Byron Center, MI*

Prep: 25 min. + marinating
Cook: 20 min./batch • **Makes:** 8 servings

- 2 cups buttermilk
- 2 Tbsp. Dijon mustard
- 2 tsp. salt
- 2 tsp. hot pepper sauce
- 1½ tsp. garlic powder
- 8 bone-in chicken breast halves, skin removed (8 oz. each)
- 2 cups soft bread crumbs
- 1 cup cornmeal
- 2 Tbsp. canola oil
- ½ tsp. poultry seasoning
- ½ tsp. ground mustard
- ½ tsp. paprika
- ½ tsp. cayenne pepper
- ¼ tsp. dried oregano
- ¼ tsp. dried parsley flakes

1. Preheat air fryer to 375°. In a large bowl, combine the first 5 ingredients. Add chicken and turn to coat. Refrigerate, covered, for 1 hour or overnight.

2. Drain the chicken, discarding marinade. Combine remaining ingredients in a shallow dish and stir to combine. Add the chicken, 1 piece at a time, and turn to coat. Place in a single layer in air-fryer basket sprayed with cooking spray. Air-fry until a thermometer reads 170°, about 20 minutes, turning halfway. Repeat with remaining chicken. When the last batch of chicken is cooked, return all chicken to basket and air-fry for 2-3 minutes longer to heat through.

1 chicken breast half: 352 cal., 9g fat (2g sat. fat), 104mg chol., 562mg sod., 23g carb. (3g sugars, 1g fiber), 41g pro.

TEST KITCHEN TIP
In our testing, we have found cook times vary dramatically between brands of air fryers. As a result, we have given wider than normal ranges on suggested cook times. Begin checking at the first time listed and adjust as needed.

5i

ROSEMARY ROASTED LAMB

Who knew so few ingredients could result in such an elegant make-ahead entree? One bite will make this a favorite in your home.
—*Matthew Lawrence, Vashon, WA*

- -

Prep: 10 min. + chilling • **Bake:** 2 hours 5 min.

  ½ **cup olive oil**
  3 **garlic cloves, minced**
  1 **tablespoon kosher salt**
  1 **tablespoon minced fresh rosemary**
  1 **leg of lamb (7 to 9 pounds)**

1. Preheat oven to 425°. In a small bowl, combine the oil, garlic, salt and rosemary; rub over the lamb. Cover and refrigerate overnight. Place lamb, fat side up, on a rack in a shallow roasting pan.
2. Bake, uncovered, 20 minutes. Reduce heat to 350°; bake 1¾-2¼ hours longer or until meat reaches desired doneness (for medium-rare, a thermometer should read 135°; medium, 140°; medium-well, 145°), basting occasionally with pan juices. Let stand 15 minutes before slicing.
1 serving (5 ounces): 357 cal., 21g fat (6g sat. fat), 143mg chol., 629mg sod., 0 carb., 40g pro.

COFFEE-BRAISED ROAST BEEF

The recipe is quick and the meat is tasty flavorful, so it's a nice welcome home.
—*Nancy Schuler, Belle Fourche, SD*

- -

Prep: 10 min. + marinating • **Cook:** 6½ hours
Makes: 10 servings

- 1 cup cider vinegar
- 4 garlic cloves, crushed, divided
- 1 boneless beef chuck roast (4 to 5 lbs.), trimmed
- 2 tsp. salt
- 1 tsp. pepper
- 1 cup strong brewed coffee
- 1 cup beef broth
- 1 medium onion, sliced
- 3 Tbsp. cornstarch
- ¼ cup cold water
  Mashed potatoes

1. In a large shallow dish, combine vinegar and 2 garlic cloves. Add roast; turn to coat. Cover and refrigerate overnight, turning occasionally.
2. Drain roast, discarding marinade. Pat roast dry; sprinkle with salt and pepper. Place roast in a 5- or 6-qt. slow cooker; add coffee, broth, onion and remaining garlic. Cook, covered, on low until the meat is tender, 6-7 hours.
3. Remove roast and keep warm. Strain cooking juices, discarding onion and garlic; skim fat. In a small bowl, mix cornstarch and cold water until smooth; gradually stir into slow cooker. Cook, covered, on high until gravy is thickened, 30 minutes. Slice roast; serve with mashed potatoes and gravy.
5 oz. cooked beef with ½ cup gravy: 324 cal., 17g fat (7g sat. fat), 118mg chol., 636mg sod., 3g carb. (0 sugars, 0 fiber), 36g pro.

LIGHTENED-UP BEEF-STUFFED SHELLS

I love that I can make this meal ahead of time or bake it for dinner right away. Either way, it's a lighter take on a much-loved dish.
—*Blair Lonergan, Rochelle, VA*

- -

Prep: 45 min. + chilling • **Bake:** 45 min.
Makes: 10 servings

- 20 uncooked jumbo pasta shells
- 1 lb. lean ground beef (90% lean)
- 1 large onion, chopped
- 1 medium green pepper, chopped
- 1¼ cups reduced-fat ricotta cheese
- 1½ cups shredded reduced-fat Italian cheese blend, divided
- ¼ cup grated Parmesan cheese
- ¼ cup prepared pesto
- 1 large egg, lightly beaten
- 1 can (14½ oz.) Italian diced tomatoes, undrained
- 1 can (8 oz.) no-salt-added tomato sauce
- 1 tsp. Italian seasoning

1. Cook pasta according to the package directions for al dente; drain and rinse in cold water. In a large skillet, cook the beef, onion and green pepper over medium heat until meat is no longer pink; drain. In a large bowl, combine the ricotta cheese, 1 cup Italian cheese blend, Parmesan cheese, pesto, egg and half of the beef mixture.
2. In a small bowl, combine the tomatoes, tomato sauce and Italian seasoning. Spread ¾ cup into a 13x9-in. baking dish coated with cooking spray. Spoon cheese mixture into pasta shells; place in baking dish. Combine the remaining beef mixture and tomato mixture; spoon over shells. Sprinkle with the remaining cheese. Cover and refrigerate overnight.
3. Remove from the refrigerator 30 minutes before baking. Cover and bake at 350° for 40 minutes. Uncover; bake 5-10 minutes longer or until cheese is melted.
2 stuffed shells: 295 cal., 12g fat (5g sat. fat), 70mg chol., 436mg sod., 23g carb. (7g sugars, 2g fiber), 22g pro. **Diabetic exchanges:** 3 lean meat, 1½ starch, 1 fat.

BOMBAY CHICKEN

This dinner always turns out moist and tender. The marinade has a slightly exotic flair, giving the dish a zesty flavor. It makes a beautiful presentation as well.
—*June Thomas, Chesterton, IN*

- -

Prep: 10 min. + marinating • **Grill:** 25 min.
Makes: 8 servings

1½ **cups plain yogurt**
¼ **cup lemon juice**
2 **Tbsp. chili powder**
2 **Tbsp. paprika**
2 **Tbsp. olive oil**
1½ **tsp. salt**
½ **to 1 tsp. cayenne pepper**
½ **tsp. garlic powder**
¼ **tsp. ground ginger**
¼ **tsp. ground cardamom**
⅛ **tsp. ground cinnamon**
4 **to 5 lbs. bone-in chicken thighs and legs, skin removed**

1. In a large shallow dish, combine the first 11 ingredients. Add the chicken; turn to coat. Refrigerate, covered, overnight.
2. Drain chicken, discarding the marinade.
3. On a lightly oiled grill rack, grill chicken, covered, over medium-hot heat for 10-15 minutes on each side or until a thermometer reads 170°-175°.
1 serving (4 oz.): 255 cal., 13g fat (3g sat. fat), 106mg chol., 344mg sod., 3g carb. (0 sugars, 1g fiber), 31g pro.

HAM & SWISS POTATO CASSEROLE

When I wanted to use up ingredients I had on hand, I started experimenting—and hit a home run! The classic trio of ham, Swiss cheese and potatoes comes together in this comforting bake, which is now one of my go-to recipes.

—*Sarah Wilham, Elkhart, IL*

Prep: 25 min. • **Bake:** 20 min.
Makes: 8 servings

5	large potatoes (about 4 lbs.), peeled and cut into ¾-in. pieces
¼	cup butter, cubed
1	medium onion, chopped
1	garlic clove, minced
⅓	cup all-purpose flour
2	cups 2% milk
1⅓	cups roasted red pepper Alfredo sauce
1	tsp. dried basil
¼	tsp. salt
¼	tsp. dill weed
¼	tsp. pepper
2	cups cubed fully cooked ham
2	cups shredded Swiss cheese
¼	cup seasoned bread crumbs
1	Tbsp. butter, melted

1. Preheat oven to 375°. Place potatoes in a large saucepan; add water to cover. Bring to a boil. Reduce heat; simmer, covered, until crisp-tender, 8-10 minutes. Meanwhile, in a large skillet, heat butter over medium-high heat. Add onion; cook and stir 6-8 minutes or until tender. Add garlic; cook and stir for 1 minute. Stir in the flour until blended; gradually whisk in the milk. Bring to a boil, stirring constantly; cook and stir 1-2 minutes or until thickened. Stir in Alfredo sauce and seasonings; heat through.

2. Drain potatoes; transfer to a greased 13x9-in. baking dish. Layer with ham, cheese and sauce. In a small bowl, combine bread crumbs and butter. Sprinkle over top. Bake, uncovered, 18-22 minutes or until topping is golden brown and cheese is melted. Let stand 5 minutes before serving.

To Make Ahead: Prepare the recipe as directed, layering ham, cheese and sauce in baking dish. Cover and refrigerate overnight. Remove from the refrigerator 30 minutes before baking. Prepare crumb topping; sprinkle over top. Bake as directed.

1 serving: 456 cal., 22g fat (13g sat. fat), 93mg chol., 897mg sod., 45g carb. (7g sugars, 3g fiber), 22g pro.

THAI CHICKEN & SLAW

Because of the hint of sweetness from the honey, this one-dish meal has become very popular with my friends and family. I love that I can make it ahead when I have guests.
—*Karen Norris, Philadelphia, PA*

Prep: 25 min. + marinating • **Cook:** 30 min.
Makes: 8 servings

- ½ cup canola oil
- ½ cup white wine vinegar
- ½ cup honey
- 2 Tbsp. minced fresh gingerroot
- 2 Tbsp. reduced-sodium soy sauce
- 2 garlic cloves, minced
- 1 tsp. sesame oil
- 8 boneless skinless chicken thighs (about 2 lbs.)

SLAW
- 6 cups coleslaw mix
- 1 cup frozen shelled edamame, thawed
- 1 medium sweet pepper, chopped
- 1 Tbsp. creamy peanut butter
- ½ tsp. salt
- 4 green onions, sliced

1. In a small bowl, whisk first 7 ingredients until blended. Pour 1 cup marinade into a bowl or shallow dish. Add chicken and turn to coat. Refrigerate, covered, overnight. Cover and refrigerate remaining marinade.
2. Preheat oven to 350°. Drain chicken, discarding marinade from the bowl. Place chicken in a 13x9-in. baking dish coated with cooking spray. Bake, uncovered, until a thermometer reads 170°, 30-40 minutes.
3. Meanwhile, place coleslaw mix, edamame and pepper in a large bowl. Add the peanut butter and salt to reserved marinade; whisk until blended. Pour over coleslaw mixture; toss to coat. Refrigerate until serving.
4. Serve chicken with slaw. Sprinkle with green onions.
3 oz. cooked chicken with ⅔ cup slaw: 326 cal., 18g fat (3g sat. fat), 76mg chol., 171mg sod., 16g carb. (12g sugars, 2g fiber), 24g pro. **Diabetic exchanges:** 3 lean meat, 2 fat, 1 vegetable, ½ starch.

BEEF KABOBS WITH CHUTNEY SAUCE

I created this entree for our daughter, a fan of Indian food. The chutney and subtle curry give the beef a sweet and spicy flair.
—*Judy Thompson, Ankeny, IA*

- -

Prep: 15 min. + marinating • **Grill:** 5 min.
Makes: 8 kabobs (about ½ cup sauce)

¼	cup mango chutney
1	Tbsp. water
1	Tbsp. cider vinegar
1	tsp. curry powder
¼	tsp. cayenne pepper
1	lb. beef top sirloin steak, cut into ¼-in. strips

CHUTNEY SAUCE

½	cup plain yogurt
3	Tbsp. mango chutney
1	tsp. lemon juice
½	tsp. curry powder
¼	tsp. ground cumin
⅛	tsp. cayenne pepper

1. In a large shallow dish, combine the first 5 ingredients. Add the beef; turn to coat. Refrigerate, covered, overnight.

2. In a small bowl, combine the sauce ingredients. Cover and refrigerate sauce until serving.

3. Drain beef, discarding the marinade. Thread beef onto 8 metal or soaked wooden skewers.

4. On a lightly oiled grill rack, grill kabobs, covered, over medium heat or broil 4 in. from the heat for 4-6 minutes or until the meat reaches desired doneness, turning occasionally. Serve with the sauce.

2 skewers with 2 Tbsp. sauce: 258 cal., 6g fat (2g sat. fat), 50mg chol., 321mg sod., 23g carb. (15g sugars, 0 fiber), 25g pro. **Diabetic exchanges:** 3 lean meat, 1½ starch.

FREEZER MEAL PREPS

SIMPLIFY LIFE WITH FREEZER-TO-TABLE
FAVORITES ANY TIME OF DAY.

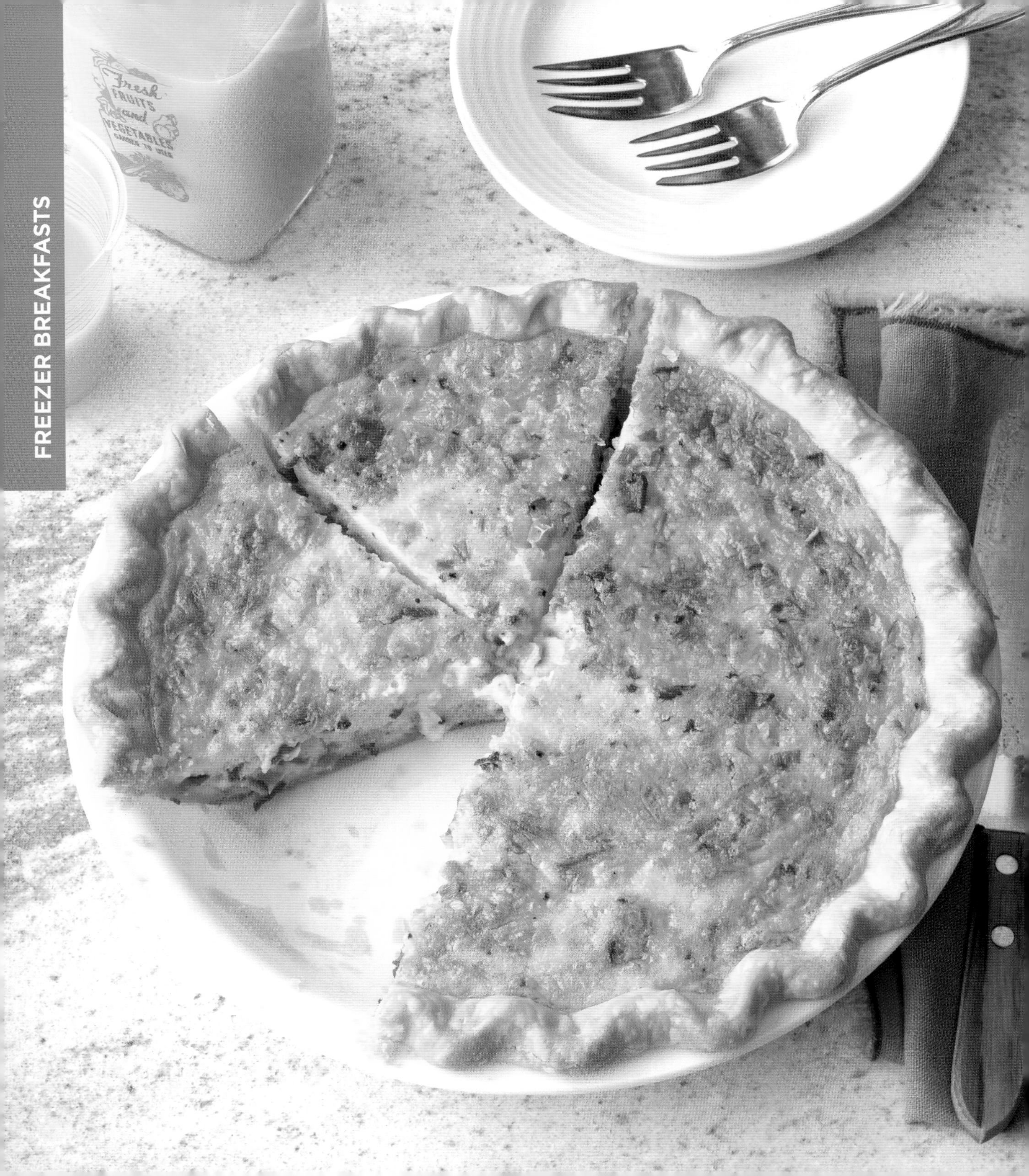
Fresh
FRUITS
and
VEGETABLES

❄ BACON SWISS QUICHE

With a quiche like this, you don't need a lot of heavy side dishes. It's got everything on the inside!
—*Colleen Belbey, Warwick, RI*

Prep: 15 min. • **Bake:** 40 min. + standing
Makes: 6 servings

- 1 sheet refrigerated pie crust
- ¼ cup sliced green onions
- 1 Tbsp. butter
- 6 large eggs
- 1½ cups heavy whipping cream
- ¼ cup unsweetened apple juice
- 1 lb. sliced bacon, cooked and crumbled
- ⅛ tsp. salt
- ⅛ tsp. pepper
- 2 cups shredded Swiss cheese

1. Preheat oven to 350°. Line a 9-in. pie plate with crust; trim and flute edges. Set aside. In a small skillet, saute green onions in butter until tender.
2. In a large bowl, whisk eggs, cream and juice. Stir in bacon, salt, pepper and green onions. Pour into the crust; sprinkle with the cheese.
3. Bake 40-45 minutes or until a knife inserted in the center comes out clean. Let stand 10 minutes before cutting.
Freeze option: Securely wrap individual portions of cooled quiche in plastic wrap and foil; freeze. To use, partially thaw in refrigerator overnight. Remove from refrigerator 30 minutes before baking. Preheat oven to 350°. Unwrap quiche; reheat in oven until heated through and a thermometer inserted in center reads 165°.
1 slice: 739 cal., 60g fat (31g sat. fat), 359mg chol., 781mg sod., 22g carb. (4g sugars, 0 fiber), 27g pro.

🍎 ❄ PIGS IN A POOL

My kids love sausage and pancakes, but making them on a busy weekday was out of the question. My homemade version of pigs in a blanket is a thrifty alternative to the packaged kind, and they freeze like a dream.
—*Lisa Dodd, Greenville, SC*

Prep: 45 min. • **Bake:** 20 min.
Makes: 4 dozen

- 1 lb. reduced-fat bulk pork sausage
- 2 cups all-purpose flour
- ¼ cup sugar
- 1 Tbsp. baking powder
- 1 tsp. salt
- ½ tsp. ground cinnamon
- ¼ tsp. ground nutmeg
- 1 large egg, room temperature, lightly beaten
- 2 cups fat-free milk
- 2 Tbsp. canola oil
- 2 Tbsp. honey
  Maple syrup, optional

1. Preheat oven to 350°. Coat 48 mini muffin cups with cooking spray.
2. Shape sausage into forty-eight ¾-in. balls. Place meatballs on a rack coated with cooking spray in a shallow baking pan. Bake until cooked through, 15-20 minutes. Drain on paper towels. In a large bowl, whisk flour, sugar, baking powder, salt and spices. In another bowl, whisk egg, milk, oil and honey until blended. Add to flour mixture; stir just until moistened.
3. Place a sausage ball in each mini muffin cup; cover with batter. Bake until lightly browned, 20-25 minutes. Cool 5 minutes before removing from pans to wire racks. Serve warm, with syrup if desired.
Freeze option: Freeze cooled muffins in airtight freezer containers. To use, microwave each muffin on high until heated through, 20-30 seconds.
4 mini muffins: 234 cal., 10g fat (3g sat. fat), 45mg chol., 560mg sod., 26g carb. (9g sugars, 1g fiber), 10g pro. **Diabetic exchanges:** 1½ starch, 1 medium-fat meat, ½ fat.

GINGERBREAD BUTTERMILK WAFFLES

Now you can enjoy the heartwarming flavor of gingerbread at breakfast.
—Taste of Home *Test Kitchen*

- -

Takes: 30 min. • **Makes:** 8 waffles

- 1 cup all-purpose flour
- 1½ tsp. baking powder
- 1 tsp. ground ginger
- ¾ tsp. ground cinnamon
- ½ tsp. baking soda
- ¼ tsp. salt
- ⅛ tsp. ground cloves
- ⅓ cup packed brown sugar
- 1 large egg, separated, room temperature
- ¾ cup buttermilk
- ¼ cup molasses
- 3 Tbsp. butter, melted
- ⅛ tsp. cream of tartar
  Confectioners' sugar, optional

1. In a large bowl, combine the first 7 ingredients. In a small bowl, beat the brown sugar and egg yolk until fluffy; add the buttermilk, molasses and butter. Stir into dry ingredients just until combined.
2. In small bowl, beat egg white and cream of tartar until stiff peaks form. Fold into batter. Spoon onto a preheated waffle maker. Bake according to manufacturer's directions until golden brown. Sprinkle with confectioners' sugar if desired.

Freeze option: Freeze cool waffles between layers of waxed paper in a resealable freezer container. To use, reheat waffles in a toaster on medium setting. Or, microwave each waffle on high for 30-60 seconds or until heated through.

2 waffles: 357 cal., 11g fat (6g sat. fat), 71mg chol., 672mg sod., 60g carb. (35g sugars, 1g fiber), 7g pro.

ORANGE CRANBERRY BREAD

The beauty of this festive quick bread is that it makes a delicious post-dinner snack as well as breakfast the next day. I like to toast leftover slices and spread them with cream cheese or butter for breakfast.
—Ron Gardner, Grand Haven, MI

- -

Prep: 20 min. • **Bake:** 50 min. + cooling
Makes: 2 loaves (16 slices each)

- 2¾ cups all-purpose flour
- ⅔ cup sugar
- ⅔ cup packed brown sugar
- 3½ tsp. baking powder
- 1 tsp. salt
- ½ tsp. ground cinnamon
- ¼ tsp. ground nutmeg
- 1 large egg, room temperature
- 1 cup 2% milk
- ½ cup orange juice
- 3 Tbsp. canola oil
- 2 to 3 tsp. grated orange zest
- 2 cups coarsely chopped fresh or frozen cranberries
- 1 large apple, peeled and chopped

1. In a large bowl, combine the flour, sugars, baking powder, salt, cinnamon and nutmeg. Whisk the egg, milk, orange juice, oil and orange zest; stir into dry ingredients just until blended. Fold in cranberries and apple.
2. Pour into 2 greased 8x4-in. loaf pans. Bake at 350° for 50-55 minutes or until a toothpick inserted in the center comes out clean. Cool for 10 minutes before removing from pans to wire racks.

Freeze option: Securely wrap cooled loaves in foil and freeze. To use, thaw the loaves at room temperature.

1 slice: 98 cal., 2g fat (0 sat. fat), 8mg chol., 125mg sod., 19g carb. (10g sugars, 1g fiber), 2g pro.

SMOKED SALMON QUICHE

My mother passed this recipe on to me because I'm always looking for new ways to cook the fish my son catches. You can use regular salmon, but the smoked flavor simply can't be beat.

—*Rose Marie Cherven, Anchorage, AK*

Prep: 30 min. • **Bake:** 35 min. + standing
Makes: 8 servings

- 1 **sheet refrigerated pie crust**
- 1 **cup shredded reduced-fat Swiss cheese**
- 1 **Tbsp. all-purpose flour**
- 3 **plum tomatoes, seeded and chopped**
- 2 **Tbsp. finely chopped onion**
- 2 **tsp. canola oil**
- 3 **oz. smoked salmon fillet, flaked (about ½ cup)**
- 4 **large eggs**
- 1 **cup 2% milk**
- ¼ **tsp. salt**

1. On a lightly floured surface, unroll crust. Transfer to a 9-in. pie plate. Trim the crust to ½ in. beyond edge of plate; flute edges.

2. In a small bowl, combine cheese and flour. Transfer to crust.

3. In a large skillet, saute the tomatoes and onion in oil just until tender. Remove from the heat; stir in the salmon. Spoon over the cheese mixture.

4. In a small bowl, whisk the eggs, milk and salt. Pour into crust. Bake at 350° for 35-40 minutes or until a knife inserted in the center comes out clean. Let stand for 15 minutes before cutting.

Freeze option: Securely wrap and freeze cooled quiche in plastic wrap and foil. To use, partially thaw in refrigerator overnight. Remove from the refrigerator 30 minutes before baking. Preheat oven to 350°. Unwrap the quiche; reheat in oven until heated through and a thermometer inserted in center reads 165°.

1 slice: 235 cal., 13g fat (5g sat. fat), 122mg chol., 348mg sod., 17g carb. (4g sugars, 0 fiber), 12g pro. **Diabetic exchanges:** 2 medium-fat meat, 1 starch.

WHY YOU'LL LOVE IT:
"This quiche is absolutely amazing! My husband and I thought it was great, and I can't wait to make it again!"
—SGRONHOLZ, TASTEOFHOME.COM

FREEZER BREAKFAST SANDWICHES

On busy mornings, these hearty freezer breakfast sandwiches save the day.
—*Christine Rukavena, Milwaukee, WI*

Prep: 25 min. • **Cook:** 15 min.
Makes: 12 sandwiches

    12 large eggs
    ⅔ cup 2% milk
    ½ tsp. salt
    ¼ tsp. pepper
SANDWICHES
    12 English muffins, split
     4 Tbsp. butter, softened
    12 slices Colby-Monterey Jack cheese
    12 slices Canadian bacon

1. Preheat oven to 325°. In a large bowl, whisk eggs, milk, salt and pepper until blended. Pour into a 13x9-in. baking pan coated with cooking spray. Bake until set, 15-18 minutes. Cool on a wire rack.
2. Meanwhile, toast English muffins (or bake at 325° for 12-15 minutes or until lightly browned). Spread 1 tsp. butter on each muffin bottom.
3. Cut eggs into 12 portions. Layer muffin bottoms with an egg portion, a cheese slice (tearing cheese to fit) and Canadian bacon. Replace muffin tops. Wrap sandwiches in foil; freeze in a freezer container.
To use frozen sandwiches: Remove foil. Wrap a sandwich in a paper towel and microwave at 50% power until thawed, 1-2 minutes. Turn the sandwich over; microwave at 100% power 30-60 seconds or until hot and a thermometer reads at least 160°. Let sandwich stand 2 minutes before serving.
1 sandwich: 334 cal., 17g fat (9g sat. fat), 219mg chol., 759mg sod., 26g carb. (3g sugars, 2g fiber), 19g pro.

BUTTERMILK PUMPKIN WAFFLES

My girlfriend loves pumpkin, so I like to incorporate it into recipes. In fall, I freeze pumpkin puree just to make these waffles later in the year.
—*Charles Insler, Silver Spring, MD*

Prep: 20 min. • **Cook:** 5 min./batch
Makes: 12 waffles

- ¾ cup all-purpose flour
- ½ cup whole wheat flour
- 2 Tbsp. brown sugar
- 1 tsp. baking powder
- 1 tsp. ground cinnamon
- ½ tsp. ground ginger
- ¼ tsp. baking soda
- ¼ tsp. salt
- ¼ tsp. ground cloves
- 2 large eggs, room temperature
- 1¼ cups buttermilk
- ½ cup fresh or canned pumpkin
- 2 Tbsp. butter, melted
  Optional: Butter and maple syrup

1. In a large bowl, combine the first 9 ingredients. In a small bowl, whisk eggs, buttermilk, pumpkin and melted butter. Stir into dry ingredients just until moistened.
2. Bake in a preheated waffle maker according to manufacturer's directions until golden brown. Serve with butter and syrup if desired.
Freeze option: Cool waffles on wire racks. Freeze between layers of waxed paper in a resealable freezer container. To use, reheat waffles in a toaster on medium setting. Or, microwave each waffle on high until heated through, 30-60 seconds.
2 waffles: 194 cal., 6g fat (3g sat. fat), 83mg chol., 325mg sod., 28g carb. (8g sugars, 3g fiber), 7g pro. **Diabetic exchanges:** 2 starch, 1 fat.

MEDITERRANEAN VEGGIE BRUNCH PUFF

I make breakfast casseroles with whatever I have, and that's often spinach, sweet red pepper and cheddar. I give this puff a burst of flavor with a little homemade Greek vinaigrette served on the side.

—Angela Robinson, Findlay, OH

- -

Prep: 25 min. + chilling • **Bake:** 25 min.
Makes: 8 servings

- 6   large eggs
- 2   large egg whites
- 1   cup 2% milk
- 1   garlic clove, minced
- ½   tsp. salt
- ¼   tsp. pepper
- 5   cups cubed croissants (about 6 oz.)
- ¾   cup chopped roasted sweet red peppers, divided
- ½   cup finely chopped sweet onion
- 1   pkg. (10 oz.) frozen chopped spinach, thawed and squeezed dry
- 1   cup shredded cheddar cheese
- ½   cup crumbled feta cheese
- 3   Tbsp. Greek vinaigrette

1. In a large bowl, whisk first 6 ingredients until blended. Place the croissant pieces in a single layer in a greased 11x7-in. baking dish; top with ½ cup red pepper, onion and spinach. Pour egg mixture over top. Sprinkle with cheddar and feta cheeses. Refrigerate, covered, overnight.

2. Finely chop remaining red pepper; place in a jar with a tight-fitting lid. Add the vinaigrette; shake to combine and refrigerate until serving.

3. Preheat oven to 350°. Remove casserole from refrigerator while oven heats. Bake, uncovered, 25-30 minutes or until a knife inserted in the center comes out clean. Let stand 5-10 minutes before cutting. Serve with vinaigrette mixture.

Freeze option: Cover and freeze unbaked casserole and remaining chopped sweet red pepper separately. To use, partially thaw both in refrigerator overnight. Remove from the refrigerator 30 minutes before baking. Preheat oven to 350°. Bake casserole as directed, increasing time as necessary to heat through and for a thermometer inserted in center to read 165°. Combine vinaigrette and chopped sweet red pepper; serve with casserole.

1 piece with 1½ tsp. vinaigrette mixture: 281 cal., 17g fat (8g sat. fat), 175mg chol., 656mg sod., 16g carb. (6g sugars, 2g fiber), 14g pro.

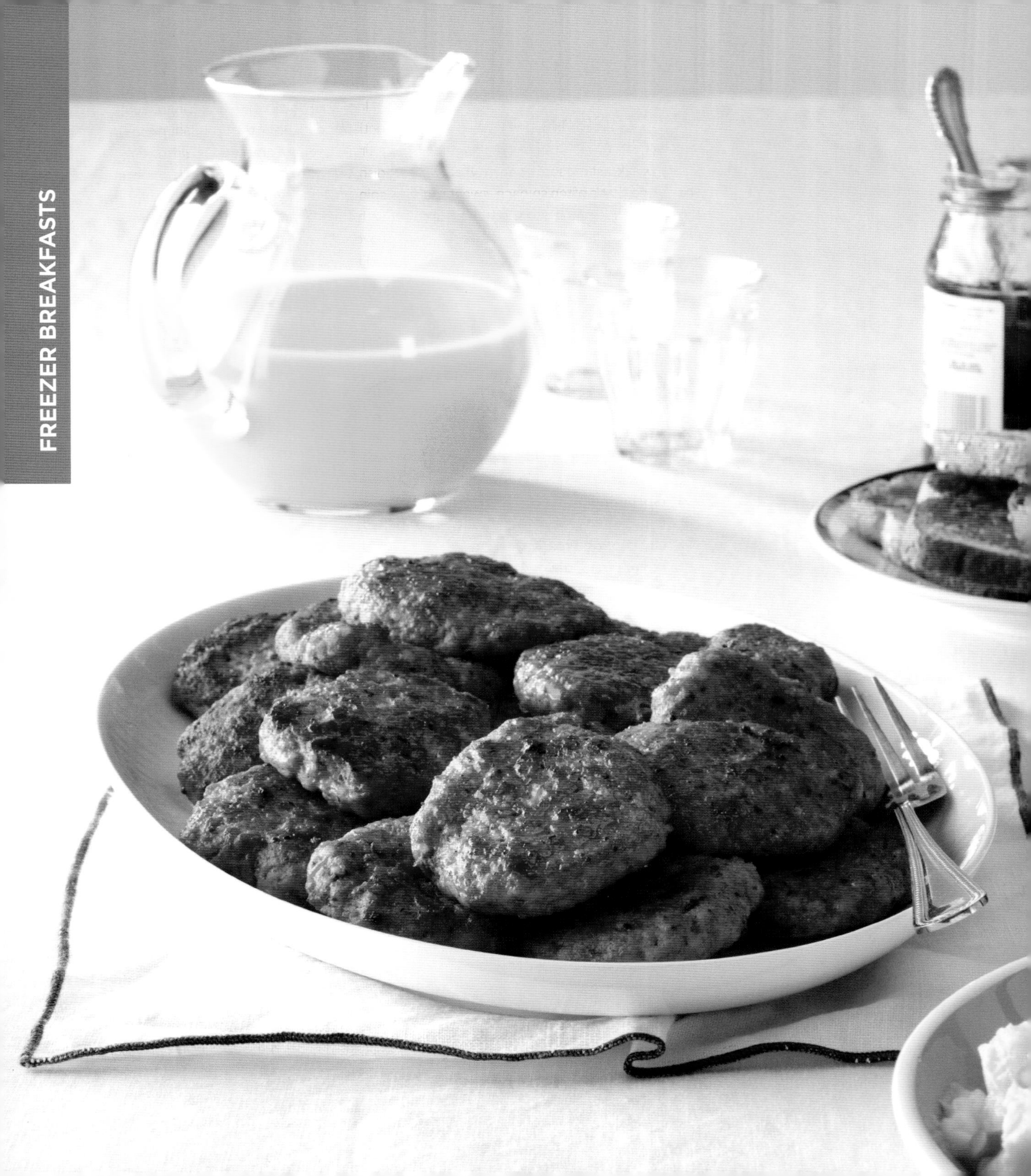

❄ HOMEMADE BREAKFAST SAUSAGE PATTIES

Buttermilk is the secret to keeping these easy pork patties moist, while a blend of seasonings create a wonderful flavor that complements any breakfast menu.

—*Harvey Keeney, Mandan, ND*

Prep: 30 min. • **Cook:** 10 min./batch
Makes: 20 patties

¾   cup buttermilk
2¼ tsp. kosher salt
1½ tsp. rubbed sage
1½ tsp. brown sugar
1½ tsp. pepper
¾   tsp. dried marjoram
¾   tsp. dried savory
¾   tsp. cayenne pepper
¼   tsp. ground nutmeg
2½ lbs. ground pork

1. In a large bowl, combine the first 9 ingredients. Add pork; mix lightly but thoroughly. Shape into twenty 3-in. patties.
2. In a large skillet coated with cooking spray, cook the patties in batches over medium heat until a thermometer reads 160°, 5-6 minutes on each side. Remove to paper towels to drain.

Freeze option: Wrap each cooked, cooled patty; transfer to an airtight container. May be frozen for up to 3 months. To use, unwrap patties and place on a baking sheet coated with cooking spray. Bake at 350° until heated through, about 15 minutes on each side. To use, unwrap patties and place on a baking sheet coated with cooking spray. Bake at 350° for 15 minutes on each side or until heated through.

1 sausage patty: 126 cal., 8g fat (3g sat. fat), 38mg chol., 251mg sod., 1g carb. (1g sugars, 0 fiber), 11g pro.

5ⁱ 🍎 ❄ WHOLE WHEAT PANCAKES

To fix a large batch of tender pancakes for my five children, I rely on this fuss-free recipe. It calls for whole wheat flour and buttermilk, which make the pancakes very filling but also very light. Serve them with hot chocolate for a breakfast that's sure to delight little ones.

—*Line Walter, Wayne, PA*

Takes: 25 min. • **Makes:** 20 pancakes

2   cups whole wheat flour
½   cup toasted wheat germ
1   tsp. baking soda
½   tsp. salt
2   large eggs, room temperature
3   cups buttermilk
1   Tbsp. canola oil

1. In a large bowl, combine the flour, wheat germ, baking soda and salt. In another bowl, whisk the eggs, buttermilk and oil. Stir into dry ingredients just until blended.
2. Pour batter by ¼ cupfuls onto a hot griddle coated with cooking spray; turn when bubbles form on top. Cook until the second side is golden brown.

Freeze option: Freeze cooled pancakes between layers of waxed paper in an airtight freezer container. To use, place the pancakes on an ungreased baking sheet, cover with foil, and reheat in a preheated 375° oven for 6-10 minutes. Or, place a stack of 3 pancakes on a microwave-safe plate and microwave on high until heated through, 45-90 seconds.

2 pancakes: 157 cal., 4g fat (1g sat. fat), 45mg chol., 335mg sod., 24g carb. (4g sugars, 4g fiber), 9g pro. **Diabetic exchanges:** 1½ starch, 1 fat.

BRUNCH BUDDIES ENCHILADAS

In our women's group, we take turns making brunch. I was tired of the same casseroles so I invented this Mexican-style bake. The recipe requests keep coming.
—*Julia Huntington, Cheyenne, WY*

Prep: 40 min. • **Bake:** 40 min. + standing
Makes: 12 servings

- 3 **cups shredded Mexican cheese blend, divided**
- 2 **cups cubed fully cooked ham**
- 1 **small green pepper, chopped**
- 1 **small onion, chopped**
- 1 **medium tomato, chopped**
- 12 **flour tortillas (6 in.)**
- 10 **large eggs**
- 2 **cups half-and-half cream**
- 2 **Tbsp. all-purpose flour**
- ½ **tsp. salt**
- ½ **tsp. onion powder**
- ½ **tsp. pepper**

TOPPINGS
- 4 **green onions, thinly sliced**
- ½ **cup cherry tomatoes, quartered**
- 1 **can (2¼ oz.) sliced ripe olives, drained, optional**

1. Preheat oven to 350°. Place 2 cups cheese, ham, green pepper, onion and tomato in a large bowl; toss to combine. Place ½ cup mixture off center on each tortilla. Roll up and place in a greased 13x9-in. baking dish, seam side down.

2. In another bowl, whisk eggs, cream, flour and seasonings until blended; pour over the enchiladas. Sprinkle with remaining cheese; add toppings.

3. Bake, covered, 30 minutes. Uncover; bake until cheese is melted and a knife inserted in egg portion comes out clean, 10-15 minutes longer. Let stand 10 minutes before serving.

Freeze option: Cover and freeze unbaked casserole. To use, partially thaw in the refrigerator overnight. Remove from refrigerator 30 minutes before baking. Preheat oven to 350°. Cover casserole with foil; bake as directed, increasing uncovered time to 25-35 minutes or until cheese is melted and a thermometer inserted in center reads 165°.

1 enchilada: 375 cal., 22g fat (10g sat. fat), 214mg chol., 832mg sod., 22g carb. (3g sugars, 2g fiber), 21g pro.

WHOLE WHEAT PECAN WAFFLES

We bought a new waffle maker, and a recipe came with it. We finally decided to try it and, after a few changes, we came up with these delicious waffles.
—*Sarah Morris, Joplin, MO*

- -

Takes: 30 min. • **Makes:** 16 waffles

- 2 **cups whole wheat pastry flour**
- 2 **Tbsp. sugar**
- 3 **tsp. baking powder**
- ½ **tsp. salt**
- 2 **large eggs, separated, room temperature**
- 1¾ **cups fat-free milk**
- ¼ **cup canola oil**
- ½ **cup chopped pecans**

1. Preheat waffle maker. Whisk together first 4 ingredients. In another bowl, whisk together egg yolks, milk and oil; add to flour mixture, stirring just until moistened.

2. In a clean bowl, beat the egg whites on medium speed until stiff but not dry. Fold into batter. Bake the waffles according to manufacturer's directions until golden brown, sprinkling the batter with pecans after pouring.

Freeze option: Cool waffles on wire racks. Freeze between layers of waxed paper in a freezer container. Reheat waffles in a toaster or toaster oven on medium setting.

2 (4-in.) waffles: 241 cal., 14g fat (1g sat. fat), 48mg chol., 338mg sod., 24g carb. (6g sugars, 3g fiber), 7g pro. **Diabetic exchanges:** 2½ fat, 1½ starch.

5i ❄

LANCE'S OWN FRENCH TOAST

When my young son, Lance, helps me make this French toast, he knows what order to add the ingredients and even how much to measure out. It's great for the whole family!
—*Janna Steele, Magee, MA*

Prep: 10 min. • **Cook:** 15 min.
Makes: 6 servings

- 4   large eggs
- 1   cup 2% milk
- 1   tablespoon honey
- ½   teaspoon ground cinnamon
- ⅛   teaspoon pepper
- 12   slices whole wheat bread
  Cinnamon sugar, optional
  Vanilla frosting, optional

1. In a shallow bowl, whisk eggs, milk, honey, cinnamon and pepper. Dip both sides of the bread in egg mixture. Cook on a greased hot griddle 3-4 minutes on each side or until golden brown.

2. If desired, sprinkle with cinnamon sugar or frost with vanilla icing.

Freeze option: Cool French toast on wire racks. Freeze between layers of waxed paper in a resealable freezer container. To use, reheat French toast in a toaster oven on medium setting. Or, microwave each French toast on high for 30-60 seconds or until heated through.

2 slices: 218 calories, 6g fat (2g saturated fat), 144mg cholesterol, 331mg sodium, 28g carbohydrate (8g sugars, 4g fiber), 13g protein. **Diabetic exchanges:** 2 starch, 1 medium-fat meat.

EASY MORNING WAFFLES

Making your own fluffy waffles from scratch takes no time at all, and the touch of cinnamon takes them way beyond any store-bought variety. Mix up your meal plan with the different versions.
—Taste of Home *Test Kitchen*

Prep: 20 min. • **Cook:** 5 min./batch
Makes: 14 waffles (1 cup syrup)

    2   cups all-purpose flour
    1   Tbsp. brown sugar
    2   tsp. baking powder
    ½   tsp. salt
    ½   tsp. ground cinnamon
    3   large eggs, separated,
        room temperature
    2   cups 2% milk
    ¼   cup canola oil
    ¾   tsp. vanilla extract
SYRUP
    ½   cup butter, cubed
    ½   cup honey
    1   tsp. ground cinnamon

1. In a large bowl, combine the flour, brown sugar, baking powder, salt and cinnamon. In a small bowl, whisk the egg yolks, milk, oil and vanilla; stir into dry ingredients just until moistened. In a small bowl, beat egg whites until stiff peaks form; fold into batter.
2. Bake in a preheated waffle maker according to manufacturer's directions until golden brown.
3. In a microwave, melt the butter, honey and cinnamon; stir until smooth. Serve waffles with syrup.

Freeze option: Arrange waffles in a single layer on sheet pans. Freeze overnight or until frozen. Transfer to a freezer container. Pour remaining syrup into a freezer container. Freeze up to 2 months. To use, reheat waffles in a toaster. Microwave syrup until heated through, and serve with waffles.
2 waffles: 464 cal., 25g fat (10g sat. fat), 130mg chol., 442mg sod., 53g carb. (26g sugars, 1g fiber), 9g pro.
Chocolate Waffles: Stir ¼ cup unsweetened baking cocoa into the flour mixture and proceed as directed.
Bacon-Cheddar Waffles: Prepare batter as directed, eliminating vanilla extract and cinnamon. Stir in 4 cooked and crumbled bacon strips and ½ cup shredded sharp cheddar cheese. Cook as directed.
Dairy-Free Orange-Almond Waffles: Use unsweetened almond milk instead of 2% milk. Prepare recipe as directed, adding 2 tsp. orange zest and ½ tsp. almond extract.
Pesto-Parmesan Waffles: Prepare batter as directed, eliminating vanilla extract and cinnamon. Stir in ⅓ cup grated Parmesan cheese and 2 Tbsp. prepared pesto. Cook as directed.

❄ QUICHE PASTRY CUPS

My grandmother used to make egg cup surprises for family brunches on special occasions. The added fillings were always a surprise, as she never seemed to use the same combination of ingredients twice. As children, we had a guessing game as to what we'd find in the tender crust, which added an aspect of family fun to our meal. Now I can stash some in the freezer for my own family fun!
—*Denalee Standart, Rancho Mureta, CA*

- -

Prep: 30 min. • **Bake:** 15 min.
Makes: 1½ dozen

- 1 **pkg. (17.3 oz.) frozen puff pastry, thawed**
- 4 **large eggs, divided use**
- 1 **cup plus 2 Tbsp. half-and-half cream, divided**
- 1 **Tbsp. minced fresh thyme**
- ½ **tsp. salt**
- ½ **tsp. pepper**
- ¼ **tsp. ground nutmeg**
- 1½ **cups shredded Gruyere cheese**
- 1½ **cups chopped fresh spinach**
- 1 **medium sweet red pepper, chopped**
- 8 **bacon strips, cooked and crumbled**

1. Preheat oven to 400°. On a lightly floured surface, unfold puff pastry. Roll each sheet into a 12-in. square; cut each into 9 squares. Place in ungreased muffin cups, pressing gently onto bottoms and up sides, allowing corners to point up.

2. In a small bowl, whisk 3 eggs, 1 cup cream, thyme and seasonings. In another bowl, combine cheese, spinach, red pepper and bacon; divide among pastry cups. Pour egg mixture over cheese mixture.

3. In a small bowl, whisk remaining egg with remaining cream; brush over pastry edges. Bake 15-18 minutes or until golden brown. Remove to wire racks. Serve warm.

Freeze option: Cover and freeze baked pastries on greased baking sheets until firm. Transfer to resealable freezer containers; return to freezer. To use, reheat frozen pastries on ungreased baking sheets in a preheated 375° oven 17-20 minutes or until heated through.

1 quiche: 226 cal., 14g fat (5g sat. fat), 62mg chol., 312mg sod., 16g carb. (1g sugars, 2g fiber), 8g pro.

FROZEN FRUIT CUPS

Add some sparkle to your next gathering with these make-ahead citrus treats. The petite cups burst with color and fresh flavor, and they look so cute served in shiny foil containers. They make great after-school snacks, too!
—*Sue Ross, Casa Grande, AZ*

Prep: 30 min. + freezing • **Makes:** 9½ dozen

  5 **pkg. (3 oz. each) lemon gelatin**
10 **cups boiling water**
  5 **cans (20 oz. each) unsweetened pineapple tidbits, undrained**
  5 **cans (11 oz. each) mandarin oranges, drained**
  5 **cans (6 oz. each) frozen orange juice concentrate, partially thawed**
  5 **large firm bananas, sliced**

1. In a very large bowl, dissolve the gelatin in boiling water; cool for 10 minutes. Stir in the remaining ingredients.

2. Spoon mixture into foil cups. Freeze until firm. Remove from the freezer 30 minutes before serving.

1 fruit cup: 48 cal., 0 fat (0 sat. fat), 0 chol., 11mg sod., 12g carb. (11g sugars, 1g fiber), 1g pro. **Diabetic exchanges:** 1 fruit.

FRENCH TOAST STICKS

You can keep these French toast sticks in the freezer for an instant breakfast. The convenient size makes them an ideal buffet item, but they're hearty enough to satisfy the entire family on busy mornings.
—Taste of Home *Test Kitchen*

- -

Prep: 20 min. + freezing • **Bake:** 20 min.
Makes: 1½ dozen

6	slices day-old Texas toast
4	large eggs
1	cup 2% milk
2	Tbsp. sugar
1	tsp. vanilla extract
¼	to ½ tsp. ground cinnamon
1	cup crushed cornflakes, optional
	Confectioners' sugar, optional
	Maple syrup

1. Cut each piece of bread into thirds; place in an ungreased 13x9-in. dish. In a large bowl, whisk the eggs, milk, sugar, vanilla and cinnamon. Pour over the bread; soak for 2 minutes, turning once. If desired, coat bread with cornflake crumbs on all sides.

2. Place the sticks in a greased 15x10x1-in. baking pan. Freeze 45 minutes or until firm. Transfer to an airtight freezer container and store in the freezer.

To use frozen French toast sticks: Place desired number on a greased baking sheet. Bake at 425° for 8 minutes. Turn; bake 10-12 minutes longer or until golden brown. Sprinkle with confectioners' sugar if desired. Serve with syrup.

3 sticks: 183 cal., 6g fat (2g sat. fat), 145mg chol., 251mg sod., 24g carb. (8g sugars, 1g fiber), 8g pro.

CARAMELIZED BACON TWISTS

Whenever my grandchildren come over, these sweet chewy bacon strips are a big hit. Lining the pan with foil before baking helps cut down on cleanup.
—Jane Paschke, University Park, FL

- -

Takes: 30 min. • **Makes:** about 3 dozen

½	cup packed brown sugar
2	tsp. ground cinnamon
1	lb. bacon strips

1. Preheat oven to 350°. Line a 15x10x1-in. pan with foil.

2. In a shallow bowl, mix brown sugar and cinnamon. Cut bacon strips crosswise in half; dip in sugar mixture to coat. Twist 2 or 3 times, then place in prepared pan. Bake until browned and crisp, 15-20 minutes.

Freeze option: Freeze cooled bacon twists in freezer containers, separating layers with waxed paper. If desired, reheat bacon in a microwave oven or on a foil-lined baking sheet in a preheated 350° oven. Bake at 350° for 6-8 minutes or until heated through.

1 bacon twist: 35 cal., 2g fat (1g sat. fat), 5mg chol., 81mg sod., 3g carb. (3g sugars, 0 fiber), 2g pro.

❄ ITALIAN QUICHES

This hearty dish tastes like pizza and can be enjoyed for breakfast as well as supper. The recipe makes two, so get more bang for your buck on your meal plan!
—*Bernice Hancock, Greenville, PA*

Prep: 25 min. • **Bake:** 35 min. + standing
Makes: 2 quiches (6 servings each)

- 2 **unbaked pastry shells**
- 1 **lb. bulk Italian sausage**
- 4 **cups (16 oz.) finely shredded part-skim mozzarella cheese**
- 1 **medium onion, thinly sliced**
- 1 **medium green pepper, thinly sliced**
- 1 **medium sweet red pepper, thinly sliced**
- 6 **large eggs**
- 2 **cups 2% milk**
- 1 **tsp. minced garlic**
- ¼ **cup grated Parmesan cheese**

1. Preheat oven to 400°. Line unpricked crusts with a double thickness of heavy-duty foil. Bake 4 minutes. Remove the foil; bake 4 minutes longer. Remove from oven; leave oven on.

2. In a large skillet, cook sausage over medium heat until no longer pink; drain. Spoon sausage into crusts; sprinkle with mozzarella cheese. Top with onion and peppers. In a large bowl, whisk eggs, milk and garlic. Pour over peppers; sprinkle with Parmesan cheese.

3. Cover edges of quiches loosely with foil; place on a baking sheet. Bake at 400° for 35-40 minutes or until a knife inserted in the center comes out clean. Let stand for 10 minutes before cutting.

Freeze option: Cover and freeze unbaked quiches up to 3 months. To use, remove from the freezer 30 minutes before baking (do not thaw). Preheat oven to 400°. Cover edges of crust loosely with foil; place on a baking sheet. Bake 50-60 minutes or until a knife inserted in the center comes out clean. Let stand 10 minutes before cutting.

1 slice: 395 cal., 25g fat (11g sat. fat), 155mg chol., 565mg sod., 23g carb. (6g sugars, 1g fiber), 20g pro.

WHY YOU'LL LOVE IT:
"It was delicious. I enjoyed it for breakfast, dinner and even took some to work for lunch! So glad I have a second one in the freezer to bake on a busy weeknight."
—ERUTLEDGE17, TASTEOFHOME.COM

CINNAMON RAISIN QUICK BREAD

Cinnamon and raisin bring heartwarming flavor to this mildly sweet bread. It's ideal for an on-the-go breakfast or a quick snack before dinner.
—*Flo Burtnett, Gage, OK*

- -

Prep: 15 min. • **Bake:** 55 min. + cooling
Makes: 2 loaves (12 slices each)

- 4   **cups all-purpose flour**
- 2   **cups sugar, divided**
- 2   **tsp. baking soda**
- 1   **tsp. salt**
- 2   **large eggs, room temperature**
- 2   **cups buttermilk**
- ½   **cup canola oil**
- ½   **cup raisins**
- 3   **tsp. ground cinnamon**

1. Preheat oven to 350°. In a large bowl, combine flour, 1½ cups sugar, soda and salt. In a small bowl, whisk eggs, buttermilk and oil. Stir into the dry ingredients just until moistened. Fold in the raisins. Combine cinnamon and remaining sugar; set aside.
2. Spoon half the batter into 2 greased 8x4-in. loaf pans. Sprinkle with half of the reserved cinnamon sugar; repeat layers. Cut through batter with a knife to swirl.
3. Bake 55-60 minutes or until a toothpick inserted in center comes out clean. Cool for 10 minutes before removing from pans to wire racks.

Freeze option: Wrap cooled bread in foil and freeze for up to 3 months. To use, thaw at room temperature.

1 slice: 204 cal., 5g fat (1g sat. fat), 18mg chol., 231mg sod., 36g carb. (20g sugars, 1g fiber), 3g pro.

5i ❄

SAUSAGE BALLS

These are a fun variation from regular sausage links or patties. Have the kids help shape them into balls, then serve with eggs, pancakes or any other breakfast item on extra crazy mornings.
—*Dinah Overlein, Jim Falls, WI*

Prep: 30 min. • **Bake:** 25 min.
Makes: 3 dozen

1	lb. bulk pork sausage
3	cups biscuit/baking mix
2	cups shredded sharp cheddar cheese
2	large eggs, lightly beaten

1. In a bowl, combine all ingredients. Shape into 1-in. balls and place on a rack in a shallow baking pan.
2. Bake at 375° for 25-30 minutes or until golden brown.
Freeze option: Freeze uncooked sausage balls in airtight freezer containers. To use, bake frozen at 425° for 15-20 minutes or until golden brown.
3 sausage balls: 278 cal., 18g fat (8g sat. fat), 69mg chol., 657mg sod., 20g carb. (1g sugars, 1g fiber), 10g pro.

FLUFFY BANANA PANCAKES

I love to make pancakes for my family on Saturday mornings. Since we often have ripe bananas, I decided to add them to a batch of pancake batter. The results were absolutely delicious!

—*Lori Stevens, Riverton, UT*

- -

Takes: 30 min. • **Makes:** 14 pancakes

1	cup all-purpose flour
1	cup whole wheat flour
3	Tbsp. brown sugar
1	tsp. baking powder
1	tsp. baking soda
1	tsp. ground cinnamon
½	tsp. salt
2	large eggs, room temperature
2	cups buttermilk
2	Tbsp. canola oil
1	tsp. vanilla extract
1	ripe medium banana, finely chopped
⅓	cup finely chopped walnuts

1. In a large bowl, combine the first 7 ingredients. In another bowl, whisk eggs, buttermilk, oil and vanilla until blended. Add to the dry ingredients, stirring just until moistened. Fold in banana and walnuts.

2. Pour batter by ¼ cupfuls onto a hot griddle coated with cooking spray. Cook until bubbles begin to form on top and bottoms are golden brown. Turn; cook until second side is golden brown.

Freeze option: Freeze cooled pancakes between layers of waxed paper in a freezer container. To use, place pancakes on an ungreased baking sheet, cover with foil and reheat in a preheated 375° oven for 5-10 minutes. Or, place 2 pancakes on a microwave-safe plate and microwave on high for 40-50 seconds or until heated through.

2 pancakes: 283 cal., 10g fat (2g sat. fat), 63mg chol., 503mg sod., 40g carb. (12g sugars, 4g fiber), 9g pro. **Diabetic exchanges:** 2½ starch, 1½ fat.

Fluffy Strawberry Pancakes: Replace chopped banana with ¾ cup chopped fresh strawberries; proceed as directed.

Fluffy Peach Pancakes: Replace chopped banana with ¾ cup chopped fresh or frozen peaches; proceed as directed.

Fluffy Blueberry Pancakes: Replace chopped banana with ¾ cup chopped fresh or frozen blueberries; proceed as directed.

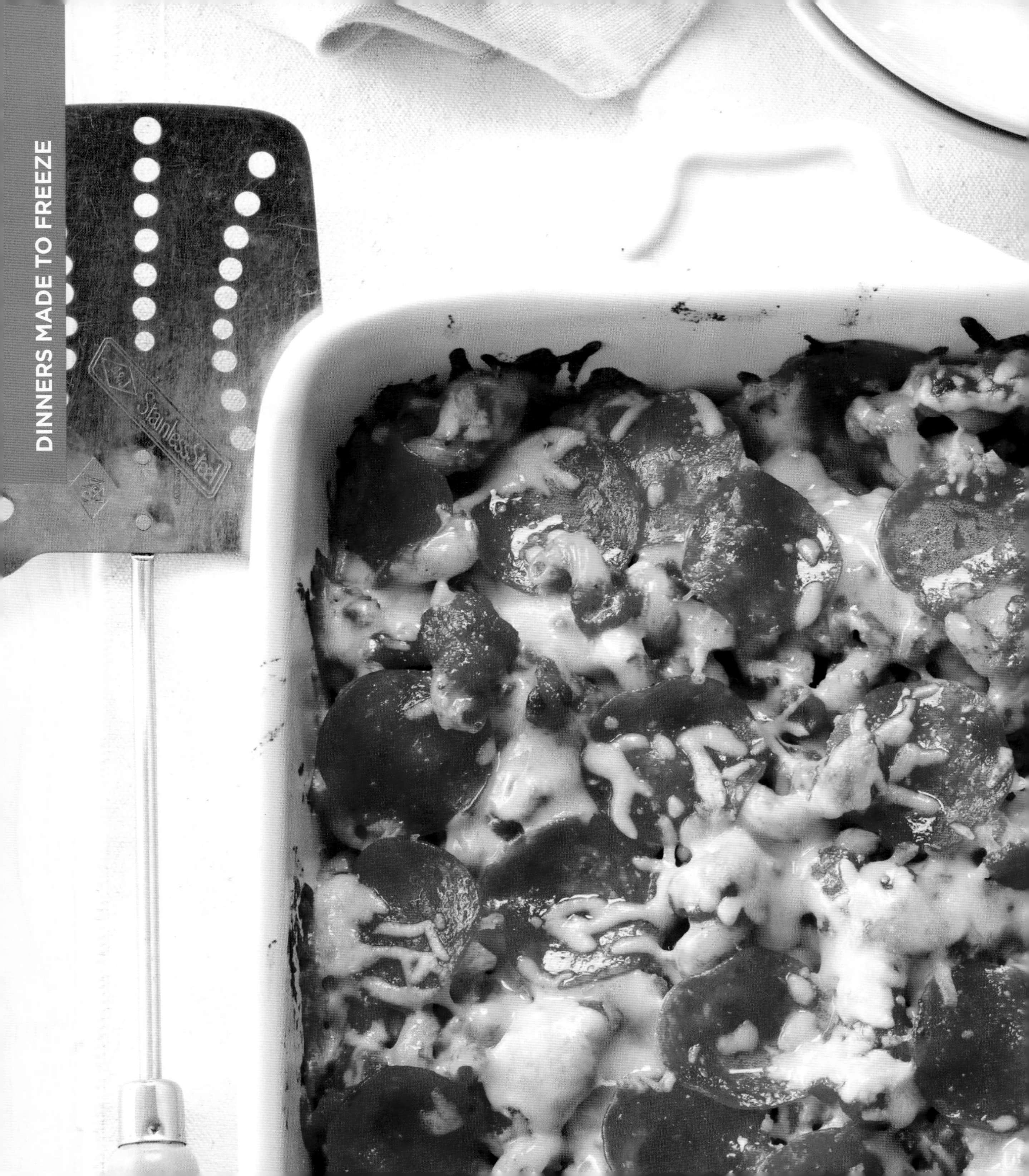
Stainless Steel

PIZZA PASTA CASSEROLE

Kids will line up for this zippy pizza-flavored dish. The recipe makes two casseroles, so you can serve one to your family right away and keep the other in the freezer for an extra busy evening.
—*Nancy Scarlett, Graham, NC*

- -

Prep: 20 min. • **Bake:** 25 min.
Makes: 2 casseroles (10 servings each)

- 2   lbs. ground beef
- 1   large onion, chopped
- 3½ cups spaghetti sauce
- 1   pkg. (16 oz.) spiral or cavatappi pasta, cooked and drained
- 4   cups shredded part-skim mozzarella cheese
- 8   oz. sliced pepperoni

1. Preheat oven to 350°. In a large skillet, cook beef and onion over medium heat until meat is no longer pink; drain. Stir in spaghetti sauce and pasta.
2. Transfer to 2 greased 13x9-in. baking dishes. Sprinkle with cheese. Arrange pepperoni over the top.
3. Bake, uncovered, 25-30 minutes or until heated through.
Freeze option: Cool unbaked casseroles; cover and freeze up to 3 months. To use, partially thaw in the refrigerator overnight. Remove from refrigerator 30 minutes before baking. Preheat the oven to 350°. Bake as directed, increasing time to 35-40 minutes or until heated through and a thermometer inserted in center reads 165°.
1 serving: 301 cal., 15g fat (6g sat. fat), 46mg chol., 545mg sod., 22g carb. (4g sugars, 1g fiber), 19g pro.

❄ ITALIAN SAUSAGE CALZONE

This calzone with spinach and sausage is definitely a favorite. Using a refrigerated pizza crust, it's a cinch to prepare one for us or several to freeze.
—*Terri Gallagher, King George, VA*

- -

Prep: 20 min. • **Bake:** 30 min. + standing
Makes: 6 servings

- 1   tube (13.8 oz.) refrigerated pizza crust
- 1   can (8 oz.) pizza sauce
- 1   pkg. (10 oz.) frozen chopped spinach, thawed and squeezed dry
- 1   lb. bulk Italian sausage, cooked and drained
- 1   jar (4½ oz.) sliced mushrooms, drained
- 2   cups shredded part-skim mozzarella cheese

1. Unroll pizza dough onto an ungreased baking sheet; pat into a 14x11-in. rectangle. Spread pizza sauce over 1 long side of dough to within ½ in. of edges.
2. Layer the spinach, sausage, mushrooms and cheese over sauce. Fold the dough over filling; pinch seams to seal.
3. Bake at 400° for 30-35 minutes or until golden brown. Let stand for 10-15 minutes before slicing.
Freeze option: Freeze the cooled unsliced calzone in a freezer container. To use, place on an ungreased baking sheet, cover with foil and reheat in a preheated 375° oven for 10 minutes. Uncover; bake the calzone until heated through.
1 slice: 322 cal., 15g fat (6g sat. fat), 44mg chol., 870mg sod., 28g carb. (4g sugars, 3g fiber), 17g pro.

❄ CHICKEN BURRITOS

This mouthwatering southwestern recipe makes enough for two casseroles, so you can enjoy one today and freeze the other for a busy weeknight. These burritos are super to have on hand for quick meals or to take to potlucks.

—*Sonya Nightingale, Burley, ID*

Prep: 20 min. • **Bake:** 35 min.
Makes: 2 casseroles (6 servings each)

6	Tbsp. butter
1	large onion, chopped
¼	cup chopped green pepper
½	cup all-purpose flour
3	cups chicken broth
1	can (10 oz.) diced tomatoes and green chiles, undrained
1	tsp. ground cumin
1	tsp. chili powder
½	tsp. garlic powder
½	tsp. salt
2	Tbsp. chopped jalapeno pepper, optional
1	can (15 oz.) chili with beans
1	pkg. (8 oz.) cream cheese, cubed
8	cups cubed cooked chicken
24	flour tortillas (6 in.), warmed
6	cups shredded Colby-Monterey Jack cheese Salsa, optional

1. Preheat oven to 350°. In a Dutch oven, heat butter over medium-high heat. Add the onion and pepper; cook and stir until tender. Stir in flour until blended; gradually stir in the broth. Bring to a boil; cook and stir for 2 minutes. Reduce heat; stir in tomatoes, seasonings and, if desired, jalapeno. Cook 5 minutes. Add the chili and cream cheese; stir until cream cheese is melted. Stir in the cubed chicken.

2. Spoon about ½ cup filling across center of each tortilla; sprinkle each with ¼ cup Colby-Monterey Jack cheese. Fold the bottom and sides over filling and roll up. Place in 2 greased 13x9-in. baking dishes.

3. Bake, covered, 35-40 minutes or until heated through. If desired, serve burritos with salsa.

Freeze option: Cool unbaked casserole; cover and freeze. To use, partially thaw in the refrigerator overnight. Remove from refrigerator 30 minutes before baking. Preheat oven to 350°. Cover casserole with foil; bake as directed, increasing the baking time to 50-55 minutes or until heated through and a thermometer inserted in the center reads 160°.

Note: Wear disposable gloves when cutting hot peppers; the oils can burn skin. Avoid touching your face.

2 burritos: 760 cal., 44g fat (23g sat. fat), 177mg chol., 1608mg sod., 40g carb. (2g sugars, 2g fiber), 51g pro.

BEANS & FRANKS BAKE

Here's a kid-pleasing beans-and-hot dog combination with a unique and delicious cornbread topping.
—*Roxanne VanGelder, Rochester, NH*

- -

Prep: 20 min. • **Bake:** 40 min.
Makes: 2 casseroles (4 servings each)

2	pkg. (8½ oz. each) cornbread/muffin mix
1	can (28 oz.) baked beans
4	hot dogs, sliced
½	lb. sliced bacon, cooked and crumbled
1	cup ketchup
½	cup packed brown sugar
½	cup chopped onion
2	cups shredded part-skim mozzarella cheese

1. Prepare the cornbread batter according to package directions; set aside. In a large bowl, combine the baked beans, hot dogs, bacon, ketchup, brown sugar and onion. Transfer to 2 greased 8-in. square baking dishes. Sprinkle with the cheese; top with cornbread batter.

2. Cover and freeze 1 casserole for up to 3 months. Bake the second casserole, uncovered, at 350° for 40-45 minutes or until a toothpick inserted in the center comes out clean.

To use frozen casserole: Remove from the freezer 30 minutes before baking. Cover and bake at 350° for 40 minutes. Uncover; bake the casserole 15-20 minutes longer or until heated through.

1 serving: 687 cal., 28g fat (11g sat. fat), 96mg chol., 1886mg sod., 88g carb. (36g sugars, 10g fiber), 24g pro.

❄ POLISH CASSEROLE

When I first made this dish, my 2-year-old liked it so much that he wanted it for every meal! You can use almost any pasta that will hold the sauce.

—*Crystal Jo Bruns, Iliff, CO*

Prep: 25 min. • **Bake:** 45 min.
Makes: 2 casseroles (6 servings each)

- 4 cups uncooked penne pasta
- 1½ lbs. smoked Polish sausage or kielbasa, cut into ½-in. slices
- 2 cans (10¾ oz. each) condensed cream of mushroom soup, undiluted
- 1 jar (16 oz.) sauerkraut, rinsed and well drained
- 3 cups shredded Swiss cheese, divided
- 1⅓ cups 2% milk
- 4 green onions, chopped
- 2 Tbsp. Dijon mustard
- 4 garlic cloves, minced

1. Preheat oven to 350°. Cook penne pasta according to package directions; drain and transfer to a large bowl. Stir in the sausage, soup, sauerkraut, 2 cups Swiss cheese, milk, onions, mustard and garlic.

2. Spoon into 2 greased 8-in. square baking dishes; sprinkle with the remaining cheese. Bake, uncovered, until golden brown and bubbly, 45-50 minutes.

Freeze option: Cover and freeze unbaked casserole up to 3 months. Thaw in the refrigerator overnight. Remove from refrigerator 30 minutes before baking. Preheat oven to 350°. Bake, uncovered, until golden brown and bubbly, 50-55 minutes.

1 cup: 428 cal., 26g fat (11g sat. fat), 69mg chol., 1193mg sod., 28g carb. (4g sugars, 3g fiber), 19g pro.

❄ CHEESY VEGGIE LASAGNA

This is my daughter-in-law's recipe. It's tasty and a little different from usual lasagna recipes. You won't even miss the meat!
—*Alyce Wyman, Pembina, ND*

- -

Prep: 30 min. • **Bake:** 40 min. + standing
Makes: 2 lasagnas (9 servings each)

- 18 uncooked lasagna noodles
- 2 large eggs
- 2 large egg whites
- 2 cartons (15 oz. each) reduced-fat ricotta cheese
- 4 tsp. dried parsley flakes
- 2 tsp. dried basil
- 2 tsp. dried oregano
- 1 tsp. pepper
- 8 cups garden-style spaghetti sauce
- 4 cups shredded part-skim mozzarella cheese
- 2 pkg. (16 oz. each) frozen cut green beans or 8 cups cut fresh green beans
- ⅔ cup grated Parmesan cheese

1. Cook the noodles according to package directions. Meanwhile, in a small bowl, whisk the eggs, egg whites, reduced-fat ricotta cheese, parsley, basil, oregano and pepper; set aside.

2. In each of two 13x9-in. baking dishes coated with cooking spray, spread 1 cup spaghetti sauce. Drain the noodles; place 3 noodles over spaghetti sauce in each dish.

3. Layer each with a quarter of the ricotta mixture, 1 cup spaghetti sauce, 1 cup mozzarella cheese, 3 more lasagna noodles and half of green beans. Top each with the remaining ricotta mixture and 1 cup spaghetti sauce. Layer with remaining lasagna noodles, spaghetti sauce and mozzarella cheese. Sprinkle Parmesan cheese over each.

4. Cover and freeze 1 casserole for up to 3 months. Bake remaining lasagna, uncovered, at 375° for 40-45 minutes or until bubbly and the edges are lightly browned. Let lasagna stand for 10 minutes before serving.

To use frozen lasagna: Thaw in the refrigerator overnight. Remove from the refrigerator 30 minutes before baking. Cover and bake at 375° for 1¼-1½ hours or until bubbly. Let stand for 10 minutes before serving.

1 piece: 320 cal., 10g fat (5g sat. fat), 56mg chol., 713mg sod., 38g carb. (14g sugars, 5g fiber), 18g pro. **Diabetic exchanges:** 2 starch, 2 lean meat, 2 vegetable.

❄ TATER TOT CASSEROLES

Ground beef, sausage, cheese and, of course, Tater Tots make this casserole a crowd-pleaser. Cayenne pepper and hot Italian sausage give it an extra punch.
—*Ryan Jones, Chillicothe, IL*

- -

Prep: 25 min. • **Bake:** 45 min.
Makes: 2 casseroles (6 servings each)

- ¾ **lb. bulk hot Italian sausage**
- ¾ **lb. lean ground beef (90% lean)**
- 1 **small onion, chopped**
- 2 **cans (10¾ oz. each) condensed cream of celery soup, undiluted**
- 2 **cups frozen cut green beans, thawed**
- 1 **can (15¼ oz.) whole kernel corn, drained**
- 2 **cups shredded Colby-Monterey Jack cheese, divided**
- ½ **cup 2% milk**
- 1 **tsp. garlic powder**
- ¼ **tsp. seasoned salt**

- ¼ **to ½ tsp. cayenne pepper**
- 1 **pkg. (32 oz.) frozen Tater Tots**

1. In a Dutch oven, cook the sausage, beef and onion over medium heat until meat is no longer pink; drain. Add the soup, beans, corn, 1 cup Colby-Monterey Jack cheese, milk, garlic powder, seasoned salt and cayenne. Transfer to 2 greased 11x7-in. baking dishes. Top with the Tater Tots; sprinkle with the remaining cheese.
2. Cover and freeze 1 casserole for up to 3 months. Cover and bake the remaining casserole at 350° for 40 minutes. Uncover and bake casserole for 5-10 minutes longer or until bubbly.
To use frozen casserole: Thaw in the refrigerator overnight. Remove from the refrigerator 30 minutes before baking. Cover and bake at 350° for 50 minutes. Uncover and bake 5-10 minutes longer or until bubbly.
1 serving: 370 cal., 22g fat (8g sat. fat), 48mg chol., 1085mg sod., 30g carb. (4g sugars, 3g fiber), 16g pro.

❄ CHICKEN PIZZA

Your family will never guess that this fun twist on typical pizza relies on a packaged crust and prepared pesto. Loaded with chicken and black beans, hearty slices fill everyone up fast!
—Taste of Home *Test Kitchen*

- -

Prep: 20 min. • **Cook:** 10 min.
Makes: 6 servings

- 1 **pound boneless skinless chicken breasts, cut into 1-inch pieces**
- 1 **tablespoon olive oil**
- 1 **prebaked 12-inch pizza crust**
- ¼ **cup prepared pesto**
- 1 **large tomato, chopped**
- ½ **cup canned black beans, rinsed and drained**
- 1 **cup shredded part-skim mozzarella cheese**
- ½ **cup shredded Parmesan cheese**

1. In a large skillet, cook chicken in oil over medium heat for 10-15 minutes or until no longer pink.
2. Place the crust on a lightly greased 12-in. pizza pan. Spread with pesto; top with the chicken, tomato, beans and cheeses. Bake at 400° for 10-12 minutes or until cheese is melted.
Freeze option: Securely wrap and freeze unbaked pizza. To use, unwrap pizza; bake as directed, increasing time as necessary.
1 slice: 431 cal., 18g fat (6g sat. fat), 65mg chol., 692mg sod., 35g carb. (1g sugars, 1g fiber), 32g pro.

TWO-FOR-ONE CHICKEN TETRAZZINI

A good friend shared a version of this recipe with me 35 years ago. I pay it forward by bringing the second casserole to friends when they are unable to cook.
—*Helen McPhee, Savoy, IL*

Prep: 30 min. • **Bake:** 20 min.
Makes: 2 casseroles (4 servings each)

1	pkg. (12 oz.) **spaghetti**
⅓	cup **butter,** cubed
⅓	cup **all-purpose flour**
¾	tsp. **salt**
¼	tsp. **white pepper**
1	can (14½ oz.) **chicken broth**
1½	cups **half-and-half cream**
1	cup **heavy whipping cream**
4	cups **cubed cooked chicken**
3	cans (4 oz. each) **mushroom stems and pieces,** drained
1	jar (4 oz.) **sliced pimientos,** drained
½	cup grated **Parmesan cheese**

1. Cook the spaghetti according to package directions. Meanwhile, in a Dutch oven, melt butter. Stir in the flour, salt and pepper until smooth. Gradually add broth, half-and-half and whipping cream. Bring to a boil; cook and stir until thickened, about 2 minutes.

2. Remove from the heat. Stir in the cubed chicken, mushrooms and pimientos. Drain spaghetti; add to the chicken mixture and toss to coat.

3. Transfer to 2 greased 11x7-in. baking dishes. Sprinkle with cheese. Cover and freeze 1 casserole for up to 2 months. Bake the second casserole, uncovered, at 350° until heated through, 20-25 minutes.

To use frozen casserole: Thaw in the refrigerator overnight. Cover and bake at 350° for 30 minutes. Uncover; bake until heated through, 15-20 minutes longer. Stir before serving.

1 cup: 572 cal., 31g fat (17g sat. fat), 150mg chol., 746mg sod., 40g carb. (4g sugars, 2g fiber), 31g pro.

LONE STAR CHICKEN ENCHILADAS

Start with deli-roasted chicken to speed up the prep for this family-friendly casserole. For a milder version, use Monterey Jack cheese in place of pepper jack.

—*Avanell Hewitt, North Richland Hills, TX*

- -

Prep: 30 min. + freezing • **Bake:** 35 min.
Makes: 6 servings

3	cups shredded cooked chicken breast
1	can (10 oz.) diced tomatoes with mild green chiles, drained
¾	cup salsa verde
1	can (4 oz.) chopped green chiles
1	can (2¼ oz.) sliced ripe olives, drained
1	tsp. ground cumin
2½	cups heavy whipping cream
¾	tsp. salt
12	corn tortillas (6 in.), warmed
2	cups shredded pepper Jack cheese

1. In a large bowl, combine the first 6 ingredients. In a shallow bowl, combine cream and salt.

2. Dip both sides of each tortilla in cream mixture; top with ¼ cup chicken mixture. Roll up and place seam side down in a greased 13x9-in. baking dish. Pour the remaining cream mixture over the top; sprinkle with cheese. Cover and freeze up to 6 months.

To use frozen casserole: Thaw in the refrigerator overnight. Remove from the refrigerator 30 minutes before baking. Cover and bake at 350° for 35-40 minutes or until heated through.

2 enchiladas: 897 cal., 65g fat (37g sat. fat), 270mg chol., 1437mg sod., 36g carb. (4g sugars, 4g fiber), 45g pro.

BOW TIES & HAM

We love casseroles! Just pop one in the oven to warm your home and fill your tummy. Here's a favorite recipe from our family cookbook.
—*Suzette Jury, Keene, CA*

Prep: 20 min. • **Bake:** 25 min.
Makes: 2 casseroles (6 servings each)

- 4 cups uncooked bow tie pasta
- 6 cups frozen broccoli florets
- 4 cups cubed fully cooked ham
- 2 cartons (10 oz. each) refrigerated Alfredo sauce
- 2 cups shredded Swiss cheese
- 1 can (8 oz.) mushroom stems and pieces, drained

1. Cook the pasta according to package directions, adding the broccoli during the last 5 minutes of cooking. Meanwhile, in a large bowl, combine ham, Alfredo sauce, cheese and mushrooms. Drain the pasta mixture; add to the ham mixture and toss to coat.

2. Transfer to 2 greased 11x7-in. baking dishes. Cover and freeze 1 casserole for up to 3 months. Cover and bake the remaining casserole at 375° for 20 minutes. Uncover; bake casserole for 5-10 minutes longer or until bubbly.

To use frozen casserole: Thaw in the refrigerator overnight. Remove from the refrigerator 30 minutes before heating. Cover and microwave on high roughly 8-10 minutes or until heated through, stirring once.

1 cup: 384 cal., 23g fat (10g sat. fat), 60mg chol., 1178mg sod., 24g carb. (3g sugars, 2g fiber), 20g pro.

BREADSTICK PIZZA

Make Monday fun-day with a hassle-free homemade pizza featuring refrigerated breadsticks as the crust. Feeding the kids? Slice the pieces into small strips and let them dip each strip into marinara sauce. They'll love it!

—*Mary Hankins, Kansas City, MO*

- -

Prep: 25 min. • **Bake:** 20 min.
Makes: 12 servings

- 2 tubes (11 oz. each) refrigerated breadsticks
- ½ lb. sliced fresh mushrooms
- 2 medium green peppers, chopped
- 1 medium onion, chopped
- 1½ tsp. Italian seasoning, divided
- 4 tsp. olive oil, divided
- 1½ cups shredded cheddar cheese, divided
- 5 oz. Canadian bacon, chopped
- 1½ cups shredded part-skim mozzarella cheese
  Marinara sauce

1. Unroll breadsticks into a greased 15x10x1-in. baking pan. Press onto the bottom and up the sides of pan; pinch seams to seal. Bake at 350° until set, 6-8 minutes.

2. Meanwhile, in a large skillet, saute the mushrooms, peppers, onion and 1 tsp. Italian seasoning in 2 tsp. oil until vegetables are crisp-tender; drain.

3. Brush crust with remaining oil. Sprinkle with ¾ cup shredded cheddar cheese; top with the vegetable mixture and Canadian bacon. Combine the shredded mozzarella cheese and remaining cheddar cheese; sprinkle over top. Sprinkle with remaining Italian seasoning.

4. Bake until cheese is melted and crust is golden brown, 20-25 minutes. Serve with marinara sauce.

Freeze option: Bake crust as directed, add toppings and cool. Securely wrap and freeze unbaked pizza. To use, unwrap the pizza; bake as directed, increasing time as necessary.

1 piece: 267 cal., 11g fat (6g sat. fat), 27mg chol., 638mg sod., 29g carb. (5g sugars, 2g fiber), 13g pro.

❄ CHEESY SCALLOPED POTATOES & HAM

Creamy, cheesy and easy to make, this casserole is the definition of comfort food. This makes two casseroles, so it's great for a crowd; it freezes nicely, too.
—*Salina Bontrager, Kalona, IA*

- -

Prep: 45 min. • **Bake:** 1¾ hours
Makes: 2 casseroles (8 servings each)

 2   cans (10¾ oz. each) condensed cream of chicken soup, undiluted
 2   cups sour cream
⅔   cup butter, melted
 1   tsp. garlic powder
 1   tsp. pepper
6½   lbs. potatoes, peeled and cut into ¼-in. slices
 6   cups cubed fully cooked ham (about 2½ lbs.)
 1   pkg. (16 oz.) Velveeta, cubed

1. Preheat oven to 350°. Mix the first 5 ingredients. Stir in potatoes, ham and cheese. Transfer to 2 greased 13x9-in. baking dishes.
2. Bake, covered, 1 hour. Uncover and bake 45-55 minutes or until potatoes are tender.
Freeze option: Cover and freeze unbaked casseroles. To use, partially thaw casseroles in refrigerator overnight. Remove from refrigerator 30 minutes before baking. Preheat oven to 350°. Bake casseroles as directed, increasing time as necessary to heat through and for a thermometer inserted in center to read 165°.
1½ cups: 491 cal., 28g fat (15g sat. fat), 106mg chol., 1664mg sod., 34g carb. (5g sugars, 2g fiber), 23g pro.

ITALIAN SAUSAGE RIGATONI BAKE

Here's a dish that combines all of our favorite Italian flavors, but the fresh mozzarella really sets it apart!
—*Blair Lonergan, Rochelle, VA*

- -

Prep: 30 min. • **Bake:** 25 min.
Makes: 2 casseroles (4 servings each)

 1   pkg. (16 oz.) rigatoni
 1   lb. bulk Italian sausage
½   lb. sliced fresh mushrooms
 1   medium sweet red pepper, chopped
 5   cups marinara sauce
¼   cup grated Parmesan cheese
 2   Tbsp. half-and-half cream
 1   lb. sliced part-skim mozzarella cheese

1. Preheat oven to 375°. Cook rigatoni according to package directions; drain.
2. In a large skillet, cook the sausage, mushrooms and pepper over medium-high heat until sausage is no longer pink and vegetables are tender, breaking up sausage into crumbles, 8-10 minutes; drain. Stir in the marinara sauce, Parmesan cheese and cream. Add the rigatoni and toss to coat.
3. In each of 2 greased 8-in. square baking dishes, layer one-fourth of the rigatoni mixture and one-fourth of the mozzarella cheese. Repeat layers. Bake, uncovered, until heated through and cheese is melted, 25-35 minutes. (Cover loosely with foil if tops brown too quickly.)
Freeze option: Cool unbaked casseroles; cover and freeze. To use, partially thaw in refrigerator overnight. Remove from refrigerator 30 minutes before baking. Preheat oven to 375°. Bake casseroles as directed, increasing time as necessary to heat through and for a thermometer inserted in center to read 165°.
1 piece: 535 cal., 26g fat (11g sat. fat), 71mg chol., 774mg sod., 48g carb. (4g sugars, 3g fiber), 29g pro.

MEATBALLS IN HONEY BUFFALO SAUCE

My family loves a sweet-spicy combo and declared this recipe an instant favorite just for that reason. The meatballs start sweet but finish with a little heat!
—Anne Ormond, Dover, NH

Prep: 45 min. • **Cook:** 2 hours
Makes: about 2½ dozen

- 2 large eggs, lightly beaten
- 15 Ritz crackers, crushed
- ½ medium onion, finely chopped
- ¼ cup 2% milk
- 4 tsp. brown sugar
- ½ tsp. garlic powder
- ½ tsp. ground chipotle pepper
- ¼ tsp. smoked paprika
- ¼ tsp. salt
- ⅛ tsp. pepper
- ½ lb. ground beef
- ½ lb. ground pork
- ½ lb. ground veal

SAUCE

- ½ cup honey
- ¼ cup Buffalo wing sauce
- ¼ cup packed brown sugar
- 2 Tbsp. orange marmalade
- 2 Tbsp. apricot spreadable fruit
- 2 Tbsp. reduced-sodium soy sauce
- ¼ tsp. crushed red pepper flakes
  Hot cooked rice or pasta
  Sliced celery, optional

1. Preheat oven to 400°. Combine the first 10 ingredients. Add meat; mix lightly but thoroughly. Shape the meat mixture into 1½-in. balls; bake on a greased rack in a 15x10x1-in. baking pan lined with foil until lightly browned, 12-15 minutes. Meanwhile, in a small saucepan over medium heat, whisk together sauce ingredients until the brown sugar is dissolved.

2. Transfer the meatballs to a 3-qt. slow cooker; add sauce. Cook, covered, on low until the meatballs are cooked through, about 2 hours. Serve with hot cooked rice or pasta and, if desired, sliced celery.

Freeze option: Freeze cooled meatballs and sauce in freezer containers. To use, partially thaw in refrigerator overnight. Heat through in a covered saucepan, stirring gently; add water or broth if necessary. Serve meatballs as directed.

3 meatballs with 2 Tbsp. sauce: 258 cal., 10g fat (3g sat. fat), 81mg chol., 459mg sod., 30g carb. (26g sugars, 0 fiber), 14g pro.

❄

CREAMY CHICKEN CASSEROLE

I created this noodle casserole when my husband was craving a dish his aunt used to make. It's is now a staple at our house.
—*Mari Warnke, Fremont, WI*

Prep: 20 min. • **Bake:** 40 min.
Makes: 2 casseroles (5 servings each)

    4   cups uncooked egg noodles
    4   cups cubed cooked chicken
    1   pkg. (16 oz.) frozen
        peas and carrots
    2   cups whole milk
    2   cans (10¾ oz. each) condensed
        cream of celery soup, undiluted
    2   cans (10¾ oz. each) condensed
        cream of chicken soup, undiluted
    1   cup chopped onion
    2   Tbsp. butter, melted
    ½   tsp. salt
    ½   tsp. pepper

1. Preheat oven to 350°. Cook the egg noodles according to package directions. Meanwhile, in a large bowl, combine the remaining ingredients. Drain the noodles; add to the chicken mixture.
2. Transfer to 2 greased 8-in. square baking dishes. Cover and bake the casseroles for 30 minutes. Uncover and bake until heated through, 10-15 minutes longer.
Freeze option: Cover and freeze unbaked casseroles up to 3 months. To use, partially thaw in refrigerator overnight. Remove from the refrigerator 30 minutes before baking. Cover and microwave casseroles on high for 10-12 minutes or until heated through and a thermometer inserted in center reads 165°, stirring twice.
1⅓ cups: 355 cal., 15g fat (5g sat. fat), 81mg chol., 1106mg sod., 30g carb. (7g sugars, 3g fiber), 24g pro.

INDIVIDUAL SHEPHERD'S PIES

These comforting little pies are easy to freeze and eat later on busy weeknights.
—*Ellen Osborne, Clarksville, TN*

- -

Prep: 30 min. • **Bake:** 20 min.
Makes: 10 mini pies

- 1   lb. ground beef
- 3   Tbsp. chopped onion
- ½   tsp. minced garlic
- ⅓   cup chili sauce or ketchup
- 1   Tbsp. cider vinegar
- 2   cups hot mashed potatoes (with added milk and butter)
- 3   oz. cream cheese, softened
- 1   tube (12 oz.) refrigerated buttermilk biscuits
- ½   cup crushed potato chips Paprika, optional

1. Preheat oven to 375°. In a large skillet, cook beef and onion over medium heat until beef is no longer pink, 5-7 minutes, breaking up beef into crumbles. Add garlic; cook for 1 minute or until tender. Drain. Stir in chili sauce and vinegar.
2. In a small bowl, mix mashed potatoes and cream cheese until blended. Press 1 biscuit onto bottom and up sides of each of 10 greased muffin cups. Fill with beef mixture. Spread potato mixture over tops. Sprinkle with potato chips, pressing down lightly.
3. Bake until golden brown, 20-25 minutes. If desired, sprinkle with paprika.
Freeze option: Freeze cooled shepherd's pies in a single layer in freezer containers. To use, partially thaw in refrigerator overnight. Bake on a baking sheet in a preheated 375° oven until heated through, 15-18 minutes.
2 mini pies: 567 cal., 30g fat (12g sat. fat), 84mg chol., 1378mg sod., 51g carb. (9g sugars, 2g fiber), 23g pro.

GROUND BEEF SPIRAL BAKE

We got this recipe from a restaurant cook who lived in the duplex beside my mother-in-law. It was one of his favorites. It's easy to make, tastes fantastic and freezes well. Both my mother-in-law and her neighbor are gone now, but this recipe always brings back memories!
—*Monika Rahn, Dillsburg, PA*

- -

Prep: 40 min. • **Bake:** 25 min.
Makes: 2 casseroles (8 servings each)

- 1   pkg. (16 oz.) spiral pasta
- 2   lbs. ground beef
- ⅔   cup chopped onion
- 1   tsp. minced garlic
- 2   jars (26 oz. each) spaghetti sauce
- 2   Tbsp. tomato paste
- 1   tsp. dried basil
- 1   tsp. dried oregano
- 4   cups shredded part-skim mozzarella cheese

1. Cook spiral pasta according to package directions; drain. Meanwhile, in a Dutch oven, cook beef and onion over medium heat until meat is no longer pink. Add garlic; cook 1 minute longer. Drain. Stir in the spaghetti sauce, tomato paste, basil and oregano. Bring to a boil. Reduce heat; simmer, uncovered, for 5-10 minutes.
2. Stir pasta into meat mixture. Transfer to 2 greased 13x9-in. baking dishes. Sprinkle each with 2 cups cheese. Cover and freeze 1 casserole for up to 3 months.
3. Bake the remaining casserole, uncovered, at 350° for 25-30 minutes or until casserole is heated through.
To use frozen casserole: Thaw in the refrigerator overnight. Bake, uncovered, at 350° for 35-40 minutes or until casserole is heated through.
¾ cup: 359 cal., 15g fat (6g sat. fat), 54mg chol., 627mg sod., 32g carb. (8g sugars, 3g fiber), 23g pro.

WILD RICE MUSHROOM CHICKEN

I use a wild rice mix to put a tasty spin on a traditional chicken and rice bake. It's simple and delicious with leftover chicken or even cooked turkey.

—*Jacqueline Graves, Lawrenceville, GA*

Prep: 15 min. • **Cook:** 20 min.
Makes: 2 casseroles (4 servings each)

- 2 **pkg. (6 oz. each) long grain and wild rice mix**
- 8 **boneless skinless chicken breast halves (6 oz. each)**
- 5 **Tbsp. butter, divided**
- 1 **large sweet red pepper, chopped**
- 2 **jars (4½ oz. each) sliced mushrooms, drained**

1. Prepare the rice according to package directions. Meanwhile, in a large skillet, cook the chicken in 3 Tbsp. butter for 6-8 minutes on each side or until browned and a meat thermometer reads 170°. Remove chicken and keep warm.

2. Add remaining butter to pan drippings; saute red pepper until tender. Stir in the mushrooms; heat through. Add to rice. Serve 4 chicken breasts with half of the rice mixture.

3. Place the remaining chicken in a greased 11x7-in. baking dish; top with remaining rice mixture. Cool. Cover and freeze for up to 3 months.

To use frozen casserole: Thaw in the refrigerator. Cover and bake at 350° for 35-40 minutes or until heated through.

1 serving: 319 cal., 11g fat (6g sat. fat), 109mg chol., 504mg sod., 17g carb. (1g sugars, 1g fiber), 36g pro.

TACO-FILLED PASTA SHELLS

I've been stuffing pasta shells with different fillings for years, but my family enjoys this version with taco-seasoned meat the most. The frozen shells are convenient, because you can take out only the number you need. Just add zippy taco sauce and bake.
—*Marge Hodel, Roanoke, IL*

Prep: 20 min. + chilling • **Bake:** 45 min.
Makes: 2 casseroles (6 servings each)

```
2    lbs. ground beef
2    envelopes taco seasoning
1½   cups water
1    pkg. (8 oz.) cream cheese, cubed
24   uncooked jumbo pasta shells
¼    cup butter, melted
```

ADDITIONAL INGREDIENTS (FOR EACH CASSEROLE)

```
1    cup salsa
1    cup taco sauce
1    cup shredded cheddar cheese
1    cup shredded Monterey
     Jack cheese
1½   cups crushed tortilla chips
1    cup sour cream
3    green onions, chopped
```

1. In a Dutch oven, cook ground beef over medium heat until no longer pink; drain. Stir in the taco seasoning and water. Bring to a boil. Reduce heat; simmer, uncovered, for 5 minutes. Stir in cream cheese until melted. Transfer to a bowl; cool. Chill for 1 hour.

2. Cook pasta shells according to package directions; drain. Gently toss with butter. Fill each shell with about 3 Tbsp. of meat mixture. Place half of the shells in a freezer container. Cover and freeze for up to 3 months.

3. To prepare remaining shells, spoon 1 cup salsa into a greased 9-in. square baking dish. Top with remaining stuffed shells and 1 cup taco sauce. Cover and bake at 350° for 30 minutes. Uncover; sprinkle with 1 cup each of cheeses and 1½ cups chips. Bake 15 minutes longer or until heated through. Serve with sour cream and onions.

To use frozen shells: Thaw in the refrigerator for 24 hours (shells will be partially frozen). Remove from dish. Add salsa to dish; top with shells and taco sauce. Cover and bake at 350° for 40 minutes. Uncover; continue as directed.

2 shells: 492 cal., 31g fat (16g sat. fat), 98mg chol., 982mg sod., 29g carb. (4g sugars, 1g fiber), 23g pro.

MEXICAN-STYLE MEAT LOAVES

On a vacation to Arizona, I fell in love with *albondigas,* Latin American meatballs. After playing with a number of different spices I came up with a version that's amazing as a meat loaf.
—*James Schend, Pleasant Prairie, WI*

Prep: 20 min. • **Bake:** 50 min. + standing
Makes: 2 loaves (8 servings each)

3	large eggs, lightly beaten
⅔	cup 2% milk
⅔	cup thick and zesty tomato sauce
2	Tbsp. Worcestershire sauce
1	large onion, finely chopped
2	cans (2¼ oz. each) sliced ripe olives, drained
¾	cup dry bread crumbs
⅓	cup minced fresh cilantro
2½	tsp. ground cumin
2½	tsp. chili powder
1	tsp. salt
1	tsp. pepper
3	lbs. lean ground beef (90% lean)
	Optional: Salsa and additional cilantro

1. Preheat oven to 350°. In a large bowl, combine the first 12 ingredients. Add beef; mix lightly but thoroughly. Transfer the mixture to 2 greased 9x5-in. loaf pans.

2. Bake meat loaves 50-55 minutes or until a thermometer reads 160°. Let stand for 10 minutes before slicing. If desired, top with salsa and cilantro.

Freeze option: Shape meat loaves in plastic wrap-lined loaf pans; cover and freeze until firm. Remove from pans and wrap securely in foil; return to freezer. To use, unwrap and bake the meat loaves in pans as directed, increasing time to 1¼-1½ hours or until a thermometer inserted in center reads 160°.

1 slice: 196 cal., 10g fat (3g sat. fat), 89mg chol., 453mg sod., 7g carb. (2g sugars, 1g fiber), 19g pro. **Diabetic exchanges:** 3 lean meat, ½ starch.

BEEFY CHILI DOGS

For years people have told me I make the best hot dog chili out there. It's timeless and family-friendly, and I usually carry the recipe with me because people ask for it.
—*Vicki Boyd, Mechanicsville, VA*

Prep: 5 min. • **Cook:** 25 min.
Makes: 8 servings (2 cups chili)

1   pound ground beef
1   teaspoon chili powder
½   teaspoon garlic powder
½   teaspoon paprika
¼   teaspoon cayenne pepper
1   cup ketchup
8   hot dogs
8   hot dog buns, split
     Optional: Shredded cheddar cheese
     and chopped onion

1. For the chili, in a large skillet, cook beef over medium heat 5-7 minutes or until no longer pink, breaking into crumbles; drain. Transfer the beef to a food processor; pulse until finely chopped.
2. Return beef to skillet; stir in seasonings and ketchup. Bring to a boil. Reduce heat; simmer, covered, 15-20 minutes to allow flavors to blend, stirring occasionally.
3. Meanwhile, cook hot dogs according to package directions. Serve in buns with chili. If desired, top with cheese and onion.
Freeze option: Freeze cooled chili in a freezer container. To use, partially thaw in refrigerator overnight. Heat through in a saucepan, stirring occasionally; add water if necessary.
1 hot dog with ¼ cup chili: 400 cal., 22g fat (9g sat. fat), 60mg chol., 1092mg sod., 31g carb. (11g sugars, 1g fiber), 19g pro.

CHICKEN CORDON BLEU BAKE

I freeze several pans of this casserole to share with my neighbors or for busy days.
—*Rea Newell, Decatur, IL*

Prep: 20 min. • **Bake:** 40 min.
Makes: 2 casseroles (6 servings each)

- 2   pkg. (6 oz. each) reduced-sodium stuffing mix
- 1   can (10¾ oz.) condensed cream of chicken soup, undiluted
- 1   cup 2% milk
- 8   cups cubed cooked chicken
- ½   tsp. pepper
- ¾   lb. sliced deli ham, cut into 1-in. strips
- 1   cup shredded Swiss cheese
- 3   cups shredded cheddar cheese

1. Preheat oven to 350°. Prepare stuffing mixes according to package directions. Meanwhile, whisk together soup and milk.
2. Toss the chicken with pepper; divide between 2 greased 13x9-in. baking dishes. Layer with the ham, Swiss cheese, 1 cup cheddar cheese, soup mixture and stuffing. Sprinkle with remaining cheddar cheese.
3. Bake, covered, 30 minutes. Uncover; bake until cheese is melted, 10-15 minutes.

Freeze option: Cover and freeze unbaked casseroles. To use, partially thaw in the refrigerator overnight. Remove from the refrigerator 30 minutes before baking. Preheat oven to 350°. Bake, covered, until heated through and a thermometer inserted in center reads 165°, about 45 minutes. Uncover; bake until the cheese is melted, 10-15 minutes.

1 cup: 555 cal., 29g fat (15g sat. fat), 158mg chol., 1055mg sod., 26g carb. (5g sugars, 1g fiber), 46g pro.

COMFORTING TUNA PATTIES

My grandmother and mother made these tuna patties during Lent. The patties are even good cold the next day—if there are any left, that is!
—*Ann Marie Eberhart, Gig Harbor, WA*

Prep: 25 min. + chilling • **Cook:** 5 min./batch
Makes: 6 servings

- 2   tablespoons butter
- 3   tablespoons all-purpose flour
- 1   cup evaporated milk
- 1   pouch (6.4 ounces) light tuna in water
- ⅓   cup plus ½ cup dry bread crumbs, divided
- 1   green onion, finely chopped
- 2   tablespoons lemon juice
- ½   teaspoon salt
- ¼   teaspoon pepper
     Oil for frying

1. In a small saucepan, melt butter over medium heat. Stir in flour until smooth; gradually whisk in milk. Bring to a boil, stirring constantly; cook and stir until thickened, 2-3 minutes. Remove from heat. Transfer to a small bowl; cool.
2. Stir in the tuna, ⅓ cup bread crumbs, green onion, lemon juice, salt and pepper. Refrigerate, covered, at least 30 minutes.
3. Place remaining ½ cup bread crumbs in a shallow bowl. Drop ⅓ cup tuna mixture into crumbs. Gently coat and shape into a ½-in.-thick patty. Repeat. In a large skillet, heat oil over medium heat. Add tuna patties in batches; cook 2-3 minutes on each side or until golden brown. Drain on paper towels.

Freeze option: Freeze cooled tuna patties in freezer containers, separating layers with waxed paper. To use, reheat tuna patties on a baking sheet in a preheated 325° oven until heated through.

1 tuna patty: 255 cal., 17g fat (5g sat. fat), 34mg chol., 419mg sod., 15g carb. (5g sugars, 1g fiber), 10g pro.

SAUSAGE BREAD SANDWICHES

I make these sandwiches in my spare time and freeze them so they're ready when needed, such as for last-minute dinners and tailgating parties when we attend Kansas State football games.
—*Donna Roberts, Manhattan, KS*

Prep: 30 min. • **Bake:** 20 min.
Makes: 4 sandwich loaves (3 pieces each)

- 1 pkg. (16 oz.) hot roll mix
- 2 lbs. reduced-fat bulk pork sausage
- 2 Tbsp. dried parsley flakes
- 2 tsp. garlic powder
- 1 tsp. onion powder
- ½ tsp. dried oregano
- 2 cups shredded part-skim mozzarella cheese
- ½ cup grated Parmesan cheese
- 1 large egg
- 1 Tbsp. water

1. Preheat oven to 350°. Prepare roll mix dough according to package directions.
2. Meanwhile, in a large skillet, cook the sausage over medium heat 8-10 minutes or until no longer pink, breaking into crumbles; drain. Stir in seasonings.
3. Divide dough into 4 portions. On a lightly floured surface, roll each into a 14x8-in. rectangle. Top each with 1¼ cups sausage mixture to within 1 in. of edges; sprinkle with ½ cup mozzarella cheese and 2 Tbsp. Parmesan cheese. Roll up jelly-roll style, starting with a long side; pinch seams and ends to seal.
4. Transfer to greased baking sheets, seam side down. In a small bowl, whisk egg with water; brush over loaves. Bake until golden brown and heated through, 20-25 minutes. Cool sandwiches 5 minutes before slicing.
Freeze option: Cool cooked sandwiches 1 hour on wire racks. Cut each sandwich into thirds; wrap each securely in foil. Freeze until serving. To reheat in the oven, place wrapped frozen sandwiches on a baking sheet. Heat the sandwiches in a preheated 375° oven for 20-25 minutes or until heated through.
1 piece: 432 cal., 25g fat (10g sat. fat), 103mg chol., 926mg sod., 27g carb. (5g sugars, 1g fiber), 24g pro.

BEEF TACO LASAGNA

This recipe makes two big pans. Freeze one or both to enjoy later.
—*Stacey Compton, Toledo, OH*

Prep: 30 min. • **Bake:** 35 min. + standing
Makes: 2 casseroles (8 servings each)

- 24 **lasagna noodles**
- 2 **lbs. lean ground beef (90% lean)**
- 2 **envelopes taco seasoning**
- 4 **large egg whites**
- 2 **cartons (15 oz. each) ricotta cheese**
- 8 **cups shredded cheddar cheese**
- 2 **jars (24 oz. each) chunky salsa**

1. Preheat oven to 350°. Cook the lasagna noodles according to package directions. Meanwhile, in a large skillet, cook beef over medium heat until no longer pink; drain. Stir in taco seasoning. In a small bowl, combine the egg whites and ricotta cheese. Drain the noodles.

2. In each of two 13x9-in. baking dishes, layer 4 noodles, ¾ cup ricotta mixture, one quarter of the beef mixture and 1 cup cheddar cheese. Top each with 4 more noodles, ¾ cup ricotta mixture, 1½ cups salsa and 1 cup cheese. Repeat.

3. Bake, uncovered, 35-40 minutes or until heated through. Let stand for 10 minutes before cutting.

Freeze option: Cover and freeze unbaked lasagna. To use, partially thaw lasagna in the refrigerator overnight. Remove from the refrigerator 30 minutes before baking. Bake the lasagna as directed, increasing the time as necessary to heat through and for a thermometer to read 165°.

1 piece: 545 cal., 26g fat (17g sat. fat), 109mg chol., 1198mg sod., 42g carb. (7g sugars, 1g fiber), 35g pro.

HAM & CHEESE CASSEROLES

I got this recipe from my mother and love it because it's easy and I've usually got the ingredients on hand. Also, it freezes well and I can have it handy when extra guests show up. Everyone always likes it; there are never any leftovers.
—*Jan Schoshke, Brookville, KS*

- -

Prep: 20 min. • **Bake:** 25 min.
Makes: 2 casseroles (8 servings each)

1½ lbs. uncooked egg noodles
3 lbs. cubed fully cooked ham
4 cans (10¾ oz. each) condensed cream of chicken soup, undiluted
4 cups frozen cut green beans, thawed
1 cup 2% milk
¼ cup butter, melted
2 cups shredded Colby-Monterey Jack cheese

1. Preheat oven to 350°. Cook the pasta according to package directions.
2. Meanwhile, in a large bowl, combine ham, soup, beans and milk. Drain pasta; pour over ham mixture and toss to coat. Transfer to 2 greased 13x9-in. baking dishes.
3. Drizzle each with butter; sprinkle with cheese. Bake, uncovered, 25-30 minutes or until heated through.
Freeze option: Cool unbaked casseroles; cover and freeze up to 3 months. To use, partially thaw in refrigerator overnight. Remove from the refrigerator 30 minutes before baking. Preheat oven to 350°. Bake, uncovered, 40-45 minutes or until heated through and a thermometer inserted in center reads 165°.
1⅓ cups: 470 cal., 21g fat (9g sat. fat), 109mg chol., 1786mg sod., 42g carb. (3g sugars, 3g fiber), 27g pro.

SASSY SALSA MEAT LOAVES

Here's a twist on classic meat loaf that can be made ahead and will last for a few days afterward. Make meat loaf sandwiches with the leftovers, buns and a little Monterey Jack cheese.

—*Tasha Tully, Owings Mills, MD*

Prep: 25 min. • **Bake:** 65 min. + standing
Makes: 2 loaves (6 servings each)

- ¾ cup uncooked instant brown rice
- 1 can (8 oz.) tomato sauce
- 1½ cups salsa, divided
- 1 large onion, chopped
- 1 large egg, lightly beaten
- 1 celery rib, finely chopped
- ¼ cup minced fresh parsley
- 2 Tbsp. minced fresh cilantro
- 2 garlic cloves, minced
- 1 Tbsp. chili powder
- 1½ tsp. salt
- ½ tsp. pepper
- 2 lbs. lean ground beef (90% lean)
- 1 lb. ground turkey
- ½ cup shredded reduced-fat Monterey Jack cheese or Mexican cheese blend

1. Preheat oven to 350°. Cook the rice according to package directions; cool slightly. In a large bowl, combine tomato sauce, ½ cup salsa, onion, egg, celery, parsley, cilantro, garlic and seasonings; stir in rice. Add beef and turkey; mix lightly but thoroughly.

2. Shape mixture into two 8x4-in. loaves in a greased 15x10x1-in. baking pan. Bake loaves until a thermometer inserted in the center reads 165°, 1-1¼ hours.

3. Spread with remaining salsa and sprinkle with cheese; bake until cheese is melted, about 5 minutes. Let stand for 10 minutes before slicing.

Freeze option: Bake meat loaves without topping. Securely wrap and freeze cooled meat loaf in foil. To use, partially thaw in refrigerator overnight. Unwrap the meat loaves; place in a greased 15x10x1-in. baking pan. Reheat in a preheated 350° oven until a thermometer inserted in center reads 165°, 40-45 minutes; top as directed.

1 slice: 237 cal., 11g fat (4g sat. fat), 91mg chol., 634mg sod., 9g carb. (2g sugars, 1g fiber), 25g pro. **Diabetic exchanges:** 3 lean meat, ½ starch, ½ fat.

SIMPLE CREAMY CHICKEN ENCHILADAS

This is one of the first recipes I created and cooked for my husband right after we got married. He was so impressed! Now we fix these enchiladas regularly for friends.
—*Melissa Rogers, Tuscaloosa, AL*

Prep: 30 min. • **Bake:** 30 min.
Makes: 2 casseroles (5 servings each)

- 2 cans (14½ oz. each) diced tomatoes with mild green chiles, undrained
- 2 cans (10½ oz. each) condensed cream of chicken soup, undiluted
- 1 can (10¾ oz.) condensed cheddar cheese soup, undiluted
- ¼ cup 2% milk
- 1 Tbsp. ground cumin
- 1 Tbsp. chili powder
- 2 tsp. garlic powder
- 2 tsp. dried oregano
- 5 cups shredded rotisserie chicken
- 1 pkg. (8 oz.) cream cheese, cubed and softened
- 20 flour tortillas (8 in.), warmed
- 4 cups shredded Mexican cheese blend

1. Preheat oven to 350°. For sauce, mix first 8 ingredients. For filling, in a large bowl, mix chicken and cream cheese until blended; stir in 3½ cups sauce.

2. Spread ¼ cup of the sauce into each of 2 greased 13x9-in. baking dishes. Place ⅓ cup of the filling down the center of each tortilla; roll up and place seam side down in baking dishes. Pour remaining sauce over tops; sprinkle with cheese.

3. Bake, uncovered, 30-35 minutes or until heated through and cheese is melted.

Freeze option: Cover and freeze unbaked enchiladas up to 3 months. To use, partially thaw in refrigerator overnight. Remove from the refrigerator 30 minutes before baking. Preheat oven to 350°. Cover enchiladas with greased foil; bake until heated through and a thermometer inserted in center reads 165°, about 45 minutes. Uncover; bake until cheese is melted, 5-10 minutes longer.

2 enchiladas: 828 cal., 40g fat (17g sat. fat), 132mg chol., 1738mg sod., 72g carb. (5g sugars, 7g fiber), 42g pro.

TEST KITCHEN TIP
To bring down the sodium content of this recipe, switch to no-salt-added diced tomatoes and reduced-sodium condensed soup.

SOUTHWESTERN CASSEROLE

I've been making this mild family-pleasing casserole for years. It tastes wonderful, fits nicely into our budget and, best of all, makes a second hot dish to freeze and enjoy sometime later.

—Joan Hallford, North Richland Hills, TX

Prep: 25 min. • **Bake:** 40 min.
Makes: 2 casseroles (6 servings each)

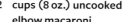

2 cups (8 oz.) uncooked elbow macaroni
2 lbs. ground beef
1 large onion, chopped
2 garlic cloves, minced
2 cans (14½ oz. each) diced tomatoes, undrained
1 can (16 oz.) kidney beans, rinsed and drained
1 can (6 oz.) tomato paste
1 can (4 oz.) chopped green chiles, drained

1½ tsp. salt
1 tsp. chili powder
½ tsp. ground cumin
½ tsp. pepper
2 cups shredded Monterey Jack cheese
2 jalapeno peppers, seeded and chopped

1. Cook macaroni according to package directions. Meanwhile, in a large saucepan, cook beef and onion over medium heat, crumbling beef, until meat is no longer pink. Add garlic; cook 1 minute longer. Drain. Stir in next 8 ingredients. Bring to a boil. Reduce heat; simmer, uncovered, for 10 minutes. Drain macaroni; stir into beef mixture.
2. Preheat oven to 375°. Transfer macaroni mixture to 2 greased 2-qt. baking dishes. Top with cheese and jalapenos. Cover and bake at 375° for 30 minutes. Uncover; bake until bubbly and heated through, for about 10 minutes longer. Serve 1 casserole. Cool the second casserole; cover and freeze up to 3 months.

To use frozen casserole: Thaw in the refrigerator 8 hours. Preheat oven to 375°. Remove from refrigerator 30 minutes before baking. Cover and bake, increasing time as necessary to heat through and for a thermometer inserted in center to read 165°, 20-25 minutes.

Note: Wear disposable gloves when cutting hot peppers; the oils can burn skin. Avoid touching your face.

1 cup: 321 cal., 15g fat (7g sat. fat), 64mg chol., 673mg sod., 23g carb. (5g sugars, 4g fiber), 24g pro.

MINIATURE MEAT PIES

I keep these pies handy in the freezer.
—*Gayle Lewis, Yucaipa, CA*

Prep: 30 min. • **Bake:** 15 min.
Makes: about 1½ dozen

- 1 **lb. ground beef**
- ½ **cup chili sauce**
- 2 **Tbsp. onion soup mix**
- 3 **cups all-purpose flour**
- 1 **to 2 Tbsp. sesame seeds, optional**
- 1 **tsp. salt**
- 1 **cup shortening**
- ¾ **cup shredded cheddar cheese**
- ¾ **cup evaporated milk**
- 1 **Tbsp. cider vinegar**

1. In a large skillet, cook beef over medium heat until no longer pink; drain. Stir in chili sauce and soup mix; set aside.
2. In a large bowl, combine the flour, sesame seeds if desired, and salt. Cut in shortening and cheese until crumbly. Combine milk and vinegar; gradually add to flour mixture, tossing with a fork until dough forms a ball.
3. Divide dough in half; roll out to ⅛-in. thickness. Cut with a lightly floured 2½-in. round cutter. Place half of the circles 2 in. apart on ungreased baking sheets; top each with a rounded tablespoon of beef mixture. Top with remaining circles. Moisten edges with water and press with a fork to seal. Cut a slit in the top of each.
4. Bake at 425° for 12-16 minutes or until golden brown. Serve immediately.
Freeze option: Freeze cooled pies in an airtight container for up to 3 months. Bake, frozen, on an ungreased baking sheet at 425° until heated through, 14-16 minutes.
2 meat pies: 508 cal., 30g fat (10g sat. fat), 41mg chol., 983mg sod., 40g carb. (6g sugars, 1g fiber), 17g pro.

ASIAN-STYLE MEAT LOAF

Here's a family-friendly meat loaf with just a hint of Asian flair. Serve it with pea pods or steamed baby bok choy and brown rice.
—Taste of Home *Test Kitchen*

Prep: 25 min. • **Bake:** 50 min. + standing
Makes: 2 loaves (8 servings each)

- 1⅓ **cups panko bread crumbs**
- 1 **small onion, finely chopped**
- 2 **large eggs, lightly beaten**
- ⅓ **cup 2% milk**
- ¼ **cup hoisin sauce**
- 1 **Tbsp. reduced-sodium soy sauce**
- 2 **garlic cloves, minced**
- 2 **tsp. prepared mustard**
- 1¼ **tsp. ground ginger**
- 1 **tsp. salt**
- 2 **lbs. extra-lean ground turkey**
- 1 **lb. Italian turkey sausage links, casings removed**

TOPPING

- 1 **cup ketchup**
- ½ **cup packed brown sugar**
- 2 **tsp. prepared mustard**

1. Preheat the oven to 350°. In a large bowl, combine first 10 ingredients. Add turkey and sausage; mix lightly but thoroughly. Transfer to 2 greased 9x5-in. loaf pans. Mix topping ingredients; spread over tops.
2. Bake until a thermometer reads 165°, 50-55 minutes. Let stand for 10 minutes before slicing.
Freeze option: Shape meat loaves in plastic wrap-lined loaf pans; cover and freeze until firm. Remove from pans and wrap securely in foil; return to freezer. To use, unwrap and bake meat loaves as directed, increasing time to 1¼-1½ hours or until a thermometer inserted in center reads 165°.
1 slice: 187 cal., 6g fat (1g sat. fat), 67mg chol., 636mg sod., 17g carb. (12g sugars, trace fiber), 16g pro. **Diabetic exchanges:** 2 lean meat, 1 starch.

MINI SAUSAGE PIES

The simple ingredients and family-friendly flavor of these little sausage cups make them a go-to dinner favorite!
—*Kerry Dingwall, Wilmington, NC*

- -

Prep: 35 min. • **Bake:** 30 min.
Makes: 1 dozen

- 1 pkg. (17.3 oz.) frozen puff pastry, thawed
- 1 lb. bulk sage pork sausage
- 6 green onions, chopped
- ½ cup chopped dried apricots
- ¼ tsp. pepper
- ⅛ tsp. ground nutmeg
- 1 large egg, lightly beaten

1. Preheat oven to 375°. On a lightly floured surface, unfold pastry sheets; roll each into a 16x12-in. rectangle. Using a floured cutter, cut twelve 4-in. circles from 1 sheet; press onto bottoms and up sides of ungreased muffin cups. Using a floured cutter, cut twelve 3½-in. circles from remaining sheet.

2. Mix sausage, green onions, apricots and spices lightly but thoroughly. Place ¼ cup mixture into each pastry cup. Brush edges of smaller pastry circles with egg; place over pies, pressing edges to seal. Brush with egg. Cut slits in top.

3. Bake the pies until golden brown and a thermometer inserted in filling reads 160°, 30-35 minutes. Cool for 5 minutes before removing from pan to a wire rack.

Freeze option: Cool baked pies and freeze in freezer containers. To use, partially thaw pies in refrigerator overnight. Reheat on a baking sheet in a preheated 350° oven until heated through, 14-17 minutes.

2 mini pies: 551 cal., 36g fat (10g sat. fat), 82mg chol., 784mg sod., 42g carb. (5g sugars, 5g fiber), 16g pro.

STUFFED BANANA PEPPERS

The combination of meats gives these stuffed peppers their distinctively different flavor. Because they freeze so well, we can enjoy my home-grown peppers long after summer is over.

—*Thomas Kendzlic, Pittsburgh, PA*

- -

Prep: 50 min. • **Bake:** 35 min.
Makes: 2 dishes (6 servings each)

6	cups tomato sauce, divided
24	banana peppers
4	large eggs, lightly beaten
1	cup seasoned bread crumbs
1⅓	cups grated Parmesan cheese, divided
¼	cup minced fresh basil or 4 tsp. dried basil
6	garlic cloves, minced
½	tsp. salt
½	tsp. pepper
½	lb. ground beef
½	lb. bulk hot Italian sausage
½	lb. ground veal
¼	cup olive oil

1. Grease two 13x9-in. baking dishes. Spread ½ cup tomato sauce in each dish; set aside.

2. Cut tops off peppers and remove seeds. In a large bowl, combine the eggs, bread crumbs, ⅔ cup cheese, basil, garlic, salt and pepper. Crumble the beef, sausage and veal over mixture; mix well. Spoon into peppers.

3. In a large skillet, cook peppers in oil in batches over medium heat for 1-2 minutes on each side or until lightly browned. Arrange 12 peppers in each prepared dish. Top with remaining sauce; sprinkle with remaining cheese.

4. Cover and freeze 1 dish up to 3 months. Cover and bake the remaining dish at 350° for 35-40 minutes or until meat is no longer pink and peppers are tender.

To use frozen stuffed peppers: Thaw in the refrigerator overnight. Remove from the refrigerator 30 minutes before baking. Cover and bake at 350° for 45-50 minutes or until the meat is no longer pink and peppers are tender.

Note: Wear disposable gloves when cutting hot peppers; the oils can burn skin. Avoid touching your face.

2 stuffed pepepers: 302 cal., 16g fat (5g sat. fat), 112mg chol., 1092mg sod., 22g carb. (6g sugars, 7g fiber), 20g pro.

DEBRA'S CAVATINI

I love this recipe because it makes two hearty casseroles. I like to add a little something different every time I make it, such as extra garlic, to give it an added boost of flavor.

—*Debra Butcher, Decatur, IN*

- -

Prep: 45 min. • **Bake:** 35 min.
Makes: 2 casseroles (6 servings each)

- 1   **pkg. (16 oz.) penne pasta**
- 1   **lb. ground beef**
- 1   **lb. bulk Italian pork sausage**
- 1¾ **cups sliced fresh mushrooms**
- 1   **medium onion, chopped**
- 1   **medium green pepper, chopped**
- 2   **cans (14½ oz. each) Italian diced tomatoes**
- 1   **jar (23½ oz.) Italian sausage and garlic spaghetti sauce**
- 1   **jar (16 oz.) chunky mild salsa**
- 1   **pkg. (8 oz.) sliced pepperoni, chopped**
- 1   **cup shredded Swiss cheese, divided**
- 4   **cups shredded part-skim mozzarella cheese, divided**
- 1½ **cups shredded Parmesan cheese, divided**
- 1   **jar (24 oz.) 3-cheese spaghetti sauce**

1. Cook penne pasta according to package directions. Meanwhile, in a Dutch oven, cook beef, sausage, mushrooms, onion and green pepper over medium heat until meat is no longer pink; drain.

2. Drain pasta; add to the meat mixture. Stir in the tomatoes, sausage and garlic spaghetti sauce, salsa and pepperoni.

3. Preheat oven to 350°. Divide half the pasta mixture between 2 greased 13x9-in. baking dishes. Sprinkle each with ¼ cup Swiss cheese, 1 cup mozzarella cheese and ⅓ cup Parmesan cheese. Spread ¾ cup 3-cheese spaghetti sauce over each. Top with the remaining pasta mixture and the 3-cheese spaghetti sauce. Sprinkle with remaining cheeses.

4. Cover and bake until bubbly, about 25 minutes. Uncover; bake until cheese is melted, about 10 minutes longer.

Freeze option: Cover unbaked casserole and freeze for up to 3 months. To use, thaw in refrigerator overnight. Remove from refrigerator 30 minutes before baking. Preheat oven to 350°. Bake casserole, covered, 45 minutes. Uncover; bake for 10 minutes or until cheese is melted.

1 serving: 669 cal., 34g fat (15g sat. fat), 90mg chol., 1825mg sod., 54g carb. (20g sugars, 5g fiber), 37g pro.

1. Preheat oven to 425°. Place potatoes and carrots in a large saucepan; add water to cover. Bring to a boil. Reduce heat; cook, covered, 8-10 minutes or until vegetables are crisp-tender; drain.

2. In a large skillet, heat the butter over medium-high heat. Add onion; cook and stir until tender. Stir in flour and seasonings until blended. Gradually stir in broth and milk. Bring to a boil, stirring constantly; cook and stir 2 minutes or until thickened. Stir in the chicken, peas, corn and potato mixture; remove from heat.

3. Unroll a pie crust into each of two 9-in. pie plates; trim even with rims. Add chicken mixture. Unroll remaining crusts; place over the filling. Trim, seal and flute edges. Cut slits in tops.

4. Bake 35-40 minutes or until crust is lightly browned. Let stand 15 minutes before cutting.

Freeze option: Cover and freeze the unbaked pies. To use, remove from freezer 30 minutes before baking (do not thaw). Preheat oven to 425°. Place pies on baking sheets; cover the edges loosely with foil. Bake 30 minutes. Reduce oven setting to 350°; bake until crust is golden brown and a thermometer inserted in center reads 165°, 70-80 minutes longer.

1 serving: 475 cal., 28g fat (14g sat. fat), 74mg chol., 768mg sod., 41g carb. (5g sugars, 2g fiber), 15g pro.

FAVORITE CHICKEN POTPIE

Chock-full of chicken, potatoes, peas and corn, this autumn favorite makes two golden pies, so you can serve one at supper and save the other for another time. These potpies are perfect for company or even for a potluck.

—*Karen Johnson, Bakersfield, CA*

- -

Prep: 40 min. • **Bake:** 35 min. + standing
Makes: 2 potpies (8 servings each)

2	cups diced peeled potatoes
1¾	cups sliced carrots
1	cup butter, cubed
⅔	cup chopped onion
1	cup all-purpose flour
1¾	tsp. salt
1	tsp. dried thyme
¾	tsp. pepper
3	cups chicken broth
1½	cups whole milk
4	cups cubed cooked chicken
1	cup frozen peas
1	cup frozen corn
4	sheets refrigerated pie crust

TEST KITCHEN TIP
When the edge of the crust falls inward off the lip of the pie plate, we say it slumped. Reduce slumping by setting a fluted crust in the refrigerator for 30 to 45 minutes.

ITALIAN PORK CHOPS

A recipe that combines my slow cooker with freezer-friendly foods? I'm sold! This pork entree always comes out so tender and juicy. Keep the chops and savory sauce in the freezer for fast meals.
—*Bonnie Marlow, Ottoville, OH*

Prep: 15 min. • **Cook:** 5 hours
Makes: 6 servings

- 6 boneless pork loin chops (6 oz. each)
- 1 Tbsp. canola oil
- 1 medium green pepper, diced
- 1 can (6 oz.) tomato paste
- 1 jar (4½ oz.) sliced mushrooms, drained
- ½ cup water
- 1 envelope spaghetti sauce mix
- ½ to 1 tsp. hot pepper sauce

1. In a large skillet, brown pork chops in oil over medium heat for 3-4 minutes on each side; drain. In a 5-qt. slow cooker, combine the remaining ingredients. Top with the pork chops.
2. Cover and cook on low for 5-6 hours or until meat is tender.
Freeze option: Cool pork chop mixture. Freeze in freezer containers. To use, partially thaw in the refrigerator overnight. Heat through slowly in a covered skillet, stirring occasionally, until a thermometer inserted in pork reads 165°.
1 pork chop: 303 cal., 12g fat (4g sat. fat), 82mg chol., 763mg sod., 13g carb. (5g sugars, 3g fiber), 34g pro.

MOROCCAN BRAISED BEEF

Curry powder is a blend of up to 20 spices, herbs and seeds. In this Moroccan stew, begin with 2 teaspoons of curry, then add more to your taste.
—*Taste of Home Test Kitchen*

Prep: 20 min. • **Cook:** 7 hours
Makes: 6 servings

- ⅓ cup all-purpose flour
- 2 lbs. boneless beef chuck roast, cut into 1-in. cubes
- 3 Tbsp. olive oil
- 2 cans (14½ oz. each) beef broth
- 2 cups chopped onions
- 1 can (14½ oz.) diced tomatoes, undrained
- 1 cup dry red wine
- 1 Tbsp. curry powder
- 1 Tbsp. paprika
- 1 tsp. salt
- 1 tsp. ground cumin
- 1 tsp. ground coriander
- ½ tsp. cayenne pepper
- 1½ cups golden raisins
  Hot cooked couscous, optional

1. Place flour in a large shallow dish; add beef and turn to coat. In a large skillet, brown beef in oil. Transfer to a 5-qt. slow cooker. Stir in the broth, onions, tomatoes, wine and seasonings. Cover and cook on low for 7-8 hours or until the meat is tender.
2. During the last 30 minutes of cooking, stir in the raisins. Serve with cooked couscous if desired.
Freeze option: Freeze cooled beef mixture in freezer containers. To use, partially thaw in refrigerator overnight. Heat through in a saucepan, stirring occasionally; add broth if necessary. Serve as directed.
1⅓ cups beef mixture: 533 cal., 22g fat (7g sat. fat), 98mg chol., 620mg sod., 45g carb. (30g sugars, 5g fiber), 34g pro.

SLOW-COOKER CHICKEN TINGA

I first fell in love with this traditional Mexican dish at a taco stand inside a gas station. This is how I now make it at home. My version has a nice zing without being overly spicy.

—*Ramona Parris, Canton, GA*

- -

Prep: 25 min. • **Cook:** 4 hours
Makes: 8 servings

- 8 oz. fresh chorizo
- 1½ lbs. boneless, skinless chicken thighs
- 1 large onion, cut into wedges
- 1 can (14½ oz.) fire-roasted diced tomatoes
- ½ cup chicken broth
- 3 Tbsp. minced chipotle peppers in adobo sauce
- 3 garlic cloves, minced
- 2 tsp. ground cumin
- 1 tsp. dried oregano
- ½ tsp. salt
- 16 corn tortillas (6 in.)
  Optional: Shredded lettuce and pico de gallo

1. In a small skillet, fully cook chorizo over medium heat, breaking meat into crumbles, 6-8 minutes; drain. Transfer to a 3- or 4-qt. slow cooker. Add the next 9 ingredients; stir to combine. Cook, covered, on low until chicken is tender, 4-5 hours.

2. Remove chicken; cool slightly. Shred with 2 forks. Remove and discard onions; strain cooking juices and skim fat. Return cooking juices and chicken to slow cooker; heat through. Serve chicken in corn tortillas. If desired, top with shredded lettuce and pico de gallo.

Freeze option: Freeze cooled chicken mixture in freezer containers. To use, partially thaw in refrigerator overnight. Heat through in a saucepan, stirring occasionally; add broth if necessary.

2 tacos: 363 cal., 16g fat (5g sat. fat), 82mg chol., 800mg sod., 27g carb. (3g sugars, 4g fiber), 25g pro.

TEST KITCHEN TIP

Freezer containers are a natural for meal planners, but resealable freezer storage bags allow you to "flatten" the food out and save space in the freezer.

SUPER EASY COUNTRY-STYLE RIBS

I'm an extreme rib fanatic. When we were growing up, our mom made these for us all the time, and we still can't get enough of them. Because they freeze well, I'm able to enjoy them anytime I want!

—*Stephanie Loaiza, Layton, UT*

Prep: 10 min. • **Cook:** 5 hours
Makes: 4 servings

1½ cups ketchup
½ cup packed brown sugar
½ cup white vinegar
2 tsp. seasoned salt
½ tsp. liquid smoke, optional
2 lbs. boneless country-style pork ribs

1. In a 3-qt. slow cooker, mix the ketchup, brown sugar, vinegar, seasoned salt and, if desired, liquid smoke. Add ribs; turn to coat. Cook, covered, on low 5-6 hours or until meat is tender.

2. Remove pork to a serving plate. Skim fat from cooking liquid. If desired, transfer to a small saucepan to thicken; bring to a boil and cook 12-15 minutes or until sauce is reduced to 1½ cups. Serve with ribs.

Freeze option: In a large airtight container, combine ketchup, brown sugar, vinegar, seasoned salt and, if desired, liquid smoke. Add pork; seal bag and freeze. To use, place container in refrigerator until the ribs are completely thawed, about 48 hours. Cook as directed.

6 oz. cooked pork: 550 cal., 21g fat (8g sat. fat), 131mg chol., 2003mg sod., 51g carb. (51g sugars, 0 fiber), 40g pro.

MAPLE MUSTARD CHICKEN

My husband loves this chicken dish. It calls for only a few ingredients, and we try to have them all on hand for a delicious and cozy dinner anytime.
—*Jennifer Seidel, Midland, MI*

- -

Prep: 5 min. • **Cook:** 3 hours
Makes: 6 servings

- 6 **boneless skinless chicken breast halves (6 oz. each)**
- ½ **cup maple syrup**
- ⅓ **cup stone-ground mustard**
- 2 **Tbsp. quick-cooking tapioca**
  Hot cooked brown rice

Place the chicken in a 3-qt. slow cooker. In a small bowl, combine the syrup, mustard and tapioca; pour over chicken. Cover and cook on low for 3-4 hours or until tender. Serve with rice.

Freeze option: Cool the chicken in sauce. Freeze in freezer containers. To use, partially thaw in refrigerator overnight. Heat through in a covered skillet until a meat thermometer reads 165°, stirring occasionally; add broth or water if necessary.

1 chicken breast half: 289 cal., 4g fat (1g sat. fat), 94mg chol., 296mg sod., 24g carb. (17g sugars, 2g fiber), 35g pro.

SLOW-COOKER SWEET POTATO SOUP

I love that I can top this creamy soup with anything my heart desires, which means I can eat it several days in a row without ever having to have it the same way twice. You can substitute fresh onions and celery in this recipe if you prefer, but using the dried version makes it easy to throw together on a weekday morning before you head out the door.

—*Colleen Delawder, Herndon, VA*

- -

Prep: 15 min. • **Cook:** 5 hours
Makes: 8 servings (2½ qt.)

3	**lbs. sweet potatoes, peeled and cut into 1-in. cubes (about 8 cups)**
2	**Tbsp. butter**
1	**Tbsp. Worcestershire sauce**
1	**tsp. dried minced onion**
1	**tsp. dried celery flakes, optional**
½	**tsp. salt**
½	**tsp. pepper**
¼	**tsp. dried thyme**
⅛	**tsp. ground chipotle pepper**
6	**cups reduced-sodium chicken broth**
	Optional: Sour cream and pepitas

1. In a 4- or 5-qt. slow cooker, combine all ingredients except sour cream and pepitas. Cook, covered, on low until potatoes are tender, 5-6 hours.

2. Puree soup using an immersion blender. Or, cool slightly and puree soup in batches in a blender; return to slow cooker and heat through. If desired, top servings with sour cream and pepitas.

Freeze option: Freeze cooled soup in freezer containers. To use, partially thaw in refrigerator overnight. Heat through in a saucepan, stirring occasionally; add broth or water if necessary.

1¼ cups: 215 cal., 3g fat (2g sat. fat), 8mg chol., 637mg sod., 43g carb. (18g sugars, 5g fiber), 5g pro.

TEST KITCHEN TIP

The potatoes will be tender in 5-6 hours, but if you're away from home later and they simmer longer, they'll be perfectly fine since they'll eventually be pureed.

SWEET & SPICY PINEAPPLE CHICKEN SANDWICHES

My kids ask for chicken sloppy joes, and this version has a bonus of sweet pineapple. This is great to double for a potluck or save in the freezer for last-minute meals. We love them topped with smoked Gouda.
—*Nancy Heishman, Las Vegas, NV*

Prep: 15 min. • **Cook:** 2¾ hours
Makes: 8 servings

- 2½ **lbs. boneless skinless chicken breasts**
- 1 **bottle (18 oz.) sweet and spicy barbecue sauce, divided**
- 2 **Tbsp. honey mustard**
- 1 **can (8 oz.) unsweetened crushed pineapple, undrained**
- 8 **hamburger buns, split and toasted**
  Optional: Bibb lettuce leaves and thinly sliced red onion

1. Place the chicken breasts in a 4-qt. slow cooker. Combine ¼ cup barbecue sauce and mustard; pour over chicken. Cover and cook on low until chicken is tender, 2½-3 hours.
2. Remove chicken; discard liquid. Shred chicken with 2 forks and add back to slow cooker. Add the crushed pineapple and remaining barbecue sauce; cover and cook on high for 15 minutes.
3. Serve mixture on toasted buns with toppings as desired.
Freeze option: Place shredded chicken in freezer containers. Cool and freeze. To use, partially thaw in refrigerator overnight. Heat through in a covered saucepan, stirring gently; add broth if necessary.
1 sandwich: 415 cal., 6g fat (1g sat. fat), 78mg chol., 973mg sod., 56g carb. (30g sugars, 2g fiber), 34g pro.

ZESTY SAUSAGE & BEANS

You will love this hearty freezer-friendly dish when it comes to feeding your hungry family. Packed with sausage, beans and bacon, it's guaranteed to satisfy even the heftiest appetites.
—*Melissa Just, Minneapolis, MN*

Prep: 30 min. • **Cook:** 5 hours
Makes: 10 servings

- 2 **lbs. smoked kielbasa or Polish sausage, halved and sliced**
- 2 **cans (15 oz. each) black beans, rinsed and drained**
- 1 **can (15 oz.) great northern beans, rinsed and drained**
- 1 **can (15 oz.) thick and zesty tomato sauce**
- 1 **medium green pepper, chopped**
- 1 **medium onion, chopped**
- ½ **cup water**
- 5 **bacon strips, cooked and crumbled**
- 3 **Tbsp. brown sugar**
- 2 **Tbsp. cider vinegar**
- 3 **garlic cloves, minced**
- ¼ **tsp. dried thyme**
- ¼ **tsp. dried marjoram**
- ¼ **tsp. cayenne pepper**
  Hot cooked rice

In a large skillet, brown sausage. Transfer to a 4-qt. slow cooker; add the beans, tomato sauce, green pepper, onion, water, bacon, brown sugar, vinegar, garlic, thyme, marjoram and cayenne. Cover and cook on low for 5-6 hours or until vegetables are tender. Serve with rice.
Freeze option: Freeze cooled sausage mixture in freezer containers. To use, partially thaw in refrigerator overnight. Heat through in a saucepan, stirring occasionally; add broth or water if necessary.
¾ cup: 439 cal., 26g fat (9g sat. fat), 64mg chol., 1505mg sod., 29g carb. (7g sugars, 7g fiber), 20g pro.

VIETNAMESE CHICKEN MEATBALL SOUP WITH BOK CHOY

Throughout Vietnam there are many soups that are served all year long. I enjoy this warm, flavorful chicken soup for casual dinners, but it's also great ladled into a thermos for lunch. It's a perfect way to use bok choy.
—*Brenda Watts, Gaffney, SC*

Prep: 45 min. • **Cook:** 6 hours
Makes: 8 servings (about 2½ qt.)

- ¼   **cup panko bread crumbs**
- ¼   **cup finely chopped onion**
- 1   **large egg, lightly beaten**
- 2   **serrano peppers, seeded and minced**
- 1   **garlic clove, minced**
- ½   **lb. ground chicken**
- 2   **Tbsp. peanut oil**

SOUP
- 6   **cups chicken or vegetable stock**
- 1   **can (14½ oz.) fire-roasted diced tomatoes, undrained**
- 1   **small onion, cut into thin strips**
- 1   **cup bok choy leaves, cut into 1-in. strips**
- 1   **cup fresh baby carrots, julienned**
- 1   **cup julienned roasted sweet red peppers**
- 3   **serrano peppers, julienned**
- 2   **garlic cloves, minced**
- ½   **tsp. salt**
- ¼   **cup panko bread crumbs, optional**
- 1   **large egg, beaten**

1. In a large bowl, combine the first 5 ingredients. Add chicken; mix lightly but thoroughly. Shape into ¾-in. balls. In a large skillet, heat oil over medium heat. Brown meatballs in batches; drain. Transfer to a 4- or 5-qt. slow cooker.

2. Add stock, tomatoes, onion, bok choy, carrots, red peppers, julienned serrano peppers, garlic and salt. Cook, covered, on low until meatballs are cooked through and vegetables are tender, 6-8 hours. If desired, stir in panko. Without stirring, drizzle beaten egg into slow cooker. Let stand for 2-3 minutes or until egg is set.

Freeze option: Before adding egg, cool soup. Freeze in freezer containers. To use, partially thaw in refrigerator overnight. Heat through in a saucepan, stirring occasionally; add broth if necessary. Without stirring, drizzle beaten egg into soup. Let stand for 2-3 minutes or until egg is set.

1⅓ cups: 147 cal., 7g fat (2g sat. fat), 65mg chol., 836mg sod., 9g carb. (5g sugars, 1g fiber), 10g pro.

BUFFALO CHICKEN SLIDERS

I came up with the idea for these sliders when my mom and dad served a similar recipe at a family get-together.
—*Christina Addison, Blanchester, OH*

- -

Prep: 20 min. • **Cook:** 3 hours
Makes: 6 servings

- 1 lb. boneless skinless chicken breasts
- 2 Tbsp. plus ⅓ cup Louisiana-style hot sauce, divided
- ¼ tsp. pepper
- ¼ cup butter, cubed
- ¼ cup honey
- 12 Hawaiian sweet rolls, warmed
  Optional ingredients: Lettuce leaves, sliced tomato, thinly sliced red onion and crumbled blue cheese

1. Place chicken in a 3-qt. slow cooker. Toss with 2 Tbsp. hot sauce and pepper; cook, covered, on low 3-4 hours or until tender.
2. Remove chicken; discard cooking juices. In a small saucepan, combine butter, honey and remaining hot sauce; cook and stir over medium heat until blended. Shred chicken with 2 forks; stir into the sauce and heat through. Serve on rolls with desired optional ingredients.

Freeze option: Freeze cooled chicken mixture in freezer containers. To use, partially thaw in refrigerator overnight. Microwave, covered, on high in a microwave-safe dish until heated through, stirring occasionally; add water if necessary.

2 sliders: 396 cal., 15g fat (8g sat. fat), 92mg chol., 873mg sod., 44g carb. (24g sugars, 2g fiber), 24g pro.

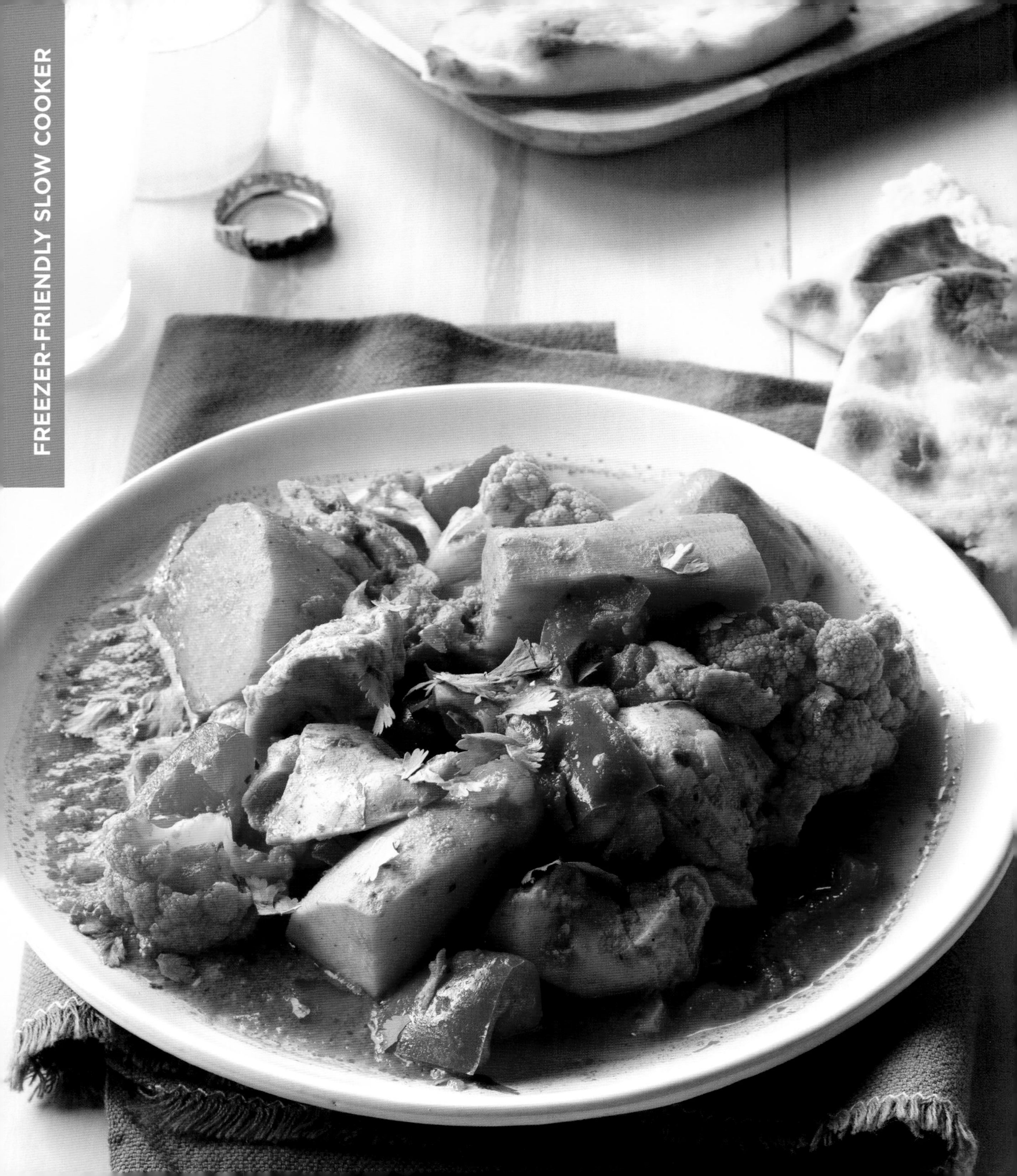

SAUCY INDIAN-STYLE CHICKEN & VEGETABLES

This easy Indian dish will be loved by all. Feel free to add more or less tikka masala sauce according to your taste.
—*Erica Polly, Sun Prairie, WI*

- -

Prep: 15 min. • **Cook:** 4 hours
Makes: 8 servings

- 2 medium sweet potatoes, peeled and cut into 1½-in. pieces
- 2 Tbsp. water
- 2 medium sweet red peppers, cut into 1-in. pieces
- 3 cups fresh cauliflowerets
- 2 lbs. boneless skinless chicken thighs, cubed
- 2 jars (15 oz. each) tikka masala curry sauce
- ¾ tsp. salt
  Minced fresh cilantro, optional
  Naan flatbreads, warmed

1. Microwave sweet potatoes and water, covered, on high just until potatoes begin to soften, 3-4 minutes.
2. In a 5- or 6-qt. slow cooker, combine vegetables and chicken; add sauce and salt. Cook, covered, on low until meat is tender, 4-5 hours. If desired, top with cilantro; serve with warmed naan.

Freeze option: Omitting cilantro and naan, freeze cooled chicken and vegetable mixture in freezer containers. To use, partially thaw in refrigerator overnight. Microwave, covered, on high in a microwave-safe dish until mixture is heated through, stirring gently; add water if necessary. If desired, sprinkle with cilantro. Serve with warmed naan.

1¼ cups: 334 cal., 15g fat (4g sat. fat), 80mg chol., 686mg sod., 25g carb. (12g sugars, 5g fiber), 25g pro. **Diabetic exchanges:** 3 lean meat, 2 fat, 1½ starch.

BALSAMIC BEEF HOAGIES

We all love these sandwiches, but storing the meat in the freezer makes it a snap to whip up quesadillas or even pizza. Serve it over cooked rice for a one-dish meal. You can find more family-friendly recipes at my blog, theseasonedmom.com.
—*Blair Lonergan, Rochelle, VA*

- -

Prep: 25 min. • **Cook:** 5 hours
Makes: 8 servings

- 1 cup beef broth
- ½ cup balsamic vinegar
- 2 Tbsp. brown sugar
- 2 Tbsp. Worcestershire sauce
- 4 garlic cloves, minced
- 1 boneless beef chuck roast (2 lbs.)
SANDWICHES
- ½ cup mayonnaise
- 8 hoagie buns, split and toasted
- 4 medium tomatoes, sliced
- ½ cup thinly sliced fresh basil

1. In a small bowl, mix the first 5 ingredients. Place roast in a 4- or 5-qt. slow cooker. Pour broth mixture over top. Cook, covered, on low until meat is tender, 5-6 hours.
2. Remove roast; shred with 2 forks. Skim fat from cooking juices. Return beef and juices to slow cooker; heat through.
3. Spread mayonnaise on buns. Top with beef, tomatoes and basil.

Freeze option: Freeze cooled meat mixture in freezer containers. To use, partially thaw in refrigerator overnight. Heat through in a saucepan, stirring occasionally; add broth if necessary.

1 sandwich: 549 cal., 26g fat (7g sat. fat), 79mg chol., 669mg sod., 46g carb. (14g sugars, 2g fiber), 31g pro.

MARMALADE MEATBALLS

We had a potluck at work, so I started simmering these meatballs in the morning. By lunchtime they were ready. They were a big hit with everyone!
—*Jeanne Kiss, Greensburg, PA*

Prep: 10 min. • **Cook:** 4 hours
Makes: about 5 dozen

- 1 **bottle (16 oz.) Catalina salad dressing**
- 1 **cup orange marmalade**
- 3 **Tbsp. Worcestershire sauce**
- ½ **tsp. crushed red pepper flakes**
- 1 **pkg. (32 oz.) frozen fully cooked home-style meatballs, thawed**

In a 3-qt. slow cooker, combine the salad dressing, marmalade, Worcestershire sauce and pepper flakes. Stir in meatballs. Cover and cook on low for 4-5 hours or until heated through.

Freeze option: Freeze cooled meatball mixture in freezer containers. To use, partially thaw in refrigerator overnight. Microwave, covered, on high in a microwave-safe dish until heated through, gently stirring; add water if necessary.

1 meatball: 73 cal., 4g fat (1g sat. fat), 12mg chol., 126mg sod., 6g carb. (5g sugars, 0 fiber), 2g pro.

Easy Party Meatballs: Omit the first 4 ingredients. Combine 1 bottle (14 oz.) ketchup, ¼ cup A.1. steak sauce, 1 Tbsp. minced garlic and 1 tsp. Dijon mustard in slow cooker; stir in meatballs. Follow recipe as directed.

SLOW-COOKER CORDON BLEU SOUP

I've taken this creamy slow-cooker soup to potlucks and teacher luncheons, and I bring home an empty crock every time. When my son's school recently created a cookbook, this was the first recipe he asked me to submit, and his teachers were glad he did.
—*Erica Winkel, Ada, MI*

Prep: 40 min. + cooling • **Cook:** 3 hours
Makes: 8 servings (2½ qt.)

- 3   **Tbsp. butter, melted**
- ¼   **tsp. garlic powder**
- ¼   **tsp. pepper**
- 4   **cups cubed French bread**

SOUP

- 1   **small onion, diced**
- 1   **celery rib, diced**
- 1   **garlic clove, minced**
- ¼   **tsp. salt**
- ¼   **tsp. pepper**
- 3   **cans (14½ oz. each) reduced-sodium chicken broth**
- ⅓   **cup all-purpose flour**
- ⅓   **cup water**
- ¼   **cup white wine or additional reduced-sodium chicken broth**
- 8   **oz. reduced-fat cream cheese, cubed**
- 1½   **cups Swiss cheese, shredded**
- ½   **cup shredded cheddar cheese**
- ½   **lb. diced rotisserie chicken**
- ½   **lb. diced deli ham**

1. For croutons, preheat oven to 375°. In a large bowl, mix melted butter, garlic powder and pepper. Add bread cubes; toss to coat. Transfer croutons to a 15x10x1-in. baking pan; bake, stirring every 5 minutes, until golden brown, 15-20 minutes. Remove to wire racks to cool completely.

2. Meanwhile, in a 4- or 5-qt. slow cooker, combine the next 5 ingredients; pour in the broth. Cook, covered, on low until vegetables are tender, about 2 hours.

3. Increase slow cooker heat setting to high. Mix flour and water until smooth; whisk flour mixture into broth. Cook until thickened, 30-40 minutes. Stir in wine. Whisk in cheeses until melted. Add the chicken and ham; heat through. Serve with the croutons.

Freeze option: Before adding croutons, freeze cooled soup in freezer containers. Freeze croutons separately. To use, partially thaw soup in refrigerator overnight. Heat the soup through in a saucepan, stirring occasionally; add water if necessary. While soup is heating, thaw the croutons at room temperature; sprinkle over soup.

1¼ cups plus ½ cup croutons: 384 cal., 23g fat (13g sat. fat), 100mg chol., 1112mg sod., 15g carb. (3g sugars, 1g fiber), 29g pro.

TEST KITCHEN TIP

Thick, creamy soups may separate slightly when thawed and reheated. A good stir usually does the trick in smoothing it all out again.

EASY CARNITAS

These flavor-packed tacos are so good, I put them on my blog, manilaspoon.com! The slow cooker makes them a snap.
—*Abigail Raines, Hamden, CT*

- -

Prep: 25 min. • **Cook:** 8 hours
Makes: 12 servings

- ½ cup salsa
- 3 bay leaves
- 1 Tbsp. salt
- 2 tsp. ground cumin
- 2 tsp. dried oregano
- 2 tsp. pepper
- 1½ tsp. garlic powder
- 4 whole cloves
- 1¼ cups water
- 2 medium onions, chopped
- 1 bone-in pork shoulder roast (6 to 7 lbs.)
- 24 corn tortillas (6 in.) or taco shells, warmed
  Optional toppings: Shredded cheese, sour cream and chopped tomato, onion and cilantro

1. In a small bowl, mix first 9 ingredients. Place onions in a 6-qt. oval slow cooker. Place roast over onions; pour salsa mixture over roast. Cook, covered, on low until pork is tender, 8-10 hours.
2. Remove roast; remove and discard bone. Shred pork with 2 forks. Serve in tortillas with toppings as desired.

Freeze option: Freeze cooled pork mixture in freezer containers. To use, partially thaw in refrigerator overnight. Microwave, covered, on high in a microwave-safe dish until heated through, stirring occasionally; add water or broth if necessary.

2 tacos: 393 cal., 18g fat (6g sat. fat), 100mg chol., 757mg sod., 25g carb. (2g sugars, 4g fiber), 32g pro.

SWEET & TANGY CHICKEN WINGS

Here's a festive recipe that's perfect for parties. Stash these wings in your freezer and you'll always have a great snack or casual dinner at the ready.
—*Ida Tuey, South Lyon, MI*

- -

Prep: 20 min. • **Cook:** 2¼ hours
Makes: 2 dozen

- 12 chicken wings (about 3 lbs.)
- ½ tsp. salt, divided
  Dash pepper
- 1½ cups ketchup
- ¼ cup packed brown sugar
- ¼ cup red wine vinegar
- 2 Tbsp. Worcestershire sauce
- 1 Tbsp. Dijon mustard
- 1 tsp. minced garlic
- 1 tsp. liquid smoke, optional
  Optional: Sliced jalapeno peppers, finely chopped red onion and sesame seeds

1. Using a sharp knife, cut through the 2 wing joints; discard wing tips. Sprinkle chicken with a dash of salt and pepper. Broil 4-6 in. from the heat for 6-8 minutes on each side or until golden brown. Transfer to a greased 5-qt. slow cooker.
2. Combine the ketchup, brown sugar, vinegar, Worcestershire sauce, mustard, garlic, liquid smoke, if desired, and the remaining salt; pour over wings. Toss to coat.
3. Cover and cook on low until chicken is tender, 2-3 hours. If desired, top with the jalapenos, onion and sesame seeds to serve.

Freeze option: Freeze cooled fully cooked wings in freezer containers. To use, partially thaw in refrigerator overnight. Reheat wings in a foil-lined 15x10x1-in. baking pan in a preheated 325° oven until heated through, covering if necessary to prevent browning. Serve as directed.

1 piece: 74 cal., 3g fat (1g sat. fat), 14mg chol., 282mg sod., 7g carb. (6g sugars, 0 fiber), 5g pro.

SPICY QUINOA STUFFED PEPPERS

Banana peppers can be very tricky: Sometimes they are hot and sometimes they are not. If you want to be on the safe side, try using Bianca peppers instead, which are a sweeter pepper.
—*Danielle Lee, Sewickley, PA*

Prep: 45 min. • **Cook:** 3½ hours
Makes: 4 servings

6	Tbsp. water
3	Tbsp. uncooked red or white quinoa, rinsed
½	lb. bulk spicy Italian sausage
½	lb. lean ground beef (90% lean)
½	cup tomato sauce
2	green onions, chopped
2	garlic cloves, minced
1½	tsp. Sriracha chili sauce
½	tsp. chili powder
¼	tsp. salt
⅛	tsp. pepper
16	mild banana peppers
2	cups reduced-sodium spicy V8 juice

1. In a small saucepan, bring water to a boil. Add quinoa. Reduce heat; simmer, covered, until the liquid is absorbed, 12-15 minutes. Remove from heat; fluff with a fork.

2. In a large bowl, combine sausage, beef, tomato sauce, green onions, garlic, chili sauce, chili powder, salt, pepper and cooked quinoa. Cut and discard tops from peppers; remove seeds. Fill the peppers with the meat mixture.

3. Stand peppers upright in a 4-qt. slow cooker. Pour V8 juice over top. Cook, covered, on low until peppers are tender, 3½-4½ hours.

Freeze option: Freeze cooled stuffed peppers and sauce in freezer containers. To use, partially thaw in refrigerator overnight. Microwave, covered, on high in a microwave-safe dish until heated through.

4 stuffed peppers: 412 cal., 22g fat (7g sat. fat), 74mg chol., 965mg sod., 29g carb. (11g sugars, 13g fiber), 26g pro.

TEST KITCHEN TIP

This is a smart way to use up any leftover quinoa you may have worked into your meal plan. Simply use ½ cup of cooked quinoa in the filling.

FAMILY-FAVORITE ITALIAN BEEF

With only a few ingredients, this roast beef is a snap to throw together. We use the tender meat on sandwiches, but keep it in the freezer for nachos and wraps.
—*Lauren Adamson, Layton, UT*

- -

Prep: 10 min. • **Cook:** 8 hours
Makes: 12 servings

- 1 jar (16 oz.) sliced pepperoncini, undrained
- 1 can (14½ oz.) diced tomatoes, undrained
- 1 medium onion, chopped
- ½ cup water
- 2 pkg. Italian salad dressing mix
- 1 tsp. dried oregano
- ½ tsp. garlic powder
- 1 beef rump roast or bottom round roast (3 to 4 lbs.)
- 12 Italian rolls, split

1. In a bowl, mix the first 7 ingredients. Place roast in a 5- or 6-qt. slow cooker. Pour the pepperoncini mixture over the top. Cook, covered, on low 8-10 hours or until the meat is tender.

2. Remove roast; cool slightly. Skim fat from cooking juices. Shred beef with 2 forks. Return beef and cooking juices to slow cooker; heat through. Serve on rolls.

Freeze option: Freeze the cooled, cooked beef mixture in freezer containers. To use, partially thaw in refrigerator overnight. Heat through in a saucepan, stirring occasionally; add water if necessary.

1 sandwich: 278 cal., 7g fat (2g sat. fat), 67mg chol., 735mg sod., 24g carb. (3g sugars, 2g fiber), 26g pro. **Diabetic exchanges:** 3 lean meat, 2 starch.

BRAZILIAN STEW

I introduced this recipe to my family, and it has become one of our favorite comforts.
—*Andrea Romanczyk, Magna, UT*

- -

Prep: 15 min. + soaking • **Cook:** 7 hours
Makes: 8 servings

1½ cups dried black beans
1 lb. smoked kielbasa or Polish sausage, sliced
1 lb. boneless country-style pork ribs
1 pkg. (12 oz.) fully cooked Spanish chorizo links, sliced
1 smoked ham hock
1 large onion, chopped
3 garlic cloves, minced
2 bay leaves
¾ tsp. salt
½ tsp. pepper
5 cups water
Hot cooked rice

1. Rinse and sort the beans; soak according to the package directions. Drain and rinse, discarding soaking liquid.

2. In a 6-qt. slow cooker, combine beans with next 9 ingredients. Add water; cook, covered, on low until meat and beans are tender, 7-9 hours.

3. Remove pork ribs and ham hock. When cool enough to handle, remove meat from bones; discard bones and bay leaves. Shred meat with 2 forks; return to slow cooker. Serve with hot cooked rice.

Freeze option: Freeze cooled stew in freezer containers. To use, partially thaw in refrigerator overnight. Heat through in a saucepan, stirring occasionally; add water if necessary.

1½ cups: 531 cal., 33g fat (11g sat. fat), 101mg chol., 1069mg sod., 27g carb. (3g sugars, 6g fiber), 33g pro.

SLOW-COOKER BEEF BARBACOA

I love this beef barbacoa because the meat is fall-apart tender and the sauce is smoky, slightly spicy and oh, so flavorful. It's an amazing alternative to ground beef tacos or even pulled pork carnitas. It's also versatile. Keep it in the freezer for fast Mexican pizza or popular rice bowls.

—*Holly Sander, Lake Mary, FL*

- -

Prep: 20 min. • **Cook:** 6 hours
Makes: 8 servings

1	beef rump or bottom round roast (3 lbs.)
½	cup minced fresh cilantro
⅓	cup tomato paste
8	garlic cloves, minced
2	Tbsp. chipotle peppers in adobo sauce plus 1 Tbsp. sauce
2	Tbsp. cider vinegar
4	tsp. ground cumin
1	Tbsp. brown sugar
1½	tsp. salt
1	tsp. pepper
1	cup beef stock
1	cup beer or additional stock
16	corn tortillas (6 in.)
	Pico de gallo
	Optional toppings: Lime wedges, queso fresco and additional cilantro

1. Cut roast in half. Mix next 9 ingredients; rub over roast. Place in a 5-qt. slow cooker. Add stock and beer. Cook, covered, until meat is tender, 6-8 hours.

2. Remove roast; shred with 2 forks. Reserve 3 cups cooking juices; discard remaining juices. Skim fat from reserved juices. Return beef and reserved juices to slow cooker; heat through.

3. Serve with tortillas and pico de gallo. If desired, serve with lime wedges, queso fresco and additional cilantro.

Freeze option: Place shredded beef in freezer containers. Cool and freeze. To use, partially thaw in refrigerator overnight. Heat through in a covered saucepan, stirring gently; add broth if necessary.

2 filled tortillas: 361 cal., 10g fat (3g sat. fat), 101mg chol., 652mg sod., 28g carb. (4g sugars, 4g fiber), 38g pro. **Diabetic exchanges:** 5 lean meat, 2 starch.

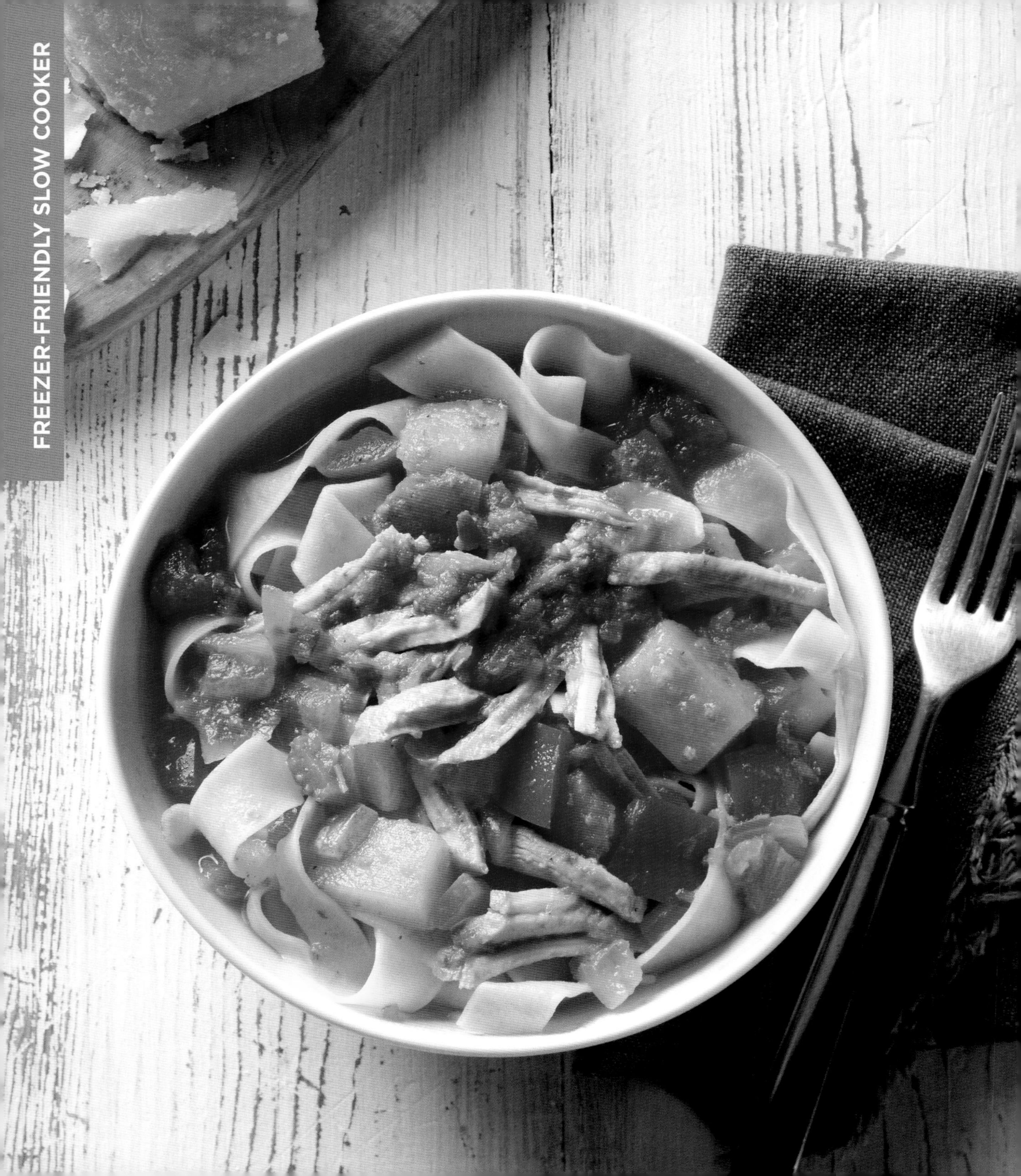

SPICY PORK & BUTTERNUT SQUASH RAGU

This recipe is a marvelously spicy combo that's perfect for cooler fall weather and satisfying after a day spent outdoors.
—Monica Osterhaus, Paducah, KY

Prep: 20 min. • **Cook:** 5 hours
Makes: 10 servings

- 2   cans (14½ oz. each) stewed tomatoes, undrained
- 1   pkg. (12 oz.) frozen cooked winter squash, thawed
- 1   large sweet onion, cut into ½-in. pieces
- 1   medium sweet red pepper, cut into ½-in. pieces
- 1½ tsp. crushed red pepper flakes
- 2   lbs. boneless country-style pork ribs
- 1   tsp. salt
- ¼   tsp. garlic powder
- ¼   tsp. pepper
     Hot cooked pasta
     Shaved Parmesan cheese, optional

1. Combine first 5 ingredients in bottom of a 6- or 7-qt. slow cooker. Sprinkle ribs with salt, garlic powder and pepper; place in slow cooker. Cook, covered, on low until pork is tender, 5-6 hours.

2. Remove cover; stir to break pork into smaller pieces. Serve with pasta. If desired, top with Parmesan cheese.

Freeze option: Freeze cooled sauce in freezer containers. To use, partially thaw in refrigerator overnight. Heat through in a saucepan, stirring occasionally.

1 cup ragu: 195 cal., 8g fat (3g sat. fat), 52mg chol., 426mg sod., 13g carb. (6g sugars, 2g fiber), 17g pro. **Diabetic exchanges:** 2 lean meat, 1 starch.

DELUXE WALKING NACHOS

This slow-cooked potluck chili makes an awesome filling for a little bag of walk-around nachos. Cut the bag lengthwise to make it easier to load up your fork.
—Mallory Lynch, Madison, WI

Prep: 20 min. • **Cook:** 6 hours
Makes: 18 servings

- 1   lb. lean ground beef (90% lean)
- 1   large sweet onion, chopped
- 3   garlic cloves, minced
- 2   cans (14½ oz. each) diced tomatoes with mild green chiles
- 2   cans (15 oz. each) pinto beans, rinsed and drained
- 2   cans (15 oz. each) black beans, rinsed and drained
- 2   to 3 Tbsp. chili powder
- 2   tsp. ground cumin
- ½   tsp. salt
- 18 pkg. (1 oz. each) nacho-flavored tortilla chips

Optional toppings: Shredded cheddar cheese, sour cream, chopped tomatoes and pickled jalapeno slices

1. In a large skillet, cook beef, onion and garlic over medium heat until beef is no longer pink, breaking up beef into crumbles, 6-8 minutes; drain.

2. Transfer beef mixture to a 5-qt. slow cooker. Drain 1 can tomatoes, discarding liquid; add to slow cooker. Stir in the beans, chili powder, cumin, salt and the remaining tomatoes. Cook, covered, on low 6-8 hours to allow flavors to blend. Mash beans to desired consistency.

3. Just before serving, cut open tortilla chip bags. Divide chili among bags; add toppings as desired.

Freeze option: Freeze cooled chili in a freezer container. To use, partially thaw in refrigerator overnight. Heat through in a saucepan, stirring occasionally; add water if necessary.

1 serving: 282 cal., 10g fat (2g sat. fat), 16mg chol., 482mg sod., 36g carb. (5g sugars, 6g fiber), 12g pro.

SWEET-AND-SOUR BEEF STEW

This chunky meal in a bowl makes terrific use of nutrient-packed vegetables. It has a deliciously sweet and tangy taste.
—*Frances Conklin, Cottonwood, ID*

Prep: 25 min. • **Cook:** 8 hours
Makes: 8 servings

- 2 lbs. beef top round steak, cut into 1-in. cubes
- 2 Tbsp. olive oil
- 1 can (15 oz.) tomato sauce
- 2 large onions, chopped
- 4 medium carrots, thinly sliced
- 1 large green pepper, cut into 1-in. pieces
- 1 cup canned pineapple chunks, drained
- ½ cup cider vinegar
- ¼ cup packed brown sugar
- ¼ cup light corn syrup
- 2 tsp. chili powder
- 2 tsp. paprika
- ½ tsp. salt
  Hot cooked rice, optional

1. In a large skillet, brown beef in oil in batches; drain. Transfer to a 4- or 5-qt. slow cooker.
2. In a large bowl, combine the tomato sauce, onions, carrots, green pepper, pineapple, vinegar, brown sugar, corn syrup, chili powder, paprika and salt; pour over beef.
3. Cover and cook on low for 8-10 hours or until beef is tender. Serve with cooked rice if desired.
Freeze option: Freeze cooled stew in freezer containers. To use, partially thaw in refrigerator overnight. Heat through in a saucepan, stirring occasionally; add broth or water if necessary.
1 cup: 290 cal., 7g fat (2g sat. fat), 64mg chol., 465mg sod., 29g carb. (17g sugars, 3g fiber), 28g pro. **Diabetic exchanges:** 3 lean meat, 2 vegetable, 1 starch, ½ fat.

PULLED PORK SANDWICHES

These simple sandwiches tastes like something you'd order from a local barbecue joint.
—*Lauren Adamson, Layton, UT*

Prep: 15 min. • **Cook:** 8 hours
Makes: 10 servings

- ⅓ cup liquid smoke
- 3 Tbsp. paprika
- 3 tsp. salt
- 3 tsp. pepper
- 1 tsp. garlic powder
- 1 tsp. ground mustard
- 1 boneless pork shoulder butt roast (3 to 4 lbs.)
- 1 bottle (18 oz.) barbecue sauce
- 10 hamburger buns, split

1. In a small bowl, whisk first 6 ingredients; rub over roast. Place roast in a 5- or 6-qt. slow cooker. Cook, covered, on low until meat is tender, 8-10 hours.
2. Remove roast; cool slightly. Discard cooking juices. Shred pork with 2 forks; return to slow cooker. Stir in barbecue sauce; heat through. Serve on buns.
To make ahead: In a small bowl, whisk the first 6 ingredients; rub over roast. Place roast in a freezer container and freeze. To use, place roast in refrigerator 48 hours or until roast is completely thawed. Cook and serve as directed.
Freeze option: Freeze cooled meat mixture in freezer containers. To use, partially thaw in refrigerator overnight. Heat through in a saucepan, stirring occasionally; add water if necessary.
1 sandwich: 436 cal., 16g fat (5g sat. fat), 81mg chol., 827mg sod., 44g carb. (20g sugars, 2g fiber), 28g pro.

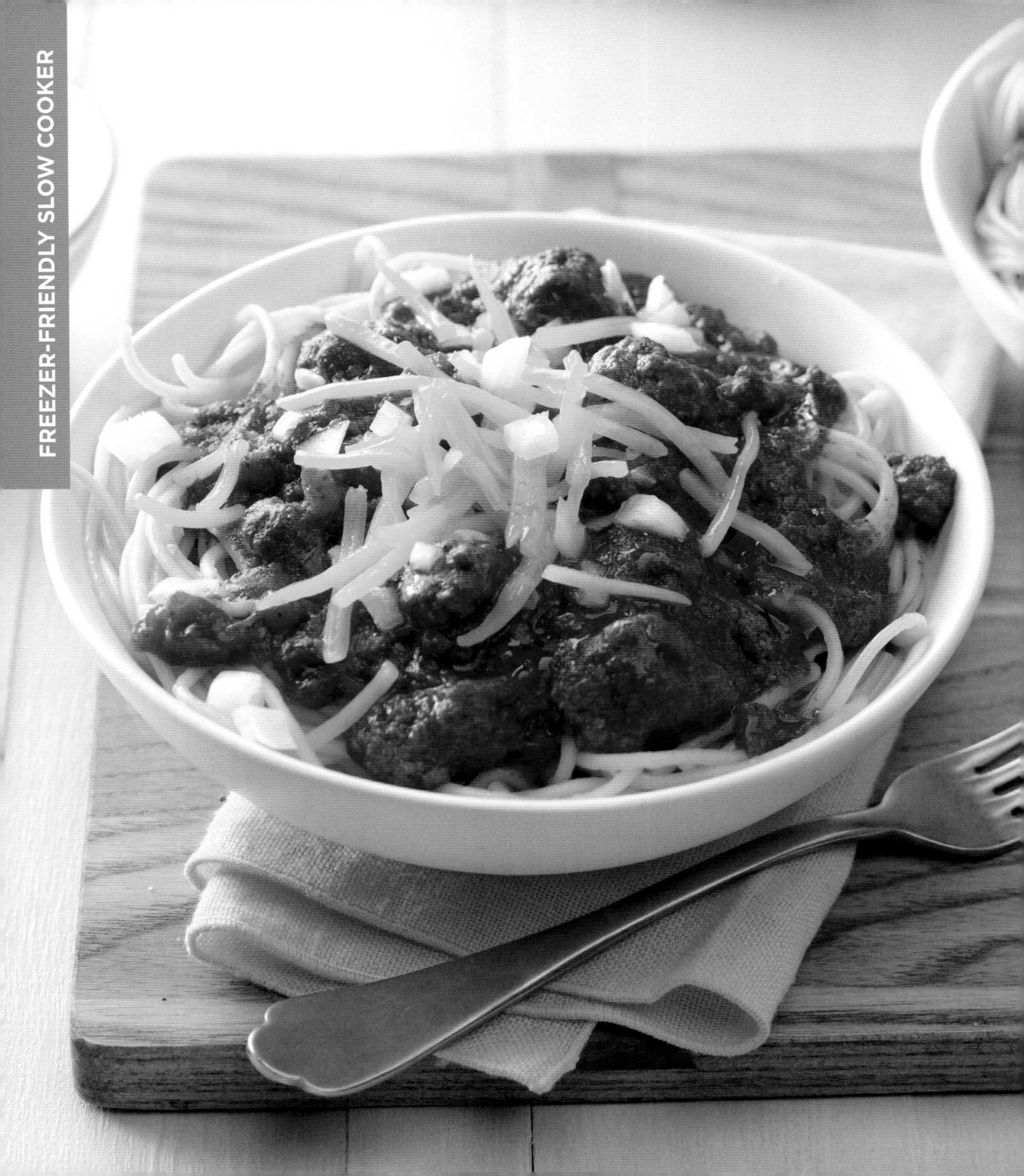

CINCINNATI CHILI

My husband convinced me to enter this in a contest, and I won third place!
—*Carrie Birdsall, Dallas, GA*

- -

Prep: 20 min. • **Cook:** 6 hours
Makes: 6 servings (1½ qt.)

1½ lbs. ground beef
1 small onion, chopped
1 can (29 oz.) tomato puree
1 can (14½ oz.) whole
 tomatoes, crushed
2 Tbsp. brown sugar
4 tsp. chili powder
1 Tbsp. white vinegar
1 tsp. salt
¾ tsp. ground cinnamon
½ tsp. ground allspice
½ tsp. pepper
1 garlic clove, crushed
3 bay leaves
 Hot cooked spaghetti
 Shredded cheddar cheese, optional
 Additional chopped onion, optional

1. In a large skillet over medium heat, cook beef and onion, crumbling meat, until the beef is no longer pink and onion is tender, 6-8 minutes; drain. Transfer to a 3- or 4-qt. slow cooker. Add next 11 ingredients.
2. Cook, covered, on low 6-8 hours. Discard garlic clove and bay leaves. Serve on hot cooked spaghetti; if desired, top with shredded cheddar cheese and additional chopped onion.

Freeze option: Freeze the chili, without toppings, in freezer containers. To use, partially thaw in refrigerator overnight. Heat through in a saucepan, stirring occasionally; add water if necessary. Serve as directed.

1 cup: 315 cal., 14g fat (5g sat. fat), 70mg chol., 644mg sod., 19g carb. (9g sugars, 4g fiber), 23g pro.

CHEESY TURKEY MEAT LOAF

Nothing says comfort food better than meat loaf! Get this one started in the afternoon and you'll have a delicious hot meal ready by dinner.
—*Deanna Martinez, Wake Forest, NC*

- -

Prep: 15 min. • **Cook:** 3 hours + standing
Makes: 6 servings

1 large egg, lightly beaten
1 cup crushed saltines
1 cup ketchup
2 garlic cloves, minced
1 tsp. salt
1 tsp. pepper
2 lbs. ground turkey
2½ cups shredded cheddar
 cheese, divided
½ cup shredded Parmesan cheese

1. Fold an 18-in. square piece of heavy-duty foil in half to make an 18x9-in. strip. Place strip on bottom and up sides of a 5- or 6-qt. slow cooker. Coat strip with cooking spray.
2. In a large bowl, combine the first 6 ingredients. Add turkey, 2 cups cheddar cheese and Parmesan cheese; mix lightly but thoroughly (mixture will be moist). Shape meat into an 8x5-in. loaf; place in center of strip.
3. Cook, covered, on low 3-4 hours or until a thermometer reads 165°. Sprinkle with remaining cheese during the last 20 minutes of cooking. Using the ends of foil strip as handles, remove meat loaf to a platter. Let stand 15 minutes.

Freeze option: Prepare the meat loaf as directed, omitting cheddar cheese over top. Securely wrap cooled meat loaf in foil, then freeze; freeze remaining ½ cup cheddar cheese in a freezer container. To use, partially thaw in refrigerator overnight. Unwrap meat loaf; reheat on a greased 15x10x1-in. baking pan in a preheated 350° oven until heated through and a thermometer inserted in center reads 165°. Sprinkle with cheese.

1 serving: 540 cal., 31g fat (14g sat. fat), 184mg chol., 1522mg sod., 21g carb. (11g sugars, 0 fiber), 45g pro.

BEER-BRAISED STEW

Friends and family will never guess that the secret ingredient in this wonderful stew is beer! What a nice meal to come home to—just cook the noodles and dinner is ready.
—*Geri Faustich, Appleton, WI*

- -

Prep: 20 min. • **Cook:** 6 hours
Makes: 8 servings

3	bacon strips, diced
2	lbs. beef stew meat, cut into 1-in. cubes
½	tsp. pepper
¼	tsp. salt
2	Tbsp. canola oil
2	cups fresh baby carrots
1	medium onion, cut into wedges
1	tsp. minced garlic
1	bay leaf
1	can (12 oz.) beer or nonalcoholic beer
1	Tbsp. soy sauce
1	Tbsp. Worcestershire sauce
1	tsp. dried thyme
2	Tbsp. all-purpose flour
¼	cup water
	Hot cooked noodles
	Chopped fresh parsley, optional

1. In a large skillet, cook bacon over medium heat until crisp. Remove to paper towels; drain, discarding drippings. Sprinkle beef with pepper and salt. In the same skillet, brown beef in oil in batches; drain.

2. Transfer to a 5-qt. slow cooker. Add the carrots, bacon, onion, garlic and bay leaf. In a small bowl, combine the beer, soy sauce, Worcestershire sauce and thyme. Pour over beef mixture.

3. Cover and cook on low for 5½-6 hours or until meat and vegetables are tender.

4. In a small bowl, combine the flour and water until smooth. Gradually stir into slow cooker. Cover and cook on high for 30 minutes or until thickened. Discard bay leaf. Serve beef with noodles. If desired, top with chopped parsley.

Freeze option: Freeze the cooled stew in freezer containers. To use, partially thaw in refrigerator overnight. Heat through in a saucepan, stirring occasionally; add broth or water if necessary.

½ cup: 258 cal., 13g fat (4g sat. fat), 74mg chol., 340mg sod., 8g carb. (4g sugars, 1g fiber), 24g pro.

TURKEY SAUSAGE SOUP

This favorite gives me plenty of time to have fun with my kids and grandkids.
—*Nancy Heishman, Las Vegas, NV*

Prep: 30 min. • **Cook:** 6 hours
Makes: 10 servings (about 3¼ qt.)

- 1 pkg. (19½ oz.) Italian turkey sausage links, casings removed
- 3 large tomatoes, chopped
- 1 can (15 oz.) garbanzo beans or chickpeas, rinsed and drained
- 3 medium carrots, thinly sliced
- 1½ cups cut fresh green beans (1-in. pieces)
- 1 medium zucchini, quartered lengthwise and sliced
- 1 large sweet red or green pepper, chopped
- 8 green onions, chopped
- 4 cups chicken stock
- 1 can (12 oz.) tomato paste
- ½ tsp. seasoned salt
- ⅓ cup minced fresh basil

1. In a large skillet, cook the sausage over medium heat 8-10 minutes or until no longer pink, breaking into crumbles; drain and transfer to a 6-qt. slow cooker.

2. Add the next 7 ingredients. In a bowl, whisk stock, tomato paste and seasoned salt; pour over vegetables.

3. Cook, covered, on low 6-8 hours or until vegetables are tender. Just before serving, stir in basil.

Freeze option: Freeze cooled soup in freezer containers. To use, partially thaw in refrigerator overnight. Heat through in a saucepan, stirring occasionally; add stock if necessary.

1⅓ cups: 167 cal., 5g fat (1g sat. fat), 20mg chol., 604mg sod., 21g carb. (8g sugars, 5g fiber), 13g pro.

SWEET POTATO CHILI WITH TURKEY

Swapping ground turkey for ground beef lightens up this chili.
—*Rachel Lewis, Danville, VA*

Prep: 20 min. • **Cook:** 5 hours
Makes: 6 servings (2¼ qt.)

- 1   lb. ground turkey
- 1   small onion, chopped
- 2   cups chicken broth
- 1   can (15 oz.) sweet potato puree or canned pumpkin
- 1   can (4 oz.) chopped green chiles
- 1   Tbsp. chili powder
- 1   tsp. garlic powder
- 1   tsp. ground cumin
- 1   tsp. curry powder
- ½   tsp. dried oregano
- ½   tsp. salt
- 1   can (15½ oz.) great northern beans, rinsed and drained
  Optional: Sour cream, fresh cilantro and sliced red onions

1. In a large skillet, cook turkey and onion over medium heat until turkey is no longer pink and onion is tender, 5-7 minutes, breaking up turkey into crumbles; drain. Transfer to a 3- or 4-qt. slow cooker.
2. Stir in broth, sweet potato puree, chiles and seasonings. Cook, covered, on low for 4-5 hours. Stir in beans; cook until heated through, about 1 hour. If desired, top with sour cream, cilantro and red onions.
Freeze option: Freeze cooled chili in freezer containers. To use, partially thaw in chili in refrigerator overnight. Heat through in a saucepan, stirring occasionally; add broth if necessary.
1½ cups: 243 cal., 6g fat (1g sat. fat), 52mg chol., 606mg sod., 27g carb. (5g sugars, 7g fiber), 20g pro.

CHUNKY CHICKEN CACCIATORE

This recipe is so versatile. It's perfect for meal planning because you can look in your fridge and toss in any extras such as red pepper, mushrooms or extra zucchini. And if you're a vegetarian, go ahead and simply leave out the chicken.
—*Stephanie Loaiza, Layton, UT*

Prep: 10 min. • **Cook:** 4 hours
Makes: 6 servings

- 6   boneless skinless chicken thighs (about 1½ lbs.)
- 2   medium zucchini, cut into 1-in. slices
- 1   medium green pepper, cut into 1-in. pieces
- 1   large sweet onion, coarsely chopped
- ½   tsp. dried oregano
- 1   jar (24 oz.) garden-style spaghetti sauce
  Hot cooked spaghetti
  Optional: Sliced ripe olives and shredded Parmesan cheese

1. Place chicken and vegetables in a 3-qt. slow cooker; sprinkle with oregano. Pour sauce over top. Cook, covered, on low for 4-5 hours or until chicken is tender.
2. Remove chicken; break up slightly with 2 forks. Return to slow cooker. Serve with spaghetti. If desired, top with the olives and cheese.
Freeze option: Place the first 6 ingredients in a freezer container and freeze. To use, place container in refrigerator 48 hours or until contents are completely thawed. Cook and serve as directed.
1 serving: 285 cal., 11g fat (2g sat. fat), 76mg chol., 507mg sod., 21g carb. (14g sugars, 3g fiber), 24g pro. **Diabetic exchanges:** 3 lean meat, 1½ starch.

CHICKEN MERLOT WITH MUSHROOMS

A dear friend who liked cooking as much as I do shared this recipe with me, and I think of her every time I make it.
—*Shelli McWilliam, Salem, OR*

Prep: 10 min. • **Cook:** 5 hours
Makes: 8 servings

- ¾ lb. sliced fresh mushrooms
- 1 large onion, chopped
- 2 garlic cloves, minced
- 3 lbs. boneless skinless chicken thighs
- 1 can (6 oz.) tomato paste
- ¾ cup chicken broth
- ¼ cup merlot or additional chicken broth
- 2 Tbsp. quick-cooking tapioca
- 2 tsp. sugar
- 1½ tsp. dried basil
- ½ tsp. salt
- ¼ tsp. pepper
- 2 Tbsp. grated Parmesan cheese
  Hot cooked pasta, optional

1. Place the mushrooms, onion and garlic in a 5-qt. slow cooker. Top with the chicken.
2. In a small bowl, combine tomato paste, broth, wine, tapioca, sugar, basil, salt and pepper. Pour over chicken. Cover and cook on low for 5-6 hours until chicken is tender.
3. Sprinkle with the cheese. Serve with pasta if desired.

Freeze option: Freeze cooled chicken mixture in freezer containers. To use, partially thaw in refrigerator overnight. Heat through in a saucepan, stirring occasionally; add broth or water if necessary.
5 oz. cooked chicken with ½ cup sauce: 310 cal., 13g fat (4g sat. fat), 115mg chol., 373mg sod., 11g carb. (5g sugars, 1g fiber), 35g pro. **Diabetic exchanges:** 5 lean meat, ½ starch.

SLOW-COOKER SWEET-AND-SOUR PORK

Chinese food is a big temptation for us, so I re-created a favorite. As the pork cooks, the aroma is beyond mouthwatering.
—*Elyse Ellis, Layton, UT*

Prep: 15 min. • **Cook:** 6¼ hours
Makes: 4 servings

- ½ cup sugar
- ½ cup packed brown sugar
- ½ cup chicken broth
- ⅓ cup white vinegar
- 3 Tbsp. lemon juice
- 3 Tbsp. reduced-sodium soy sauce
- 3 Tbsp. tomato paste
- ½ tsp. garlic powder
- ¼ tsp. ground ginger
- ¼ tsp. pepper
- 1½ lbs. boneless pork loin chops, cut into 1-in. cubes
- 1 large onion, cut into 1-in. pieces
- 1 large green pepper, cut into 1-in. pieces
- 1 can (8 oz.) pineapple chunks, drained
- 3 Tbsp. cornstarch
- ⅓ cup chicken broth
  Hot cooked rice

1. In a 3- or 4-qt. slow cooker, mix the first 10 ingredients. Stir in pork, onion, green pepper and pineapple. Cook, covered, on low 6-8 hours or until pork is tender.
2. In a small bowl, mix cornstarch and broth until smooth; gradually stir into cooking juices. Cook, covered, on low 15-20 minutes longer or until sauce is thickened. Serve with rice.

Freeze option: In a large resealable plastic freezer bag, combine first 10 ingredients. Add pork, onion, green pepper and pineapple; seal bag, turn to coat, then freeze. To use, place filled freezer bag in refrigerator 48 hours or until contents are completely thawed. Cook as directed.
1⅓ cups: 531 cal., 10g fat (4g sat. fat), 83mg chol., 705mg sod., 75g carb. (63g sugars, 2g fiber), 35g pro.

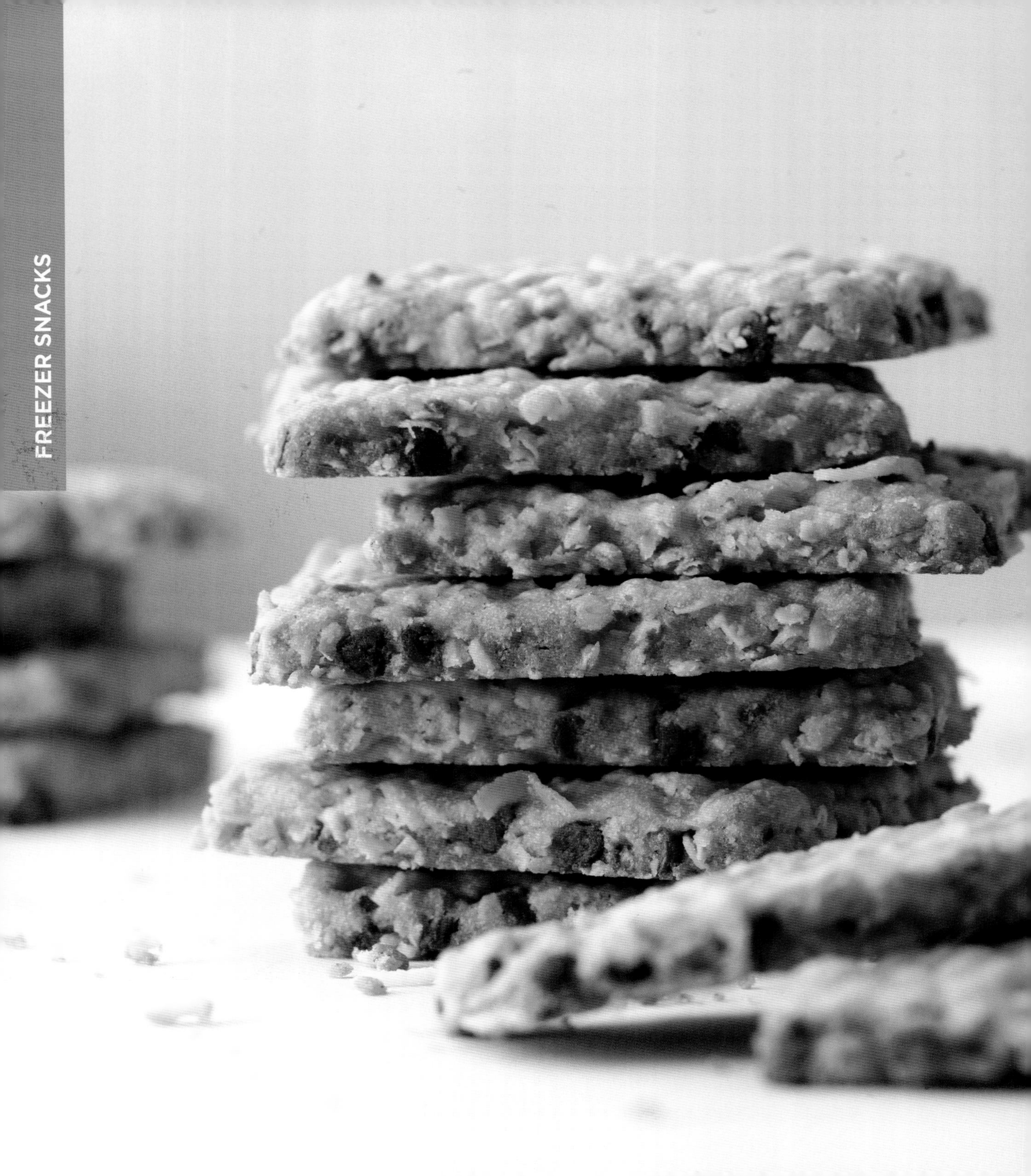

❄ CHOCOLATE COCONUT OATIES

On one of those nights when I just needed a treat, I hit the pantry and improvised this recipe. The mini chocolate chips give you melty goodness in every single bite.
—*Emily Tyra, Traverse City, MI*

Prep: 30 min. + chilling • **Bake:** 10 min./batch
Makes: about 4½ dozen

1¼ cups butter, softened
1 cup packed brown sugar
1 large egg, room temperature
2 cups all-purpose flour
2 cups quick-cooking oats
1 tsp. salt
1 cup miniature semisweet chocolate chips
1 cup sweetened shredded coconut

1. In a large bowl, cream butter and brown sugar until light and fluffy. Beat in egg. In another bowl, whisk the flour, oats and salt; gradually beat into creamed mixture. Stir in chocolate chips and coconut.
2. Divide dough in half. Shape each into a disk. Wrap and refrigerate 1 hour or until firm enough to roll.
3. Preheat the oven to 350°. On a lightly floured surface, roll each portion of dough to ¼-in. thickness. Cut with a floured 2¼-in. square cookie cutter. Place 1 in. apart on parchment paper-lined baking sheets.
4. Bake 9-11 minutes or until the edges are light brown. Remove from pans to wire racks to cool.
Freeze option: Transfer wrapped dough to a freezer container; freeze. To use, thaw the dough in refrigerator until soft enough to roll. Proceed as directed.
1 cookie: 106 cal., 6g fat (4g sat. fat), 15mg chol., 85mg sod., 12g carb. (7g sugars, 1g fiber), 1g pro.

❄ SAUSAGE WONTON CUPS

Here's a tasty hot snack for all those parties that feature fun finger foods. I've made this recipe several times, and these bites always disappear so fast. It's really easy.
—*Shirley Van Allen, High Point, NC*

Takes: 30 min. • **Makes:** 2 dozen

1 lb. Italian turkey sausage links, casings removed
1 can (15 oz.) tomato sauce
½ tsp. garlic powder
½ tsp. dried basil
24 wonton wrappers
1 cup shredded Italian cheese blend

1. In a large skillet, cook the sausage over medium heat until no longer pink; drain. Stir in tomato sauce, garlic powder and basil. Bring to a boil. Reduce the heat; simmer, uncovered, until thickened, 8-10 minutes.
2. Meanwhile, press wonton wrappers into miniature muffin cups coated with cooking spray. Bake at 350° until lightly browned, 8-9 minutes.
3. Spoon the sausage mixture into cups. Sprinkle with cheese. Bake until cheese is melted, 5-7 minutes longer. Serve warm.
Freeze option: Freeze cooled filled wonton cups in freezer containers, separating layers with waxed paper. To use, reheat wonton cups in coated muffin pans in a preheated 350° oven until crisp and heated through.
1 wonton cup: 68 cal., 3g fat (1g sat. fat), 15mg chol., 270mg sod., 6g carb. (0 sugars, 0 fiber), 5g pro. **Diabetic exchanges:** ½ starch, ½ fat.

BROCCOLI-CHEDDAR TASSIES

Our family adores broccoli casserole. I wanted to try it as an appetizer, so I used a pecan tassie recipe for the crust. The result? We're talking scrumptious.
—*Gail Gaiser, Ewing, NJ*

- -

Prep: 45 min. + chilling • **Bake:** 20 min./batch
Makes: about 4 dozen

- 1 cup butter, softened
- 6 oz. cream cheese, softened
- 2 cups all-purpose flour

FILLING
- 1 pkg. (16 oz.) frozen chopped broccoli
- 1 large egg, lightly beaten
- 1 can (10¾ oz.) condensed cream of celery soup, undiluted
- ¼ cup 2% milk
- ¼ cup mayonnaise
- ½ cup shredded sharp cheddar cheese

TOPPING
- ¼ cup dry bread crumbs
- 1 Tbsp. butter, melted

1. In a small bowl, cream the butter and cream cheese until smooth. Gradually beat flour into creamed mixture. Divide dough in half. Shape each into a disk. Cover and refrigerate for 1 hour or until firm enough to handle.

2. Preheat oven to 350°. Shape dough into 1-in. balls; place in greased mini-muffin cups. Using floured fingers, press evenly onto bottoms and up sides of cups.

3. Cook broccoli according to package directions; drain. In a large bowl, combine egg, condensed soup, milk and mayonnaise; stir in cheese and cooked broccoli. Spoon about 1 Tbsp. filling into each cup. For topping, mix bread crumbs and melted butter; sprinkle over filling.

4. Bake until the edges are golden brown, 18-22 minutes. Cool in pans for 2 minutes before removing to wire racks. Serve warm.

To make ahead: Dough can be made 2 days in advance.

Freeze option: Freeze cooled pastries on waxed paper-lined baking sheets until firm. Transfer to resealable freezer containers. To use, reheat the pastries on ungreased baking sheets in a preheated 350° oven for 14-16 minutes or until lightly browned and heated through.

1 tassie: 92 cal., 7g fat (4g sat. fat), 21mg chol., 101mg sod., 6g carb. (0 sugars, 1g fiber), 2g pro.

�)❄ CHEDDAR CORN DOG MUFFINS

I wanted a change from hot dogs, so I created these corn dog muffins. I added jalapenos to this kid-friendly snack, and that won my husband over, too.
—*Becky Tarala, Palm Coast, FL*

Takes: 25 min. • **Makes:** 9 muffins

1   pkg. (8½ oz.) cornbread/muffin mix
⅔   cup 2% milk
1   large egg, room temperature, lightly beaten
5   turkey hot dogs, sliced
½   cup shredded sharp cheddar cheese
2   Tbsp. finely chopped pickled jalapeno, optional

1. Preheat oven to 400°. Line 9 muffin cups with foil liners or grease 9 nonstick muffin cups.

2. In a small bowl, combine muffin mix, milk and egg; stir in hot dogs, cheese and, if desired, jalapeno. Fill the prepared cups three-fourths full.

3. Bake until a toothpick inserted in center comes out clean, 14-18 minutes. Cool for 5 minutes before removing from pan to a wire rack. Serve warm. Refrigerate any leftovers.

Freeze option: Freeze cooled muffins in freezer containers. To use, microwave each muffin on high 30-60 seconds or until muffin is heated through.

1 muffin: 216 cal., 10g fat (4g sat. fat), 46mg chol., 619mg sod., 23g carb. (7g sugars, 2g fiber), 8g pro.

🍲🍎❄ SLOW-COOKED PEACH SALSA

Fresh peaches and tomatoes make my salsa a hands-down winner over store versions. As a treat, I give my co-workers several jars throughout the year.
—*Peggi Stahnke, Cleveland, OH*

Prep: 20 min. • **Cook:** 3 hours + cooling
Makes: 11 cups

4   lbs. tomatoes (about 12 medium), chopped
1   medium onion, chopped
4   jalapeno peppers, seeded and finely chopped
½   to ⅔ cup packed brown sugar
¼   cup minced fresh cilantro
4   garlic cloves, minced
1   tsp. salt
4   cups chopped peeled fresh peaches (about 4 medium), divided
1   can (6 oz.) tomato paste

1. In a 5-qt. slow cooker, combine the first 7 ingredients; stir in 2 cups peaches. Cook, covered, on low 3-4 hours or until the onion is tender.

2. Stir tomato paste and remaining peaches into slow cooker. Cool. Transfer salsa to covered containers.

Freeze option: Fill freezer-safe containers to within ½ in. of tops. Freeze for up to 12 months. Thaw the frozen salsa in the refrigerator before serving.

Note: Wear disposable gloves when cutting hot peppers; the oils can burn skin. Avoid touching your face.

¼ cup: 28 cal., 0 fat (0 sat. fat), 0 chol., 59mg sod., 7g carb. (5g sugars, 1g fiber), 1g pro.
Diabetic exchanges: ½ starch.

MARTHA WASHINGTON CANDY

Passed down by my grandmother and mother, this recipe is a cherished family tradition. We've even had each grandchild and great-grandchild take a turn stirring the candy mixture.
—*Cindi Boger, Ardmore, AL*

Prep: 45 min. + chilling
Makes: about 5½ dozen

- 1 **cup butter, softened**
- 4 **cups confectioners' sugar**
- 1 **can (14 oz.) sweetened condensed milk**
- 1 **tsp. vanilla extract**
- 3 **cups sweetened shredded coconut**
- 2 **cups chopped pecans, toasted**
- 6 **cups (36 oz.) semisweet chocolate chips**
- ¼ **cup shortening**

1. In a large bowl, beat softened butter, confectioners' sugar, milk and vanilla until blended. Stir in coconut and pecans. Divide dough in half; refrigerate, covered, 1 hour.

2. Working with half the dough at a time, shape mixture into 1-in. balls; place on waxed paper-lined baking sheets. Refrigerate 30 minutes longer.

3. In top of a double boiler or a metal bowl over barely simmering water, melt the chocolate chips and shortening; stir until smooth. Dip balls in melted chocolate; allow excess to drip off. Return to waxed paper. Refrigerate until set.

Freeze option: Freeze candy, layered between pieces of waxed paper, in freezer containers. To use, thaw in refrigerator 2 hours before serving.

1 piece: 196 cal., 13g fat (7g sat. fat), 9mg chol., 43mg sod., 23g carb. (21g sugars, 1g fiber), 2g pro.

TEST KITCHEN TIP

For this recipe, make sure to use sweetened condensed milk. This type of milk has most of the water cooked off and added sugar. It's generally used in candy and dessert recipes. Evaporated milk is concentrated in the same way, but doesn't contain added sugar.

5i ❄

GORGONZOLA PHYLLO CUPS

You need only a few minutes to put these bites together. The flavor combo of rich Gorgonzola, apples and cranberries is especially good in the colder months.
—*Trisha Kruse, Eagle, ID*

- -

Takes: 20 min. • **Makes:** 2½ dozen

    2   pkg. (1.9 oz. each) frozen
        miniature phyllo tart shells
  1⅓ cups crumbled Gorgonzola cheese
   ½   cup chopped apple
   ⅓   cup dried cranberries
   ⅓   cup chopped walnuts

1. Preheat oven to 350°. Place tart shells on a 15x10x1-in. baking pan. In a small bowl, mix remaining ingredients; carefully spoon into tart shells.
2. Bake 6-8 minutes or until lightly browned. Serve warm or at room temperature. Refrigerate leftovers.
Freeze option: Freeze cooled pastries in a freezer container, separating layers with waxed paper. To use, reheat pastries on a greased baking sheet in a preheated 350° oven until crisp and heated through.
1 appetizer: 54 cal., 3g fat (1g sat. fat), 4mg chol., 77mg sod., 4g carb. (1g sugars, 0 fiber), 2g pro.

🧀 ❄ CHEESE CRISPIES

For years I've taken these crispy, crunchy snacks to work. They get high marks from everybody in the teachers lounge.
—*Eileen Ball, Cornelius, NC*

Prep: 15 min. + chilling • **Bake:** 15 min./batch
Makes: about 4½ dozen

   1   cup unsalted butter, softened
 2½   cups shredded extra-
        sharp cheddar cheese
   2   cups all-purpose flour
   ¾   tsp. salt
   ½   tsp. cayenne pepper
 2½   cups Rice Krispies
        Pecan halves, optional

1. Beat butter and cheese until blended. In another bowl, whisk flour, salt and cayenne; gradually beat into cheese mixture. Stir in the Rice Krispies. If necessary, turn onto a lightly floured surface and knead 4-6 times, forming a stiff dough.

2. Divide dough in half; shape each into a 7-in.-long roll. Wrap and refrigerate 1 hour or overnight.

3. Preheat oven to 350°. Unwrap and cut dough crosswise into ¼-in. slices. Place 1 in. apart on parchment-lined baking sheets. If desired, top each slice with a pecan half. Bake 14-16 minutes or until the edges are golden brown. Remove from pans to wire racks to cool.

To make ahead: Dough can be made 2 days in advance and stored in the refrigerator.

Freeze option: Freeze wrapped logs in an airtight container. To use, unwrap frozen logs and cut into slices. Bake as directed.

1 cracker: 73 cal., 5g fat (3g sat. fat), 15mg chol., 73mg sod., 5g carb. (0 sugars, 0 fiber), 2g pro.

MUSHROOM PALMIERS

I found this recipe a long time ago while attending a fundraiser for the small-town museum in West Texas where I worked. It is still a huge hit at parties. Frozen puff pastry helps make it easy and impressive. The cute palmiers freeze well, too.

—Judy Lock, Panhandle, TX

Prep: 20 min. + cooling • **Bake:** 15 min./batch
Makes: 4 dozen

- 2   Tbsp. butter
- ¾   lb. fresh mushrooms, finely chopped
- 1   small onion, finely chopped
- 1   tsp. minced fresh thyme or ¼ tsp. dried thyme
- ¾   tsp. lemon juice
- ¾   tsp. hot pepper sauce
- ¼   tsp. salt
- 1   pkg. (17.3 oz.) frozen puff pastry, thawed
- 1   large egg
- 2   tsp. water

1. Preheat oven to 400°. In a large skillet, heat butter over medium heat. Add the mushrooms and onion; cook and stir until tender. Stir in thyme, lemon juice, hot pepper sauce and salt. Cool completely.

2. Unfold 1 pastry sheet. Spread half of the mushroom mixture to within ½ in. of edges. Roll up the left and right sides toward the center, jelly-roll style, until rolls meet in the middle. Cut into 24 slices. Repeat with the remaining pastry and mushroom mixture.

3. Place on greased baking sheets. In a small bowl, whisk the egg and water; brush over pastries. Bake 15-20 minutes or until golden brown. Serve the palmiers warm or at room temperature.

Freeze option: Freeze cooled appetizers in freezer containers, separating layers with waxed paper. To use, preheat oven to 400°. Reheat appetizers on a greased baking sheet until crisp and heated through.

1 palmier: 58 cal., 3g fat (1g sat. fat), 5mg chol., 52mg sod., 6g carb. (0 sugars, 1g fiber), 1g pro.

� TURKEY EMPANADAS

Turn Thanksgiving leftovers into tasty empanadas using refrigerated pie pastry. We make these savory pastries after the holidays and freeze them for quick fixes on busy weeknights.
—*Cheryl Marinaccio, Webster, NY*

- -

Prep: 30 min. • **Bake:** 15 min.
Makes: about 1½ dozen

- 1 cup cubed cooked turkey
- ½ cup cooked stuffing
- 2 Tbsp. whole-berry cranberry sauce
- 2 Tbsp. turkey gravy
- 2 pkg. (14.1 oz. each) refrigerated pie pastry
- 1 large egg
- 1 Tbsp. water
  Rubbed sage, optional
  Additional turkey gravy or whole-berry cranberry sauce, optional

1. Preheat oven to 400°. In a small bowl, combine turkey, stuffing, cranberry sauce and gravy.
2. On a lightly floured surface, unroll 1 pastry. Roll out into a 12-in. circle. Cut with a floured 4-in. biscuit cutter. Repeat with remaining pastry.
3. In a small bowl, whisk egg with water; brush over edges of pastry circles. Place 1 Tbsp. filling on 1 side. Fold dough over filling. Press edges with a fork to seal.
4. Place 2 in. apart on greased baking sheets. Brush tops with remaining egg mixture; sprinkle with sage if desired. Bake 12-15 minutes or until golden brown. Serve empanadas warm, with gravy or cranberry sauce if desired.
Freeze option: Freeze cooled pastries in resealable freezer containers. To use, reheat the pastries on a greased baking sheet in a preheated 400° oven 8-10 minutes or until lightly browned and heated through.
1 empanada: 185 cal., 10g fat (4g sat. fat), 23mg chol., 175mg sod., 19g carb. (2g sugars, 0 fiber), 4g pro.

5i ❄ MINI PHYLLO TACOS

Crispy phyllo cups are the secret to creating an appetizer with all the flavor and appeal of a taco—and much easier to eat! These two-bite treats of spicy ground beef and zesty shredded cheese will be a surefire hit with a hungry crowd.
—*Roseann Weston, Philipsburg, PA*

- -

Prep: 30 min. • **Bake:** 10 min.
Makes: 2½ dozen

- 1 lb. lean ground beef (90% lean)
- ½ cup finely chopped onion
- 1 envelope taco seasoning
- ¾ cup water
- 1¼ cups shredded Mexican cheese blend, divided
- 2 pkg. (1.9 oz. each) frozen miniature phyllo tart shells

1. Preheat oven to 350°. In a small skillet, cook beef and onion over medium heat until meat is no longer pink; drain. Stir in the taco seasoning and water. Bring to a boil. Reduce the heat; simmer, uncovered, 5 minutes. Remove from the heat; stir in ½ cup of the cheese blend.
2. Place the tart shells in an ungreased 15x10x1-in. baking pan. Fill shells with the taco mixture.
3. Bake 6 minutes. Sprinkle with remaining cheese blend; bake until cheese is melted, 2-3 minutes longer.
Freeze option: Freeze cooled taco cups in a freezer container, separating layers with waxed paper. To use, reheat on a baking sheet in a preheated 350° oven until crisp and heated through.
1 appetizer: 63 cal., 3g fat (1g sat. fat), 11mg chol., 156mg sod., 4g carb. (0 sugars, 0 fiber), 4g pro.

PEPPERONI PIZZA TWISTS

My stepsister gave me this handy recipe. I tweaked it just a bit to suit my taste, and you can as well. You can add diced green peppers, olives or whatever you like!
—Lisa Worley, Adairsville, GA

Prep: 20 min. • **Bake:** 30 min. + standing
Makes: 8 servings

- 2 pkg. (11 oz. each) refrigerated crusty French loaf
- 1 Tbsp. all-purpose flour
- 1 cup shredded part-skim mozzarella cheese
- 1 pkg. (3½ oz.) sliced pepperoni, finely chopped
- 1 jar (14 oz.) pizza sauce, divided
- 1 large egg white, beaten
- 2 Tbsp. grated Parmesan cheese
- ½ tsp. Italian seasoning

1. Place 1 loaf on a lightly floured surface. With a sharp knife, make a lengthwise slit down the center of loaf to within ½ in. of bottom. Open dough so it lies flat; sprinkle with half of flour. Roll into a 14x5-in. rectangle. Repeat with remaining loaf.

2. In a large bowl, combine mozzarella cheese and pepperoni. Spread half of the mozzarella mixture down the center of each rectangle. Drizzle each with 3 Tbsp. pizza sauce.

3. Roll up jelly-roll style, starting from a long side; seal seams and ends. Place 1 loaf seam side down on a greased baking sheet. Place the remaining loaf seam side down next to the first loaf. Twist the loaves together 3 times.

4. With a sharp knife, make 3 shallow 3-in. slashes across top of each loaf; brush with egg white. Sprinkle with Parmesan cheese and Italian seasoning.

5. Bake at 350° for 25 minutes. Cover loosely with foil. Bake 4 minutes longer or until golden brown. Let stand for 10 minutes before slicing. Serve with remaining pizza sauce.

Freeze option: Freeze the cooled unsliced bread in heavy-duty foil. To use, remove from freezer 30 minutes before reheating. Remove from foil and reheat on a greased baking sheet in a preheated 325° oven until heated through. Serve as directed.

1 slice: 319 cal., 11g fat (5g sat. fat), 20mg chol., 1016mg sod., 38g carb. (7g sugars, 2g fiber), 14g pro.

❄

SPANAKOPITA SPRING ROLLS

I was inspired to turn spanakopita into a hand-held hors d'oeuvre. I use wonton wrappers in place of phyllo dough, and now these are the biggest hit among my friends.
—*Jade Randall, Las Vegas, NV*

Prep: 15 min. • **Cook:** 5 min./batch
Makes: 14 spring rolls

2   **pkg. (10 oz. each) frozen chopped spinach, thawed and squeezed dry**
2   **cups crumbled feta cheese**
4   **garlic cloves, minced**
2   **tsp. dill weed**
¼   **tsp. salt**
¼   **tsp. pepper**
14 **refrigerated egg roll wrappers**
    Oil for deep-fat frying

1. Mix first 6 ingredients. With a corner of an egg roll wrapper facing you, place about ⅓ cup filling just below center of wrapper. (Cover the remaining wrappers with a damp paper towel until ready to use.) Fold bottom corner over filling; moisten the remaining wrapper edges with water. Fold side corners toward center over the filling. Roll up tightly, pressing at tip to seal. Repeat.
2. In an electric skillet or deep-fat fryer, heat oil to 375°. Fry spring rolls, a few at a time, until golden brown, 3-4 minutes, turning occasionally. Drain on paper towels.
Freeze option: Freeze uncooked spring rolls in freezer containers, spacing them so they don't touch and separating the layers with waxed paper. To use, fry frozen spring rolls as directed, increasing time as necessary.
1 spring roll: 245 cal., 12g fat (4g sat. fat), 20mg chol., 568mg sod., 22g carb. (0 sugars, 3g fiber), 10g pro.

HAM & BRIE PASTRIES

Growing up, I loved pocket pastries. Now, with a busy family, I need quick bites. My spin on the classic ham and cheese delivers as a snack or for supper.
—*Jenn Tidwell, Fair Oaks, CA*

- -

Takes: 30 min. • **Makes:** 16 pastries

1	**sheet frozen puff pastry, thawed**
⅓	**cup apricot preserves**
4	**slices deli ham, quartered**
8	**oz. Brie cheese, cut into 16 pieces**

1. Preheat oven to 400°. On a lightly floured surface, unfold puff pastry. Roll pastry to a 12-in. square; cut into sixteen 3-in. squares. Place 1 tsp. preserves in center of each square; top with ham, folding as necessary, and cheese. Overlap 2 opposite corners of pastry over filling; pinch tightly to seal.
2. Place on a parchment-lined baking sheet. Bake 15-20 minutes or until golden brown. Cool the pastries on pan at least 5 minutes before serving.

Freeze option: Freeze cooled pastries in a freezer container, separating layers with waxed paper. To use, reheat pastries on a baking sheet in a preheated 400° oven until heated through.

1 pastry: 144 cal., 8g fat (3g sat. fat), 17mg chol., 192mg sod., 13g carb. (3g sugars, 1g fiber), 5g pro.

SOFT BEER PRETZELS

What goes together better than beer and pretzels? Not much that I can think of. That's why I put them together into one delicious recipe. I'm always looking for new ways to combine fun flavors, and this pretzel certainly fits the bill.
—*Alyssa Wilhite, Whitehouse, TX*

- -

Prep: 1 hour + rising • **Bake:** 10 min.
Makes: 8 pretzels

1	bottle (12 oz.) amber beer or nonalcoholic beer
1	pkg. (¼ oz.) active dry yeast
2	Tbsp. unsalted butter, melted
2	Tbsp. sugar
1½	tsp. salt
4	to 4½ cups all-purpose flour
10	cups water
⅔	cup baking soda

TOPPING
1	large egg yolk
1	Tbsp. water
	Coarse salt, optional

1. In a small saucepan, heat the beer to 110°-115°; remove from heat. Stir in yeast until dissolved. In a large bowl, combine butter, sugar, 1½ tsp. salt, yeast mixture and 3 cups flour; beat on medium speed until smooth. Stir in enough remaining flour to form a soft dough (dough will be sticky).
2. Turn dough onto a floured surface; knead until smooth and elastic, 6-8 minutes. Place in a greased bowl, turning once to grease the top. Cover and let rise in a warm place until doubled, about 1 hour.

3. Preheat oven to 425°. Punch dough down. Turn onto a lightly floured surface; divide and shape into 8 balls. Roll each into a 24-in. rope. Curve ends of each rope to form a circle; twist ends once and lay over opposite side of circle, pinching the ends to seal.
4. In a Dutch oven, bring water and baking soda to a boil. Drop pretzels, 2 at a time, into boiling water. Cook for 30 seconds. Remove with a slotted spoon; drain well on paper towels.
5. Place 2 in. apart on greased baking sheets. In a small bowl, whisk egg yolk and water; brush over pretzels. Sprinkle with coarse salt if desired. Bake 10-12 minutes or until golden brown. Remove from pans to a wire rack to cool.

Freeze option: Freeze cooled pretzels in freezer containers. To use, thaw at room temperature or microwave each pretzel on high until heated through, 20-30 seconds.

1 pretzel: 288 cal., 4g fat (2g sat. fat), 16mg chol., 604mg sod., 53g carb. (6g sugars, 2g fiber), 7g pro.

To Make Pretzel Bites: Divide and shape into 8 balls; roll each into a 12-in. rope. Cut each rope into 1-in. pieces. Boil and top as directed; bake at 400° for 6-8 minutes or until golden brown. Yield: 8 dozen.

ALMOND CHEDDAR APPETIZERS

I always try to have a supply of these savory bites on hand in the freezer. If guests drop in, I just pull some out and reheat to serve. They work great as a snack, for brunch or along with a lighter lunch.
—Linda Thompson, Southampton, ON

- -

Takes: 25 min. • **Makes:** about 4 dozen

- 1 cup mayonnaise
- 2 tsp. Worcestershire sauce
- 1 cup shredded sharp cheddar cheese
- 1 medium onion, chopped
- ¾ cup slivered almonds, chopped
- 6 bacon strips, cooked and crumbled
- 1 loaf (1 lb.) French bread

1. In a bowl, combine the mayonnaise and Worcestershire sauce; stir in cheese, onion, almonds and bacon.
2. Cut bread into ½-in. slices; spread with cheese mixture. Cut slices in half; place on a greased baking sheet. Bake at 400° until bubbly, 8-10 minutes.
Freeze option: Place unbaked appetizers in a single layer on a baking sheet; freeze for 1 hour. Remove from pan and store in an airtight container for up to 2 months. When ready to use, place thawed appetizers on a greased baking sheet. Bake at 400° for 10 minutes or until bubbly.
1 piece: 81 cal., 6g fat (1g sat. fat), 4mg chol., 116mg sod., 6g carb. (1g sugars, 0 fiber), 2g pro.

PIZZA PUFFS

What's more fun than a pizza puff? Skip the kind sold in the frozen aisle and try this homemade version. You can substitute any meat or vegetable for the pepperoni and any cheese for the mozzarella.
—Vivi Taylor, Middleburg, FL

- -

Takes: 30 min. • **Makes:** 20 servings

- 1 loaf (1 lb.) frozen pizza dough, thawed
- 20 slices pepperoni
- 8 oz. part-skim mozzarella cheese, cut into 20 cubes
- ¼ cup butter
- 2 small garlic cloves, minced
  Dash salt
  Marinara sauce, warmed
  Optional: Crushed red pepper flakes and grated Parmesan cheese

1. Preheat oven to 400°. Shape dough into 1½-in. balls; flatten into ⅛-in. thick circles. Place 1 pepperoni slice and 1 cheese cube in center of each circle; wrap dough around pepperoni and cheese. Pinch edges to seal; shape into a ball. Repeat with remaining dough, cheese and pepperoni. Place seam side down on greased baking sheets; bake until light golden brown, 10-15 minutes. Cool slightly.
2. Meanwhile, in a small saucepan, melt butter over low heat. Add garlic and salt, taking care not to brown butter or garlic; brush over puffs. Serve with marinara sauce; if desired, sprinkle with red pepper flakes and Parmesan.
Freeze option: Cover and freeze unbaked pizza puffs on waxed paper-lined baking sheets until firm. Transfer to a freezer container; seal and return to freezer. To use, preheat oven to 325°; bake pizza puffs on greased baking sheets as directed, increasing time as necessary to heat through.
1 puff: 120 cal., 6g fat (3g sat. fat), 15mg chol., 189mg sod., 11g carb. (1g sugars, 0 fiber), 5g pro.

MOROCCAN EMPANADAS

My family goes for Moroccan flavors, so I make empanadas using apricot preserves and beef in pastry. A spicy dipping sauce adds to the appeal of these flaky hand pies.
—*Arlene Erlbach, Morton Grove, IL*

Prep: 30 min. • **Bake:** 15 min.
Makes: 20 servings

- ¾ lb. ground beef
- 1 medium onion, chopped
- 3 oz. cream cheese, softened
- ⅓ cup apricot preserves
- ¼ cup finely chopped carrot
- ¾ tsp. Moroccan seasoning (ras el hanout) or ½ tsp. ground cumin plus ¼ tsp. ground coriander and dash cayenne pepper
- ¼ tsp. salt
- 3 sheets refrigerated pie crust
- 1 large egg yolk, beaten
- 1 Tbsp. sesame seeds

SAUCE
- ½ cup apricot preserves
- ½ cup chili sauce

1. Preheat oven to 425°. In a large skillet, cook beef and onion over medium heat until beef is no longer pink, breaking up beef into crumbles, 5-7 minutes; drain. Stir in cream cheese, preserves, carrot and seasonings. Cool slightly.

2. On a lightly floured work surface, unroll sheets of pie crust. Cut 40 circles with a floured 3-in. cookie cutter, rerolling crust as necessary. Place half of the circles 2 in. apart on parchment-lined baking sheets. Top each with 1 rounded Tbsp. beef mixture. Top with remaining crust circles; press edges with a fork to seal.

3. Brush tops with egg yolk; sprinkle with sesame seeds. Cut slits in tops. Bake until golden brown, 12-15 minutes. Remove from pan to a wire rack.

4. Meanwhile, in a microwave, warm the sauce ingredients, stirring to combine. Serve with empanadas.

Freeze option: Cover and freeze unbaked empanadas on waxed paper-lined baking sheets until firm. Transfer to a freezer container; return to freezer. To use, bake empanadas as directed, increasing time as necessary. Prepare sauce as directed.

Note: This recipe was tested with McCormick Gourmet Moroccan Seasoning (ras el hanout).

1 empanada with about 2 tsp. sauce: 215 cal., 11g fat (5g sat. fat), 30mg chol., 256mg sod., 25g carb. (8g sugars, 0 fiber), 5g pro.

CHEESY CHIVE CRISPS

These snack bites are great to keep on hand for guests. Since the recipe makes a lot, you might want to freeze some of the cheese logs for future use. Be sure to thaw them in the refrigerator for 2 or 3 hours before slicing and baking.
—*Eve McNew, St. Louis, MO*

Prep: 10 min. + chilling • **Bake:** 20 min./batch
Makes: about 9 dozen

- 1 cup butter, softened
- 3 cups shredded sharp cheddar cheese
- 2 cups all-purpose flour
- ¼ cup minced chives
- ½ tsp. salt
- ½ tsp. hot pepper sauce
  Dash garlic salt
- 2 cups crisp rice cereal

1. In a large bowl, cream butter and cheese until light and fluffy. Beat in the flour, chives, salt, pepper sauce and garlic salt. Stir in cereal. Shape into four 6½x1½-in. logs. Wrap securely and refrigerate for 1 hour or until firm.

2. Unwrap and cut into ¼-in. slices. Place on ungreased baking sheets. Bake at 325° for 20-25 minutes or until edges are crisp and lightly browned. Remove to wire racks to cool. Store in the refrigerator or freezer.

2 crisps: 73 cal., 5g fat (3g sat. fat), 16mg chol., 106mg sod., 5g carb. (0 sugars, 0 fiber), 2g pro.

MEDITERRANEAN PASTRY PINWHEELS

These quick appetizers are irresistible on the plate, and the flavors of sun-dried tomatoes and pesto balance beautifully.
—*Kristen Heigl, Staten Island, NY*

Prep: 20 min. + freezing • **Bake:** 15 min.
Makes: 16 appetizers

- 1 sheet frozen puff pastry, thawed
- 1 pkg. (8 oz.) cream cheese, softened
- ¼ cup prepared pesto
- ¾ cup shredded provolone cheese
- ½ cup chopped oil-packed sun-dried tomatoes
- ½ cup chopped ripe olives
- ¼ tsp. pepper

1. Preheat oven to 400°. Unfold puff pastry; roll and trim into a 10-in. square.
2. Beat cream cheese and pesto until smooth; stir in remaining ingredients. Spread cheese mixture on pastry to within ½ in. of edges. Roll up jelly-roll style. Freeze 30 minutes. Cut crosswise into 16 slices.
3. Bake cut side down on a parchment-lined baking sheet until pinwheels are golden brown, 12-15 minutes.

Freeze option: Cover and freeze unbaked pastry slices on waxed paper-lined baking sheets until firm. Transfer to an airtight container; return to freezer. To use, preheat oven to 400°; bake pastries until golden brown, 15-20 minutes.

1 pinwheel: 170 cal., 13g fat (5g sat. fat), 18mg chol., 227mg sod., 11g carb. (1g sugars, 2g fiber), 4g pro.

BUTTER CHICKEN MEATBALLS

My husband and I love meatballs, and we love butter chicken. Before an appetizer party, we had the brilliant idea to combine these two all-time favorites, and they got rave reviews.
—*Shannon Dobos, Calgary, AB*

Prep: 30 min. • **Cook:** 3 hours
Makes: about 3 dozen

- 1½ lbs. ground chicken or turkey
- 1 large egg, lightly beaten
- ½ cup soft bread crumbs
- 1 tsp. garam masala
- ½ tsp. tandoori masala seasoning
- ½ tsp. salt
- ¼ tsp. cayenne pepper
- 3 Tbsp. minced fresh cilantro, divided
- 1 jar (14.1 oz.) butter chicken sauce

1. Combine the first 7 ingredients plus 2 Tbsp. cilantro; mix lightly but thoroughly. With wet hands, shape into 1-in. balls. Place the meatballs in a 3-qt. slow cooker coated with cooking spray. Pour butter sauce over the meatballs.
2. Cook, covered, on low until meatballs are cooked through, 3-4 hours. Top with remaining cilantro.

Freeze option: Omitting remaining cilantro, freeze cooled meatball mixture in freezer containers. To use, partially thaw meatballs in refrigerator overnight. Microwave, covered, on high in a microwave-safe dish until heated through, stirring gently and adding a little water if necessary. To serve, sprinkle with remaining cilantro.

1 meatball: 40 cal., 2g fat (1g sat. fat), 18mg chol., 87mg sod., 1g carb. (1g sugars, 0 fiber), 3g pro.

FROSTY ORANGE CREAM CHEESE CUPS

Stash these frozen citrus-flavored bites in the freezer for cute last-minute treats. White chocolate and chopped pistachios make them seem special.
—*Roxanne Chan, Albany, CA*

Prep: 35 min. + freezing • **Makes:** 2 dozen

- 1¼ cups crushed gingersnap cookies (about 25 cookies)
- 5 Tbsp. butter, melted
- 4 oz. cream cheese, softened
- 2 Tbsp. confectioners' sugar
- 2 Tbsp. plus ½ cup heavy whipping cream, divided
- ½ cup orange marmalade
- 4 oz. white baking chocolate, chopped
- ⅓ cup salted pistachios, chopped

1. In a small bowl, mix cookie crumbs and butter; press onto bottoms and up sides of ungreased mini-muffin cups. Freeze 20 minutes.

2. In a small bowl, beat cream cheese, confectioners' sugar and 2 Tbsp. cream until smooth. Stir in marmalade; drop by scant tablespoonfuls into cups. Freeze 2 hours or until set.

3. In a double boiler or metal bowl over hot water, melt white chocolate with remaining cream; stir until smooth. Cool slightly. Spoon or drizzle over cups. Sprinkle with pistachios. Freeze, covered, overnight or until firm. Serve frozen.

1 cup: 142 cal., 9g fat (5g sat. fat), 18mg chol., 87mg sod., 15g carb. (10g sugars, 0 fiber), 2g pro.

PULLED PORK DOUGHNUT HOLE SLIDERS

This slider recipe was created by accident when we had a surplus of root beer from a party. Now we can't have barbecue any other way!

—*Eden Dranger, Los Angeles, CA*

Prep: 55 min. • **Cook:** 8 hours.
Makes: 5 dozen

  1 bottle (2 liters) root beer
1½ cups barbecue sauce
1½ tsp. salt
  1 tsp. minced fresh gingerroot
  1 bone-in pork shoulder
       roast (about 3 lbs.)
SLAW:
  ½ cup mayonnaise
  2 Tbsp. white vinegar
  1 Tbsp. maple syrup
  1 pkg. (14 oz.) coleslaw mix
ASSEMBLY:
 60 plain doughnut holes
 60 appetizer skewers
       Additional barbecue sauce, optional

1. In a large saucepan, bring root beer to a boil. Reduce heat to medium-high; cook, uncovered, until liquid is reduced by half, 30-45 minutes. Transfer to a 5- or 6-qt. slow cooker. Stir in barbecue sauce, salt and ginger. Add roast, turning to coat.

2. Cook, covered, on low until the pork is tender, 8-10 hours. For slaw, in a large bowl, mix mayonnaise, vinegar and syrup. Stir in coleslaw mix. Refrigerate, covered, until flavors are blended, at least 1 hour.

3. Remove pork from slow cooker; skim fat from cooking juices. Remove meat from bones; shred with 2 forks. Return the juices and pork to slow cooker; heat through.

4. To serve, cut doughnut holes in half; cut a thin slice off bottoms to level. Serve pork and slaw in doughnut holes; secure with skewers. If desired, serve with additional barbecue sauce.

Freeze option: Freeze cooled pork mixture in freezer containers. To use, partially thaw in refrigerator overnight. Heat through in a covered saucepan, stirring gently.

1 slider: 138 cal., 7g fat (2g sat. fat), 13mg chol., 218mg sod., 14g carb. (10g sugars, 0 fiber), 5g pro.

PLANNED OVERS

COOK ONCE, EAT ALL WEEK WITH DISHES THAT USE UP LEFTOVERS.

BEEF

ITALIAN POT ROAST

This delicious pot roast is a favorite of my husband's. Prepare the tender beef on the weekend, and then use leftovers to speed up workweek dinners.
—*Debbie Daly, Buckingham, IL*

Prep: 20 min. • **Cook:** 5 hours
Makes: 8 servings

- 1   boneless beef chuck roast (3 to 4 lbs.)
- 1   can (28 oz.) diced tomatoes, drained
- ¾   cup chopped onion
- ¾   cup Burgundy wine or beef broth
- 1½ tsp. salt
- 1   tsp. dried basil
- ½   tsp. dried oregano
- 1   garlic clove, minced
- ¼   tsp. pepper
- ¼   cup cornstarch
- ½   cup cold water

1. Cut the roast in half. Place in a 5-qt. slow cooker. Add the tomatoes, onion, wine, salt, basil, oregano, garlic and pepper. Cover and cook on low for 5-6 hours or until the meat is tender.

2. Remove meat to a serving platter; keep warm. Skim fat from the cooking juices; transfer to a small saucepan. Combine the cornstarch and water until smooth. Gradually stir into pan. Bring to a boil; cook and stir until thickened, about 2 minutes. Serve with meat.

5 oz. cooked beef: 345 cal., 16g fat (6g sat. fat), 111mg chol., 641mg sod., 10g carb. (4g sugars, 2g fiber), 34g pro.

BEEFY MUSHROOM SOUP

This is a tasty way to use leftover roast and get a delicious supper on the table in about a half hour. The heartwarming, rich flavor of this mushroom soup is sure to please.
—*Ginger Ellsworth, Caldwell, ID*

Takes: 30 min. • **Makes:** 3 cups

- 1   medium onion, chopped
- ½   cup sliced fresh mushrooms
- 2   Tbsp. butter
- 2   Tbsp. all-purpose flour
- 2   cups reduced-sodium beef broth
- ⅔   cup cubed cooked roast beef
- ½   tsp. garlic powder
- ¼   tsp. paprika
- ¼   tsp. pepper
- ⅛   tsp. salt

   Dash hot pepper sauce
   Shredded part-skim mozzarella cheese, optional

1. In a large saucepan, saute onion and mushrooms in butter until onion is tender; remove with a slotted spoon and set aside. In a small bowl, whisk flour and broth until smooth; gradually add to the pan. Bring to a boil; cook and stir until thickened, 1-2 minutes.

2. Add the roast beef, garlic powder, paprika, pepper, salt, pepper sauce and onion mixture; cook and stir until heated through. Garnish with cheese if desired.

1 cup: 180 cal., 9g fat (5g sat. fat), 52mg chol., 470mg sod., 9g carb. (3g sugars, 1g fiber), 14g pro. **Diabetic exchanges:** 2 lean meat, 2 fat, 1 vegetable.

ROAST BEEF WITH CHIVE ROASTED POTATOES

It's hard to believe that last night's beef roast could get any better, but it shines in this heartwarming dish.
—Taste of Home *Test Kitchen*

- -

Prep: 20 min. • **Bake:** 25 min.
Makes: 6 servings

- 2   lbs. red potatoes, cut into 1-in. cubes
- 2   Tbsp. olive oil
- 2   tsp. minced chives
- ¾   tsp. salt, divided
- 2   medium onions, halved and thinly sliced
- 1   lb. sliced fresh mushrooms
- ¼   cup butter, cubed
- 1   garlic clove, minced
- 1   tsp. dried rosemary, crushed
- ¼   tsp. pepper
- ⅓   cup dry red wine or beef broth
- 2   cups cubed cooked roast beef
- 1   cup beef gravy

1. Place potatoes in a greased 15x10x1-in. baking pan. Drizzle with oil and sprinkle with chives and ¼ tsp. salt; toss to coat. Bake, uncovered, at 425° for 25-30 minutes or until tender, stirring occasionally.
2. Meanwhile, in a large skillet, saute onions and mushrooms in butter until tender. Add the garlic, rosemary, pepper and remaining ½ tsp. salt; cook 1 minute longer. Stir in the wine. Add the beef and gravy; heat through. Serve with potatoes.
1 serving: 379 cal., 15g fat (6g sat. fat), 66mg chol., 591mg sod., 35g carb. (6g sugars, 5g fiber), 24g pro.

ASPARAGUS BEEF CASHEW STIR-FRY

As appetizing to the eye as it is to the palate, this fast entree features lots of vegetables, beef and cashews. A local restaurant once handed out asparagus recipes, including this one, and now it's a favorite.
—Joyce Huebner, Marinette, WI

- -

Prep: 20 min. • **Cook:** 25 min.
Makes: 6 servings

- 2   Tbsp. cornstarch
- 1   cup beef broth
- 3   Tbsp. soy sauce
- ½   tsp. sugar
- 2   Tbsp. canola oil
- 2   whole garlic cloves
- 2   lbs. fresh asparagus, trimmed and cut into 2½-in. pieces
- 2   medium onions, halved and thinly sliced
- 1   medium sweet red pepper, julienned 1 large carrot, cut into 2½-in. strips
- 2½ cups sliced cooked roast beef (2½-in. strips)
- 1   cup salted cashew halves
     Hot cooked rice

1. In a small bowl, combine cornstarch and broth until smooth. Stir in the soy sauce and sugar; set aside. In a wok or large skillet, heat oil; add the garlic. Cook and stir until lightly browned, about 1 minute; discard garlic.
2. Stir-fry the asparagus, onions, red pepper and carrot for 15-20 minutes or until crisp-tender. Add roast beef heat through. Stir reserved sauce; add to the pan. Bring to a boil; cook and stir until thickened, about 2 minutes. Sprinkle with cashews. Serve with rice.
¾ cup: 382 cal., 21g fat (4g sat. fat), 54mg chol., 815mg sod., 18g carb. (7g sugars, 4g fiber), 30g pro.

ROAST BEEF PASTA SKILLET

Leftover beef is the star in a skillet dinner that's perfect for two. Chopped tomato adds a burst of fresh flavor.
—*Bill Hilbrich, St. Cloud, MN*

- -

Takes: 20 min. • **Makes:** 2 servings

 1 cup uncooked spiral pasta
 ½ cup chopped onion
 1 tsp. olive oil
 1 tsp. butter
 1 cup cubed cooked roast beef
 1 tsp. pepper
 ½ cup chopped tomato
 ½ cup grated Parmesan cheese

Cook pasta according to package directions. Meanwhile, in a large skillet, saute onion in oil and butter until tender. Add roast beef and pepper; heat through. Drain pasta; add to beef mixture. Stir in tomato and cheese.
2 cups: 448 cal., 14g fat (6g sat. fat), 87mg chol., 358mg sod., 38g carb. (4g sugars, 3g fiber), 40g pro.

GRILLED BUTTERMILK CHICKEN

I created this main course years ago after one of our farmers-market customers, a chef, shared the idea of marinating chicken in buttermilk. The chicken is easy to prepare and always turns out moist and delicious. Best of all, the recipe makes a lot so you can use the cooked chicken breasts in all sorts of dishes later in the week. Don't feel like grilling? Bake the chicken to perfection in the oven!
—Sue Gronholz, Beaver Dam, WI

Prep: 10 min. + marinating • **Grill:** 10 min.
Makes: 12 servings

- 1½ cups buttermilk
- 4 fresh thyme sprigs
- 4 garlic cloves, halved
- ½ tsp. salt
- 12 boneless skinless chicken breast halves (about 4½ lbs.)

1. Place the buttermilk, thyme, garlic and salt in a large bowl or shallow dish. Add chicken and turn to coat. Refrigerate for 8 hours or overnight, turning occasionally.
2. Drain the chicken, discarding marinade. Grill, covered, over medium heat until a thermometer reads 165°, 5-7 minutes per side.

1 chicken breast half: 189 cal., 4g fat (1g sat. fat), 95mg chol., 168mg sod., 1g carb. (1g sugars, 0 fiber), 35g pro. **Diabetic exchanges:** 5 lean meat.

CREAMY CHICKEN SOUP

Kids won't think twice about eating their veggies with this creamy and cheesy soup.
—LaVonne Lundgren, Sioux City, IA

Takes: 30 min. • **Makes:** 8 servings (2¾ qt.)

- 4 cups cubed cooked chicken breast
- 3½ cups water
- 2 cans (10¾ oz. each) condensed cream of chicken soup, undiluted
- 1 pkg. (16 oz.) frozen mixed vegetables, thawed
- 1 can (14½ oz.) diced potatoes, drained
- 1 pkg. (16 oz.) Velveeta, cubed

In a Dutch oven, combine first 5 ingredients. Bring to a boil. Reduce heat; cover and simmer until the vegetables are tender, 8-10 minutes. Stir in cubed cheese just until melted (do not boil).

1⅓ cups: 429 cal., 22g fat (11g sat. fat), 116mg chol., 1464mg sod., 23g carb. (6g sugars, 4g fiber), 33g pro.

CHICKEN, NECTARINE & AVOCADO SALAD

This tasty, refreshing entree salad comes together very quickly. Using granola adds crunch and makes it different. I've tried it with a few different types of granola, and our favorites have been ones with a lot of nuts and that aren't extremely sweet.
—*Elisabeth Larsen, Pleasant Grove, UT*

- -

Takes: 15 min. • **Makes:** 4 servings

6	oz. fresh baby spinach (about 8 cups)
2	medium nectarines, thinly sliced
2	cups cubed cooked chicken
1	cup crumbled feta cheese
½	cup poppy seed salad dressing
1	medium ripe avocado, peeled and sliced
1	cup granola with fruit and nuts

In a large bowl, combine the baby spinach, nectarines, chicken and feta. Drizzle with dressing; toss to coat. Top with avocado and granola. Serve immediately.

1½ cups: 561 cal., 32g fat (7g sat. fat), 87mg chol., 539mg sod., 38g carb. (18g sugars, 7g fiber), 30g pro.

TEST KITCHEN TIP
Remember that if you do not have time for Grilled Buttermilk Chicken on page 341, you can still plan on these recipes by using a prepared rotisserie chicken from the store.

❄ FLAKY CHICKEN WELLINGTON

Because it starts with chicken that's already cooked, this impressive Wellington is super easy! I like to cook the chicken a day or so ahead of time to make it even simpler to throw together on busy nights.
—*Kerry Dingwall, Wilmington, NC*

Prep: 30 min. • **Bake:** 15 min.
Makes: 6 servings

2   **cups cubed cooked chicken**
1   **pkg. (10 oz.) frozen chopped spinach, thawed and squeezed dry**
3   **hard-boiled large eggs, chopped**
½   **cup finely chopped dill pickles**
⅓   **cup finely chopped celery**
2   **tubes (8 oz. each) refrigerated crescent rolls**
2   **tsp. prepared mustard, divided**
1   **cup sour cream**
2   **Tbsp. dill pickle juice**

1. Preheat oven to 350°. In a large bowl, combine the first 5 ingredients. Unroll 1 tube of crescent dough into 1 long rectangle; press perforations to seal.
2. Spread half the mustard over dough; top with half the chicken mixture to within ¼ in. of edges. Roll up jelly-roll style, starting with a long side; pinch seam to seal. Place cut side down on a parchment-lined baking sheet. Cut slits in top. Repeat with the remaining crescent dough, mustard and chicken mixture.
3. Bake until golden brown, 15-20 minutes. Meanwhile, combine sour cream and pickle juice; serve with pastries.

Freeze option: Cover and freeze unbaked pastries on a parchment-lined baking sheet until firm. Transfer to a freezer container; return to freezer. To use, bake pastries on a parchment-lined baking sheet in a preheated 350° oven until Wellingtons are golden brown, 30-35 minutes. Prepare the sauce as directed.

⅓ pastry with about 3 Tbsp. sauce: 495 cal., 28g fat (6g sat. fat), 144mg chol., 830mg sod., 37g carb. (10g sugars, 2g fiber), 25g pro.

PORK

🍲 ⑤ᵢ
GARLIC-APPLE PORK ROAST

This is the meal I have become famous for, and it is so simple to prepare in the slow cooker. The garlic and apple flavors really complement the pork. It is just wonderful served alongside steamed asparagus and roasted red potatoes.

—*Jennifer Loos, Washington Boro, PA*

- -

Prep: 10 min. • **Cook:** 8 hours + standing
Makes: 12 servings

1 boneless pork loin roast
   (3½ to 4 lbs.)
1 jar (12 oz.) apple jelly
½ cup water
2½ tsp. minced garlic
1 Tbsp. dried parsley flakes
1 to 1½ tsp. seasoned salt
1 to 1½ tsp. pepper

1. Cut the roast in half; place in a 5-qt. slow cooker. In a small bowl, combine the jelly, water and garlic; pour over roast. Sprinkle with parsley, salt and pepper.
2. Cover and cook on low until the meat is tender, 8-10 hours. Let stand for 15 minutes before slicing. Serve with the cooking juices if desired.
4 oz. cooked pork: 237 cal., 6g fat (2g sat. fat), 66mg chol., 165mg sod., 19g carb. (17g sugars, 0 fiber), 26g pro.

CHINESE SPINACH-ALMOND SALAD

I use leftover pork roast in my favorite salad. It combines power-packed spinach with other veggies, lean meat and crunchy heart-healthy almonds. The flavors work well with a light Asian dressing.

—*Mary Ann Kieffer, Lawrence, KS*

- -

Takes: 10 min. • **Makes:** 4 servings

1 pkg. (6 oz.) fresh baby spinach
2 cups cubed cooked pork
1 cup bean sprouts
2 medium carrots, thinly sliced
½ cup sliced fresh mushrooms
¼ cup sliced almonds, toasted
½ cup reduced-fat sesame
   ginger salad dressing

In a large bowl, combine first 6 ingredients. Divide among 4 salad plates; drizzle each serving with 2 Tbsp. reduced-fat salad dressing. Serve immediately.
1 serving: 244 cal., 11g fat (3g sat. fat), 63mg chol., 500mg sod., 12g carb. (6g sugars, 3g fiber), 24g pro. **Diabetic exchanges:** 3 lean meat, 1 vegetable, 1 fat, ½ starch.

PORK BARBECUE SANDWICHES

Growing up, we were happy when there was pork roast on the menu because we were sure that, within the next few days, we'd be enjoying it again with these quick and tasty sandwiches.
—*George Hascher, Phoenicia, NY*

Takes: 30 min. • **Makes:** 4 servings

- 2 celery ribs, finely chopped
- 1 medium onion, finely chopped
- 1 tsp. canola oil
- 1 cup ketchup
- 1 to 1½ tsp. salt
- 1 tsp. ground mustard
- 2 cups shredded cooked pork
- 4 kaiser rolls or hamburger buns, split

In a large saucepan, saute celery and onion in oil until tender. Stir in the ketchup, salt and mustard. Add the pork. Bring to a boil. Reduce heat; cover and simmer for 20-30 minutes to allow flavors to blend. Serve on rolls.

1 sandwich: 398 cal., 10g fat (3g sat. fat), 63mg chol., 1720mg sod., 49g carb. (18g sugars, 2g fiber), 26g pro.

ROAST PORK SOUP

This well-seasoned, satisfying soup has a rich full-bodied broth brimming with tender chunks of pork, potatoes and navy beans. It has been a family favorite for years. Served with cornbread, it's one of our comfort foods in winter.
—*Sue Gulledge, Springville, AL*

Prep: 15 min. • **Cook:** 55 min.
Makes: 9 servings (2¼ qt.)

- 3 cups cubed cooked pork roast
- 2 medium potatoes, peeled and chopped
- 1 large onion, chopped
- 1 can (15 oz.) navy beans, rinsed and drained
- 1 can (14½ oz.) Italian diced tomatoes, undrained
- 4 cups water
- ½ cup unsweetened apple juice
- ½ tsp. salt
- ½ tsp. pepper
  Minced fresh basil

In a soup kettle or Dutch oven, combine the first 9 ingredients. Bring to a boil. Reduce heat; cover and simmer until vegetables are crisp-tender, about 45 minutes. Sprinkle with basil.

1 cup: 206 cal., 5g fat (2g sat. fat), 42mg chol., 435mg sod., 23g carb. (6g sugars, 4g fiber), 18g pro. **Diabetic exchanges:** 1 starch, 1 meat, 1 vegetable.

PORK

PORK SPANISH RICE

My family wasn't fond of pork roast until I used it in this yummy casserole.
—*Betty Unrau, MacGregor, MB*

Prep: 20 min. • **Bake:** 20 min.
Makes: 4 servings

- 1 **medium green pepper, chopped**
- 1 **small onion, chopped**
- 2 **Tbsp. butter**
- 1 **can (14½ oz.) diced tomatoes, drained**
- 1 **cup chicken broth**
- ½ **tsp. salt**
- ¼ **tsp. pepper**
- 1¾ **cups cubed cooked pork**
- 1 **cup uncooked instant rice**
  Optional: Lime wedge and minced cilantro

1. In a large skillet, saute green pepper and onion in butter until tender. Stir in the tomatoes, broth, salt and pepper. Bring to a boil; stir in pork and rice.
2. Transfer to a greased 2-qt. baking dish. Cover and bake at 350° until rice is tender and liquid is absorbed, 20-25 minutes. Stir before serving. If desired, serve with lime wedges and top with minced cilantro.
1 cup: 304 cal., 12g fat (6g sat. fat), 71mg chol., 756mg sod., 29g carb. (5g sugars, 3g fiber), 21g pro. **Diabetic exchanges:** 3 lean meat, 2 starch, 1½ fat.

SEASONED TACO MEAT

I got this recipe from the restaurant where I work. Everyone in town loves the blend of different seasonings, and now the secret is out for you to enjoy at home.
—*Denise Mumm, Dixon, IA*

- -

Prep: 10 min. • **Cook:** 35 min.
Makes: 6½ cups

- 3 lbs. ground beef
- 2 large onions, chopped
- 2 cups water
- 5 Tbsp. chili powder
- 2 tsp. salt
- 1 tsp. ground cumin
- ¾ tsp. garlic powder
- ¼ to ½ tsp. crushed red pepper flakes

In a large cast-iron skillet or Dutch oven, cook beef and onion over medium heat until meat is no longer pink; drain. Add water and seasonings. Bring to a boil. Reduce heat; simmer, uncovered, until the water is evaporated, about 15 minutes.

¼ cup: 113 cal., 7g fat (3g sat. fat), 35mg chol., 277mg sod., 2g carb. (1g sugars, 1g fiber), 10g pro.

TEST KITCHEN TIP

Seasoned Taco Meat can be used in a variety of ways. You can obviously use it as a filling for tacos or enchiladas, but try it as a topping for baked potatoes or mix it into scrambled eggs. Consider the recipes on the next few pages for even more ways to use the cooked taco meat.

TACO PINWHEELS

These pinwheels come together quickly when you start with leftover taco meat. They make an appealing party appetizer served with salsa, or a fun lunch option with a salad on the side.
—*Cindy Reams, Philipsburg, PA*

- -

Prep: 15 min. + chilling
Makes: 3 dozen pinwheels

- 4 oz. cream cheese, softened
- ¾ cup cooked taco meat
- ¼ cup finely shredded cheddar cheese
- ¼ cup salsa
- 2 Tbsp. mayonnaise
- 2 Tbsp. chopped ripe olives
- 2 Tbsp. finely chopped onion
- 5 flour tortillas (8 in.), room temperature
- ½ cup shredded lettuce
  Additional salsa

1. In a small bowl, beat the cream cheese until smooth. Stir in the taco meat, cheese, salsa, mayonnaise, olives and onion. Spread over tortillas. Sprinkle with lettuce; roll up tightly. Wrap securely and refrigerate for at least 1 hour.
2. Unwrap and cut into 1-in. pieces. Serve with additional salsa.
1 pinwheel: 51 cal., 3g fat (1g sat. fat), 6mg chol., 84mg sod., 4g carb. (0 sugars, 0 fiber), 2g pro.

MEAT-AND-POTATO QUICHE

This hearty dish is welcome anytime, of course, but our family especially enjoys it at breakfast! It just seems to get the day off to a great start.

—*Esther Beachy, Hutchinson, KS*

- -

Prep: 20 min. • **Bake:** 30 min.
Makes: 6 servings

- 3 Tbsp. canola oil
- 3 cups shredded peeled potatoes, well drained
- 1 cup shredded part-skim mozzarella cheese
- ¾ cup cooked taco meat
- ¼ cup chopped onion
- 1 cup heavy whipping cream
- 5 large eggs
- ½ tsp. salt
- ⅛ tsp. pepper

1. Combine oil and potatoes in a 10-in. pie plate. Press mixture down evenly to form a crust. Bake at 425° until lightly browned, about 10 minutes.

2. Layer with the mozzarella, taco meat and onion. Whisk together the cream, eggs, salt and pepper; pour over beef mixture. Bake until a knife inserted in center comes out clean, about 30 minutes.

1 slice: 377 cal., 29g fat (13g sat. fat), 242mg chol., 356mg sod., 18g carb. (3g sugars, 2g fiber), 12g pro.

TACO PIZZA SQUARES

Everyone will come running the minute you take this fun twist on pizza out of the oven. I top a convenient refrigerated pizza dough with any leftover taco meat, tomatoes and cheese, bringing a full-flavored fiesta to the table. Try it with salsa on the side.
—*Sarah Vovos, Middleton, WI*

- -

Takes: 25 min. • **Makes:** 10 servings

- 1 tube (13.8 oz.) refrigerated pizza crust
- 1 can (8 oz.) pizza sauce
- 2 cups cooked taco meat
- 2 medium tomatoes, seeded and chopped
- 2 cups shredded mozzarella cheese
    Optional: Shredded lettuce and sour cream

Unroll pizza dough and place in a 15x10x1-in. baking pan. Spread with pizza sauce; sprinkle with the taco meat, tomatoes and cheese. Bake at 400° until crust is golden brown, 15-20 minutes. Top with shredded lettuce and sour cream if desired.

1 piece: 259 cal., 11g fat (5g sat. fat), 40mg chol., 660mg sod., 23g carb. (4g sugars, 2g fiber), 17g pro.

SPICY EGG BAKE

This family favorite makes a wonderful morning meal served with muffins and fresh fruit. It's also a great way to use up extra taco meat. Adjust the heat by choosing a hotter or milder salsa.
—*Michelle Jibben, Springfield, MN*

- -

Takes: 30 min. • **Makes:** 8 servings

- 1 tube (8 oz.) refrigerated crescent rolls
- 10 large eggs
- ⅓ cup water
- 3 Tbsp. butter
- 1½ cups prepared taco meat
- 1 cup shredded cheddar cheese
- 1 cup shredded Monterey Jack cheese
- 1 cup salsa

1. Unroll crescent roll dough into a greased 13x9-in. baking dish. Seal the seams and perforations; set aside.
2. In a small bowl, whisk eggs and water. In a large skillet, heat butter until hot. Add the egg mixture; cook and stir over medium heat until eggs are almost set. Remove from the heat.
3. Sprinkle taco meat over dough. Layer with the eggs, cheeses and salsa. Bake, uncovered, at 375° until bubbly and cheese is melted, 14-16 minutes.

1 piece: 481 cal., 32g fat (14g sat. fat), 327mg chol., 981mg sod., 19g carb. (4g sugars, 3g fiber), 30g pro.

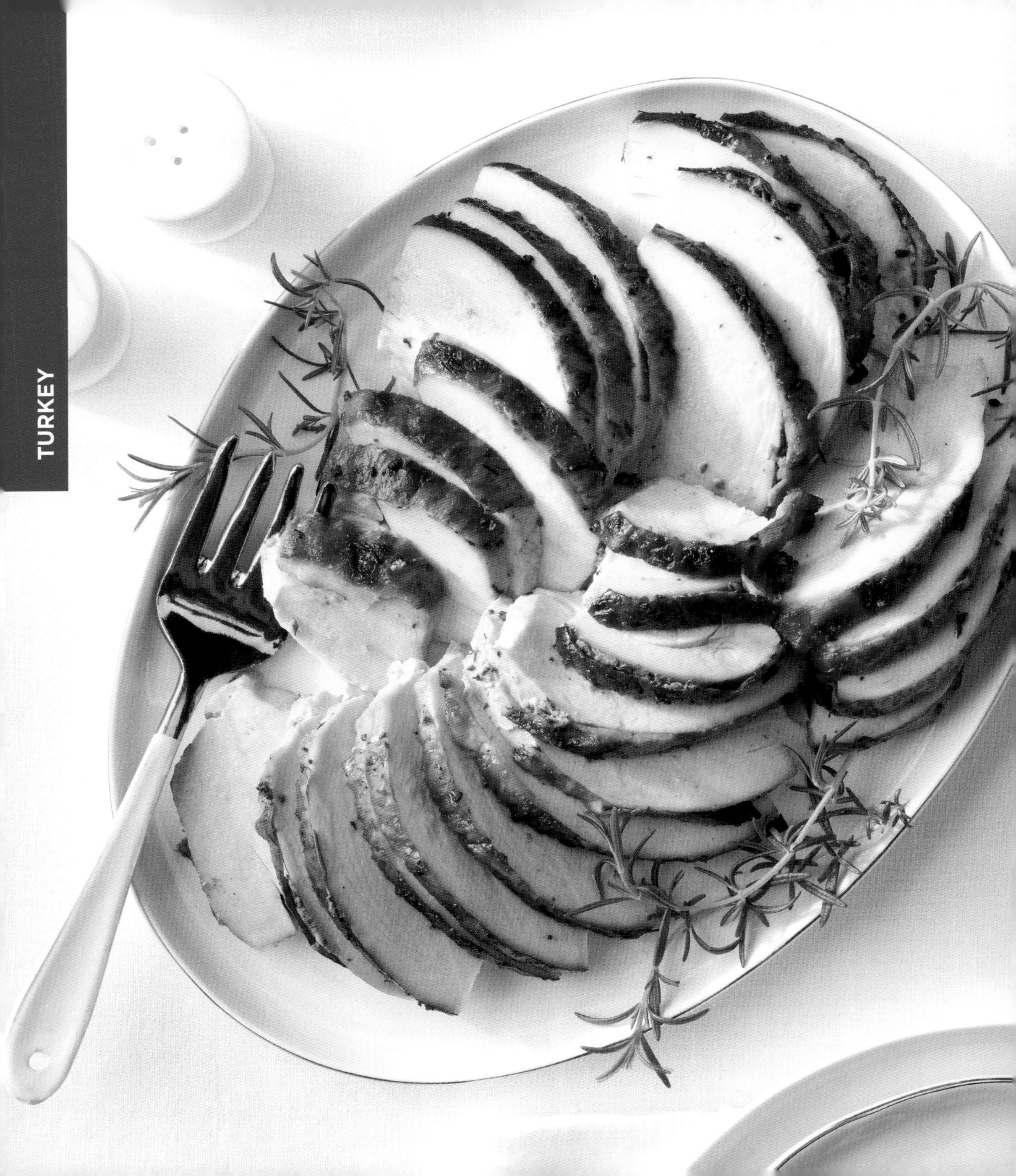

ROSEMARY TURKEY BREAST

Because I rub an herb mixture under the turkey's skin, I can remove the skin before serving and not lose any of the flavor. The result is a lower-in-fat, yet delicious entree that makes the perfect centerpiece for special meals. Best of all, the leftover meat can be used in a variety of dishes to beat the clock on busy days.
—*Dorothy Pritchett, Wills Point, TX*

Prep: 10 min. • **Bake:** 1½ hours + standing
Makes: 15 servings

- 2 Tbsp. olive oil
- 8 to 10 garlic cloves, peeled
- 3 Tbsp. chopped fresh rosemary or 3 tsp. dried rosemary, crushed
- 1 tsp. salt
- 1 tsp. paprika
- ½ tsp. coarsely ground pepper
- 1 bone-in turkey breast (5 lbs.)

1. In a food processor, combine oil, garlic, rosemary, salt, paprika and pepper; cover and process until garlic is coarsely chopped.
2. With your fingers, loosen the skin from both sides of turkey breast. Spread half the garlic mixture over the meat under the skin. Smooth the skin over meat and secure to underside of breast with toothpicks. Spread remaining garlic mixture over turkey skin.
3. Place turkey breast on a rack in a shallow roasting pan. Bake, uncovered, at 325° until a thermometer reads 170°, 1½-2 hours. Let turkey breast stand for 15 minutes before slicing. Discard toothpicks.
4 oz. cooked turkey: 148 cal., 3g fat (0 sat. fat), 78mg chol., 207mg sod., 1g carb. (0 sugars, 0 fiber), 29g pro.
Diabetic exchanges: 4 lean meat.

TURKEY LATTICE PIE

With its pretty lattice crust, this cheesy baked dish looks as good as it tastes. It's easy to make, too, since it uses cooked turkey and ready-to-go crescent roll dough.
—*Lorraine Naig, Emmetsburg, IA*

Prep: 20 min. • **Bake:** 20 min.
Makes: 12 servings

- 3 tubes (8 oz. each) refrigerated crescent rolls
- 4 cups cubed cooked turkey
- 1½ cups shredded cheddar or Swiss cheese
- 3 cups frozen chopped broccoli, thawed and drained
- 1 can (10¾ oz.) condensed cream of chicken soup, undiluted
- 1⅓ cups whole milk
- 2 Tbsp. Dijon mustard
- 1 Tbsp. dried minced onion
- ½ tsp. salt
  Dash pepper
- 1 large egg, lightly beaten

1. Preheat oven to 375°. Unroll 2 tubes of crescent roll dough; carefully separate into rectangles. Place rectangles in an ungreased 15x10x1-in. baking pan. Press onto bottom and ¼ in. up the sides of pan to form a crust, sealing seams and perforations. Bake until light golden brown, 5-7 minutes.
2. Meanwhile, in a large bowl, combine the turkey, cheese, broccoli, soup, milk, mustard, onion, salt and pepper. Spoon over crust.
3. Unroll remaining dough; divide into rectangles. Seal perforations. Cut each rectangle into four 1-in. strips. Using strips, make a lattice design on top of turkey mixture. Brush with egg. Bake until top crust is golden brown and filling is bubbly, 17-22 minutes longer.
1 piece: 396 cal., 20g fat (4g sat. fat), 81mg chol., 934mg sod., 30g carb. (8g sugars, 2g fiber), 24g pro.

TURKEY & APPLE ARUGULA SALAD IN A JAR

Join the jarred salad craze with this adaptation of a turkey and apple salad. It's a smart way to finish up last night's poultry.
—Taste of Home *Test Kitchen*

Takes: 20 min. • **Makes:** 4 servings

½ cup orange juice
3 Tbsp. red wine vinegar
1 to 3 Tbsp. sesame oil
2 Tbsp. minced fresh chives
¼ tsp. salt
¼ tsp. coarsely ground pepper
SALAD
4 cups cubed cooked turkey
4 tsp. curry powder
½ tsp. coarsely ground pepper
¼ tsp. salt
1 large apple, chopped
1 Tbsp. lemon juice
1 cup green grapes, halved
1 can (11 oz.) mandarin
  oranges, drained
½ cup pomegranate seeds
  or dried cranberries
½ cup chopped walnuts
4 cups fresh arugula or baby spinach

1. In a small bowl, whisk first 6 ingredients. Place turkey in a large bowl; sprinkle with the seasonings and toss to combine. In a separate bowl, toss chopped apple with lemon juice.

2. In each of four 1-qt. wide-mouth canning jars, divide and layer ingredients in the following order: orange juice mixture, seasoned turkey, apple, grapes, oranges, pomegranate seeds, walnuts and arugula. Cover and refrigerate until serving. Transfer salads into bowls; toss to combine.

1 serving: 471 cal., 19g fat (3g sat. fat), 141mg chol., 453mg sod., 33g carb. (25g sugars, 5g fiber), 45g pro.

TURKEY-SWEET POTATO STEW

This soup brings on the nostalgic flavors and heartwarming feel of the holidays at any time of year. We enjoy it regularly at our home for that very reason.
—*Radine Kellogg, Fairview, IL*

- -

Prep: 20 min. • **Cook:** 30 min.
Makes: 4 servings (1½ qt.)

- 2 medium sweet potatoes, peeled and cubed
- 2 cups water
- 2 tsp. sodium-free chicken bouillon granules
- 1 can (14¾ oz.) cream-style corn
- 1 Tbsp. minced fresh sage
- ¼ tsp. pepper
- 1 Tbsp. cornstarch
- 1 cup 2% milk
- 2 cups cubed cooked turkey breast

1. In a large saucepan, combine potatoes, water and bouillon; bring to a boil. Reduce heat; cook, covered, until the potatoes are tender, 10-15 minutes.
2. Stir in corn, sage and pepper; heat through. In a small bowl, mix cornstarch and milk until smooth; stir into soup. Bring to a boil; cook and stir until thickened, 1-2 minutes. Stir in turkey; heat through.
1½ cups: 275 cal., 3g fat (1g sat. fat), 65mg chol., 374mg sod., 39g carb. (13g sugars, 3g fiber), 26g pro. **Diabetic exchanges:** 3 lean meat, 2½ starch.

TURKEY WILD RICE SOUP

A dear friend brought me some of this soup when I was ill. I asked her for the recipe, and I've made it several times since. Now I take it to friends when they're not feeling well. It's filling and comforting, and goes well with a green salad. I always look forward to preparing it the day after a turkey meal. I just use the extra turkey!
—*Doris Cox, New Freedom, PA*

Prep: 15 min. • **Cook:** 20 min.
Makes: 6 servings

- 1 medium onion, chopped
- 1 can (4 oz.) sliced mushrooms, drained
- 2 Tbsp. butter
- 3 cups water
- 2 cups chicken broth
- 1 pkg. (6 oz.) long grain and wild rice mix
- 2 cups diced cooked turkey
- 1 cup heavy whipping cream
  Minced fresh parsley

In a large saucepan, saute onion and mushrooms in butter until the onion is tender. Add water, broth and rice mix with seasoning; bring to a boil. Reduce heat; simmer for 20-25 minutes or until rice is tender. Stir in turkey and cream and heat through. Sprinkle with parsley.

1 cup: 364 cal., 21g fat (12g sat. fat), 100mg chol., 857mg sod., 25g carb. (3g sugars, 1g fiber), 19g pro.

BISTRO TURKEY CALZONE

Turkey, cheddar, bacon and apple harmonize well in this family-friendly sandwich perfect for weeknight meals.
—*Donna-Marie Ryan, Topsfield, MA*

Prep: 25 min. • **Bake:** 20 min.
Makes: 6 servings

- 1 Tbsp. cornmeal
- 1 loaf (1 lb.) frozen pizza dough, thawed
- ¾ lb. thinly sliced cooked turkey
- 8 slices cheddar cheese
- 5 bacon strips, cooked and crumbled
- 1 small tart apple, peeled and thinly sliced
- 1 large egg, beaten
- ½ tsp. Italian seasoning

1. Sprinkle cornmeal over a greased baking sheet. On a lightly floured surface, roll the dough into a 15-in. circle. Transfer to prepared pan. Arrange half of turkey over half of the dough; top with cheese, bacon, apple and remaining turkey. Fold dough over filling and pinch edges to seal.
2. With a sharp knife, cut 3 slashes in the top. Brush with egg and sprinkle with Italian seasoning. Bake at 400° until golden brown, 20-25 minutes. Let stand 5 minutes before cutting into wedges.

1 slice: 481 cal., 20g fat (10g sat. fat), 124mg chol., 756mg sod., 38g carb. (3g sugars, 0 fiber), 34g pro.

SLOW-COOKED HAM

Entertaining doesn't get much easier than when you serve this tasty ham from the slow cooker. It comes together with just a few ingredients, plus the leftovers are delicious in casseroles!
—Heather Spring, Sheppard Air Force Base, TX

- -

Prep: 5 min. • **Cook:** 6 hours
Makes: 20 servings

½   cup packed brown sugar
1   tsp. ground mustard
1   tsp. prepared horseradish
2   Tbsp. plus ¼ cup cola, divided
1   fully cooked boneless ham
     (5 to 6 lbs.), cut in half

In a small bowl, combine the brown sugar, mustard, horseradish and 2 Tbsp. cola. Rub over ham. Transfer to a 5-qt. slow cooker; add remaining cola to slow cooker. Cover and cook on low until a thermometer reads 140°, 6-8 hours.

3 oz. cooked ham: 143 cal., 4g fat (1g sat. fat), 58mg chol., 1180mg sod., 6g carb. (6g sugars, 0 fiber), 21g pro.

TEST KITCHEN TIP

Ham is a great protein to keep in the freezer for quick meals. Stash some away for use in the recipes in this section. They all call for cooked ham.

QUICK ANTIPASTO SALAD

I used to work in a pizza shop, where this salad was the most popular item on the menu. It's great for nights when it's just too hot to cook.
—Webbie Carvajal, Alpine, TX

- -

Takes: 25 min. • **Makes:** 8 servings

1½   cups cubed fully cooked ham
1   jar (10 oz.) pimiento-stuffed
      olives, drained and sliced
1   can (3.8 oz.) sliced ripe
      olives, drained
1   pkg. (3½ oz.) sliced
      pepperoni, quartered
8   cups shredded lettuce
10   to 12 cherry tomatoes, quartered
1   cup Italian salad dressing
1½   cups shredded part-skim
      mozzarella cheese

In a large bowl, combine the ham, olives and pepperoni. On a platter or individual salad plates, arrange the lettuce, olive mixture and tomatoes. Drizzle with dressing; sprinkle with cheese.

1 serving: 342 cal., 29g fat (7g sat. fat), 41mg chol., 1830mg sod., 9g carb. (3g sugars, 2g fiber), 13g pro.

CHEDDAR HAM SOUP

I knew this recipe was a keeper when my mother-in-law asked for it! The filling soup—chock-full of leftover ham, veggies and cheese—is creamy and comforting. The recipe makes enough to feed a crowd but don't expect any leftovers!
—*Marty Matthews, Clarksville, TN*

- -

Takes: 30 min. • **Makes:** 7 servings (1¾ qt.)

2	cups diced peeled potatoes
2	cups water
½	cup sliced carrot
¼	cup chopped onion
¼	cup butter, cubed
¼	cup all-purpose flour
2	cups 2% milk
¼	to ½ tsp. salt
¼	tsp. pepper
2	cups shredded cheddar cheese
1½	cups cubed fully cooked ham
1	cup frozen peas

1. In a large saucepan, combine potatoes, water, carrot and onion. Bring to a boil. Reduce heat; cover and cook until tender, for 10-15 minutes.

2. Meanwhile, in another saucepan, melt butter. Stir in flour until smooth. Gradually add the milk, salt and pepper. Bring to a boil; cook and stir until thickened, about 2 minutes. Stir in cheese until melted. Stir into undrained potato mixture. Add ham and peas; heat through.

1 cup: 331 cal., 20g fat (12g sat. fat), 73mg chol., 772mg sod., 19g carb. (5g sugars, 2g fiber), 19g pro.

HAM

❄ CREAMY NOODLE CASSEROLE

My husband, Ronald, works long hours and frequently won't arrive home until well after dinner. This casserole is great for those late nights—it's just as tasty after it's been warmed in the microwave.
—*Barb Marshall, Pickerington, OH*

Takes: 25 min. • **Makes:** 8 servings

- 1 pkg. (12 oz.) egg noodles
- 1 pkg. (16 oz.) frozen broccoli cuts
- 3 cups cubed fully cooked ham
- 1 cup shredded part-skim mozzarella cheese
- 1 cup shredded Parmesan cheese
- ⅓ cup butter, cubed
- ½ cup half-and-half cream
- ¼ tsp. each garlic powder, salt and pepper

1. In a Dutch oven, cook noodles in boiling water for 5 minutes. Add the broccoli and ham; cook 5-10 minutes longer or until the noodles are tender.

2. Drain; return to pan. Stir in the remaining ingredients. Cook and stir over low heat until butter is melted and the mixture is heated through.

Freeze option: Freeze cooled noodle mixture in freezer containers. To use, partially thaw in refrigerator overnight. Microwave, covered, on high in a microwave-safe dish until heated through, gently stirring; add broth or milk if necessary.

1 serving: 428 cal., 20g fat (11g sat. fat), 112mg chol., 1087mg sod., 35g carb. (3g sugars, 3g fiber), 25g pro.

5i HAM & SPINACH CASSEROLE

This is down-home cooking at its best! Ham and veggies join forces with a creamy sauce and pretty topping to create a hearty meal-in-one.
—Taste of Home *Test Kitchen*

Prep: 25 min. • **Bake:** 20 min.
Makes: 4 servings

- 3 cups cubed fully cooked ham
- 1 pkg. (16 oz.) frozen sliced carrots, thawed
- 1 can (10¾ oz.) condensed cream of potato soup, undiluted
- 1 pkg. (10 oz.) frozen creamed spinach, thawed
- ¼ cup water
- ¼ tsp. pepper
- ⅛ tsp. salt
- 1 tube (4 oz.) refrigerated crescent rolls

1. In a large skillet coated with cooking spray, cook ham over medium heat until lightly browned. Stir in the carrots, soup, spinach, water, pepper and salt; heat through. Pour into a greased 8-in. square baking dish.

2. Unroll crescent dough; separate into 2 rectangles. Seal perforations. Cut each rectangle lengthwise into 4 strips; make a lattice crust. Bake at 375° until the filling is bubbly and the crust is golden brown, 18-22 minutes.

1 serving: 376 cal., 13g fat (3g sat. fat), 65mg chol., 2334mg sod., 37g carb. (11g sugars, 6g fiber), 28g pro.

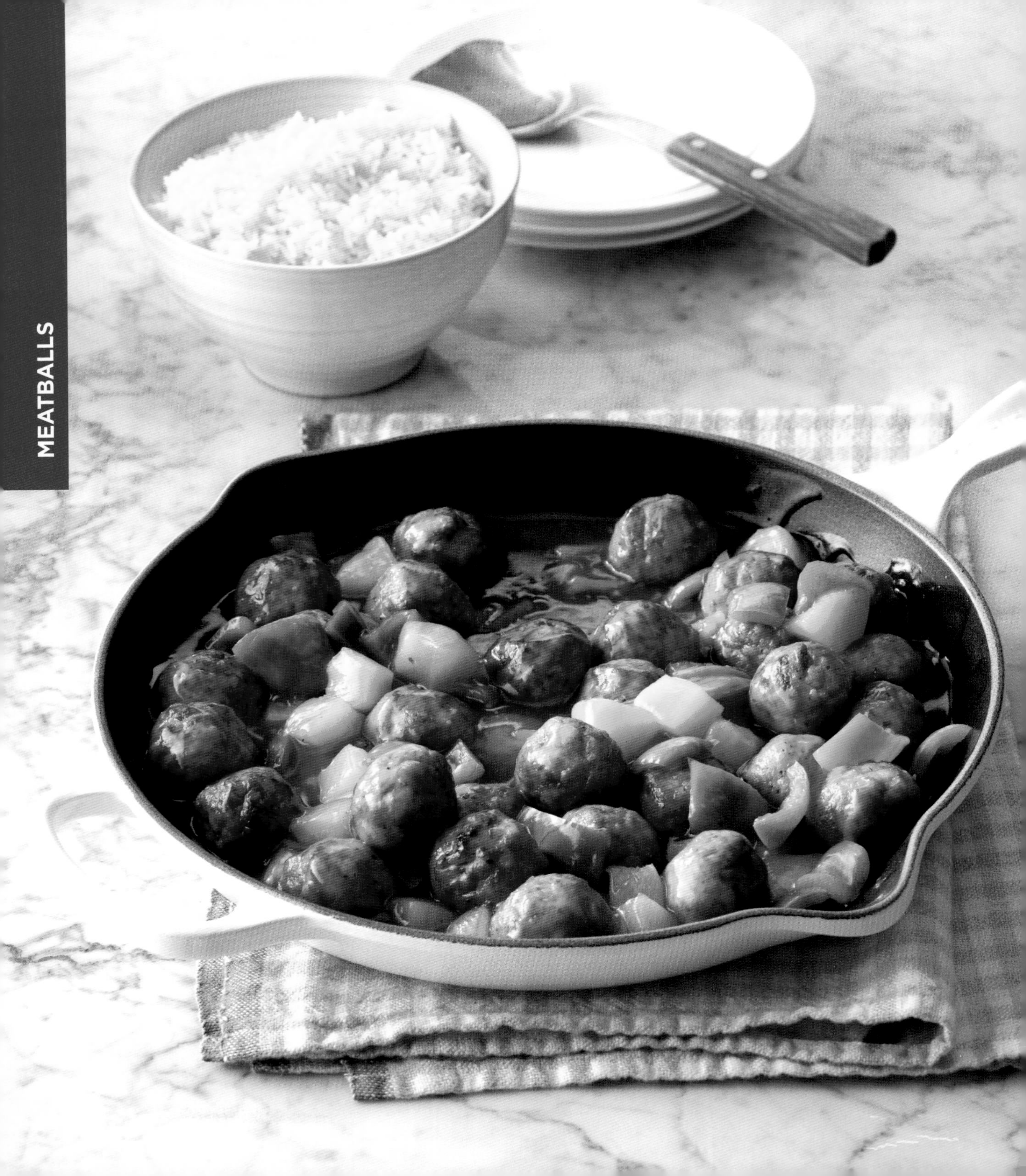

TANGY SWEET & SOUR MEATBALLS

Green pepper, pineapple and a tangy sauce transform convenient frozen meatballs into something special. Serve them over rice for a satisfying main dish.
—*Ruth Andrewson, Leavenworth, WA*

Takes: 30 min. • **Makes:** 6 servings

1 can (20 oz.) pineapple chunks
⅓ cup water
3 Tbsp. vinegar
1 Tbsp. soy sauce
½ cup packed brown sugar
3 Tbsp. cornstarch
30 frozen fully cooked Italian meatballs (about 15 oz.)
1 large green pepper, cut into 1-in. pieces
   Hot cooked rice

Drain pineapple, reserving juice. Set the pineapple aside. Add water to juice if needed to measure 1 cup; pour into a large skillet. Add ⅓ cup water, vinegar, soy sauce, brown sugar and cornstarch; stir until smooth. Cook over medium heat until thick, stirring constantly. Add the pineapple, meatballs and green pepper. Simmer, uncovered, until heated through, about 20 minutes. Serve with rice.

5 meatballs: 295 cal., 6g fat (2g sat. fat), 62mg chol., 501mg sod., 47g carb. (36g sugars, 1g fiber), 15g pro.

SLOW-COOKER MEATBALL SANDWICHES

Our approach to meatball sandwiches is a simple one: Cook the meatballs low and slow, load into hoagie buns and top with provolone and pepperoncini.
—*Stacie Nicholls, Spring Creek, NV*

Prep: 5 min. • **Cook:** 3 hours
Makes: 8 servings

2 pkg. (12 oz. each) frozen fully cooked Italian meatballs, thawed
2 jars (24 oz. each) marinara sauce
8 hoagie buns, split
8 slices provolone cheese
   Sliced pepperoncini, optional

1. Place meatballs and sauce in a 3- or 4-qt. slow cooker. Cook, covered, on low until meatballs are heated through, 3-4 hours.
2. On each bun bottom, layer cheese, meatballs and, if desired, pepperoncini; replace tops.

1 sandwich: 526 cal., 20g fat (7g sat. fat), 93mg chol., 1674mg sod., 55g carb. (15g sugars, 4g fiber), 32g pro.

RED CURRY CARROT SOUP

With its mix of delicious colors, textures and tastes, this easy soup is something special. The meatballs make it substantial enough to serve as an entree.
—*Dilnaz Heckman, Buckley, WA*

- -

Prep: 20 min. • **Cook:** 15 min.
Makes: 8 servings (2½ qt.)

5   pkg. (3 oz. each) ramen noodles
3   garlic cloves, minced
2   Tbsp. peanut oil
1   can (13.66 oz.) coconut milk, divided
2   Tbsp. red curry paste
1½ tsp. curry powder
½   tsp. ground turmeric
32 frozen fully cooked homestyle meatballs (½ oz. each)
4   cups chicken broth
1   medium zucchini, finely chopped
1   medium carrot, halved and sliced
¼   cup shredded cabbage
2   tsp. fish sauce or soy sauce
    Optional garnishes: Bean sprouts, chow mein noodles, chopped fresh basil, green onions and micro greens

1. Cook noodles according to package directions (discard seasoning packets or save for another use).
2. Meanwhile, in a Dutch oven, saute garlic in oil for 1 minute. Spoon ½ cup cream from top of coconut milk and place in the pan. Add the curry paste, curry powder and turmeric; cook and stir until oil separates from the coconut milk mixture, about 5 minutes.
3. Stir in the meatballs, broth, zucchini, carrot, cabbage, fish sauce and remaining coconut milk. Bring to a boil. Reduce heat; simmer, uncovered, 15-20 minutes or until carrot is tender and meatballs are heated through. Drain noodles; stir into soup.
4. Garnish with bean sprouts, chow mein noodles, basil, microgreens and onions if desired.

Note: This recipe was tested with regular (full-fat) coconut milk. Light coconut milk contains less cream.
1¼ cups: 438 cal., 21g fat (11g sat. fat), 52mg chol., 1059mg sod., 42g carb. (3g sugars, 1g fiber), 18g pro.

TEST KITCHEN TIP

Feel free to use your own homemade meatballs in this soup recipe if you'd like, and don't hesitate to swap in a few of your favorite veggies, too.

51

SPAGHETTI & MEATBALLS

Jazz up any purchased spaghetti sauce for a fast supper with real homemade appeal— and very little effort.

—Ruth Andrewson, Leavenworth, WA

- -

Takes: 25 min. • **Makes:** 6 servings

  1 **pkg. (12 oz.) spaghetti**
3½ **cups spaghetti sauce**
  1 **batch of 30 meatballs,**
     (frozen or thawed)
     Grated parmesan cheese, optional

Cook spaghetti according to package directions. Meanwhile, in a saucepan, combine spaghetti sauce and meatballs; cover and simmer for 15-20 minutes or until the meatballs are heated through. Serve with spaghetti; top with Parmesan cheese if desired.

1½ cups: 426 cal., 9g fat (2g sat. fat), 62mg chol., 897mg sod., 64g carb. (14g sugars, 5g fiber), 24g pro.

MEATBALL FLATBREAD

As amazing as this flatbread tastes, you would never know how quickly it comes together. A little hidden carrot, unnoticed by the kids, adds sweet texture. For a crispier crust, bake the flatbread in the oven until it is slightly crispy on top before applying tomato puree.
—*Kimberly Berg, North Street, MI*

Takes: 25 min. • **Makes:** 4 flatbreads

1   can (15 oz.) Italian tomato sauce
1   medium carrot, coarsely chopped
3   fresh basil leaves
1   garlic clove, halved
4   naan flatbreads
2   cups shredded mozzarella cheese
14   frozen fully cooked Italian meatballs, thawed and halved
     Dash each salt, pepper, dried parsley flakes and dried oregano

1. Preheat oven to 400°. Place tomato sauce, carrot, basil and garlic in a food processor; cover and process until pureed. Place flatbreads on an ungreased baking sheet. Spread with tomato sauce mixture; top with cheese and meatballs. Sprinkle with the seasonings.
2. Bake on a lower oven rack until cheese is melted, 12-15 minutes.
½ flatbread: 228 cal., 10g fat (5g sat. fat), 46mg chol., 835mg sod., 21g carb. (3g sugars, 2g fiber), 14g pro.

ITALIC MEATBALL BUNS

🖐 **ITALIAN MEATBALL BUNS**

These soft little rolls come with a surprise inside—savory Italian meatballs. They're wonderful dipped in marinara sauce, making them fun for my grandkids and adults, too. I love how easy they are to put together.
—*Trina Linder-Mobley, Clover, SC*

Prep: 30 min. + rising • **Bake:** 15 min.
Makes: 2 dozen

12   frozen bread dough dinner rolls
1   pkg. (12 oz.) frozen fully cooked Italian meatballs, thawed
2   Tbsp. olive oil
¼   cup grated Parmesan cheese
¼   cup minced fresh basil
1½   cups marinara sauce, warmed

1. Let dough stand at room temperature until softened, 25-30 minutes.
2. Cut each roll in half. Wrap each portion around a meatball, enclosing meatball completely; pinch dough firmly to seal. Place on greased baking sheets, seam side down. Cover with kitchen towel; let rise in a warm place 1½-2 hours or until the dough is almost doubled.
3. Preheat oven to 350°. Bake buns until golden brown, 12-15 minutes. Brush tops with oil; sprinkle with cheese and basil. Serve with marinara sauce.
1 bun with 1 Tbsp. sauce: 98 cal., 4g fat (1g sat. fat), 13mg chol., 253mg sod., 12g carb. (2g sugars, 1g fiber), 5g pro.

MEXICAN PORK

My first time making this dish was a hit with everyone in my family, both young and old. Serve with black beans, white rice or use as meat for tacos, enchiladas or tamales!
—*Amy Vazquez, Brandon, MS*

Prep: 20 min. • **Cook:** 8 hours
Makes: 18 servings

- 1 bone-in pork shoulder roast (4 to 5 lbs.)
- 1 can (28 oz.) enchilada sauce
- 1 large green pepper, chopped
- 1 medium onion, finely chopped
- 2 garlic cloves, minced
- ¼ cup minced fresh cilantro
- 1 Tbsp. lime juice
- 1½ tsp. grated lime zest
  Flour tortillas (8 in.), optional

1. Cut roast in half; place in a 4- or 5-qt. slow cooker. Top with the enchilada sauce, green pepper, onion and garlic. Cover and cook on low for 8-10 hours or until meat is tender.
2. Remove roast; cool slightly. Skim fat from cooking juices. Remove meat from bone; discard bone. Shred pork with 2 forks and return to slow cooker.
3. Stir in the cilantro, lime juice and lime zest; heat through. Serve with a slotted spoon on tortillas if desired.

½ cup pork: 162 cal., 9g fat (3g sat. fat), 51mg chol., 280mg sod., 4g carb. (1g sugars, 1g fiber), 17g pro.

HASH BROWN PORK SKILLET

We added potatoes and veggies to leftover pork tenderloin for an easy and creamy weeknight supper in minutes!
—*Taste of Home Test Kitchen*

Takes: 25 min. • **Makes:** 6 servings

- 4 cups frozen O'Brien potatoes, thawed
- 1 cup chopped onion
- 1 cup chopped green pepper
- 2 Tbsp. butter
- 2 cups shredded cooked pork
- 2 tsp. chicken bouillon granules
- ¼ tsp. pepper
- 2 tsp. all-purpose flour
- ½ cup 2% milk
- ¾ cup shredded cheddar cheese

1. In a large cast-iron or other heavy skillet, cook the potatoes, onion and green pepper in butter over medium heat until almost tender. Stir in the pork, bouillon and pepper; heat through.
2. In a small bowl, combine the flour and milk until smooth; add to skillet. Cook on medium-low heat until mixture is thickened, stirring frequently, 4-5 minutes.
3. Sprinkle with cheese. Remove from the heat; cover and let stand until the cheese is melted.

1 cup: 286 cal., 13g fat (7g sat. fat), 70mg chol., 449mg sod., 22g carb. (4g sugars, 3g fiber), 19g pro.`

SAVORY PORK SALAD

This meal is hearty enough for my meat-and-potatoes-loving husband, not to mention delicious! It looks beautiful in a glass bowl and comes together in a snap thanks to cooked pork.
—*Victoria Skredsvig, Snohomish, WA*

Takes: 10 min. • **Makes:** 4 servings

- 1 package (10 ounces) ready-to-serve salad greens
- 1 can (11 ounces) mandarin oranges, drained
- 1 cup cooked shredded pork, warmed
- 1 cup smoked almonds
- 1 medium apple, chopped
- ½ cup fresh snow or sugar snap peas
- ¼ cup reduced-fat balsamic vinaigrette

In large bowl combine first 6 ingredients. Drizzle salad with the balsamic vinaigrette; serve immediately.

2 cups: 441 calories, 26g fat (2g saturated fat), 15mg cholesterol, 671mg sodium, 40g carbohydrate (29g sugars, 8g fiber), 18g protein.

❄ CHUNKY CHIPOTLE PORK CHILI

This tasty, easy recipe can be made ahead and reheated. If you ask me, it's even better the second day. Feel free to use additional pepper or onion if you'd like. Or, try adding sliced mushrooms or additional beans.
—*Peter Halferty, Corpus Christi, TX*

- -

Prep: 15 min. • **Cook:** 20 min.
Makes: 4 servings

- 1   medium green pepper, chopped
- 1   small onion, chopped
- 1   chipotle pepper in adobo sauce, finely chopped
- 1   Tbsp. canola oil
- 3   garlic cloves, minced
- 1   can (16 oz.) red beans, rinsed and drained
- 1   cup beef broth
- ½   cup salsa
- 2   tsp. ground cumin
- 2   tsp. chili powder
- 2   cups shredded cooked pork
- ¼   cup sour cream
     Sliced jalapeno pepper, optional

1. In a large saucepan, saute the green pepper, onion and chipotle pepper in oil until tender. Add the minced garlic; cook 1 minute longer.

2. Add the beans, broth, salsa, cumin and chili powder. Bring to a boil. Reduce heat; simmer, uncovered, for 10 minutes or until thickened. Add pork; heat through. Serve with sour cream.

Freeze option: Cool chili and transfer to freezer containers. Freeze up to 3 months. To use, thaw in the refrigerator. Transfer to a large saucepan; heat through; add water to thin if desired. Serve with sour cream and, if desired, jalapeno slices.

1 cup: 340 cal., 14g fat (4g sat. fat), 73mg chol., 834mg sod., 24g carb. (3g sugars, 7g fiber), 27g pro.

DOUBLE-DUTY HEARTY CHILI WITHOUT BEANS

When I prepare this zesty chili, I like to combine everything the night before. Then I load the slow cooker in the morning and come home to a fabulous dinner.
—Molly Butt, Granville, OH

Prep: 25 min. • **Cook:** 6 hours
Makes: 5 servings plus leftovers

- 2   tsp. canola oil
- 1   large green pepper, chopped
- 1   large onion, chopped
- 2   garlic cloves, minced
- 3   lbs. lean ground beef (90% lean)
- 2   cans (14½ oz. each) stewed tomatoes, undrained
- 2   cans (8 oz. each) tomato sauce
- 2   cans (4 oz. each) chopped green chiles
- ½   cup minced fresh parsley
- 2   Tbsp. chili powder
- 1¼ tsp. salt
- 1   tsp. paprika
- ½   tsp. pepper
      Hot cooked rice or pasta
      Optional toppings: Shredded cheddar cheese, sour cream and sliced green onions

1. In a large skillet, heat oil over medium-high heat. Add green pepper, onion and garlic; cook and stir 3-4 minutes or until tender. Transfer to a 6-qt. slow cooker.
2. In same skillet, add beef, half at a time; cook over medium-high heat until no longer pink, 6-8 minutes, breaking into crumbles. Using a slotted spoon, transfer beef to slow cooker.
3. Stir tomatoes, tomato sauce, chiles, parsley and seasonings into beef mixture. Cook, covered, on low 6-8 hours to allow flavors to blend.

4. Reserve and refrigerate 5 cups chili for Double-Duty Layered Enchilada Casserole. Serve remaining chili with rice and toppings as desired.
Freeze option: Freeze the cooled chili in freezer containers. To use, partially thaw in refrigerator overnight. Heat through in a saucepan, stirring occasionally; add water or broth if necessary.
1 cup: 278 cal., 13g fat (5g sat. fat), 85mg chol., 863mg sod., 13g carb. (6g sugars, 3g fiber), 29g pro.

DOUBLE-DUTY LAYERED ENCHILADA CASSEROLE

Here's a heap of cozy comfort. The *Taste of Home* Test Kitchen took my recipe for chili without beans and turned it into a savory enchilada casserole.
—Molly Butt, Granville, OH

Prep: 15 min. • **Bake:** 35 min. + standing
Makes: 12 servings

- 5   cups reserved Double-Duty Hearty Chili without Beans or any thick chili without beans
- 1½   cups frozen corn (about 8 oz.)
- 1   can (15 oz.) black beans, rinsed and drained
- 1   can (15 oz.) pinto beans, rinsed and drained
- 6   flour tortillas (10 in.)
- 3   cups shredded Mexican cheese blend, divided
- 1   can (10 oz.) enchilada sauce
       Optional: Shredded lettuce and chopped fresh tomatoes

1. Preheat oven to 375°. In a large bowl, mix reserved chili, corn and beans. Spread 1 cup chili mixture into a greased 13x9-in. baking dish. Layer with 2 tortillas, 2 cups chili mixture, 1 cup cheese and ½ cup enchilada sauce. Repeat layers. Top with the remaining tortillas and chili mixture.
2. Bake, covered, 20-25 minutes or until heated through. Sprinkle with remaining cheese. Bake, uncovered, until cheese is melted, 10-15 minutes longer. Let stand for 10 minutes before cutting. If desired, serve with lettuce and tomatoes.
Freeze option: Cover and freeze unbaked casserole. To use, partially thaw in the refrigerator overnight. Remove from refrigerator 30 minutes before baking. Preheat oven to 375°. Cover casserole with foil; bake as directed, increasing covered time to 40-45 minutes or until a thermometer inserted in center reads 165°. Serve the casserole as directed.
1 piece: 409 cal., 17g fat (7g sat. fat), 60mg chol., 1031mg sod., 41g carb. (5g sugars, 6g fiber), 25g pro.

DOUBLE-DUTY CHICKEN WITH OLIVES & ARTICHOKES

My grandmother came from the region around Seville, Spain, where olives are produced. They get a starring role in her scrumptious chicken.

—*Suzette Zara, Scottsdale, AZ*

- -

Prep: 30 min. • **Cook:** 4 hours
Makes: 4 servings plus leftovers

¼ cup all-purpose flour
½ tsp. garlic salt
¼ tsp. pepper
8 bone-in chicken thighs (3 lbs.), skin removed if desired
1 Tbsp. olive oil
4 garlic cloves, thinly sliced
1 Tbsp. grated lemon zest
1 tsp. dried thyme
½ tsp. dried rosemary, crushed
1 can (14 oz.) water-packed quartered artichoke hearts, drained
½ cup pimiento-stuffed olives
1 bay leaf
1½ cups orange juice
¾ cup chicken broth
2 Tbsp. honey
GREMOLATA
¼ cup minced fresh basil
1 tsp. grated lemon zest
1 garlic clove, minced

1. In a shallow bowl, mix flour, garlic salt and pepper. Dip chicken thighs in flour mixture to coat both sides; shake off excess. In a large skillet, heat oil over medium heat. In batches, brown chicken on both sides. Transfer to a 4-qt. slow cooker.

2. Sprinkle garlic, lemon zest, thyme and rosemary over chicken. Top with artichoke hearts, olives and bay leaf. In a bowl, mix orange juice, broth and honey; pour over top. Cook, covered, on low 4-5 hours or until chicken is tender. Remove bay leaf.

3. Reserve 4 chicken thighs for Double-Duty Chicken & Feta Spinach Salad; cover and refrigerate. To serve remaining chicken, mix gremolata ingredients in a small bowl. Sprinkle gremolata over the chicken and artichoke mixture.

1 chicken thigh with ¼ cup artichoke mixture and 1 Tbsp. gremolata: 434 cal., 21g fat (4g sat. fat), 81mg chol., 971mg sod., 34g carb. (17g sugars, 1g fiber), 26g pro.

DOUBLE-DUTY CHICKEN & FETA SPINACH SALAD

In my all-purpose salad, you can change up the pasta, nuts and cheese. If you have tomatoes, leftover turkey or a fresh lemon to squeeze, go for it.
—*Donna Bardocz, Howell, MI*

- -

Takes: 25 min. • **Makes:** 6 servings

1½ cups uncooked orzo
pasta (about 8 oz.)
5 oz. fresh baby spinach (about 6 cups), finely chopped
4 reserved chicken thighs from Double-Duty Chicken with Olives & Artichokes, shredded, or 1½ cups any shredded cooked chicken
1 cup crumbled feta cheese
¾ cup sliced almonds, toasted
⅓ cup finely chopped red onion
¼ cup chicken broth
¼ cup olive oil
1 Tbsp. minced fresh basil or ¾ tsp. dried basil
¾ tsp. salt
¼ tsp. white pepper

1. Cook orzo according to the package directions for al dente. Drain orzo; rinse with cold water and drain well.
2. In a large bowl, combine spinach, orzo, chicken, cheese, almonds and onion. In a small bowl, whisk remaining ingredients until blended; add to salad and toss gently to combine.
Note: To toast nuts, bake in a shallow pan in a 350° oven for 5-10 minutes or cook in a skillet over low heat until lightly browned, stirring occasionally.
1⅓ cups: 531 cal., 26g fat (6g sat. fat), 68mg chol., 627mg sod., 44g carb. (3g sugars, 4g fiber), 29g pro.

EASY EXTRAS

SAVE TIME & MONEY WITH MEAL-PLANNING ADD-ONS.

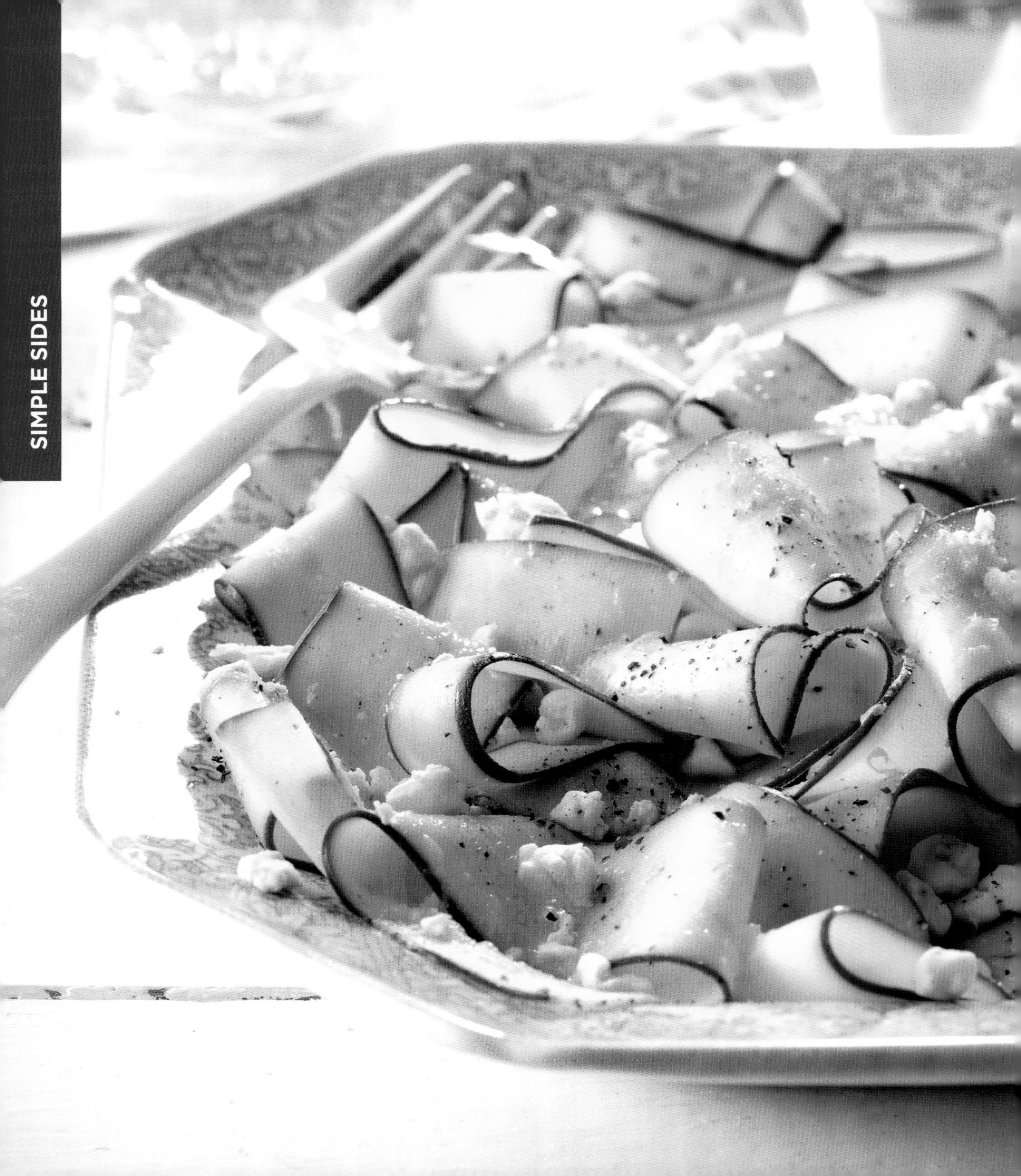

LEMONY ZUCCHINI RIBBONS

Fresh zucchini gets a festive treatment with a drizzle of lemon in this fabulous salad. Sprinkle on the goat cheese or feta and dive right in. It's perfect for nearly any entree!
—*Ellie Martin Cliffe, Milwaukee, WI*

Takes: 15 min. • **Makes:** 4 servings

- 1   Tbsp. olive oil
- ½   tsp. grated lemon zest
- 1   Tbsp. lemon juice
- ½   tsp. salt
- ¼   tsp. pepper
- 3   medium zucchini
- ⅓   cup crumbled goat or feta cheese

1. For dressing, in a small bowl, mix first 5 ingredients. Using a vegetable peeler, shave zucchini lengthwise into very thin slices; arrange on a serving plate.
2. To serve, drizzle with dressing and toss lightly to coat. Top with cheese.
¾ cup: 83 cal., 6g fat (2g sat. fat), 12mg chol., 352mg sod., 5g carb. (3g sugars, 2g fiber), 3g pro. **Diabetic exchanges:** 1 vegetable, 1 fat.

TEST KITCHEN TIP
Making this colorful salad with zucchini instead of spaghetti saves 130 calories per serving.

MINTY SUGAR SNAP PEAS

Fresh mint adds a fast and lively touch to cooked sugar snap peas. It's a great summer side with grilled entrees.
—*Alice Kaldahl, Ray, ND*

Takes: 10 min. • **Makes:** 4 servings

- 3   cups fresh sugar snap peas, trimmed
- ¼   tsp. sugar
- 2   to 3 Tbsp. minced fresh mint
- 2   Tbsp. butter

Place 1 in. of water in a large skillet. Add the peas and sugar; bring to a boil. Reduce heat; simmer, covered, until peas are crisp-tender, 4-5 minutes; drain. Stir in mint and butter.
¾ cup: 102 cal., 6g fat (4g sat. fat), 15mg chol., 45mg sod., 9g carb. (4g sugars, 3g fiber), 4g pro. **Diabetic exchanges:** 2 vegetable, 1½ fat.

GORGONZOLA-PEAR MESCLUN SALAD

This pretty salad is a tasty way to get your daily greens. To change it up, swap apples for pears and pecans for walnuts.
—*Joylyn Trickel, Helendale, CA*

Takes: 10 min. • **Makes:** 8 servings

- 2 **large pears, sliced**
- 1 **Tbsp. lemon juice**
- 6 **cups spring mix salad greens**
- 1 **cup crumbled Gorgonzola cheese**
- 1 **cup chopped walnuts, toasted**
- ½ **cup raspberry vinaigrette**

Toss pears with lemon juice. In a large bowl, combine greens, cheese, walnuts and pears. Drizzle with vinaigrette and toss to coat. Serve immediately.

Note: To toast nuts, bake in a shallow pan in a 350° oven for 5-10 minutes or cook in a skillet over low heat until lightly browned, stirring occasionally.

¾ cup: 204 cal., 14g fat (4g sat. fat), 13mg chol., 247mg sod., 17g carb. (9g sugars, 4g fiber), 6g pro.

🔟 MARJORAM GREEN BEANS

This quick and easy vegetable dish is a hit thanks to a pinch of marjoram. The taste is very subtle, yet distinctive. I like to fix beans this way for special dinners, since the bright green is so lovely on the plate.

—*Charlene Griffin, Minocqua, WI*

Takes: 20 min. • **Makes:** 8 servings

  1½ lbs. fresh green beans, trimmed
  ¾ cup water
  3 Tbsp. butter
  ½ tsp. salt
  ¼ tsp. pepper
  ⅛ to ¼ tsp. dried marjoram

Place beans and water in a large saucepan; bring to a boil. Reduce heat; cover and cook for 8-10 minutes or until crisp-tender. Drain. Add the butter, salt, pepper and marjoram; stir until butter is melted.

¾ cup: 61 cal., 4g fat (3g sat. fat), 11mg chol., 195mg sod., 5g carb. (2g sugars, 3g fiber), 1g pro.

MINI ITALIAN BISCUITS

I tasted biscuits like these at a seafood restaurant, and I really liked them. So I experimented in my own kitchen until I was able to get the same flavor in these fast little bites.

—*Elaine Whiting, Salt Lake City, UT*

Takes: 20 min. • **Makes:** about 3 dozen

  2 cups biscuit/baking mix
  ½ cup finely shredded cheddar cheese
  ½ tsp. garlic powder
  ½ tsp. dried oregano
  ½ tsp. dried basil
  ⅔ cup 2% milk

1. In a large bowl, combine the biscuit mix, cheese, garlic powder, oregano and basil. Stir in milk just until moistened.
2. Drop by rounded teaspoonfuls onto a lightly greased baking sheet. Bake at 450° for 7-8 minutes or until golden brown. Serve warm.

1 biscuit: 36 cal., 2g fat (1g sat. fat), 2mg chol., 96mg sod., 4g carb. (0 sugars, 0 fiber), 1g pro.

EASY POTATO PANCAKES

Using frozen hash browns makes these potato pancakes a snap to fix. They're a tasty companion to eggs for brunch.
—*Marlene Harguth, Maynard, MN*

Takes: 20 min. • **Makes:** 4 pancakes

- 3 cups frozen shredded hash brown potatoes
- 2 Tbsp. all-purpose flour
- 2 large eggs, room temperature, lightly beaten
- 3 Tbsp. butter, melted
- 1½ tsp. water
- ½ tsp. salt
- 1 Tbsp. canola oil

1. Place hash browns in a strainer; rinse with cold water until thawed. Drain thoroughly; transfer to a large bowl. Add the flour, eggs, butter, water and salt; mix well.
2. Heat oil in a large skillet over medium heat. Drop batter by ⅓ cupfuls into oil; fry until golden brown on both sides. Drain on paper towels.
1 pancake: 202 cal., 14g fat (7g sat. fat), 129mg chol., 421mg sod., 13g carb. (1g sugars, 1g fiber), 5g pro.

HONEY GARLIC GREEN BEANS

Green beans are great, but they can seem ordinary on their own. Just a couple of extra ingredients give them a sweet and salty attitude that everyone loves!
—*Shannon Dobos, Calgary, AB*

Takes: 20 min. • **Makes:** 8 servings

- 4 Tbsp. honey
- 2 Tbsp. reduced-sodium soy sauce
- 4 garlic cloves, minced
- ¼ tsp. salt
- ¼ tsp. crushed red pepper flakes
- 2 lbs. fresh green beans, trimmed

1. Whisk together first 5 ingredients; set aside. In a 6-qt. stockpot, bring 10 cups water to a boil. Add the beans in batches; cook, uncovered, just until crisp-tender, 2-3 minutes. Remove beans and immediately drop into ice water. Drain and pat dry.
2. Coat stockpot with cooking spray. Add beans; cook, stirring constantly, over high heat until slightly blistered, 2-3 minutes. Add sauce; continue stirring until beans are coated and sauce starts to evaporate slightly, 2-3 minutes. Remove from heat.
¾ cup: 72 cal., 0 fat (0 sat. fat), 0 chol., 225mg sod., 18g carb. (12g sugars, 4g fiber), 2g pro. **Diabetic exchanges:** 1 vegetable, ½ starch.

5i

CHEDDAR MASHED CAULIFLOWER

Want an alternative to mashed potatoes? Try cauliflower jazzed up with cheddar cheese and rosemary.

—*Chrystal Baker, Studio City, CA*

Takes: 15 min. • **Makes:** 6 servings

- 2 medium heads cauliflower, broken into florets
- ⅓ cup 2% milk
- 1 Tbsp. minced fresh rosemary
- ½ tsp. salt
- 1 cup shredded sharp cheddar cheese
  Coarsely ground black pepper, optional

In a Dutch oven, bring 1 in. of water to a boil. Add the cauliflower florets; cover and cook until tender, 5-10 minutes. Drain. Mash the cauliflower with the milk, rosemary and salt. Stir in cheese until melted. If desired, top with additional fresh rosemary and coarsely ground black pepper.

¾ cup: 122 cal., 6g fat (4g sat. fat), 21mg chol., 374mg sod., 12g carb. (5g sugars, 5g fiber), 8g pro.

SIMPLE SIDES

FESTIVE CORN & BROCCOLI

Whip up this no-fuss side dish while reheating your entree. It's the perfect addition to meal plans. If you have it, use a tablespoon of minced fresh basil instead of dried, and two to three ears of sweet corn (cut fresh from cob, about a cup) for the Mexicorn.
—Lucile Throgmorton, Clovis, NM

Takes: 15 min. • **Makes:** 5 servings

- 1   pkg. (16 oz.) frozen chopped broccoli, thawed
- 1   can (7 oz.) Mexicorn, drained
- ¼   cup butter, cubed
- 1   tsp. dried basil
- ½   tsp. salt
- ⅛   tsp. garlic powder
- ⅛   tsp. pepper

In a large cast-iron or other heavy skillet, combine the broccoli, corn and butter; cook over medium heat until butter is melted. Stir in the basil, salt, garlic powder and pepper. Cover and cook until vegetables are tender, 8-10 minutes, stirring occasionally.
⅔ cup: 135 cal., 9g fat (6g sat. fat), 24mg chol., 541mg sod., 12g carb. (3g sugars, 4g fiber), 4g pro.

MONKEY BREAD BISCUITS

Classic monkey bread is a sweetly spiced breakfast treat. I came up with an easy dinner version featuring garlic, Italian seasoning and Parmesan.
—Dana Johnson, Scottsdale, AZ

Takes: 20 min. • **Makes:** 1 dozen

- 1   tube (16.3 oz.) large refrigerated flaky biscuits
- 3   Tbsp. butter, melted
- 1   garlic clove, minced
- ½   tsp. Italian seasoning
- ¼   cup grated Parmesan cheese
    Additional Italian seasoning

1. Preheat oven to 425°. Separate biscuits; cut each into 6 pieces. In a large bowl, combine butter, garlic and Italian seasoning; add biscuit pieces and toss to coat.
2. Place 4 pieces in each of 12 greased muffin cups. Sprinkle with cheese and additional Italian seasoning. Bake until golden brown, 8-10 minutes. Serve warm.
1 biscuit: 159 cal., 9g fat (3g sat. fat), 9mg chol., 418mg sod., 16g carb. (3g sugars, 1g fiber), 3g pro.

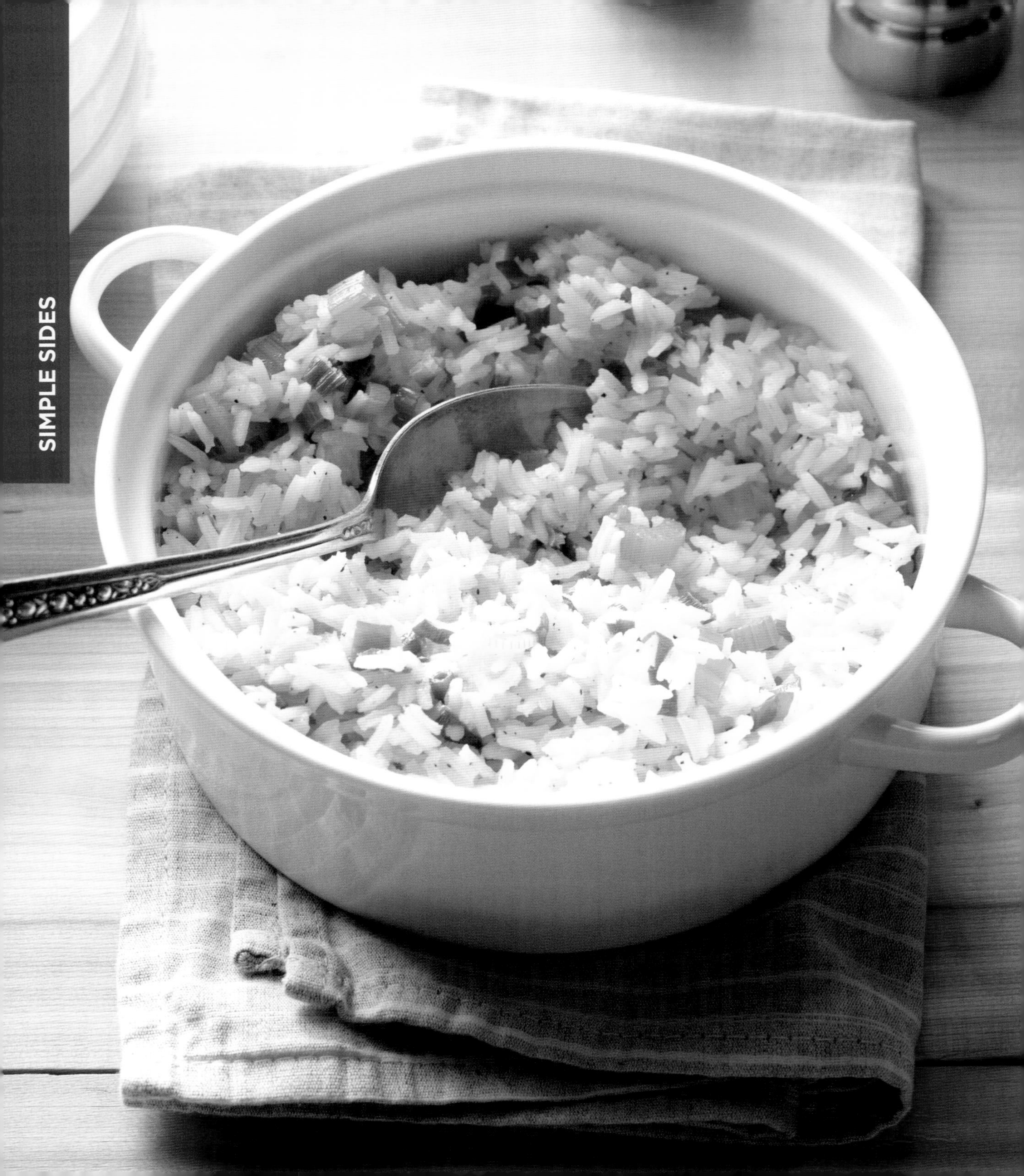

5i LEMON RICE PILAF

No need to buy premade pilaf mix when you can easily make your own in 20 minutes. The lemon zest adds a bright, welcome burst of flavor.
—Taste of Home *Test Kitchen*

Takes: 20 min. • **Makes:** 6 servings

- 1   cup uncooked jasmine or long grain white rice
- 2   Tbsp. butter
- 1   cup sliced celery
- 1   cup thinly sliced green onions
- 1   Tbsp. grated lemon zest
- 1   tsp. salt
- ¼   tsp. pepper

Cook rice according to package directions. Meanwhile, in a large skillet, heat butter over medium heat. Add celery and onions; cook until tender. Add rice, lemon zest, salt and pepper; toss lightly. Cook until the rice is heated through.

¾ cup: 155 cal., 4g fat (2g sat. fat), 10mg chol., 454mg sod., 27g carb. (1g sugars, 1g fiber), 3g pro. **Diabetic exchanges:** 2 starch, 1 fat.

WHY YOU'LL LOVE IT:
"This is such a great side dish! I served it with shredded beef. It was quick and easy."
—KIMSPACC, TASTEOFHOME.COM

5i 🍎 NECTARINE & BEET SALAD

Beets and nectarines sprinkled with feta cheese make a scrumptious new blend for a mixed green salad. The combination of ingredients may seem unlikely, but I guarantee it will become a favorite.
—Nicole Werner, Ann Arbor, MI

Takes: 10 min. • **Makes:** 8 servings

- 2   pkg. (5 oz. each) spring mix salad greens
- 2   medium nectarines, sliced
- ½   cup balsamic vinaigrette
- 1   can (14½ oz.) sliced beets, drained
- ½   cup crumbled feta cheese

On a serving dish, toss the greens and nectarines with vinaigrette. Top with beets and cheese; serve immediately.

1 cup: 84 cal., 4g fat (1g sat. fat), 4mg chol., 371mg sod., 10g carb. (6g sugars, 3g fiber), 3g pro. **Diabetic exchanges:** 2 vegetable, ½ fat.

🍎 GREEN BEANS AMANDINE

It's hard to improve on the flavor Mother Nature gives to fresh green beans, but this dish does it. My mom has been using it for years. The crunchy almonds are a super addition everyone loves.
—*Brenda DuFresne, Midland, MI*

Takes: 20 min. • **Makes:** 4 servings

1   lb. fresh or frozen green beans, cut into 2-in. pieces
½   cup water
¼   cup slivered almonds
2   Tbsp. butter
1   tsp. lemon juice
¼   tsp. seasoned salt, optional

1. Place beans and water in a large skillet or saucepan and bring to a boil. Cover and cook until crisp-tender, 10-15 minutes; drain and set aside.
2. In a large skillet, cook almonds in butter over low heat. Stir in lemon juice and, if desired, seasoned salt. Add green beans and heat through.

¾ cup: 125 cal., 9g fat (4g sat. fat), 15mg chol., 53mg sod., 10g carb. (3g sugars, 5g fiber), 4g pro. **Diabetic exchanges:** 2 fat, 1 vegetable.

SIMPLE LEMON PARSLEY POTATOES

For a simply delicious side dish, I often prepare these potatoes. I like that there are only a few ingredients and that it all goes from stove to table in so little time.
—*Dorothy Pritchett, Wills Point, TX*

Takes: 20 min. • **Makes:** 12 servings

3   lbs. small red new potatoes, quartered
½   cup butter, melted
3   Tbsp. lemon juice
3   Tbsp. minced fresh parsley

Cook potatoes in boiling salted water until tender, about 15 minutes; drain. Combine butter, lemon juice and parsley; pour over the potatoes and stir gently to coat.

1 cup: 150 cal., 8g fat (5g sat. fat), 20mg chol., 84mg sod., 18g carb. (1g sugars, 2g fiber), 2g pro.

5i ✻

OVEN-ROASTED TOMATOES

I love tomatoes, as they're both healthy and versatile. You can use these roasted bites in sandwiches or omelets, or to top broiled chicken. They really jazz up a meal plan.
—*Julie Tilney (Gomez), Downey, CA*

Prep: 20 min. • **Bake:** 3 hours + cooling
Makes: 16 servings (4 cups)

20	plum tomatoes (about 5 lbs.)
¼	cup olive oil
5	tsp. Italian seasoning
2½	tsp. salt

1. Cut tomatoes into ½-in. slices. Brush with oil; sprinkle with Italian seasoning and salt.
2. Place on racks coated with cooking spray in foil-lined 15x10x1-in. baking pans. Bake, uncovered, at 325° for 3-3½ hours or until tomatoes are deep brown around the edges and shriveled. Cool 10-15 minutes. Serve warm or at room temperature.
3. Store in an airtight container in the refrigerator for up to 1 week.
Freeze option: Place in freezer container; freeze for up to 3 months. Bring tomatoes to room temperature before using.
¼ cup: 45 cal., 4g fat (0 sat. fat), 0 chol., 373mg sod., 3g carb. (2g sugars, 1g fiber), 1g pro.

5i NUTTY GOUDA ROLLS

Here's a quick take on crescents that feels special enough for company. With Gouda, pecans and honey, these simple rolls will complement a variety of weeknight meals.
—Taste of Home *Test Kitchen*

- -

Takes: 20 min. • **Makes:** 8 rolls

- 2 oz. Gouda cheese
- 1 tube (8 oz.) refrigerated crescent rolls
- 2 Tbsp. finely chopped pecans
- 1 Tbsp. honey

1. Preheat oven to 375°. Cut cheese into eight ½-in.-wide strips. Separate crescent dough into 8 triangles; sprinkle with pecans. Place a cheese strip on the shortest side of each triangle; roll up, starting with the side with the cheese. Pinch ends to seal.
2. Place on an ungreased baking sheet. Bake until rolls are golden brown, 10-12 minutes. Immediately brush with honey. Serve warm.
1 roll: 158 cal., 9g fat (3g sat. fat), 8mg chol., 281mg sod., 14g carb. (4g sugars, 0 fiber), 4g pro.

SUMMER SALAD

This is a great meal by itself or equally refreshing as a side salad. Tart cranberries and dressing, tangy feta and crunchy pine nuts create an attractive blend.
—*Kristin Scharf, Portage, IN*

- -

Takes: 10 min. • **Makes:** 2 servings

- 1 cup fresh baby spinach
- 1 cup torn leaf lettuce
- ¼ cup crumbled feta cheese
- 2 Tbsp. dried cranberries
- 1 Tbsp. pine nuts
- 2 Tbsp. prepared reduced-fat red wine vinaigrette

In a small serving bowl, combine the first 5 ingredients. Drizzle with vinaigrette; toss to coat. Serve immediately.
1 cup: 112 cal., 7g fat (2g sat. fat), 8mg chol., 315mg sod., 10g carb. (6g sugars, 2g fiber), 4g pro. **Diabetic exchanges:** 1 vegetable, 1 fat, ½ starch.

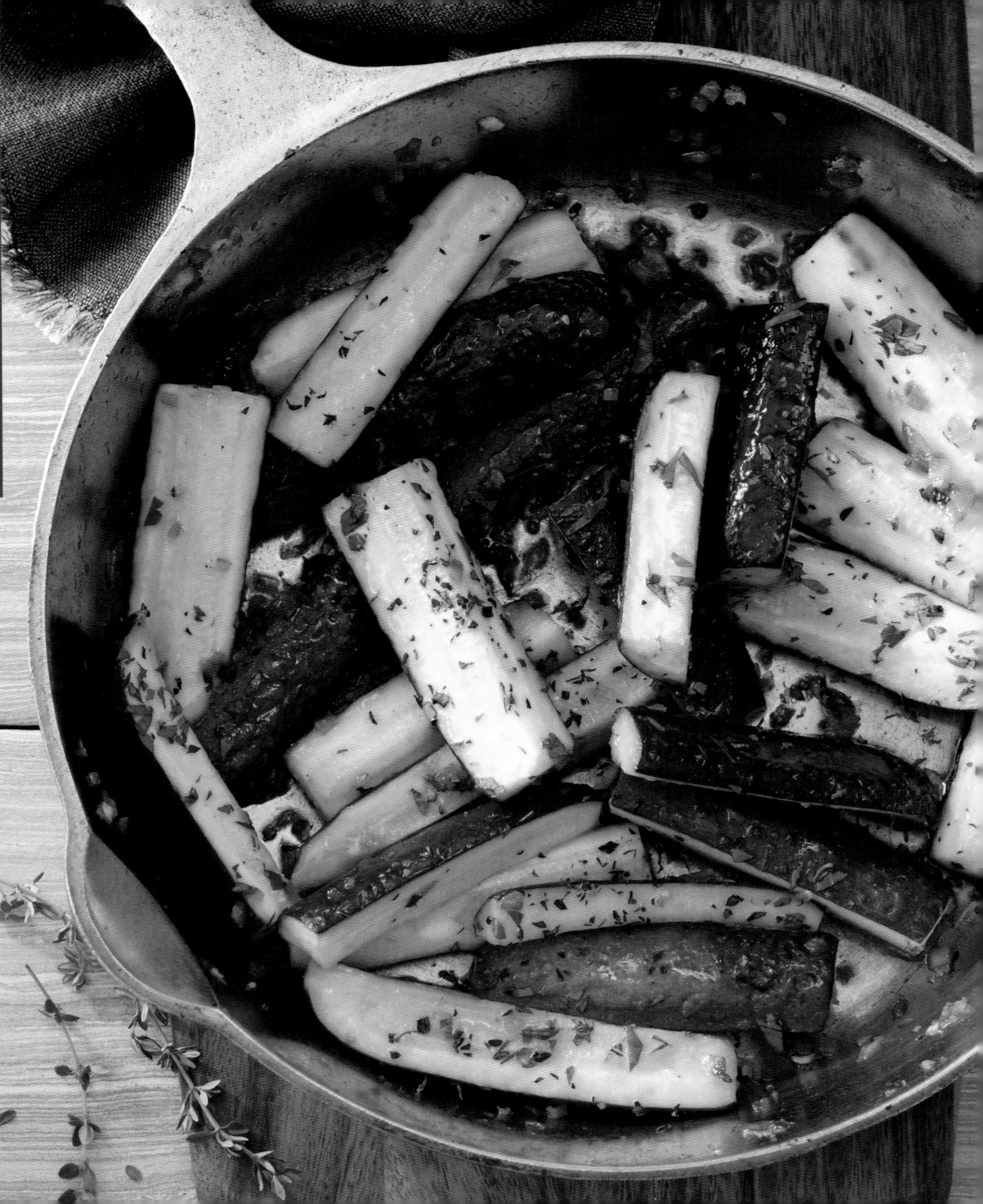

THYMED ZUCCHINI SAUTE

Simple and flavorful, this recipe is a tasty and healthy way to use up all of the zucchini taking over your end-of-summer garden. Best of all, it's ready in no time!
—*Bobby Taylor, Ulster Park, NY*

Takes: 15 min. • **Makes:** 4 servings

- 1   Tbsp. olive oil
- 1   lb. medium zucchini, quartered lengthwise and halved
- ¼   cup finely chopped onion
- ½   vegetable bouillon cube, crushed
- 2   Tbsp. minced fresh parsley
- 1   tsp. minced fresh thyme or ¼ tsp. dried thyme

In a large skillet, heat oil over medium-high heat. Add the zucchini, onion and bouillon; cook and stir for 4-5 minutes or until the zucchini is crisp-tender. Sprinkle with herbs.
Note: This recipe was prepared with Knorr vegetable bouillon.

¾ cup: 53 cal., 4g fat (1g sat. fat), 0 chol., 135mg sod., 5g carb. (2g sugars, 2g fiber), 2g pro. **Diabetic exchanges:** 1 vegetable, ½ fat.

> **WHY YOU'LL LOVE IT:**
> "*I grew up eating sliced zucchini or yellow squash dredged in egg and flour, then fried in butter. This recipe brings home all of those flavors with the added freshness of the herbs.*"
> —**TKUEHL, TASTEOFHOME.COM**

SPECIAL CREAMED CORN

This has earned a permanent place on many of our menus. While the whole family loves it, my son especially looks forward to it.
—*Deb Hauptmann, Mohnton, PA*

Takes: 20 min. • **Makes:** 8 servings

- ⅓   cup butter
- ⅓   cup all-purpose flour
- 1   cup heavy whipping cream
- 1   cup whole milk
- ¼   cup sugar
- 1   tsp. salt
     Dash white pepper
- 5   cups frozen corn, thawed
- ¼   cup grated Parmesan cheese

1. In a saucepan, melt butter over medium heat. Stir in flour until smooth. Gradually add cream, milk, sugar, salt and pepper. Bring to a boil; boil and stir for 2 minutes. Add corn; heat through.
2. Transfer mixture to an ungreased 1½-qt. broiler-proof dish. Sprinkle with Parmesan cheese. broil 5 in. from the heat until lightly browned and bubbly, 3-5 minutes.

⅔ cup: 317 cal., 21g fat (13g sat. fat), 59mg chol., 425mg sod., 31g carb. (11g sugars, 2g fiber), 6g pro.

CONFETTI CORN

This easy corn dish is sure to dress up almost any entree. The tender corn is paired with the crunch of water chestnuts, red pepper and chopped carrot in this healthy side.
—*Glenda Watts, Charleston, IL*

- -

Takes: 15 min. • **Makes:** 4 servings

¼ cup chopped carrot
1 Tbsp. olive oil
2¾ cups fresh or frozen corn, thawed
¼ cup chopped water chestnuts
¼ cup chopped sweet red pepper

In a large cast-iron or other heavy skillet, saute carrot in oil until crisp-tender. Stir in the corn, water chestnuts, and red pepper; heat through.

¾ cup: 140 cal., 4g fat (1g sat. fat), 0 chol., 7mg sod., 26g carb. (3g sugars, 3g fiber), 4g pro. **Diabetic exchanges:** 1½ starch, ½ fat.

SHAVED FENNEL SALAD

This salad tastes even more impressive than it looks. It has an incredible crunch thanks to the cucumbers, radishes and apples. And the finish of fennel fronds adds just the faintest hint of licorice flavor.
—*William Milton III, Clemson, SC*

- -

Takes: 15 min. • **Makes:** 8 servings

1 large fennel bulb, fronds reserved
1 English cucumber
1 medium Honeycrisp apple
2 Tbsp. extra virgin olive oil
½ tsp. kosher salt
¼ tsp. coarsely ground pepper
2 radishes, thinly sliced

With a mandoline or vegetable peeler, cut the fennel, cucumber and apple into very thin slices. Transfer to a large bowl; toss with olive oil, salt and pepper. Top with radishes and reserved fennel fronds to serve.

¾ cup: 55 cal., 4g fat (1g sat. fat), 0 chol., 138mg sod., 6g carb. (4g sugars, 2g fiber), 1g pro. **Diabetic exchanges:** 1 vegetable, 1 fat.

TEST KITCHEN TIP
Try adding a squeeze of lemon. The little bit of acid would complement the dressing.

SPICED SWEET POTATO FRIES

A spicy homemade seasoning blend shakes up everyone's favorite finger food in this rendition of sweet potato fries.
—Taste of Home *Test Kitchen*

- -

Takes: 25 min. • **Makes:** 6 servings

1   pkg. (19 oz.) frozen French-fried
    sweet potatoes
½   **tsp. garlic powder**
½   **tsp. curry powder**
½   **tsp. pepper**
¼   **tsp. chili powder**
⅛   **tsp. ground cinnamon**
⅛   **tsp. salt**

Bake fries according to package directions. Meanwhile, in a small bowl, combine the remaining ingredients. Sprinkle over fries; toss to coat.

1 serving: 129 cal., 3g fat (1g sat. fat), 0 chol., 241mg sod., 24g carb. (10g sugars, 2g fiber), 0 pro.

ORZO WITH PARMESAN & BASIL

Dried basil adds its rich herb flavor to this creamy and delicious skillet side dish that's table-ready in just minutes. Check out the easy variation, too!
—*Anna Chaney, Antigo, WI*

Takes: 20 min. • **Makes:** 4 servings

- 1 cup uncooked orzo pasta or pearl couscous
- 2 Tbsp. butter
- 1 can (14½ oz.) chicken broth
- ½ cup grated Parmesan cheese
- 2 tsp. dried basil
- ⅛ tsp. pepper
  Thinly sliced fresh basil, optional

1. In a large cast-iron or other heavy skillet, saute orzo in butter until lightly browned, 3-5 minutes.

2. Stir in broth. Bring to a boil. Reduce heat; cover and simmer until liquid is absorbed and orzo is tender, 10-15 minutes. Stir in the cheese, basil and pepper. If desired, top with fresh basil.

½ cup: 285 cal., 10g fat (5g sat. fat), 26mg chol., 641mg sod., 38g carb. (2g sugars, 1g fiber), 11g pro.

Corn & Pepper Orzo: Omit Parmesan cheese, basil and pepper. Prepare orzo as directed. In a large skillet coated with cooking spray, saute 1 chopped large red sweet pepper and 1 chopped medium onion in 1 Tbsp. olive oil. Stir in 2 cups thawed frozen corn, 2 tsp. Italian seasoning and ⅛ tsp. each salt and pepper. Drain the orzo; toss with vegetable mixture. Yield: 6 servings.

THREE-CHEESE CREAMED SPINACH

Cream cheese, Parmesan and mozzarella make this dish wonderfully cheesy. Sprinkle it with french-fried onions before baking for a crisp boost of flavor.
—*Kathy Vazquez, Amarillo, TX*

Takes: 20 min. • **Makes:** 6 servings

- 2 pkg. (10 oz. each) frozen chopped spinach, thawed and squeezed dry
- 1½ cups spreadable chive and onion cream cheese
- 1 cup grated Parmesan cheese
- 1 cup shredded part-skim mozzarella cheese
- ¼ cup butter, cubed
- ¼ tsp. pepper

In a large saucepan, combine all ingredients. Cook and stir the mixture over medium heat for 8-10 minutes or until blended and heated through.

⅔ cup: 415 cal., 35g fat (23g sat. fat), 103mg chol., 685mg sod., 9g carb. (5g sugars, 3g fiber), 15g pro.

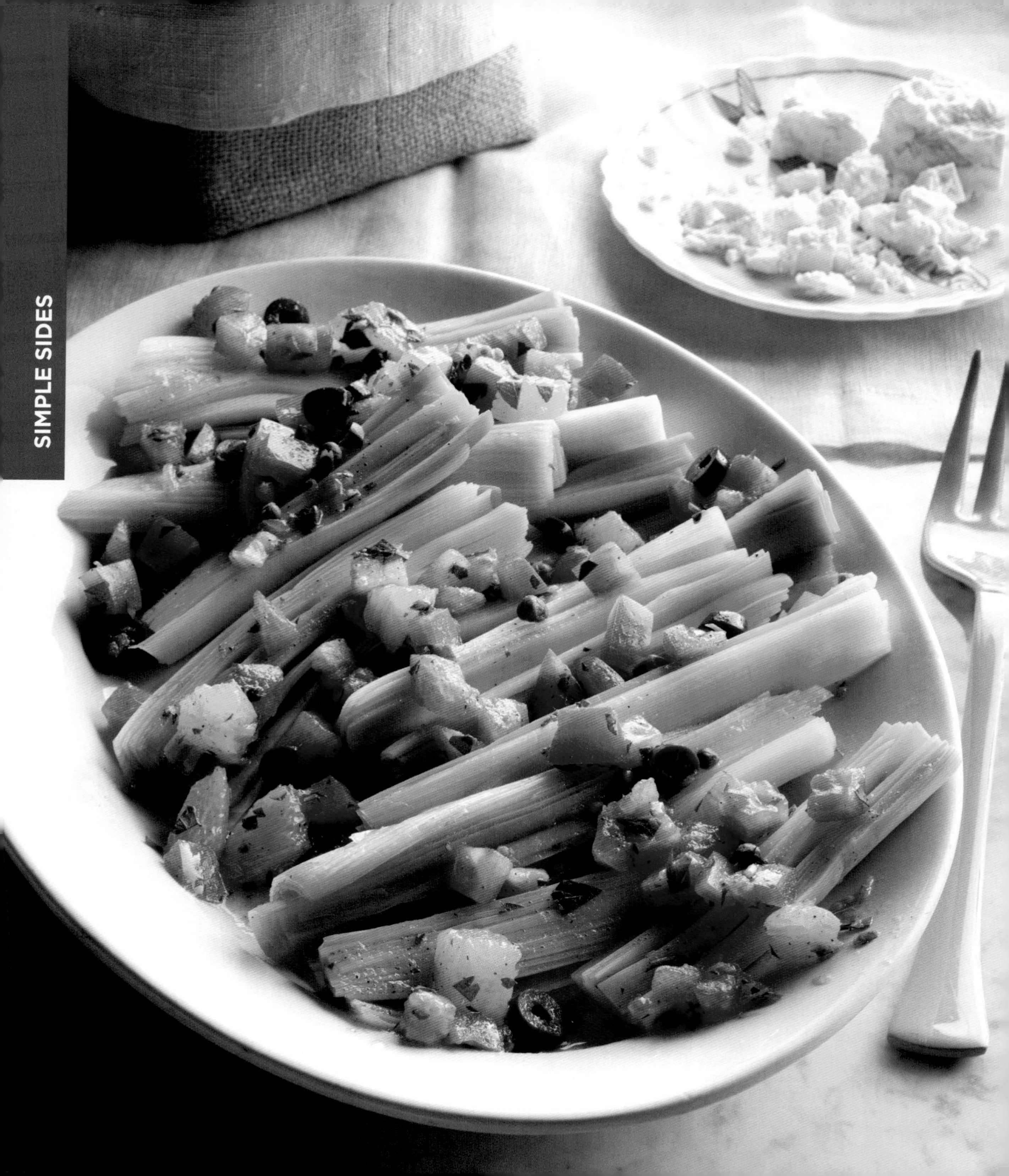

SICILIAN STEAMED LEEKS

I love the challenge of developing recipes for my garden leeks, a delicious underused vegetable. This Italian-flavored dish is a family favorite.
—*Roxanne Chan, Albany, CA*

Takes: 20 min. • **Makes:** 6 servings

- 6 medium leeks (white portion only), halved lengthwise, cleaned
- 1 large tomato, chopped
- 1 small navel orange, peeled, sectioned and chopped
- 2 Tbsp. minced fresh parsley
- 2 Tbsp. sliced Greek olives
- 1 tsp. capers, drained
- 1 tsp. red wine vinegar
- 1 tsp. olive oil
- ½ tsp. grated orange zest
- ½ tsp. pepper
  Crumbled feta cheese

In a Dutch oven, place steamer basket over 1 in. of water. Place leeks in basket. Bring water to a boil. Reduce the heat to maintain a low boil; steam, covered, until tender, 8-10 minutes. Meanwhile, combine the next 9 ingredients. Transfer leeks to a serving platter. Spoon tomato mixture over top; sprinkle with cheese.

1 serving: 83 cal., 2g fat (0 sat. fat), 0 chol., 77mg sod., 16g carb. (6g sugars, 3g fiber), 2g pro. **Diabetic exchanges:** 1 starch, ½ fat.

SHREDDED KALE & BRUSSELS SPROUTS SALAD

This salad is a simple and delicious way to eat your superfoods! It gets even better in the fridge, so I make it ahead. I use my homemade honey mustard dressing, but any type works just fine.
—*Alexandra Weisser, New York, NY*

Takes: 15 min. • **Makes:** 6 servings

- 1 small bunch kale (about 8 oz.), stemmed and thinly sliced (about 6 cups)
- ½ lb. fresh Brussels sprouts, thinly sliced (about 3 cups)
- ½ cup pistachios, coarsely chopped
- ½ cup honey mustard salad dressing
- ¼ cup shredded Parmesan cheese

Toss together all ingredients.

1 cup: 207 cal., 14g fat (2g sat. fat), 8mg chol., 235mg sod., 16g carb. (5g sugars, 4g fiber), 7g pro. **Diabetic exchanges:** 3 fat, 2 vegetable, ½ starch.

51

GLAZED BABY CARROTS

For a zippy side dish, try this recipe. These brown sugar-glazed carrots come together while the entree cooks.

—*Anita Foster, Fairmount, GA*

Takes: 15 min. • **Makes:** 4 servings

1 lb. fresh, frozen or canned whole baby carrots
   Water
2 Tbsp. butter
¼ cup brown sugar

Cook carrots in a small amount of water until tender. Drain. In a saucepan, combine butter and brown sugar; heat until sugar dissolves. Add the carrots and toss to coat. Heat through.

¾ cup: 142 cal., 6g fat (4g sat. fat), 15mg chol., 152mg sod., 23g carb. (19g sugars, 2g fiber), 1g pro.

TEST KITCHEN TIP

Dark brown sugar contains more molasses than light or golden brown sugar. The types are generally interchangeable in recipes. But if you prefer a bolder flavor, choose dark brown sugar.

ALMOND STRAWBERRY SALAD

It's easy to love this pretty salad topped with strawberries and sliced almonds. It calls for just a few ingredients but it's loaded with flavor.

—*Renae Rossow, Union, KY*

Takes: 10 min. • **Makes:** 4 servings

- 3 cups fresh baby spinach
- ½ cup sliced fresh strawberries
- ¼ cup honey-roasted sliced almonds
- 1 Tbsp. cider vinegar
- 1 Tbsp. honey
- 1½ tsp. sugar

Place the spinach, strawberries and almonds in a large bowl. Mix vinegar, honey and sugar until blended; toss with salad.

¾ cup: 75 cal., 4g fat (0 sat. fat), 0 chol., 98mg sod., 9g carb. (8g sugars, 1g fiber), 2g pro. **Diabetic exchanges:** 1 vegetable, 1 fat.

GREAT GARLIC BREAD

Reheating a pasta dish you previously froze? Whip up this tasty garlic bread topped with cheese for a complete menu.

—Taste of Home *Test Kitchen*

Takes: 15 min. • **Makes:** 8 servings

- ½ cup butter, melted
- ¼ cup grated Romano cheese
- 4 garlic cloves, minced
- 1 loaf (1 lb.) French bread, halved lengthwise
- 2 Tbsp. minced fresh parsley

1. Preheat oven to 350°. In a small bowl, mix butter, cheese and garlic; brush over cut sides of bread. Place on a baking sheet, cut side up. Sprinkle with parsley.
2. Bake 7-9 minutes or until light golden brown. Cut into slices; serve warm.

1 slice: 283 cal., 14g fat (8g sat. fat), 34mg chol., 457mg sod., 33g carb. (1g sugars, 1g fiber), 8g pro.

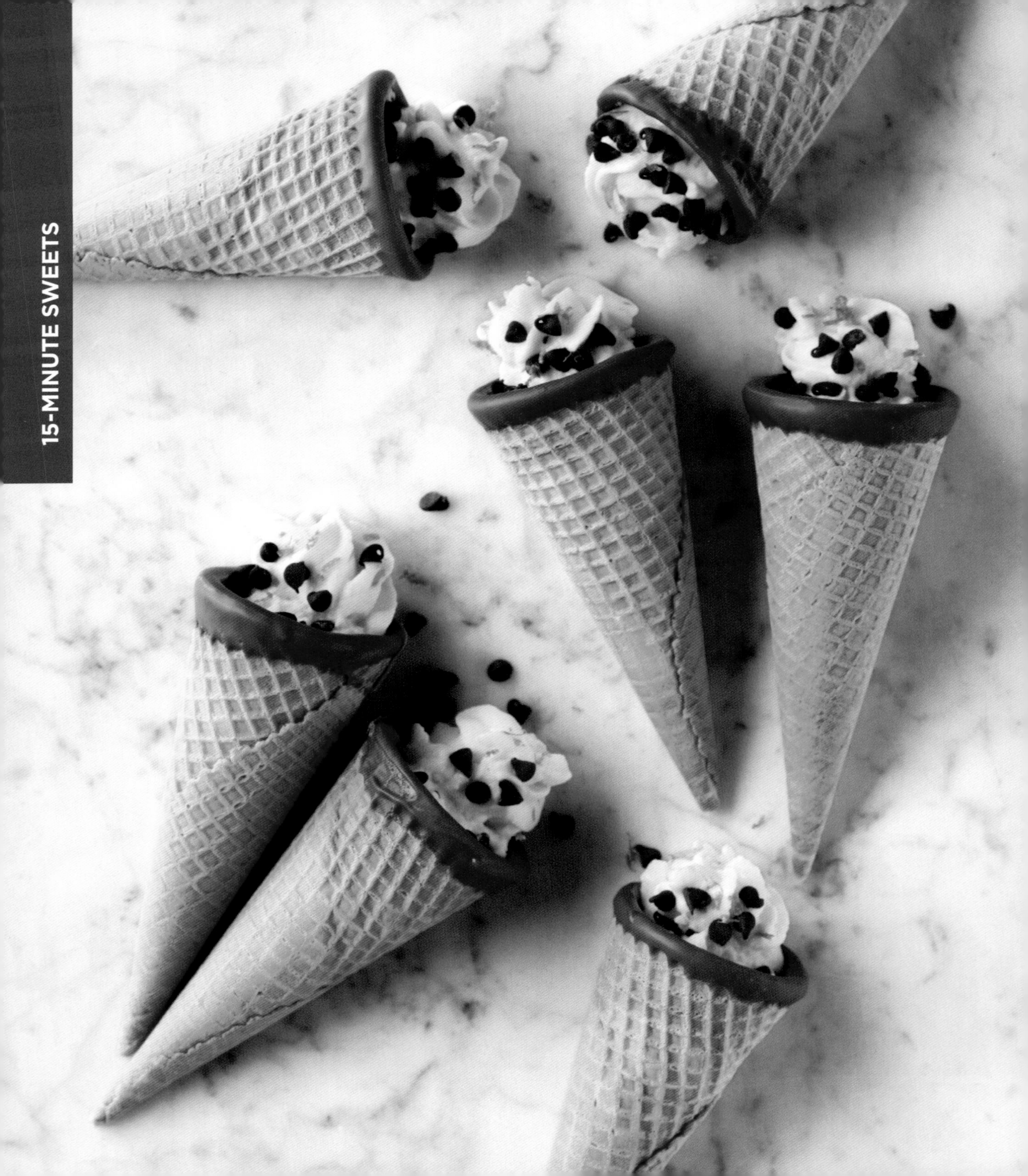

5i CANNOLI DIP

Ricotta is one of my family's favorite ingredients. I made up the cannoli filling and broke up some ice cream waffle shells to use as chips and dip—it was an instant hit! It's also good served slightly warm.
—*Ann Marie Eberhart, Gig Harbor, WA*

Takes: 10 min. • **Makes:** 8 servings

1 carton (15 oz.) whole-milk ricotta cheese
¾ cup confectioners' sugar
1 Tbsp. finely chopped candied citron
1 Tbsp. grated lime zest
Mini ice cream sugar cones, optional
Miniature semisweet chocolate chips, optional

Beat together ricotta cheese, sugar, candied citron and lime zest. If desired, scoop ricotta mixture into the cones and sprinkle with the chocolate chips.

Note: Do not use a food processor to chop the citron—it could make it too fine, and its flavor is more intense with slightly larger bits.

¼ cup: 128 cal., 5g fat (3g sat. fat), 21mg chol., 70mg sod., 16g carb. (15g sugars, 0 fiber), 6g pro.

5i CINNAMON APPLE PAN BETTY

I found this recipe soon after I was married. You'll need just a few ingredients, which you probably have on hand. It's super quick to put together, too. It's a favorite of ours during fall and winter, when apples are at their very best.
—*Shirley Leister, West Chester, PA*

Takes: 15 min. • **Makes:** 6 servings

3 medium apples, peeled and cubed
½ cup butter
3 cups cubed bread
½ cup sugar
¾ tsp. ground cinnamon

In a large skillet, saute apple in butter until tender, 4-5 minutes. Add bread cubes. Stir together sugar and cinnamon; sprinkle over apple mixture and toss to coat. Saute until bread is warmed.

½ cup: 279 cal., 16g fat (10g sat. fat), 41mg chol., 208mg sod., 34g carb. (25g sugars, 2g fiber), 2g pro.

PUMPKIN COOKIE DIP

A few moments are all you need to whip up this creamy dip that goes perfectly with store-bought gingersnaps.

—*Gloria Kirchman, Eden Prairie, MN*

Takes: 10 min. • **Makes:** 4 cups

1   pkg. (8 oz.) cream cheese, softened
2   jars (7 oz. each)
    marshmallow creme
1   can (15 oz.) solid-pack pumpkin
1   tsp. ground cinnamon
1   tsp. grated orange zest
    Gingersnaps or vanilla wafers

In a large bowl, beat cream cheese and marshmallow creme until smooth. Stir in the pumpkin, cinnamon and orange zest. Serve as a dip with cookies. Store dip in the refrigerator.

2 Tbsp.: 50 cal., 3g fat (2g sat. fat), 8mg chol., 27mg sod., 6g carb. (5g sugars, 1g fiber), 1g pro.

5j BROILED PEAR DESSERT

This sweet finale is the perfect solution for pears that aren't quite ripe. For a real treat, top it with a scoop of vanilla ice cream.

—*Kaaren Jurack, Manassas, VA*

Takes: 15 min. • **Makes:** 2 servings

2   medium ripe pears,
    halved and cored
1   Tbsp. lemon juice
2   Tbsp. brown sugar
2   Tbsp. finely chopped almonds
1   Tbsp. cold butter

1. Brush pears with lemon juice; place on a broiler pan, cut side up.
2. In a small bowl, combine brown sugar and almonds; cut in butter until crumbly. Sprinkle over pears. Broil 3-4 in. from the heat for 2-3 minutes or until topping is golden brown.

1 serving: 222 cal., 7g fat (2g sat. fat), 8mg chol., 55mg sod., 42g carb. (30g sugars, 6g fiber), 2g pro.

CINNAMON-STRAWBERRY SUNDAES

Lime adds a delicious tang to this quick and easy dessert. I'll never eat plain vanilla ice cream again!
—*Cory Roberts, Riverton, UT*

- -

Takes: 10 min. • **Makes:** 4 servings

- 1   Tbsp. butter
- 2   Tbsp. brown sugar
- 1   Tbsp. lime juice
- ¼   tsp. ground cinnamon
- 2   cups frozen unsweetened strawberries, thawed and drained, or sliced fresh strawberries
- 2   cups vanilla ice cream
- 1   tsp. grated lime zest

In a small saucepan, melt the butter over medium heat. Stir in brown sugar, lime juice and cinnamon. Cook and stir until sugar is dissolved. Add strawberries; cook until tender, about 2 minutes longer. Serve with ice cream; sprinkle with lime zest.

½ cup ice cream with 3 Tbsp. sauce: 216 cal., 10g fat (6g sat. fat), 37mg chol., 79mg sod., 30g carb. (24g sugars, 2g fiber), 3g pro.

15-MINUTE SWEETS

BANANAS FOSTER SUNDAES

I have wonderful memories of eating bananas Foster in New Orleans, and as a dietitian, wanted to find a healthier version. I combined the best of two recipes and added my own tweaks to create this southern treat.
—*Lisa Varner, El Paso, TX*

Takes: 15 min. • **Makes:** 6 servings

1   Tbsp. butter
3   Tbsp. brown sugar
1   Tbsp. orange juice
¼   tsp. ground cinnamon
¼   tsp. ground nutmeg
3   large firm bananas, sliced
2   Tbsp. chopped pecans, toasted
½   tsp. rum extract
3   cups reduced-fat vanilla ice cream

1. In an 8- or 9-in. cast-iron or other ovenproof skillet, melt the butter over medium-low heat. Stir in brown sugar, orange juice, cinnamon and nutmeg until blended. Add bananas and pecans; cook until the bananas are glazed and slightly softened, 2-3 minutes, stirring gently.
2. Remove from heat; stir in extract. Serve with ice cream.
Note: To toast nuts, cook in a skillet over low heat until nuts are lightly browned, stirring occasionally.
1 sundae: 233 cal., 7g fat (3g sat. fat), 23mg chol., 66mg sod., 40g carb. (30g sugars, 2g fiber), 4g pro.

CHOCOLATE CARAMEL FONDUE

I only need 10 minutes and just a few ingredients to whip up this instant party favorite. I serve it in punch cups so guests can carry it on dessert plates with their choice of fruit, pretzels and other dippers.
—*Cheryl Arnold, Lake Zurich, IL*

Takes: 10 min. • **Makes:** 2½ cups

1   can (14 oz.) sweetened
     condensed milk
1   jar (12 oz.) caramel
     ice cream topping
3   oz. unsweetened
     chocolate, chopped
     Assorted fresh fruit and/or pretzels

In a small saucepan, combine milk, caramel topping and chocolate; cook and stir over low heat until blended and heated through. Transfer mixture to a heated fondue pot; keep warm. Serve with fruit and/or pretzels for dipping.
2 Tbsp.: 114 cal., 3g fat (2g sat. fat), 7mg chol., 85mg sod., 22g carb. (22g sugars, 0 fiber), 2g pro.

5i
CARAMEL APPLE DIP

This four-ingredient caramel dip is so simple and yummy. People always want to know how long I worked to prepare it on the stove and are amazed to find that I made it in the microwave. When large marshmallows aren't on hand, I substitute 2 cups of mini marshmallows.
—*Becky Heiner, West Valley City, UT*

- -

Takes: 15 min. • **Makes:** 2½ cups

1	**pkg. (14 oz.) caramels**
20	**large marshmallows**
½	**cup butter, melted**
⅓	**cup heavy whipping cream**
	Apple slices

Place the caramels in a microwave-safe bowl. Microwave, uncovered, on high for 1 minute. Add marshmallows; microwave for 1 minute or until marshmallows are melted, stirring occasionally. Whisk in butter and cream until combined. Serve with apple slices. Refrigerate leftovers.

2 Tbsp.: 153 cal., 8g fat (5g sat. fat), 19mg chol., 100mg sod., 21g carb. (17g sugars, 0 fiber), 1g pro.

BLUEBERRY GRAHAM DESSERT

When you're short on time but long for cheesecake, try this fruity after-dinner treat. They make great treats to stash into a lunch bag, too. Ricotta and cream cheeses give every bit as much flavor as cheesecake without the effort. Instead of preparing individual servings, you could also layer the ingredients in a glass serving bowl.
—Taste of Home *Test Kitchen*

- -

Takes: 15 min. • **Makes:** 4 servings

¾ cup graham cracker crumbs (about 12 squares)
¼ cup chopped walnuts
2 Tbsp. sugar
¼ tsp. ground cinnamon
2 Tbsp. butter
3 oz. cream cheese, softened
⅓ cup confectioners' sugar
½ cup ricotta cheese
2 tsp. lemon juice
4 cups fresh blueberries
Whipped cream, optional

1. In a large bowl, combine graham cracker crumbs, walnuts, sugar and cinnamon. Stir in butter; set aside. In another large bowl, beat cream cheese and confectioners' sugar until smooth. Beat in ricotta cheese and lemon juice.

2. Place ½ cup blueberries in each of 4 dessert dishes. Top with cream cheese mixture, crumbs and remaining blueberries. Garnish with whipped cream if desired. Refrigerate until serving.

1 serving: 430 cal., 23g fat (11g sat. fat), 51mg chol., 255mg sod., 53g carb. (35g sugars, 4g fiber), 9g pro.

WHY YOU'LL LOVE IT:
"You can put other berries like raspberries, blackberries, strawberries and other fruit in these desserts too!"

—MUFFINMONSTER, TASTEOFHOME.COM

CREAMY PINEAPPLE PIE

Here's a light and refreshing dessert that's quick to make and impressive to serve. This is one of our favorite ways to complete a summer meal.
—*Sharon Bickett, Chester, SC*

Takes: 10 min. • **Makes:** 8 servings

- 1 **can (14 oz.) sweetened condensed milk**
- 1 **can (8 oz.) crushed pineapple, undrained**
- ¼ **cup lemon juice**
- 1 **carton (8 oz.) frozen whipped topping, thawed**
- 1 **prepared graham cracker crust**
  Optional: Chopped toasted macadamia nuts and additional crushed pineapple

Combine milk, pineapple and lemon juice; fold in whipped topping. Pour into prepared crust. Refrigerate until serving. If desired, serve with toasted macadamia nuts and additional crushed pineapple.
Note: To toast nuts, bake in a shallow pan in a 350° oven for 5-10 minutes or cook in a skillet over low heat until lightly browned, stirring occasionally.

1 slice: 367 cal., 14g fat (9g sat. fat), 17mg chol., 185mg sod., 54g carb. (46g sugars, 1g fiber), 5g pro.

PUMPKIN MILK SHAKES

My son loved this festive milk shake while growing up. It's nicely spiced and tastes like pumpkin pie. I like cutting off both ends of a licorice twist and serving it as a straw.
—*Joan Hallford, North Richland Hills, TX*

Takes: 10 min. • **Makes:** 6 servings

- 1 **cup orange juice**
- 4 **cups vanilla ice cream**
- 1 **cup canned pumpkin**
- ½ **cup packed brown sugar**
- 1 **tsp. ground cinnamon**
- ½ **tsp. ground ginger**
- ½ **tsp. ground nutmeg**
  Black licorice twists, optional

In batches, place the first 7 ingredients in a blender. Cover and process until smooth, 20-30 seconds. Serve immediately, with licorice stirrers if desired.

1 cup: 287 cal., 10g fat (6g sat. fat), 39mg chol., 78mg sod., 47g carb. (42g sugars, 2g fiber), 4g pro.

NO-BAKE PEANUT BUTTER TREATS

This quick and tasty dessert is perfect any time of day. Mix them up and keep them on hand in the refrigerator for easy snacking.
—*Sonia Rohda, Waverly, NE*

Takes: 10 min. • **Makes:** 15 treats

- ⅓ cup chunky peanut butter
- ¼ cup honey
- ½ tsp. vanilla extract
- ⅓ cup nonfat dry milk powder
- ⅓ cup quick-cooking oats
- 2 Tbsp. graham cracker crumbs

In a small bowl, combine the peanut butter, honey and vanilla. Stir in the milk powder, oats and graham cracker crumbs. Shape into 1-in. balls. Cover treats and refrigerate until serving.
1 treat: 70 cal., 3g fat (1g sat. fat), 1mg chol., 46mg sod., 9g carb. (6g sugars, 1g fiber), 3g pro. **Diabetic exchanges:** ½ starch, ½ fat.

WHY YOU'LL LOVE IT:
"You will want to double this recipe! It is so great."
—MAMAKNOWSBEST, TASTEOFHOME.COM

QUICK & EASY CHOCOLATE SAUCE

Mom made this fudgy sauce to drizzle on cake. It's also pretty darn good over ice cream. I like to keep it on hand because It keeps for several weeks in the refrigerator.
—*Janice Miller, Creston, IA*

Takes: 15 min. • **Makes:** 2¼ cups

- 12 oz. (2 cups) semisweet chocolate chips
- 1 cup heavy whipping cream
- ¾ cup sugar

1. In a small heavy saucepan, combine all ingredients. Bring to a boil over medium heat, stirring constantly. Boil and stir for 2 minutes.
2. Store in airtight containers in the refrigerator. Warm gently before serving.
2 Tbsp.: 169 cal., 11g fat (6g sat. fat), 18mg chol., 7mg sod., 21g carb. (19g sugars, 1g fiber), 1g pro.

MEXICAN CHOCOLATE DIP

Chocolate, cinnamon and a touch of heat are a classic Mexican trio. Any fruit goes well with this fudgy dip. And don't forget the churros!
—Taste of Home *Test Kitchen*

Takes: 10 min. • **Makes:** about ½ cup

- ¾ cup semisweet chocolate chips
- ⅓ cup heavy whipping cream
- ⅛ tsp. ground cinnamon
- ⅛ tsp. cayenne pepper
  Assorted fresh fruit

In a small heavy saucepan, combine the chocolate chips and cream. Using a whisk, heat and stir over medium-low heat until smooth, 4-5 minutes. Remove from heat; stir in cinnamon and cayenne. Cool slightly. Serve with fruit.
Note: Dip will become firmer as it cools. If desired, warm it gently in the microwave to soften.
2 Tbsp.: 221 cal., 17g fat (10g sat. fat), 27mg chol., 11mg sod., 21g carb. (18g sugars, 2g fiber), 2g pro.

CANTALOUPE A LA MODE

This special dessert is a refreshing finale to a warm-weather meal.
—Nancy Walker, Granite City, IL

Takes: 15 min.
Makes: 4 servings (1 cup sauce)

- ½ cup water
- ½ cup sugar
- 2 Tbsp. lemon juice
- 1 Tbsp. cornstarch
- 1 tsp. grated lemon zest
- 1 cup fresh or frozen blueberries
- 2 small cantaloupes, halved and seeded
- 4 scoops vanilla ice cream
  Fresh mint, optional

In a small saucepan, combine the first 5 ingredients; bring to a boil over medium heat. Boil and stir for 2 minutes or until thickened. Add the blueberries; cook until heated through. Fill cantaloupe with ice cream; top with sauce. Garnish with fresh mint if desired.
1 serving: 337 cal., 8g fat (5g sat. fat), 29mg chol., 74mg sod., 67g carb. (56g sugars, 3g fiber), 5g pro.

GRAPEFRUIT, LIME & MINT YOGURT PARFAIT

Tart grapefruit and lime are balanced with a bit of honey in these cool and easy parfaits.
—*Lois Enger, Colorado Springs, CO*

- -

Takes: 15 min. • **Makes:** 6 servings

4	large red grapefruit
4	cups reduced-fat plain yogurt
2	tsp. grated lime zest
2	Tbsp. lime juice
3	Tbsp. honey
	Torn fresh mint leaves

1. Cut a thin slice from the top and bottom of each grapefruit; stand fruit upright on a cutting board. With a knife, cut off peel and outer membrane from grapefruit. Cut along membrane of each segment to remove fruit.

2. In a large bowl, mix yogurt, lime zest and juice. Layer half of the grapefruit and half of the yogurt mixture into 6 parfait glasses. Repeat layers. Drizzle with honey; top with fresh mint leaves.

1 parfait: 207 cal., 3g fat (2g sat. fat), 10mg chol., 115mg sod., 39g carb. (36g sugars, 3g fiber), 10g pro.

PUMPKIN MOUSSE

Everyone will savor each creamy spoonful of this spiced dessert. It tastes so good, no one guesses it's low in fat.
—*Patricia Sidloskas, Anniston, AL*

Takes: 15 min. • **Makes:** 4 servings

- 1½ **cups cold fat-free milk**
- 1 **pkg. (1 oz.) sugar-free instant butterscotch pudding mix**
- ½ **cup canned pumpkin**
- ½ **tsp. ground cinnamon**
- ¼ **tsp. ground ginger**
- ¼ **tsp. ground allspice**
- 1 **cup fat-free whipped topping, divided**
  Coarse sugar, optional

1. In a large bowl, whisk milk and pudding mix for 2 minutes. Let stand for 2 minutes or until soft-set. Combine the pumpkin, cinnamon, ginger and allspice; fold into pudding. Fold in ½ cup whipped topping.
2. Transfer to individual serving dishes. Refrigerate until serving. Garnish with remaining whipped topping. Sprinkle with coarse sugar if desired.
⅔ cup: 95 cal., 0 fat (0 sat. fat), 2mg chol., 351mg sod., 19g carb. (8g sugars, 1g fiber), 4g pro. **Diabetic exchanges:** ½ starch, ½ fat-free milk.

EASY LEMON BERRY TARTLETS

Filled with raspberries, these flaky, sweet treats make a fun ending to a delicious weeknight meal because they come together in mere minutes.
—*Elizabeth Dehart, West Jordan, UT*

Takes: 15 min. • **Makes:** 15 tartlets

- ⅔ **cup frozen unsweetened raspberries, thawed and drained**
- 1 **tsp. confectioners' sugar**
- 1 **pkg. (1.9 oz.) frozen miniature phyllo tart shells**
- 4 **oz. reduced-fat cream cheese**
- 2 **Tbsp. lemon curd**
  Fresh raspberries, optional

1. In a small bowl, combine the raspberries and confectioners' sugar; mash with a fork. Spoon into tart shells.
2. In a small bowl, combine cream cheese and lemon curd. Pipe or spoon over filling. Top with fresh raspberries if desired.
1 tartlet: 51 cal., 3g fat (1g sat. fat), 7mg chol., 43mg sod., 5g carb. (2g sugars, 0 fiber), 1g pro. **Diabetic exchanges:** ½ starch, ½ fat.

5i S'MORES MILK SHAKE

When hunger hits, we whip up these shakes that taste like s'mores. Oven-toasted marshmallows and a blender make it happen in a snap.
—*Sarah McKenna, Centennial, CO*

- -

Takes: 15 min. • **Makes:** 4 servings

14 large marshmallows
½ cup 2% milk
3 cups vanilla ice cream
¼ cup coarsely crushed graham crackers
Chocolate syrup

1. Preheat broiler. Arrange marshmallows in a single layer on a greased foil-lined baking sheet. Broil 3-4 in. from heat 15-30 seconds on each side or until golden brown. Cool marshmallows completely.
2. Place milk and ice cream in a blender; cover and process just until combined. Add 10 toasted marshmallows; cover and pulse until blended.
3. Divide the milk shake among 4 glasses; top with crushed crackers and remaining toasted marshmallows. Drizzle with chocolate syrup; serve immediately.
¾ cup: 327 cal., 12g fat (7g sat. fat), 46mg chol., 142mg sod., 50g carb. (39g sugars, 1g fiber), 5g pro.

5i QUICK MANGO SORBET

Last summer, I decided to try my hand at making a passion fruit and mango sorbet. But fresh fruits require more prep and are difficult to find ripened at the same time. So I experimented using frozen fruit and juice, and voila! Both are readily available and inexpensive, too.
—*Carol Klein, Franklin Square, NY*

- -

Takes: 5 min. • **Makes:** 25 cups

1 pkg. (16 oz.) frozen mango chunks, slightly thawed
½ cup passion fruit juice
2 Tbsp. sugar

Place all ingredients in a blender; cover and process until smooth. Serve immediately. If desired, for a firmer texture, cover and freeze for at least 3 hours.
½ cup: 91 cal., 0 fat (0 sat. fat), 0 chol., 2mg sod., 24g carb. (21g sugars, 2g fiber), 1g pro.

5i 🍎

CHEESECAKE BERRY PARFAITS

Summer berry season is a real treat for me. It's an easy way to enjoy cheesecake and a refreshing change from traditional pudding and fruit parfaits.

—*Patricia Schroedl, Jefferson, WI*

Takes: 15 min. • **Makes:** 2 parfaits

- 2 oz. cream cheese, softened
- 4 tsp. sugar
- ⅔ cup whipped topping
- 1½ cups mixed fresh berries
  Additional whipped topping, optional

1. In a small bowl, beat the cream cheese and the sugar until smooth. Fold in the whipped topping.

2. In each of 2 parfait glasses, layer a fourth of the cream cheese mixture and a fourth of the berries. Repeat the layers. Top with additional whipped topping if desired. Chill until serving.

1 parfait: 146 cal., 4g fat (4g sat. fat), 0 chol., 1mg sod., 25g carb. (21g sugars, 3g fiber), 1g pro.

HAZELNUT CHOCOLATE MOUSSE

I love chocolate mousse, and it's so quick and easy to make that I can surprise my family with it anytime. This recipe is also good using chocolate fudge-flavored pudding mix. You can also try chocolate-flavored whipped topping instead of regular. It all depends on how much you love chocolate! Feel free to add toppings of your choice.
—*Karla Krohn, Madison, WI*

- -

Takes: 10 min. • **Makes:** 6 servings

- 1¾ **cups cold 2% milk**
- 1 **pkg. (3.9 oz.) instant chocolate pudding mix**
- ½ **cup Nutella**
- 1¾ **cups whipped topping**
  Additional whipped topping

1. Whisk the milk and pudding mix in a large bowl for 2 minutes. Let stand for 2 minutes or until soft set. Whisk in the Nutella until smooth. Fold in whipped topping.
2. Spoon into 6 dessert dishes. Chill until serving. Garnish servings with additional whipped topping.
⅔ cup: 283 cal., 12g fat (6g sat. fat), 6mg chol., 132mg sod., 40g carb. (27g sugars, 2g fiber), 4g pro.

CHOCOLATE CINNAMON TOAST

Looking for a fun dessert or snack? Toast cinnamon bread in a skillet and top with chocolate and fresh fruit. Add a small dollop of whipped cream to each slice to make it extra indulgent. What a simply delightful way to amp up meal plans.
—*Jeanne Ambrose, Milwaukee, WI*

- -

Takes: 10 min. • **Makes:** 1 serving

- 1 **slice cinnamon bread**
- 1 **tsp. butter, softened**
- 2 **Tbsp. 60% cacao bittersweet chocolate baking chips**
  Optional: Sliced banana and strawberries

Spread both sides of bread with butter. In a small skillet, toast bread over medium-high heat 2-3 minutes on each side, topping with chocolate chips after turning. Remove from heat; spread melted chocolate evenly over toast. If desired, top with fruit.
1 serving: 235 cal., 13g fat (8g sat. fat), 10mg chol., 131mg sod., 29g carb. (19g sugars, 3g fiber), 4g pro.

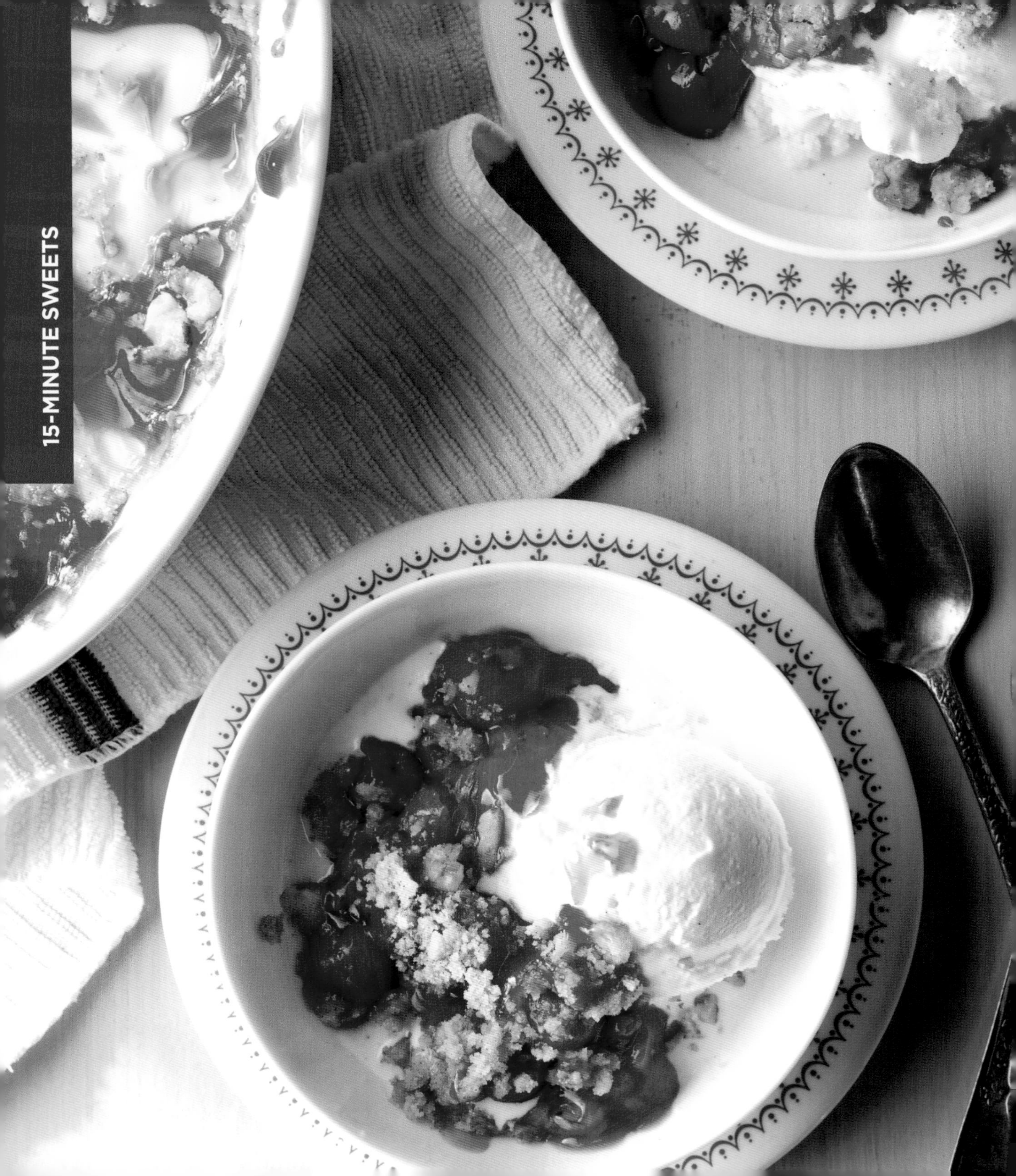

MICROWAVE CHERRY CRISP

Only 15 minutes for dessert? It's true! This treat relies on canned pie filling and takes mere minutes to heat in the microwave.
—*Laurie Todd, Columbus, MS*

Takes: 15 min. • **Makes:** 4 servings

- 1 can (21 oz.) cherry pie filling
- 1 tsp. lemon juice
- 1 cup all-purpose flour
- ¼ cup packed brown sugar
- ¾ tsp. ground cinnamon
- ¼ tsp. ground allspice
- ⅓ cup cold butter, cubed
- ½ cup chopped walnuts
    Vanilla ice cream

1. Combine the pie filling and lemon juice in an ungreased 1½-qt. microwave-safe dish; set aside.
2. In a small bowl, combine flour, brown sugar, cinnamon and allspice; cut in butter until mixture resembles coarse crumbs. Add walnuts. Sprinkle over filling.
3. Microwave, uncovered, on high until bubbly, 3-4 minutes. Serve warm with ice cream.
1 cup: 567 cal., 24g fat (10g sat. fat), 41mg chol., 187mg sod., 81g carb. (50g sugars, 3g fiber), 8g pro.

WHITE CHOCOLATE CEREAL BARS

A friend gave me this no-fuss take on classic spy treats. My husband loves them.
—*Anne Powers, Munford, AL*

Takes: 15 min. • **Makes:** about 3 dozen

- 4 cups miniature marshmallows
- 8 oz. white baking chips (about 1⅓ cups)
- ¼ cup butter, cubed
- 6 cups crisp rice cereal

1. In a Dutch oven, combine marshmallows, baking chips and butter. Cook and stir over medium-low heat until melted. Remove from heat. Add cereal; stir to coat.
2. Transfer to a greased 13x9-in. pan; gently press mixture evenly into pan. Cut into bars.
1 bar: 79 cal., 3g fat (2g sat. fat), 3mg chol., 58mg sod., 13g carb. (8g sugars, 0 fiber), 0 pro.

TEST KITCHEN TIP
Make White Chocolate Cereal Bars perfect for any holiday! Just use a shaped cookie cutter to cut the bars into shapes right out of the baking pan.

CHERRY CREAM CHEESE DESSERT

Cherries, graham crackers and a creamy filling make a festive parfait-style dessert. We sometimes substitute the cherries with blueberry pie filling or other fruits.
—*Melody Mellinger, Myerstown, PA*

Takes: 15 min. • **Makes:** 8 servings

- ¾ cup graham cracker crumbs (about 12 squares)
- 2 Tbsp. sugar
- 2 Tbsp. butter, melted

FILLING
- 1 pkg. (8 oz.) cream cheese, softened
- 1 can (14 oz.) sweetened condensed milk
- ⅓ cup lemon juice
- 1 tsp. vanilla extract
- 1 can (21 oz.) cherry pie filling

1. In a small bowl, combine the cracker crumbs, sugar and butter. Divide among 8 dessert dishes, about 4 rounded teaspoonfuls in each.

2. In a small bowl, beat cream cheese until smooth. Gradually add milk until blended. Beat in the lemon juice and vanilla. Spoon ¼ cup into each dish. Top with pie filling, about ¼ cup in each.

1 serving: 418 cal., 18g fat (11g sat. fat), 56mg chol., 228mg sod., 59g carb. (51g sugars, 1g fiber), 7g pro.

🄕 NUTTY RICE KRISPIE COOKIES

My mom and I used to make these treats regularly. Making them with the microwave means they're super easy and fun to mix up with the kids.
—*Savanna Chapdelaine, Orlando, FL*

Takes: 15 min. • **Makes:** about 2 dozen

- 1 pkg. (10 to 12 oz.) white baking chips
- ¼ cup creamy peanut butter
- 1 cup miniature marshmallows
- 1 cup crisp rice cereal
- 1 cup salted peanuts

In a large microwave-safe bowl, melt baking chips; stir until smooth. Stir in peanut butter until blended. Add the marshmallows, crisp rice cereal and peanuts. Drop by heaping tablespoonfuls onto waxed paper-lined baking sheets. Cool completely. Store in an airtight container.

1 cookie: 127 cal., 8g fat (3g sat. fat), 2mg chol., 49mg sod., 11g carb. (9g sugars, 1g fiber), 3g pro.

HOT BUTTERED CIDER MIX

Keep this mix on hand for quick warm-you-up sippers. You can omit the brandy for a kid-friendly version.
—Taste of Home *Test Kitchen*

Takes: 10 min. **Makes:** 64 servings (2 cups buttered cider mix)

- 1 cup butter, softened
- 1 cup packed brown sugar
- ½ cup honey
- 1 tsp. ground cinnamon
- ½ tsp. ground cardamom
- ¼ tsp. ground cloves

EACH SERVING
- ¾ cup hot apple cider or juice
- 1 oz. apple brandy, optional

1. Beat the butter and brown sugar until blended; beat in honey and spices. Transfer to an airtight container. Store in refrigerator up to 2 weeks.

To prepare hot cider: Place 1½ tsp. buttered cider mix in a mug. Stir in hot cider and, if desired, brandy.

¾ cup prepared cider: 136 cal., 3g fat (2g sat. fat), 8mg chol., 40mg sod., 28g carb. (25g sugars, 0 fiber), 0 pro.

5i
HOMEMADE CAJUN SEASONING

We in Louisiana love seasoned foods. I use this in gravy, over meats and with salads. It saves both time and money. Many people have asked for the recipe.
—*Onietta Loewer, Branch, LA*

Takes: 5 min. • **Makes:** about 3½ cups

- 1 carton (26 oz.) salt
- 2 containers (1 oz. each) cayenne pepper
- ⅓ cup pepper
- ⅓ cup chili powder
- 3 Tbsp. garlic powder

Combine all ingredients; store in airtight containers. Use to season pork, chicken, seafood, steaks or vegetables.

¼ tsp.: 1 cal., 0 fat (0 sat. fat), 0 chol., 433mg sod., 0 carb. (0 sugars, 0 fiber), 0 pro.

ALL-STAR MUFFIN MIX

I keep this handy mix in my pantry so I'm always ready to whip up muffins for a fast bite. The muffins are great plain, but there are so many easy variations you can make to keep menu plans interesting. Best of all, the mix saves me money in the long haul.
—Nancy Mackey, Madison, OH

Prep: 20 min. • **Bake:** 20 min.
Makes: 1 dozen per batch

- 8 cups all-purpose flour
- 3 cups sugar
- 3 Tbsp. baking powder
- 2 tsp. salt
- 2 tsp. ground cinnamon
- 2 tsp. ground nutmeg

ADDITIONAL INGREDIENTS
- 1 large egg, room temperature
- 1 cup 2% milk
- ½ cup butter, melted

1. In a large bowl, whisk first 6 ingredients until well blended. Store mix in airtight containers in a cool, dry place or in the freezer up to 6 months. Yield: 4 batches (11 cups mix).

2. To prepare plain muffins: Preheat oven to 400°. Whisk together egg, milk and melted butter. Add 2¾ cups muffin mix, stirring just until moistened. Fill paper-lined muffin cups three-fourths full. Bake 18-21 minutes or until a toothpick inserted in center comes out clean. Cool 5 minutes before removing from pan to a wire rack. Serve warm.

1 plain muffin: 208 cal., 9g fat (5g sat. fat), 39mg chol., 244mg sod., 30g carb. (14g sugars, 1g fiber), 3g pro.

Blueberry Muffins: Prepare muffins as directed, folding 1 cup fresh or frozen blueberries into prepared batter.

Rhubarb-Orange Muffins: Prepare the muffins as directed, adding ⅓ cup orange marmalade to the egg mixture and folding ¾ cup diced fresh or frozen rhubarb into prepared batter.

Banana Muffins: Prepare the muffins as directed, adding 1 cup mashed ripe bananas to egg mixture.

Cranberry-Pecan Muffins: Prepare the muffins as directed, tossing 1 cup chopped fresh or frozen cranberries, ½ cup chopped pecans and 3 Tbsp. sugar with muffin mix before adding to egg mixture.

Apricot-Cherry Muffins: Prepare muffins as directed, tossing ½ cup each chopped dried apricots and dried cherries with muffin mix before adding to egg mixture

Cappuccino Muffins: Prepare muffins as directed, tossing 1 cup miniature semisweet chocolate chips and 2 tsp. instant coffee granules with muffin mix before adding to egg mixture.

Carrot-Raisin Muffins: Prepare muffins as directed, tossing ¾ cup shredded carrots and ⅓ cup golden raisins with muffin mix before adding to egg mixture.

Apple-Cheese Muffins: Prepare muffins as directed, tossing ½ cup each shredded peeled apple and shredded Colby-Monterey Jack cheese with muffin mix before adding to egg mixture.

PANCAKE MIX IN A JAR

Mornings are bit easier when you have this pancake mix ready to go. The pancakes are fluffy and fruity.

—*Diane Musil, Lyons, IL*

Takes: 30 min.
Makes: 8 pancakes per batch

  3   cups all-purpose flour
  3   Tbsp. sugar
  2   Tbsp. baking powder
4½   tsp. ground cinnamon
  1   tsp. salt
ADDITIONAL INGREDIENTS (FOR
      EACH BATCH)
  1   large egg, room temperature
  ¾   cup milk
  3   Tbsp. canola oil
  ¼   cup chopped dried apples
      or cranberries, optional

1. Combine the first 5 ingredients. Transfer to a 1-qt. jar with a tight-fitting lid. Cover and store in a cool, dry place for up to 6 months. Yield: 2 batches (3 cups total).
2. To prepare pancakes: Place 1½ cups mix in a large bowl. In another bowl, whisk egg, milk and oil. Stir in dried fruit if desired. Stir into pancake mix just until moistened. Pour batter by ¼ cupfuls onto a greased hot griddle. Turn pancakes when bubbles on top begin to pop; cook until second side is golden brown.
2 pancakes: 329 cal., 13g fat (3g sat. fat), 59mg chol., 634mg sod., 44g carb. (8g sugars, 2g fiber), 8g pro.

ESPRESSO STEAK RUB

I'm always entering cooking contests and experimenting with big, bold flavor combinations. This espresso-laced spice rub is equal parts sweet, hot and exotic— it's awesome for grilled ribeye. Keep it on hand to dress up weeknight dinners quickly and easily.
—*Sandi Sheppard, Norman, OK*

- -

Takes: 5 min. • **Makes:** about 1 cup

⅓	cup instant espresso powder
¼	cup packed brown sugar
3	tsp. kosher salt
3	tsp. lemon-pepper seasoning
1	tsp. cayenne pepper
¼	tsp. Chinese five-spice powder
¼	tsp. garlic powder

Mix all ingredients until well blended. Transfer to an airtight container. Store in a cool, dry place for up to 6 months.
1½ tsp.: 9 cal., 0 fat (0 sat. fat), 0 chol., 211mg sod., 2g carb. (2g sugars, 0 fiber), 0 pro.

HEARTY PASTA SOUP MIX

Prepare a few batches of this soup mix one weekend, and then work the soup into your monthly meal plan. It's a hearty treat that warms up the whole family.
—Taste of Home *Test Kitchen*

- -

Prep: 15 min. • **Cook:** 1¼ hours
Makes: 14 servings (3½ qt.)

- ½ cup dried split peas
- 2 Tbsp. chicken bouillon granules
- ½ cup dried lentils
- 2 Tbsp. dried minced onion
- 1 tsp. dried basil
- 1 tsp. dried parsley flakes
- 1 envelope savory herb with garlic soup mix or vegetable soup mix
- 2 cups uncooked tricolor spiral pasta

ADDITIONAL INGREDIENTS
- 10 cups water
- 3 cups cubed cooked chicken
- 1 can (28 oz.) diced tomatoes, undrained

1. In a half-pint glass container, layer the first 7 ingredients in the order listed; seal tightly. Place the pasta in a 1-pint resealable jar; seal. Yield: 1 batch (3 cups).
2. To prepare soup: Place water in a Dutch oven; stir in the soup mix. Bring to a boil. Reduce the heat; cover and simmer for 45 minutes. Add chicken, tomatoes and pasta. Cover and simmer until pasta, peas and lentils are tender, 15-20 minutes longer.
1 cup: 173 cal., 3g fat (1g sat. fat), 27mg chol., 613mg sod., 22g carb. (3g sugars, 5g fiber), 15g pro.

5i 🍎 RASPBERRY-HERB VINAIGRETTE

Raspberry vinegar and fresh herbs make this dressing light and refreshing. It's perfect for mixed green salads topped with fresh berries or citrus segments.
—Taste of Home *Test Kitchen*

- -

Takes: 10 min. • **Makes:** about 1 cup

- ¾ cup olive oil
- ⅓ cup raspberry vinegar
- 2 tsp. sugar
- 2 tsp. minced fresh parsley
- 2 tsp. minced fresh basil
- ⅛ tsp. pepper

Combine all ingredients in a jar with a tight-fitting lid; shake well. Store in the refrigerator. Just before serving, shake dressing again.
2 Tbsp.: 163 cal., 18g fat (2g sat. fat), 0 chol., 1mg sod., 1g carb. (1g sugars, 0 fiber), 0 pro.

APPLE-CINNAMON OATMEAL MIX

Oatmeal is a breakfast staple at our house, It's a warm, nutritious start to the day that keeps us going all morning. We used to buy the oatmeal mixes, but we think this speedy homemade version is better! Feel free to substitute raisins or other dried fruit for the apples if you'd like.
—*Lynne Van Wagenen, Salt Lake City, UT*

Takes: 5 min. • **Makes:** 1 serving

- 6 cups quick-cooking oats
- 1⅓ cups nonfat dry milk powder
- 1 cup dried apples, diced
- ¼ cup sugar
- ¼ cup packed brown sugar
- 1 Tbsp. ground cinnamon
- 1 tsp. salt
- ¼ tsp. ground cloves

ADDITIONAL INGREDIENT (FOR EACH SERVING)
- ½ cup water

1. In a large bowl, combine the first 8 ingredients. Store the mix in an airtight container in a cool, dry place for up to 6 months. Yield: 8 cups.

2. To prepare oatmeal: Shake mix well. In a small saucepan, bring water to a boil; slowly stir in ½ cup mix. Cook and stir over medium heat for 1 minute. Remove from the heat. Cover and let stand until the oatmeal reaches desired consistency, about 1 minute.

½ cup: 171 cal., 2g fat (0 sat. fat), 1mg chol., 185mg sod., 34g carb. (13g sugars, 4g fiber), 6g pro. **Diabetic exchanges:** 2 starch.

QUICK & EASY HONEY MUSTARD

This fast, simple mustard with rice vinegar and honey has more flavor than any other honey mustard dressing I have ever tried.
—*Sharon Rehm, New Blaine, AR*

Takes: 5 min. • **Makes:** 1 cup

- ½ cup stone-ground mustard
- ¼ cup honey
- ¼ cup rice vinegar

In a small bowl, whisk all ingredients. Refrigerate until serving.

1 Tbsp.: 28 cal., 1g fat (0 sat. fat), 0 chol., 154mg sod., 6g carb. (5g sugars, 0 fiber), 0 pro.

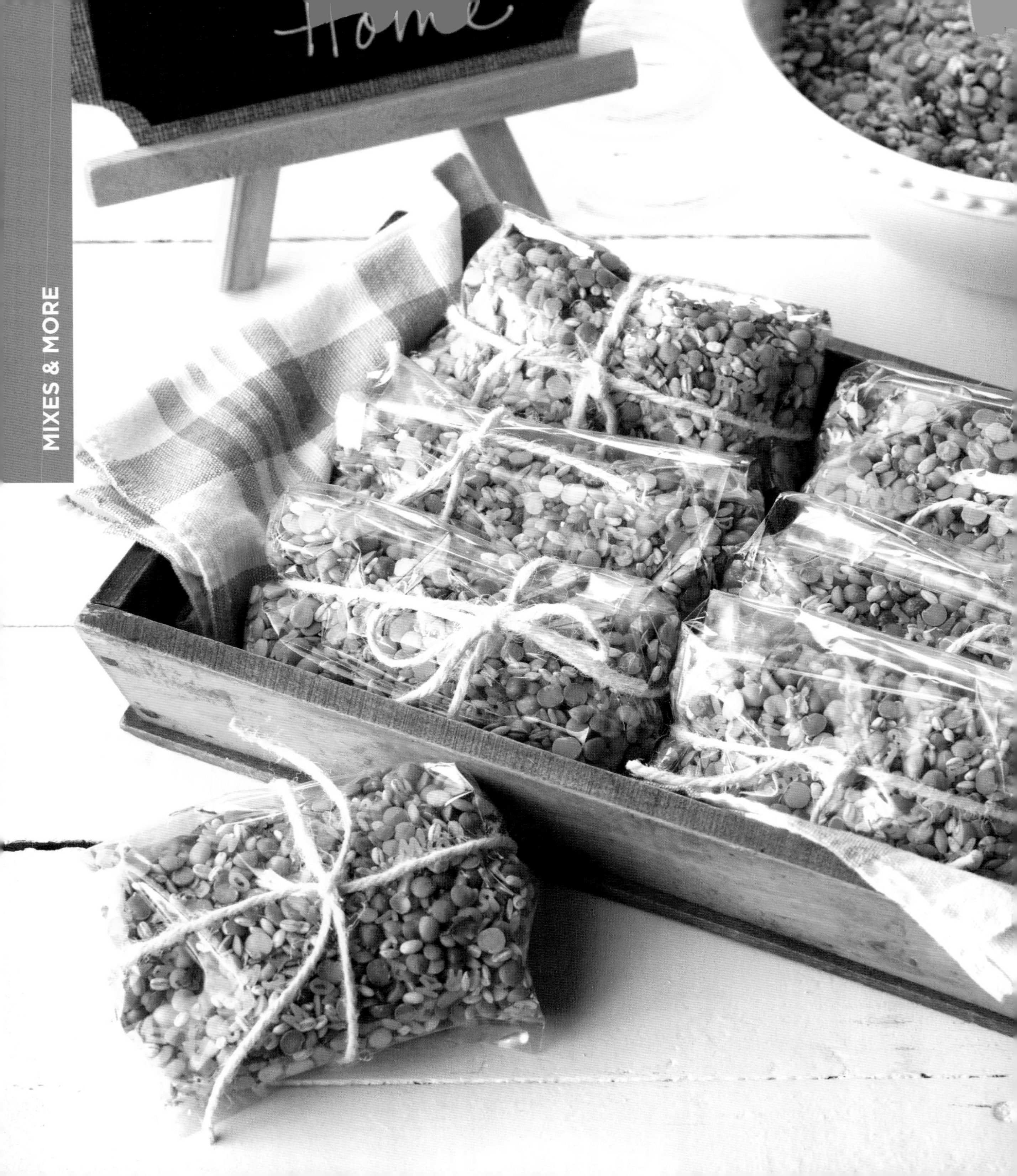
Home

SPLIT PEA SOUP MIX

My mother sent me some of this dry soup blend along with the recipe. The hearty soup is thick with lentils, barley and peas, and chicken is a nice change from the usual ham. Mix up a few batches to have on hand for no-fuss meals during the week.
—*Susan Ruckert, Tangent, OR*

Prep: 10 min. • **Cook:** 1¼ hours
Makes: 4 servings (1 qt.) per batch

- 1 pkg. (16 oz.) **dried green split peas**
- 1 pkg. (16 oz.) **dried yellow split peas**
- 1 pkg. (16 oz.) **dried lentils, rinsed**
- 1 pkg. (16 oz.) **medium pearl barley**
- 1 pkg. (12 oz.) **alphabet pasta**
- 1 jar (½ oz.) **dried celery flakes**
- ½ cup **dried parsley flakes**

ADDITIONAL INGREDIENTS
- 4 cups **chicken broth**
- ¼ tsp. **pepper**
- 1 cup **cubed cooked chicken, optional**

1. Combine the first 7 ingredients. Transfer mix to airtight containers, or divide equally among 13 plastic bags. Store in a cool, dry place for up to 1 year. Yield: 13 batches (13 cups total).

2. To prepare soup: In a large saucepan, combine 1 cup soup mix with broth, pepper and, if desired, cubed chicken. Bring to a boil. Reduce heat; simmer, covered, until peas and lentils are tender, 1-1¼ hours.

1 cup: 158 cal., 3g fat (0 sat. fat), 7mg chol., 117mg sod., 26g carb. (0 sugars, 0 fiber), 11g pro. **Diabetic exchanges:** 1½ starch, 1 lean meat.

SPICED CHAI MIX

One year, my sister-in-law mixed up this drink for a family gathering. I asked for the recipe and have been enjoying its warm, spicy flavor ever since. It goes great with a warm blanket and a good book!
—*Dee Falk, Stromsburg, NE*

Takes: 15 min. • **Makes:** about 5 cups mix (26 servings)

- 3 cups **nonfat dry milk powder**
- 1½ cups **sugar**
- 1 cup **unsweetened instant tea**
- ¾ cup **vanilla powdered nondairy creamer**
- 1½ tsp. **ground ginger**
- 1½ tsp. **ground cinnamon**
- ½ tsp. **ground cardamom**
- ½ tsp. **ground cloves**

OPTIONAL GARNISH
- **Whipped cream**

1. In a food processor, combine all dry ingredients; cover and process until powdery. Store in an airtight container in a cool, dry place for up to 6 months.

2. To prepare 1 serving: Dissolve 3 Tbsp. mix in ¾ cup of boiling water; stir well. Dollop with whipped cream if desired.

3 Tbsp.: 114 cal., 1g fat (1g sat. fat), 3mg chol., 75mg sod., 21g carb. (19g sugars, 0 fiber), 5g pro. **Diabetic exchanges:** 1½ starch.

EASY BALSAMIC VINAIGRETTE

If you have the time to spare, let the flavors meld for about one hour before using this dressing. Be sure to give it a quick shake before drizzling over your favorite greens.
—Taste of Home *Test Kitchen*

- -

Takes: 5 min. • **Makes:** 1 cup

- ⅔ **cup olive oil**
- ¼ **cup balsamic vinegar**
- 1 **Tbsp. finely chopped shallot**
- ¾ **tsp. ground mustard**
- ¾ **tsp. salt**
- ⅛ **tsp. pepper**

Combine all ingredients in a jar with a tight-fitting lid; shake well. Store in the refrigerator. Just before serving, shake dressing again.

2 Tbsp.: 169 cal., 18g fat (2g sat. fat), 0 chol., 222mg sod., 2g carb. (2g sugars, 0 fiber), 0 pro.

GLUTEN-FREE FLOUR MIX

My son and I have celiac disease, and I use this flour mix to make our favorite dishes. I prepare it in 2-quart batches and store it in airtight jars.
—*Bernice Fenskie, Wexford, PA*

- -

Takes: 5 min. • **Makes:** 3 cups

- 2 **cups white rice flour**
- ⅔ **cup potato starch flour**
- ⅓ **cup tapioca flour**

In a small bowl, combine all ingredients. Store in an airtight container in a cool, dry place for up to 1 year.

Note: Read all ingredient labels for possible gluten content prior to use. Ingredient formulas can change, and production facilities vary among brands. If you're concerned that your brand may contain gluten, contact the company. Contents of mix may settle during storage. When preparing the recipe, spoon mix into measuring cup.

1 Tbsp.: 29 cal., 0 fat (0 sat. fat), 0 chol., 0 sod., 7g carb. (0 sugars, 0 fiber), 0 pro.

SWEET & SPICY BARBECUE SAUCE

I've never cared much for store-bought barbecue sauce. I like to make things from scratch, so I save a bit of money having this homemade sauce on hand.
—*Helena Georgette Mann, Sacramento, CA*

- -

Prep: 30 min. • **Cook:** 35 min. + cooling
Makes: 1½ cups

- 1   medium onion, chopped
- 1   Tbsp. canola oil
- 1   garlic clove, minced
- 1   to 3 tsp. chili powder
- ¼   tsp. cayenne pepper
- ¼   tsp. coarsely ground pepper
- 1   cup ketchup
- ⅓   cup molasses
- 2   Tbsp. cider vinegar
- 2   Tbsp. Worcestershire sauce
- 2   Tbsp. spicy brown mustard
- ½   tsp. hot pepper sauce

1. In a large saucepan, saute onion in oil until tender. Add the garlic; cook 1 minute. Stir in the chili powder, cayenne and pepper; cook 1 minute longer.

2. Stir in the ketchup, molasses, vinegar, Worcestershire sauce, mustard and pepper sauce. Bring to a boil. Reduce heat; simmer, uncovered, for 30-40 minutes or until the sauce reaches desired consistency. Cool for 15 minutes.

3. Strain sauce through a fine mesh strainer over a large bowl, discarding vegetables and seasonings. Store in an airtight container in the refrigerator for up to 1 month. Use as a basting sauce for grilled meats.

2 Tbsp.: 68 cal., 1g fat (0 sat. fat), 0 chol., 325mg sod., 14g carb. (11g sugars, 1g fiber), 0 pro.

ALL-AROUND SEASONING MIX

I always keep this mixture on hand; it's good on anything, especially grilled pork, chicken and vegetables, so it's a great way to jazz up boring entrees.

—*Greg Fontenot, The Woodlands, TX*

- -

Takes: 10 min. • **Makes:** 1⅔ cups

½	cup paprika
3	Tbsp. onion powder
3	Tbsp. garlic powder
3	Tbsp. cayenne pepper
2	Tbsp. white pepper
2	Tbsp. pepper
4	tsp. salt
4	tsp. dried thyme
4	tsp. dried oregano
4	tsp. ground cumin
4	tsp. chili powder

In a small bowl, combine all ingredients. Store in an airtight container in a cool, dry place for up to 6 months.

1 tsp.: 7 cal., 0 fat (0 sat. fat), 0 chol., 120mg sod., 1g carb. (0 sugars, 1g fiber), 0 pro

HOMEMADE RANCH DRESSING & DIP MIX

Keep this versatile blend on hand to whip up a delicious veggie dip or salad dressing at a moment's notice.

—*Joan Hallford, North Richland Hills, TX*

- -

Prep: 10 min. + chilling
Makes: 1 cup dressing or 2 cups dip per batch

- 2 **Tbsp. dried parsley flakes**
- 1 **Tbsp. garlic powder**
- 1 **Tbsp. dried minced chives**
- 2 **tsp. lemon-pepper seasoning**
- 1½ **tsp. dried oregano**
- 1½ **tsp. dried tarragon**
- 1 **tsp. salt**

ADDITIONAL INGREDIENTS FOR SALAD
    DRESSING (FOR EACH BATCH)
- ½ **cup mayonnaise**
- ½ **cup buttermilk**

ADDITIONAL INGREDIENTS FOR DIP
    (FOR EACH BATCH)
- 1 **cup mayonnaise**
- 1 **cup sour cream**

1. Mix the seasonings until well blended. Transfer to an airtight container. Store in a cool, dry place for up to 1 year. Shake to redistribute the seasonings before using. Yield: 4 batches dressing or 2 batches dip (about 4 Tbsp. mix).

2. To prepare salad dressing: Whisk together mayonnaise, buttermilk and 1 Tbsp. mix. Refrigerate, covered, at least 1 hour before serving.

3. To prepare dip: Mix mayonnaise, sour cream and 2 Tbsp. mix until blended. Refrigerate, covered, at least 2 hours before serving.

2 Tbsp. dressing: 108 cal., 11g fat (2g sat. fat), 6mg chol., 198mg sod., 1g carb. (1g sugars, 0 fiber), 1g pro.
¼ cup dip: 262 cal., 27 g fat (7 g sat. fat), 30 mg chol., 297 mg sod., 1 g carb., trace fiber, 1 g pro.

WHY YOU'LL LOVE IT:
"I had no ranch dressing in the house, so I used this recipe. It didn't disappoint! Great flavor, and I had all of the ingredients on hand."
—AUG2295, TASTEOFHOME.COM

⑤ⓙ
CHERRY-ALMOND TEA MIX

Once you prepare this mix, all you need is water to enjoy the heartwarming tea for months to come. My family loves it!
—*Andrea Horton, Kelso, WA*

Takes: 10 min. • **Makes:** 40 servings (2½ cups tea mix)

- 2¼ cups iced tea mix with lemon and sugar
- 2 envelopes (0.13 oz. each) unsweetened cherry Kool-Aid mix
- 2 tsp. almond extract

EACH SERVING
- 1 cup boiling or cold water

Place tea mix, Kool-Aid mix and extract in a food processor; pulse until blended. Store in an airtight container in a cool, dry place up to 6 months. To prepare tea: Place 1 Tbsp. tea mix in a mug. Stir in 1 cup boiling or cold water until blended.

1 cup prepared tea: 41 cal., 0 fat (0 sat. fat), 0 chol., 1mg sod., 10g carb. (10g sugars, 0 fiber), 0 pro.

⑤ⓙ
SWEET MUSTARD PORK MARINADE

I marinate pork chops overnight using this homemade creation. It really brings out the best in the chops, and it takes only a few minutes to stir together.
—*DeAnn Alleva, Hudson, WI*

Takes: 5 min. • **Makes:** about 1 cup

- ½ cup mayonnaise
- ⅓ cup red wine vinegar
- ¼ cup packed brown sugar
- ¼ cup prepared mustard
- 2 tsp. seasoned salt

In a small bowl, whisk all ingredients until blended. Use to marinate pork.

2 Tbsp.: 121 cal., 10g fat (2g sat. fat), 1mg chol., 535mg sod., 8g carb. (7g sugars, 0 fiber), 0 pro.

VERSATILE ONION SOUP MIX

You can prepare soup, make dips and even season veggies with this handy mix. We enjoy it on oven-roasted potatoes, but try it all three ways. I even use it to season meats from time to time. It's an inexpensive substitute for store-bought soup mixes.
—*June Mullins, Livonia, MO*

- -

Takes: 5 min. • **Makes:** 2 cups

- ¾ **cup dried minced onion**
- ⅓ **cup beef bouillon granules**
- ¼ **cup onion powder**
- ¼ **tsp. sugar**
- ¼ **tsp. celery seed**

FOR ONION SOUP
- 4 **cups water**

FOR ROASTED POTATOES
- 6 **medium potatoes (about 2 lbs.), cut into ½-in. cubes**
- ⅓ **cup olive oil**

FOR ONION DIP
- 2 **cups sour cream**
  Assorted raw vegetables, chips or crackers

1. Combine first 5 ingredients. Store in an airtight container in a cool, dry place for up to 1 year. Yield: 4 batches (20 Tbsp. total).

2. To prepare onion soup: In a saucepan, combine water and 5 Tbsp. onion soup mix. Bring to a boil over medium-high heat, stirring occasionally. Reduce the heat; simmer, uncovered, for 10 minutes, stirring occasionally. Yield: 3 servings.

3. To prepare roasted potatoes: In a bowl, toss potatoes and oil. Sprinkle with 5 Tbsp. onion soup mix; toss to coat. Transfer to an ungreased 15x10x1-in. baking pan. Bake, uncovered, at 450° for 35-40 minutes or until tender, stirring occasionally. Yield: 6 servings.

4. To prepare onion dip: In a bowl, combine sour cream and 5 Tbsp. onion soup mix; mix well. Refrigerate for at least 2 hours. Serve with vegetables, chips or crackers.

1 Tbsp. mix: 15 cal., 0 fat (0 sat. fat), 0 chol., 3mg sod., 3g carb. (0 sugars, 0 fiber), 0 pro.

BARBECUE SEASONING

I use this rub on country-style ribs, pork and chicken. You'll likely have all of the seasonings on hand to make a batch, and if you don't use it all, it will keep for up to 6 months!

—*Rose Rainier, Sheridan, WY*

Takes: 10 min. • **Makes:** 1 cup

- ¼ cup beef bouillon granules
- ¼ cup chili powder
- ¼ cup paprika
- 1 Tbsp. sugar
- 1 Tbsp. garlic salt
- 1 Tbsp. onion salt
- 1 tsp. celery salt
- 1 tsp. cayenne pepper
- 1 tsp. pepper
- ½ tsp. curry powder
- ½ tsp. dried oregano

In a small bowl, combine all ingredients. Store in an airtight container in a cool, dry place up to 6 months.

1 tsp.: 6 cal., 0 fat (0 sat. fat), 0 chol., 476mg sod., 1g carb. (0 sugars, 0 fiber), 0 pro.

INDEX

EQUIVALENT MEASURES

3 TEASPOONS	= 1 tablespoon		**16 TABLESPOONS**	= 1 cup
4 TABLESPOONS	= ¼ cup		**2 CUPS**	= 1 pint
5⅓ TABLESPOONS	= ½ cup		**4 CUPS**	= 1 quart
8 TABLESPOONS	= ½ cup		**4 QUARTS**	= 1 gallon

FOOD EQUIVALENTS

MACARONI		1 cup (3½ ounces) uncooked	= 2½ cups cooked		
NOODLES, MEDIUM		3 cups (4 ounces) uncooked	= 4 cups cooked		
POPCORN		3 cups (4 ounces) uncooked	= 8 cups popped		
RICE, LONG GRAIN		1 cup uncooked	= 3 cups cooked		
RICE, QUICK-COOKING		1 cup uncooked	= 2 cups cooked		
SPAGHETTI		1 cup uncooked	= 4 cups cooked		
BREAD		1 slice	= ¾ cup soft crumbs, ¼ cup fine dry crumbs		
GRAHAM CRACKERS		7 squares	= ½ cup finely crushed		
BUTTERY ROUND CRACKERS		12 crackers	= ½ cup finely crushed		
SALTINE CRACKERS		14 crackers	= ½ cup finely crushed		
BANANAS		1 medium	= ⅓ cup mashed		
LEMONS		1 medium	= 3 tablespoons juice, 2 teaspoons grated zest		
LIMES		1 medium	= 2 tablespoons juice, 1½ teaspoons grated zest		
ORANGES		1 medium	= ¼–⅓ cup juice, 4 teaspoons grated zest		
CABBAGE	1 head = 5 cups shredded		**GREEN PEPPER**	1 large = 1 cup chopped	
CARROTS	1 pound = 3 cups shredded		**MUSHROOMS**	½ pound = 3 cups sliced	
CELERY	1 rib = ½ cup chopped		**ONIONS**	1 medium = ½ cup chopped	
CORN	1 ear fresh = ⅔ cup kernels		**POTATOES**	3 medium = 2 cups cubed	
ALMONDS	1 pound = 3 cups chopped		**PECAN HALVES**	1 pound = 4½ cups chopped	
GROUND NUTS	3¾ ounces = 1 cup		**WALNUTS**	1 pound = 3¾ cups chopped	

EASY SUBSTITUTIONS

WHEN YOU NEED...		USE...
BAKING POWDER	1 teaspoon	½ teaspoon cream of tartar + ¼ teaspoon baking soda
BUTTERMILK	1 cup	1 tablespoon lemon juice or vinegar + enough milk to measure 1 cup (let stand 5 minutes before using)
CORNSTARCH	1 tablespoon	2 tablespoons all-purpose flour
HONEY	1 cup	1¼ cups sugar + ¼ cup water
HALF-AND-HALF CREAM	1 cup	1 tablespoon melted butter + enough whole milk to measure 1 cup
ONION	1 small, chopped (⅓ cup)	1 teaspoon onion powder or 1 tablespoon dried minced onion
TOMATO JUICE	1 cup	½ cup tomato sauce + ½ cup water
TOMATO SAUCE	2 cups	¾ cup tomato paste + 1 cup water
UNSWEETENED CHOCOLATE	1 square (1 ounce)	3 tablespoons baking cocoa + 1 tablespoon shortening or oil
WHOLE MILK	1 cup	½ cup evaporated milk + ½ cup water